D1739379

A Passion for the Past

A Passion

IVOR NOËL HUME

for the Past

The Odyssey of a
Transatlantic Archaeologist

Ivor Noël Hume (signature)

University of Virginia Press   *Charlottesville and London*

University of Virginia Press
© 2010 by the Rector and Visitors of the University of Virginia
Printed in the United States of America on acid-free paper

9 8 7 6 5 4 3 2 1

LIBRARY OF CONGRESS CATALOGING-IN-PUBLICATION DATA

Noël Hume, Ivor.
   A passion for the past : the odyssey of a transatlantic archaeologist / Ivor Noël Hume.
      p.   cm.
   Includes index.
   ISBN 978-0-8139-2977-4 (cloth : alk. paper) — ISBN 978-0-8139-2996-5 (e-book)
   1. Noël Hume, Ivor. 2. Archaeologists—Great Britain—Biography. 3. Archaeologists—
United States—Biography. 4. London (England)—Antiquities. 5. Virginia—Antiquities.
6. Colonial Williamsburg (Williamsburg, Va.)—Antiquities. 7. Excavations (Archaeology)—
England—London. 8. Excavations (Archaeology)—Virginia. 9. Excavations (Archaeology)—
Virginia—Williamsburg. I. Title.
   CC115.N64A3 2010
   930.1092—dc22
   [B]   2009051784

For
Audrey and Carol
Two wives
Who together made
One happy man

CONTENTS

PREFACE

HAVING SPENT MORE than forty years as a professional archaeologist, I have been paid for doing something I would gladly have done for nothing—had I been able to afford that luxury. In short, I have been remarkably fortunate and also marvelously lucky. I do not know whether chance has played a greater role in my career than in that of most people, but I suspect that it has, for archaeology has similarities to prospecting: many dig but few find treasure. Archaeological treasure, however, tends to be written with a small *t*. Mine certainly has. I have only found two gold coins, and I do not recall deriving any Eureka!-style satisfaction from either. Indeed, I remember them only because I have so often been asked, "What's it like to find gold?" My treasures have lacked the Midas glow and came in the shape of information, bits and pieces of knowledge that, when fitted together, helped weave missing threads into the tapestry of the past.

Webster's Ninth New Collegiate Dictionary (1983) defines archaeology as "the scientific study of material remains of past human life and activities," and it follows, therefore, that the archaeologist's function is no different from that of the police detective asking, "Who done it?" The splintered window, the fingerprint on the glass, the bloody blade, are important only if they lead to the killer; in archaeology the shattered pitcher and the stained earth are only valuable if they help us determine who did what, why, and to whom. But when they do, they are far more satisfying than any shipwreck's gold.

Among the questions most often put to me is this one: What is the most exciting find you ever made? To which I reply: The last one. On the surface that response may sound more flippant than satisfying, yet it is very close to the truth. For me, there have been so many great moments, so many times that the puzzle's pieces have dropped into place, that it is impossible to put them into a hierarchical order. The blood can only race so fast and the temples throb so loudly, and both have been in high gear every time my trowel scraped the earth. I have made no secret of that shortcoming, arguing that studying "past human life and activities" is best done by live and active people who think in populist rather than computerized terms. The smoke of heresy hangs over such thinking. That confession (or something equally outrageous) may have prompted two professors lunching in a university cafeteria to conclude that I was "just a popular archaeologist, not a professional." A student who knew my secretary was sitting at a nearby table, and he overheard the remark. Not understanding it, he called her to ask what it meant. She, in turn, referred the question to me. "What is a popular archaeologist," she asked, "and why is it bad to be one?"

I forget how I answered her, but the question was valid, and my search for an honest answer led me toward this book. Had I come to the archaeological profession through the same educational process as those faculty fellows, I would have been able to assure them that their elitist view was hopelessly wrong and could do the future of archaeology no good. But because more of my lessons were learned in the trenches than in the lecture hall, my critics would almost certainly have countered that my opinion was tarnished by ignorance. Besides, it is only natural that academics in what purports to be an academic profession should frown on those who suggest that the field is the best classroom.

The gulf between amateur and professional archaeologists has widened as technology has made fieldwork increasingly and, for many amateurs, prohibitively expensive. The notion that equipped only with self-taught knowledge and common sense, amateur archaeologists could competently excavate, record, interpret, and publish their work to the profession's satisfaction has fewer proponents today than it did thirty or forty years ago.

It may be that members of most professions have reason to claim that theirs is the most cutthroat of all. Archaeology certainly has had its share of assassins, and has never lacked for young Turks eager to clamber to prominence over the ruins of their predecessors' reputations. Pioneers are by definition leaders, and anyone who leads at the beginning can expect to be damned in the end—for failing to have begun with the wisdom born of long experience. Had I the time for introspection when I lurched into a career in the hitherto nonexistent field of historical (in Britain, post-medieval) archaeology, I might have done well to recall that three of the best-known pioneers and onetime popular heroes of archaeology would eventually stand condemned.

The most recent, and the least vilified, of the three was Sir Arthur Evans, whose discoveries in Crete beginning in 1900 put the Minoan civilization on the historical map, and in the process made him the most famous archaeologist of his day. Evans was described by a colleague as having an amazing gift for visualizing the past, for reconstructing in his imagination the appearance of a room based only on a few tumbled stones and fragments of fresco. Others disagreed and condemned his literal reconstructions of parts of the Palace of Minos at Knossos as a travesty. They have demonstrated that the site's most famous artifact, the snake goddess figurine whose bare breasts have so long titillated the public's imagination, is as much hypothetical restoration as it is Cretan. Equally famous are the Minoan bull and acrobat frescoes, but these, too, have been assailed as "difficult and dubious" restorations. When my own archaeological career ended with the partial reconstruction of America's Wolstenholme Towne, public approbation could not entirely drown out the message from Knossos.

Sir Arthur Evans's excavations were compared by the London *Times* to the discoveries of the German archaeologist Heinrich Schliemann forty years before. It was Schliemann whose amateur acumen and earned fortune had turned a bleak Turkish hill into Homeric Troy and made him the friend of a prime minister and the toast of antiquarian London. Alas, his lack of archaeological knowledge (which few possessed at the time) and flaws in his character would combine to enable critics to dash his memory from its niche in the archaeological hall of heroes. They would prove that Schliemann's lack of artifactual knowledge and of soil stratigraphy had caused him to cut clean through the Troy on which his fame rested, that his autobiography was laced with lies, and that in all probability his fabled account of finding King Priam's Treasure was precisely that—a fable. Historical detectives have gathered evidence to show that the treasure was assembled from several sources, and have used Schliemann's own diary to prove that when, according to his published writings, his beautiful Greek wife, Sophia, was beside him at Troy gathering up the treasures into her shawl, she was in Athens mourning the death of her father.

Just as Schliemann, for all his faults, had lifted Homeric Troy from classic mythology and placed it on the table of archaeological reality, so nearly sixty years earlier another amateur's discoveries had done as much for Ancient Egypt. But unlike Schliemann and Sir Arthur Evans, both rich men whose own money financed their excavations, Giovanni Battista Belzoni began his brief archaeological career with barely more than the clothes on his and his wife's backs. At six feet eight inches, Belzoni, an unemployed hydraulic engineer, had performed as a circus strongman in England before trying to take his act to Constantinople. Instead, he found himself in Egypt collecting antiquities on behalf of the British consul. In the space of three years, not only did Belzoni assemble the finest collection of Egyptian sculptures ever to reach the British Museum, but he also became enough of a student of Ancient Egyptian art and artifacts to seek recognition in British academic circles. He never got it—there being no place among English gentleman antiquaries for an oversized showman with a thick Italian accent.

Rejected in London, Belzoni returned to Africa and died while trying to prove that the Niger and Nile rivers had a common source. His reputation might have grown in the years since his death had he not been as honest as Schliemann was devious. Belzoni made the mistake of describing how, while searching for antiquities in the cliff-hewn catacombs of Gournou, he had fallen through stacked sarcophagi, shattering and scattering mummy bits as he went. That, in 1817, no one was interested in run-of-the mill mummies, and even the most "professional" antiquaries were almost exclusively object oriented, has been ignored by more recent scholars who have damned the unfortunate Belzoni as being of "Beelzebubish memory," and "the greatest plunderer of them all." Nevertheless, this was the man who, in 1820, built detailed reconstructions of the tomb of the Egyptian king Seti I, and who mounted an exhibition of his discoveries that gave London a bout of Egyptomania unequaled until Howard Carter found Tutankhamen.

Belzoni's 1820 *Narrative of the Operations and Recent Discoveries in Egypt and Nubia* introduced the reading public to the romance of archaeological discovery, and I confess that after decades of digging I have been unable to banish the thrill of it. That is not a confession of which I am particularly ashamed, however; on the contrary, I contend that there has to be a bit of Belzoni's naive enthusiasm, Schliemann's desire, and Evans's showmanship in every successful archaeologist. In spite of those pioneers' mistakes and whatever character flaws their less famous critics can dig up, Belzoni's sculptures remain the centerpiece of the British Museum's Egyptian collection, Schliemann's Troy is where he said it was, and Sir Arthur Evans's concrete reconstructions at Knossos still make the Palace of Minos understandable to countless visitors in a way that its tumbled stones could not.

Of the three men, Belzoni was alone in having trodden the boards of English stages and having basked in the uninhibited applause of a popular audience (albeit while supporting a dozen carefully selected adults on his shoulders); but both Schliemann and Evans courted the same approbation—through the intermediary of the press, and both have been chided for having done so. The critics invariably have been those who recognize no responsibility on the part of archaeologists to share their discoveries with the public, and so view encouraging the press to report new discoveries as a quest for self-, rather than archaeological, promotion. There is no denying that, for better or ill, they are two legs of the same trousers and that where one goes so must the other. But it is also true that the public's interest in what is found owes much to its recognition of the finder. Thus, for example, Sir Leonard Woolley, the discoverer of the royal cemetery at Ur, became a household name in England in 1929 by giving a series of six talks on the BBC describing the principles of archaeology and how he used them to excavate in Mesopotamia. The lectures were later published as a little volume titled *Digging Up the Past,* which became one of the most famous of all popular books on archaeology. The BBC did no less for another British archaeologist who would never have been known outside the academic world had it not been for a television game show called *Animal, Vegetable, Mineral?* (an anglicized version of the American program *What in the World?*). The program pitted the wits of archaeologists, anthropologists, and other specialists against museums whose curators submitted tricky objects for identification. Eric Mortimer Wheeler flashed like a beacon amid the field of sometimes lackluster "experts," making the program the most popular on British television in 1954—and propelling himself into "Television Personality of the Year."

My own admiration for Sir Mortimer Wheeler (he was knighted in 1952) was no less enthusiastic. His knowledge was prodigious, his academic credentials were impeccable, yet he brought to everything he did, wrote, or said such enthusiasm that the past became a game in which we all could play. His biographer and fellow archaeologist, Jacquetta Hawkes, coined the best imaginable title for her book: she called it *Adventure in Archaeology.* Wheeler was at his popular zenith in the early 1950s when my own career was just beginning. His excavation techniques so plainly demonstrated in his book *Archaeology from the Earth* (1954) became the cornerstone of my own methods, and thirty years later I continued to tell students that if they were to be allowed only one textbook, that should be it. To my regret, I never had the opportunity to tell him so (though Audrey, my first wife, had been one of his students at London's Institute of Archaeology); but my adulation was not universally shared. I heard much criticism of him among museum professionals who claimed that his television performances and flamboyant press interviews damaged the standing of our profession. I listened but failed to learn, for it seemed to me that Wheeler's television-won popularity had made the British public more supportive of archaeology and museums than it had ever been before. If people like jolly old "Sir Mortimer" worked in museums, they reasoned, museums couldn't be all that dull. It certainly made sense to me, though in my own relations with the press I was soon to learn that dining with the devil can result in severe heartburn.

I am not at all sure that Sir Mortimer would have appreciated being tossed into the same satchel with Belzoni, Schliemann, and Evans. Nevertheless, the careers of all four have influenced my own, both as warnings and models, and I hope that as this book unfolds, the reasons for each will become self-evident. Indeed, that is my principal reason for writing it—the hope that as we advance ever deeper into the Age of High Technology readers may not lose sight of the humanity of antiquity.

On December 5, 1707, a small group of gentlemen with antiquarian interests met at the Bear Tavern in London's Strand to found what would later become the Society of Antiquaries of London. Their purpose was to discuss "the History and Antiquities of Great Britain preceding the reign of James Ist," albeit "without excluding any other remarkable antiquities that might be offered to them." The process of archaeological digging was but one activity within the society's sphere of antiquarian interest, and as I shall try to demonstrate, we who call ourselves archaeologists need to share the breadth of interest and knowledge that brought those gentlemen of curiosity to gather at the Bear "every Friday at six in the evening and sit till ten at farthest."

I trust that you (who used to be called "dear reader") will not find this memoir to be an exercise in prolonged pedantry but rather a narrative sufficiently improbable to be read as first-person fiction—regardless of the fact that it happens to be true. I hope, too, that it has merit as social history, since it chronicles the disintegration of a 1920s English family skating on the thin ice of transatlantic fantasies.

ACKNOWLEDGMENTS

A LIFE REMEMBERED IS a thing of shreds and patches, of vivid but some-times inaccurate recollections, of events of marginal importance firmly documented and others of great moment not documented at all. Of such stuff mine is made. Enigmatic one-line diary entries, pages from manuscripts that have survived only as sheets whereon my wife's kitchen recipes are pasted, rolls of brittle newsreel film, tattered broadcast scripts, faded theater programs and newspaper clippings, scratched shellac recordings, and boxes of curling and un-cataloged photographs have all played their part in putting Humpty Dumpty together. Here and there are gaping holes left by memories rendered uncertain by time or stilled by death.

For one whose job in life has been to reconstruct a much more remote past, this exercise has been sobering indeed. If, in our age of endless paper, it has been impossible to check facts about one's own life, with what accuracy, one wonders, can we hope to reconstruct events that happened two thousand or even only two hundred years ago? When chance dictates which letters shall burn and which shall last, and which lies shall be read as truth and which truths shall be forgotten, it is small wonder that each generation can rewrite history to enshrine new saints and topple old ones.

It has become fashionable for winners of anything to hide self-satisfaction behind a screen of thanks to everyone from the delivery-room staff to the deity of one's choice. By that yardstick the writer of a memoir should thank anyone and everyone who has ever crossed his path for good or ill—the ill bits often being more interesting than the good. Brevity, however, requires that I offer them a collective "thank-you," and limit myself to recognizing those who have consciously contributed to the book.

Few wives have been as totally involved in the life of their husband as was my first wife, Audrey, my right hand throughout my archaeological career, whose criticism of the manuscript in its early stages prevented me from making silly mistakes. Carol, my second wife, has done as much for the later chapters and salvaged my life in the process. The late Adrian Oswald, to whom I owe my archaeological career, read the London chapters and provided invaluable background information about his own life at the City's museum. Sir Hereward and Lady Wake of Courteenhall have been valued friends and hosts through more years than I care to remember, as have Sir David and Lady Burnett of Tandridge: Toby and Julia generously scraping the recesses of their memories to help me recapture details of my schoolboy years at Courteenhall, and David and Betty helping to recall digging days in London when David was chairman of Hays' Wharf. I am obliged, too, to Dr. L. I. Rimmer, headmaster of Framlingham College, to bursar Commander Fawcett, and to college historian L. Gillet for valued information and hospitality. My thanks also go to Tim C. Powell for welcoming me into his home and the house where I was born and for pursuing the records of Chelsea Old Church, and to B. Curle, local studies librarian for the Royal Boroughs of Kensington and Chelsea.

To Bea and her husband, Fred Watson, onetime owners of Blurridge, I owe much more than a visit to their home, for in a series of long letters Bea shared with me both her family's experiences at the house and many others no less inexplicable that have punctuated their lives. To the late Douglas Walton, dear friend and most enduring of the Guildhall Irregulars, I am indebted for his recollections of long and dirty days on the Upchurch Marshes.

I am obliged to Graham Payn and the estate of the late Sir Noël Coward for permission to quote lyrics from "Little Women" and "Dance Little Lady," both from *This Year of Grace,* as well as "The Party's Over Now," from *Words and Music.*

For very personal recollections from the early war years, I am deeply grateful to Renée Redfern, without whose help my life's course would have been very different. But I owe most of all to Joan, my father's second wife and my "stepmother," who, to help me reconstruct my infant years, opened doors in her memory that she would much prefer to have left closed. My gratitude to my late father is inexpressible. Knowing in the 1960s that I was about to make a first stab at these memoirs, he wrote an outline of such parts of his own history before his second marriage as he thought useful. Without that or the notes and letters passed to me by Joan after his death, legends might have continued to wear the mantle of fact.

I want to express my appreciation to all the Guildhall Irregulars, some of whose names to my shame I do not remember, but all of whom labored long, hard, and lovingly to save the remains of London's history—a past which the City itself did so little to protect. Several are dead, and others scattered I know not where. Although their names do not figure on plaques in the Museum of London, the survivors have the satisfaction of being able to point to some of the best of the museum's Roman and medieval objects and say, "I was there the day we found that!" So, to Johnny Johnson, H. E. "Skip" Allen, Don Bailey, Peter Clark, Cynthia and Diana, Douglas Walton, Peter DeBrant, H. Sibson "Peter" Drury, Charlie LeFevre, Lord Noël Buxton, and of course to Audrey—thanks for the memories.

I am indebted, also, to editor Kenny Marotta, who employed such tact and dexterity when he chose to use a surgeon's scalpel in preference to a butcher's cleaver in paring unwanted fat from my overfed hog.

Unless otherwise stated in the captions, the photographs in the gallery are derived from the Noël Hume family archive (boxes in the attic). I am indebted to the Colonial Williamsburg Foundation for the use of the photographs on gallery pages 10 and 11; to my friend the late William Gordon Davis for the photographs on gallery pages 6, 8, and 9; to the late Allan J. Wingood for the photograph on gallery page 12; to the National Geographic Society for the photograph on gallery page 13; and to British Ceremonial Arts Ltd. for the photograph on gallery page 13.

Finally, here in the New World, I am indebted to all my archaeological friends and colleagues whose names inhabit these pages.

ACT ONE

In the Old World

1   *Off the Tumbrel*

"Never forget that you've Bourbon blood in your veins."

Had I been born where I wound up I might have deduced that my parents had a taste for Virginia Gentleman. In reality my mother was referring to the French royal family.

"Your father's mother was Princess Marie de Bourbon, but she made the mistake of marrying beneath her. He was just a poor Scotsman," Mother explained in one of her familiar lectures on the importance of breeding. "Had it not been for the War, your father would have had an estate in Jersey. But as it is, all we have is the name. Noël de Galichamps was one of your great-grandmother's many titles. It goes right back through the centuries."

Having a name that did that (as well as being part of a title) provided emotional armor to stiffen my spine through childhood years when I had little else of which to be proud. Indeed, its aura lasted much longer, as a yellowing manuscript in my attic still attests—the work of aspiring playwright Noël de Galichamps.

"Noël who?" my literary agent demanded. "What's this Galichamps stuff?" I winced when he pronounced the name to rhyme with lamps. "What's the matter with plain Hume?"

What indeed? The promotional value of being the great-grandson of a Bourbon princess had in any case been limited by the fact that nobody I knew thought much of the French. Nevertheless, the knowledge that I was related to characters in *The Scarlet Pimpernel* and *A Tale of Two Cities* brought history alive when most boys of my age were more at home with Billy Bunter and Tom Cherry in the weekly *Magnet*. Knowledge implies truth; but as politicians and clergymen understand better than most of us, belief is quite as useful. I believed what my mother had told me. To me, therefore, it was so, and such benefits as were to be derived from it were mine.

I was thirty-six before I learned the truth. My father, who I had barely known as a child, broke the news that my French great-grandmother was not a princess—though the family had a lineage guaranteed to bring a gleam to the eye of every ancestor-chasing genealogist. Louise Matilda Noël de Galichamps was the daughter of Georges Noël de Galichamps Centenier of Jersey, and was descended from Matilda, wife of William the Conqueror, in commemoration of which the name had remained in the family's female line until my grandmother's death in 1914. Through several centuries Noëls had lived in Normandy, owning twenty farms in the vicinity of Caen. They apparently lived well off their rents until 1791 when the word got around that the lynching of landlords was preferable to renting. The then head of the family (my father could not remember whether it was his "great-granddad or great-great ditto") was killed in a Pimpernel-style effort to rescue his wife from a tumbrel on its way to the guillotine. Escaping with the coachman to Jersey, she wisely married him. As for the rest of the family, realizing that gentry were no longer in fashion, they crept away from Caen and out of French history. The Noël farms eventually became the property of their erstwhile tenants. French law dictated that if agricultural rents remained uncollected for twenty years, the land could be claimed by the occupant. In the aftermath of the Revolution, no one in the family felt inclined to draw attention to themselves by pressing their claims. Thus, my father explained, "all we had left were six sacks of worthless title deeds."

So much for Princess Marie de Bourbon.

Nevertheless, my mother's story did contain some truth. My paternal grandmother, Louise Matilda etc. etc. Centenier (presumably the name of the coachman), did marry a Scot; he was poor, but even if he wasn't directly descended from William the Conqueror, she could hardly be said to have married beneath her. Charles Hume's mother was Isabel Twells, daughter of a partner in the firm of Barclay, Bevan, Tritton and Twells, the founders of Barclay's Bank; he had been educated at Eton, one of England's three best schools, spent his working life in the diplomatic corps, and before retiring from government became night controller of the postal service of Great Britain. That was the part that looked good in an obituary. The reality was less glittering; for diplomatic corps read civil servant—and a monstrously poorly paid one at that. Grandfather Hume was 3rd secretary in the British embassy at St. Petersburg with a salary of only £150 a year, so little that his wife could not afford to be with him. This had been true throughout their marriage, her family life restricted to the brief periods of her husband's leave between long months of loneliness at her father's home in

Jersey. She was there when a telegram was dispatched to St. Petersburg reporting that she was terminally ill. Charles hastened back from Russia to be at her bedside—bringing the news that a devastating European war was inevitable. Louise Matilda died on June 20, 1914, eight days before Archduke Francis Ferdinand was assassinated at Sarajevo.

Exactly one month later Austria-Hungary declared war on Serbia. In the meantime, my father, who had only recently been sent to England to be educated at Eton (old Etonians invariably bred young Etonians), was abruptly hauled home to Jersey as a result of what he rather vaguely described as "wartime fears of invasion." Unfortunately, I never asked him to be more explicit, and so it remains anybody's guess whether the invaders were expected to have their eye on Jersey or on Eton. There is, however, some evidence that fear of war was no more than a face-saving cover for the humiliating truth that 3rd Secretary Hume had discovered that he couldn't afford to send his son to so exclusive a school.

The Hume lineage had some bluish blood of its own, being descended on the male side from earls of Home (or Hume), but not on the female. Infant great-grandfather was found in a bundle on the steps of Edinburgh Castle with a label pinned to his blanket that read "Son of Hume" (or Home), a foundling believed to be the product of the earl's indiscretion.

My father was born in 1900 in the convent at Caen, where his mother had been educated. He was christened Cecil by his father (pronounced Sessle not Seasle—a name he detested and never used), and Noël by his mother to keep alive her family's historic name. My father's early childhood differed from those of most Edwardian families, which, regardless of class, tended to be large and gregarious. An only child with an absentee father, living with his mother in the home of aging grandparents on an island singularly short of cultural activity, it is hardly surprising that he described those years "as rather lonely." With few other children to play with, the most excitement he could expect from the adults was watching grandfather Centenier restoring antiques. Consequently, his admission to Eton meant escape into a new and exhilarating world of knowledge, sport, and camaraderie. Perhaps because he had previously had little to do but read, my father reportedly showed considerable academic promise—which made his precipitous withdrawal both educationally tragic and psychologically traumatic.

The scant records of my father's early life (derived largely from a single narrative letter in 1963 and my stepmother's recollections in 1978) provide endless opportunities for idle speculation. One wonders what kind of a marriage Charles Hume from Scotland and Louise Matilda from France enjoyed or, indeed, whether there was any joy in it. Of my father's fierce and abiding love for his mother there can be no doubt, but he made no secret of the fact that he barely knew his father. The latter's bereavement cannot be said to have been protracted. Within months he had remarried, wedding the much younger daughter of a Baltimore newspaper owner. Just what happened in Jersey thereafter remained a dark corner in my father's life. He would say only that the marriage "was hopeless as far as I was concerned and thereafter the relationship—with my father of whom I had seen so little, was never very close—ceased."

Marooned in Jersey in a new household that seemed to mock the memory of his mother, my father counted the weeks until he would be old enough to leave and go to war. Late in 1916 he obtained a commission in the Scots Guards and thus returned to the life he had tasted with such relish in his brief sojourn at Eton. Thin, fair-haired, good-looking, and sporting a youthful moustache which he likened to a cricket match (eleven a side), my father was a carbon copy of a generation of young Englishmen who waded through the shell-wracked Flanders mud brandishing walking sticks. But when, decades later, my stepmother would embarrass him by describing him as a very brave soldier, he vehemently denied it, saying "that he loved the excitement and companionship, helped by the fact that he left not a soul who cared about him—or any responsibilities behind."

Among the thousands who responded to the posters reminding young men and old that "Your Country Needs You!" was another sixteen-year-old who posed as seventeen and joined up without his parents' permission, although he was promptly bought out by his grandfather. Several months later he joined again, and was shipped to France as a private in the Essex Regiment. John Cecil Baines never met my father, and the two had in common only that both were escaping from stepmothers, and both were named Cecil and wished they weren't. Gassed within weeks of entering the line, John Baines was invalided home, and in a wry irony joined his family business (the Harwich Gas Company) as a gas engineer. In August 1927 he would become the father of an only daughter, a month before Cecil Noël Hume had a son who would eventually marry her.

Although my father's childhood can only be sketched in with a few broad strokes, his wartime experiences survive in more detail, though characteristically he chose only to dwell on those he described as "in the lighter vein." Nevertheless, they are valuable as an insight, into the character and style both of the young men who fought in the bloodiest of all wars and of the survivors who played England into the Jazz Age—into which I was to be born. A single extract from my father's notes for a history of his wartime experiences will suffice:

> Monty Hocker was the most serious "looker-after" of his unit possible.
>
> We were always trained that "men first—horses second and officers last." In one difficult bit of the line two orderlies were killed bringing up my rations. Monty came over the top with his eye-glass in his eye and carrying my rations, as he said he would not have one of his officers starved. . . .

Lieutenant (later Captain) Hume led his men over the top—out of their trenches into no-man's-land—thirty-six times without suffering a scratch, and when the war ended he and his surviving brother officers returned to their Scots Guards base at Guildford. With little to do throughout the summer of 1919, the returned heroes made the most of their good fortune. It was, my father said, "a gay summer"—the word then used in its naive and joyous sense to describe a lightness of spirit for which there is no other. There was boating on the river, bridge parties, endless tennis, riding, cub hunting, and the regimental dance "with the Savoy band and champagne all night." Why or when my father resigned his commission I do not know, but he apparently had not yet done so in the spring of 1920 when he made a decision that would mark the end of the halcyon postwar months, the end of youth, and the beginning of a life on the fast track in the era of saxophones and syncopation—all this from unwisely accepting an invitation to spend an afternoon at a suburban tennis club.

2 🖋 Pour le Sport

THE EALING TENNIS CLUB was eminently respectable, stolidly middle-class, and stupifyingly dull—at least to a butterfly in suburbia yearning for the bright life of Belgravia. Gladys Mary Bagshaw Mann (a name that might have been coined by Noël Coward for any young lady from Ealing) preferred to be called "Dimps," an abbreviation for dimples. She had two, and used them to winning effect—to the horror of her family (which persisted in calling her Glad) and the delight of the "Tennis, anyone?" crowd at the Ealing Club. She was rail thin, yet robustly athletic; she played tennis of championship caliber, sat a horse like a man, danced like thistledown, read the right magazines, and knew all the society scandal (albeit secondhand), and at twenty-two had had a "tragic affair" with a Canadian, the telling of which provided her with an intriguing aura of experience and fragile vulnerability. The combination was as lethal as Stilton in a penny mousetrap.

And my father reached for it.

The Mann family background is as fragmentary as my father's. Legend had it (or rather my mother had it) that her grandfather had been the last of twenty-one children, a brilliant man who became the youngest-ever director of a major London hospital. However, his brilliance teetered on the edge of madness, and when he began to fill his house with so much newly bought furniture that no space remained for his family, his wife suspected that all was not well. With the furniture wagons still coming, and amid the yet-to-be-uncrated tables and chairs, he shot himself. This does not explain the source of the Manns' modest, really very modest, fortune, but it did make a good, attention-grabbing story. My mother's father's achievements were not the stuff of which legends were woven, and he made his exit quite unspectacularly some years before I was born. He survives only as the maker of a mildly saucy joke intended to bring blushes to the cheeks of Edwardian ladies, and as the creator of a memorably patriotic line when his wife (who had been educated abroad) spoke German at the dinner table. "Enough of this ushen, gushen, gerfleischen!" he roared, slamming the table with the flat of his hand. My grandmother was said never to have uttered another word in German.

The joke: If s-c-h-e-m-e-s spells schemes, what does c-h-e-m-i-s-e spell? Female undergarments were then truly unmentionables, and the fun was to trip the lady into answering the question before realizing what she had uttered. It was, as I said, only mildly saucy—and only marginally funny.

I have often pondered the capriciousness of immortality, and have wondered how my grandfather would have felt had he been told that this pair of gems was to be his only legacy. His widow must have had more worthy memories, but although she lived until 1944, she kept them to herself. My grandmother was always kind to me, and I remember her with affection—in spite of her rather formidable appearance. A champion badminton player in her youth, she had been hit by a shuttlecock and blinded in one eye. Henceforth, she always wore dark glasses, and those, coupled with the black or navy blue bonnet and voluminous clothes of the same hue worn in perpetual mourning for her husband, could cast a chill over the liveliest gathering. She also had strangely gray skin, which greatly enhanced the funereal effect. I called her "Ahmoo," presumably because she entered my vocabulary when it was quite small.

Ahmoo had three children. The eldest, Harold, did something ghastly, was banished to Mexico, and thereafter was classified as the family's black sheep. Before departing, however, Uncle Harold revealed the depth of his affection for his youngest sister when he warned my father: "If you take my advice, you'll drop her like a hot cake. She'll bring you nothing but trouble." The Manns' second child, Marian, was large, red-haired, desperately plain, and walked as though she had something stuck between her legs. Like Harold, she made a career of condemning her younger sister for being all the things she was not. It was not, by and large, a happy family. Aunt May married a kind but mousy little man who spent his life behind steel-rimmed spectacles amid the steam and pigeons of Paddington Station as an accountant for the Great Western Railway. My mother claimed that he was "chief clerk," but she was prone to making her own promotions. Thus, Uncle Harold became "chief engineer" for Henry Ford in Detroit—a contribution to automotive history overlooked by the Ford Motor Company, which has been unable to find any record of his service.

If my father had been a better tennis player, the encounter at the Ealing Club might have ended on the day it began. But he was not, and Dimps undertook to improve his game, a course which led quickly and unexpectedly to a marriage license and a registry office. In retrospect neither claimed to be in love, and both expressed surprise that it had happened. But while that was true of my father, it is unlikely that my mother was that naive. Her talent for living dangerously led to numerous miscalculations, but rarely, if ever, to no calculations at all. My father was her ticket to Shangri-la, or at least to the bright young people of Belgravia and to dining at the Dorchester.

Had it been necessary for my father to try to indulge his bride's taste for everything she saw in the pages of the *Tatler* or on the counters of Fortnum and Mason through his army pay alone, their marriage might have run its course before it did either of them any lasting harm. As it turned out, however, through the help of his friends my father obtained a civilian job that ensured the marriage's continuation through eleven years and one son. My yet-to-be-father soon became the London representative for the New York–based Central Hanover Bank and Trust Company. The job had less to do with banking than with playing host to the bank's international customers, and one that relied heavily not only on the man's personality but on the charm of his wife, the all-important hostess. In the eyes of the Americans, they had found the ideal couple—and the couple had found a goose that laid the smoothest eggs. The salary had a noble look to it, and the expense account was even better. Now the dimpled butterfly from Ealing could spread her wings—glittering dinner parties, the best theater seats, race meetings at Ascot, driving expensive cars—all desperately exhausting, but all bravely born, and all on behalf of the bank.

Like the cinematic cliché wherein leaves from a calendar blow away to mark the passage of time, so the growing number of hotel and Cunard and White Star steamship labels multiplied on the sides of the Humes' cabin trunks. Business trips to New York and Paris, vacations in Switzerland and the south of France, and every year a rented house by the sea at fashionable Eastbourne became the world-wearying lot of poor Dimps. Year by year she was finding being nice to Americans increasingly tiresome, and discovering new amusements testingly difficult. Nevertheless, in spite of the General Strike of 1926, the British economy seemed strong, and the word from America was business—and more business. For the Hanover Bank's fun couple in England the jazz bands played on. But the cracks beneath the rouge and the powder were beginning to show. Perhaps spurred by thin-lipped and celluloid-collared clerks in New York who had to review the London office's expenses, my father began to chide Dimps for her extravagance. He wasn't amusing anymore. Then he made her pregnant—right in middle of the tennis season.

My mother had an almost embarrassing penchant for telling the truth about herself and did so to people she barely knew. A friend recalled how she confessed that she both swam and played tennis the week before I was born and how angry was the doctor who had warned her in no uncertain terms the harm she might be doing. In one of her last letters my mother remembered me as "quite the most beautiful baby anyone had ever seen! So much so that men in Hyde Park wanted nurse to allow them to photograph and paint you, and at Eastbourne, too!!" Throughout her life she spoke in exclamation points, but these seem to have been justified, though one wonders about men who stop nurses in the park. The never-lying camera captured a curly-haired cherub of cathedral innocence; and sitting in my gleaming perambulator under a neatly arranged rug I must have been every mother's vision of what a boy child should be. Had they removed the rug, however, they would have found a cripple.

I was born with rickets, and spent the first two years of my life with my lower legs encased in plaster. Consequently, I was destined to endure the embarrassment of walking through most of my childhood with ankles supported by boots—an embarrassment because boots were the mark of working-class boys. Unable to take part in the sports that were the traditional route to health and happiness at school, I would have to look elsewhere for contentment. But that was way off in the future. First, I needed a name.

There seemed to be no rush. My mother used to joke that until my christening I was identified either as "it," which is understandable, or as "Tweezle"—which isn't. The discovery that I was not christened at St. George's Hanover Square and my subsequent failure to locate the right parish records have prevented me from determining exactly how long I remained nameless—probably about five weeks, for my birth certificate is dated November 4, 1927. I do know, however, that it was my godmother, Lady "Tiny" North, who, on the morning of my becoming, as it were, official, pointed out that it would be a mistake to turn up at the church without something a little more appropriate than the third-person pronoun. Lady North carried considerable weight. She was the mother of my father's wartime and dance band friend Vivian North, and the widow of Sir Henry North, who was known to the cheaper newspapers as "Harry, the Nitrate King." A fortune based on the export of Peruvian guano having provided him entrée into the circle of Edward, Prince of Wales, who knighted him upon succeeding to the throne, Sir Harry North had been a larger-than-life figure whose close-to-the-throne hijinks made his widow a friend of great worth. Consequently, her demand that serious thought be given to providing Dimps's baby with a name other than "it" or Tweezle produced hasty action.

Retaining the French connection by holding on to my father's Noël took care of the middle name, but rustling up a first in the midst of last-minute preparations for the postchristening party was infinitely more taxing. Casting around for inspiration, my mother spotted 1924's best seller, Michael Arlen's *The Green Hat*, subtitled *A Romance for a Few People*. She opened it at random and lighted on the name of the novel's hero—Ivor. "That's it! We'll call him Ivor." And so they did.

Although Ivor is a perfectly good name in Wales, I wasn't Welsh, nor was I a homosexual matinee idol. In England, Ivor Novello was everybody's Ivor of the 1930s. Consequently, I grew up to dislike the name as fervently as my father loathed Cecil. He, however, could escape it by always using his middle name, and at the moment of my christening, so could I. But by the time I left the church I had been finessed. I no longer had a middle name. Although today hyphenated names are adopted by steely-eyed and socially conscious brides as a mark of retained independence, in the 1920s double-barreled names were acquired by upwardly mobile members of the middle class who became Skeffington-Smythe (having kicked off as Smith) or Baskerville-Brown. Thus, when signing the register my mother deftly shifted the Noël out of the middle name slot into the surname—then left out the hyphen.

Any sleuth checking the accuracy of this nomenclatorial narrative can readily find a flaw in it. In block 7 of my birth certificate under the heading "Signature, Description and Resident of Informant" will be found my father's name, indicating that it was he and not my mother who filled out the form. But detectives and historians might do well to look closely at this example as a warning that even so straightforward a document as a birth certificate may not be as honest as it seems. In the two places where my father's name appears, it is given as C. Noël Hume or Cecil over Noël Hume, and one might argue that he was simply recording his Hume surname and both his Christian names. Indeed, he styled himself in that way throughout his later life. The clue that it was my mother who provided the information to the registrar lurks in block 5, under "Name and Maiden Surname of Mother," and reads "Gladys Mary Noël Hume formerly Bagshaw Mann." To no one's recollection did my maternal grandmother ever call herself anything but Mann. Evidently, therefore, in upgrading the Humes my mother Bagshawed the Manns—something my father would never have done. Thus was I reduced to one unacceptable Christian name and had my surname expanded into two unconnected bits, ensuring that I should forever be billed twice or be impenetrably filed.

Dimps would recount the *Green Hat* story whenever anyone asked why the little lad with Scots forebears had been given a Welsh name. I don't remember how old I was when I first heard it or whether it occurred to me that, rather than being comic, the tale was saying something sad about the Hume household. The latter certainly did not occur to my mother, who saw the story as a demonstration of the worldly sophistication that was the trademark of her circle, if not of her class. On March 22, 1928, when the curtain rose on Noël Coward's *This Year of Grace*, with lyrics as brash and brittle as its audience, one refrain said it all:

> We're little women,
> Alluring little women,
> Cute but cold fish
> Just like goldfish
> Looking for a bowl to swim in.
> We lead ornamental
> But uncreative lives,
> We may be little women
> But we're not good wives.

Fifty years later I asked Joan, my father's widow (and my beloved stepmother) whether she remembered the *Green Hat* explanation, and whether it was true. She replied that she did and supposed it to be so. She added that there was still a copy of the book in my father's bookcases, perhaps *the* copy. It proved to be a small brown book with thick, opulent pages of the kind that had to be cut by hand and thereafter went through life with slightly shaggy edges. Holding it was a memorable experience. Like the archaeologist reaching out to pick up a thousand-year-old potsherd, I had come within a hand's touch of a moment in history—my own history, a moment that has had its impact on every day of it.

Michael Arlen was the darling of his day. A reviewer in *Cassell's Weekly* called him "Belgravia's best seller"; the *Daily Express* declared that "for sheer wit and cynicism Mr. Arlen stands alone." Arlen's characters and settings were the mirror of young London society in the '20s, and like all mirrors, his had the ability to reproduce itself through an infinity of reflections. He chronicled, and in his readers created more, bright young people saying all the fashionable things that his typewriter had put into their mouths. He was young England's pied piper—which was odd, because Michael Arlen was really Dikran Kuyumjian, an Armenian born, not in Belgravia, but in Bulgaria.

What kind of an Ivor would I find between the pages of *The Green Hat*, and would I be seeing in him the kind of individual my mother dreamed I would become? Both questions were front and center as I opened the book and began to read. In the first paragraph I learned that the hat "was bright green, of a sort of felt, and bravely worn: being, no doubt, one of those that women who have many hats affect *pour le sport.*" The italics were the author's, but they otherwise would have been mine. The words were also Dimps's; she had used them countless times to explain her own unfortunate decisions as well as the games that capricious fate played upon her. The novel's tragic heroine was Iris—Iris Storm, Iris of the green hat, Iris at whom young men looked furtively "in the way that decent men will at a woman who is said to have had lovers," Iris the "slave of freedom." Long before she drove away into the night at the wheel of her yellow Hispano-Suiza and the sound of the metal-rending crash echoed across the silent English fields, I knew that my mother had looked into Michael Arlen's mirror and seen Iris Storm.

Looking for Ivor, I encountered Iris's war hero husband (murdered by the Sinn Fein in Ireland); her weak brother Gerald, who accosted the wrong woman in Hyde Park, got his name in the Sunday papers, and shot himself; Billy Swift (found dead near Dover); and several more elegant names-about-town, Boy Fenwick, Guy, Napier, and Hilary. "Suddenly the moaning of the wrecked car ceased, and in the silence Hilary walked into the darkness about the great tree." And so did I. The book was over, and no one named Ivor had so much as tooted a party blower or cut his throat in the ladies loo at Victoria Station.

How, I wondered, could Dimps have concocted so specific a story, and more importantly, why? For some minutes after reading the final sentence I sat with the book open on my knee pondering those questions. Slowly, perhaps caught by a draft or as the reflex result of having spent decades pressed against page 328, number 329 turned to reveal a page of advertising for another Michael Arlen book:

"PIRACY"

Fifth Printing   *7/6 & 3/6 Net*
This is the story of Ivor Pelham Marley, between the ages of eighteen
and thirty-two, and the period is . . .

So there I was, not a reincarnation of *The Green Hat*'s hero, but an identity unceremoniously fished out of the ads at the back. Had my mother remembered to append that final detail to her story, it would almost certainly have made her point recognizably—as the *Daily Sketch* critic said of Michael Arlen—"vivid, amusing, alive, intensely modern." Smart people took babies in their stride, delivering them like corks from champagne bottles, then went back to the party, leaving the infant to the nursery staff. And so it was for me.

The legend of Ivor and *The Green Hat* provided both a commentary on an era and a useful lesson for novice historians: folk tales should not be lightly dismissed as too preposterous, for although they may have been embellished and adapted into falsehood, somewhere within them hides a kernel of truth.

I, Ivor Noël (no hyphen) Hume, was born on September 30, 1927, at our rented home, Number 4, Upper Cheyne Row; the street where Thomas Carlyle had his home, and down which most of the great literary figures of the nineteenth century had driven to get there: Dickens, Huxley, Kingsley, John Stuart Mill, to drop the names of but a few. No one would deny that Upper Cheyne Row in the historic heart of Chelsea (within a stone's cast from the old Chelsea porcelain factory) was a good place to be born, not as grand as Mayfair, but fashionably chic at a time when Chelsea was a far cry from the punk-ridden sink much of it would become forty years later. Nevertheless, to American bankers with middle-American minds, bohemian London was not an appropriate setting for their ideal Limey and his charming wife. Shortly after the christening we moved uptown into Michael Arlen's Belgravia, to Knightsbridge and the imposing brick houses of Hans Place, and within dollar-tossing distance of the American Mecca—Harrods.

My own recollections of my first five years are few, but sharply etched. To be precise, there are four.

Within days of my birth I was put in the charge of a trained nurse and relegated to the top of the house and out of the way of my parents and their guests. There was nothing unusual about that; it was the normal procedure for any family with the money to employ a nurse and with a house large enough to provide a day and night nursery, as well as quarters for the nurse and for a nursery maid. In our case, I suspect that the latter did double duty as a kitchen maid, for the house was no mansion. Nevertheless, there had to be a nursery maid; no nurse worth her pabulum would take a position where she had to do her own chores. Besides, I know that we had such a maid for she starred in one of my four recollections.

With my legs encased in plaster of Paris I was a fairly immobile infant and did not require to be continuously caged in a playpen. My recollection, therefore, is of lying on a rug on the nursery floor and being introduced by the maid to a curious game of hide-and-seek. Standing astride me as I lay on my back, with her rough black stockings and white thighs looming above me, she would squat down, enveloping me in the darkness of her skirts. In the movie business this is known as "going to black," and for me the recollection ends there. I have no idea whether I was frightened or amused, or whether it happened once or often. I would like to believe that the maid got more out of it than I did. Why then, I have wondered, was this incident chosen as one of my four free looks into my infancy?

Of my parents, an old friend recalled, "They had been married some years before you were born. I saw you only about twice; you were entirely taken over by a grand Norlan nurse, and never seemed to be with them." Norlan nurses were, and still are, the best trained of any, and the name and the graduates' brown uniforms carried considerable weight in the nannying world, and, indeed, in the world of those who hired them. I had several (one at a time), not all of them, I think, from the same stable. The source of the one who figures in Recollections Nos. 2 and 3 is lost in the mists, though I have sometimes looked at the surviving photographs in which such a guardian appears and have asked, "Was it you, you with the chubby cheeks and the jolly smile? Was it you who shut my fingers in the door?"

"Master Ivor, you will learn . . ." I don't remember what. Indeed, the words may not be part of the recollection. They, and variations on them, belong to a recurring nightmare in which the waking memory is relived and expanded upon, though never to the pain of the door closing. As I say, I do not recall what it was that I was to be taught, perhaps not to try to crawl through the open doorway. I remember only being carried screaming toward it, the door of a light color and opening to the right, and beyond it a room or corridor in darkness. My wrist is gripped and my hand thrust out into the shadows and pressed against the door jamb. Then the light of the painted door spreads across my vision narrowing the darkness, and I know that when the black line disappears the door will have closed on my fingers. I suspect that the lesson was never carried to its bone-damaging conclusion, but as a reminder it evidently did the trick.

The third image is almost certainly by courtesy of the same nanny. I am held up to look into the nursery fire. The grate is iron and has black lateral bars, and behind them the coals glow an orange red. The nurse takes my teddy bear, an unusual bear made of wood, dark brown and scaly like bark, with limbs that dangle and click when shaken, and she throws it into the fire. I am forced to watch the flames erupt around it. It must have been of some hard wood, for instead of disappearing, it turns black amid the flames and then a glowing red like the coals around it. Again, I have no idea what I had done or not done to deserve the punishment, nor do I recall this incident returning in my dreams. It has simply stayed on an open shelf in my mental library throughout my life. Many years later my mother told me that one of my nurses had been dismissed after being deemed emotionally unsuitable.

Trying to get my infant recollections in order, I thought that if I were to visit the houses in Upper Cheyne Row and at Hans Place, seeing the nursery rooms might stir other memories and prove which recollection belonged where. In 1985, therefore, I wrote to the present owner of the Chelsea house, who graciously agreed to show me around. It had been built in the 1920s and so was relatively new when my father leased it. Waiting in the drawing room while the owner took a phone call, I wondered whether someone with psychic powers could recapture the electricity of the emotional crises that had wracked my parents' marriage in that room nearly fifty years earlier. Upstairs, alas, no ghosts were stirring. The master bedroom, in which I was born, said nothing to me, nor did the nursery rooms above. No door-window-fireplace relationship matched the room of my memories. I had to conclude, therefore, that the memories related to my second home, the house in Hans Place.

The Chelsea house location I knew from my birth certificate, but I would have to go back to the London telephone directories for the Hans Place number. But they did me no good. For reasons no longer explainable, they contained only my father's office address. Our home was unlisted. One clue remained, however. The pouch of aging photographs retrieved after my mother's death included a picture of the house taken from within the iron-fenced residents' garden. All I had to do was to reconstruct the camera position based on the garden details, and I would be looking straight at the old family home.

I found the garden details easily enough and had no trouble recognizing the house next door; but "ours" in the photograph did not match the one I was looking at. Number 37 had the same five stories (one shorter than those flanking it), but the details were wrong. I rang the bell and sheepishly explained my problem to the man who answered the door. "I'd like to help you," he said, "but this house wasn't built until 1952." He had no knowledge of what had been there before or what had happened to the house. "Maybe it was bombed in the war," he suggested.

ARP (Air Raid Precautions) records in the Chelsea Library's archives later proved him right. The entry in the *Bomb Incidents Book* for May 11, 1941, reads "37/38 Hans Place. HE [high explosive] direct on 37. Premises demolished. No casualties." As I disappointedly stepped away from the door of its successor, I nearly collided with a shiny black perambulator containing a ruddy-faced infant who clearly had been born with all of, if not more than, the advantages I had enjoyed. I apologized to his uniformed nurse and was told, "One should watch where one is going." She sounded as though she could have done an equally good job with "Master Ivor, you will learn," and recalling history's propensity for repetition, I hoped for the tot's sake that his parents would not discover Nanny to be emotionally unsuitable.

In 1929 emotional unsuitability was not confined to the nursery, it permeated the household, and like a Soufrière, could erupt at the most inopportune moments. For Dimps, money had not brought contentment; the good things of pre-Depression life turned to ashes in her hands, and somebody had to be blamed—even the butler. His name was Aubrey (though I never knew whether that was his Christian or his surname), and his wife was the cook. On the evening of an important bank-related dinner party, Aubrey opened the door to the first guests with his suitcase in his hand. As they entered, he left—along with his wife, leaving a note in the kitchen telling "Madam" to get her own dinner. This was another of the admissions of which my mother was unashamed, though she used it to demonstrate the unreliability of servants. Aubrey had been a person of some presence, she said, "a cut above the average," and shortly before his departure had made shockingly improper advances which had led to a noisy scene and considerable slamming of doors. One needs no Holmesian intellect to question that testimony, for it is hardly likely that a butler in a relatively small household and with his wife on the premises would make a pass at his mistress. If he was fool enough to do so and was repulsed, the result would have been his dismissal rather than a door-slamming shouting match and the simultaneous resignation of both butler and cook.

Whatever the truth may have been, the Aubrey incident was symptomatic of the tension in the Hume household. With the move to Hans Place, so wrote an old friend, "thus began a life of endless parties, but by then it was absolutely cat and dog, if ever they were alone—totally incompatible." The widow of one of my father's closest army friends confessed that they could not bear the humiliation he had to endure, and so saw less and less of him. It amused Dimps, she said, to constantly deflate him. One by one the friends crept away "until there were none, just hangers-on for the free drinks and parties."

> Let the cauldron bubble
> Justify your fate.
> Dance, dance, dance little lady,
> Leave tomorrow behind.

Although their relevance may not have been recognized, Noël Coward's lines, written in 1928, were almost certainly sung at Hans Place, for both my father and my mother were fine party pianists, my mother accompanying herself as she sang in a smoky, Dietrich-style voice. Although the international monetary cauldron was bubbling, and would boil over on October 24, 1929, the Wall Street crash had no immediate impact on the Hanover Bank's London office. For us, the band played on. At Dimps's insistence my father continued to run two rented houses, Hans Place and a large villa complete with fountain and tennis court at Eastbourne; and, when necessary, the cars got larger and faster. Like everything—or almost everything—Dimps did, she did it with style and she did it well. In an era when relatively few women had the opportunity to drive, she handled a car with enormous panache on Sussex roads better suited to a pony and trap. Photographs of only one of those cars survive, a huge convertible two-seater, a 1927 American Willys-Knight, its hood (the English call it a bonnet) half the length of the vehicle, massive black fenders (called mudguards), and wide running boards, and the body probably yellow, though one can't be sure of that in a black-and-white picture slowly turning sepia. Perched at the wheel in the picture and wearing what appears to be a white overcoat, infant Ivor looks like a marshmallow on a mountain—driving into the good life.

With my father working in the City, for Dimps the Eastbourne summers passed slowly, the days (weather permitting) spent stretched out on thick rugs, browning on the beach. The rugs had to be thick and plentiful because the beach at Eastbourne is composed entirely of chalk lumps and flint rocks; without padding, sitting on it is an experience enjoyed only by Indian fakirs. Although most of the Eastbourne beaches were open to the general public (known to my mother as "the great unwashed"), sections were set aside by consent, if not by law, to those who rented beach huts by the season—as we did. From them, the staff served lunch. It was all very civilized, and very dull. Watched over by the jolly nurse (she of the resplendent teeth) and still trapped in plaster, I was unable to paddle or collect seaweed like other children. I simply sat on the rocks, scorched an allegedly healthy nut-brown, and made "milk." This divertissement involved one bucket of seawater, two large flints, and several pieces of chalk to grind between them, the resulting powder poured into the water and stirred. It can't have been a pastime having a high satisfaction factor or much staying power, but nurse had to think of something to keep the child amused. As happens in any manufacturing plant when the workers get bored, they get sloppy and safety standards slip. Not paying sufficient attention to the correct positioning of raw material (chalk) to machinery (rocks A and B), this worker left a little finger on the anvil and whacked it with rock B. The finger burst like a ripe fruit, turning the milk to strawberry jam and ruining the afternoon. The scar that resulted from this mishap (for which the nurse was blamed and loudly reprimanded) is still clearly and jaggedly visible, my only memento of those halcyon summer days when infant Ivor's future looked very different from the way it turned out.

The small leather pouch containing the bundle of photographs that proved to be my mother's only documentary legacy included several shots of those Eastbourne summers, one of them showing the nut-brown lad sitting in his pram, and in the background the façade of the town's most exclusive and celebrated watering place, the Grand Hotel. A vast and rather somber Victorian pile by day, but by night, with its windows ablaze and its forecourt festooned with fairy lights, it became a flame to attract every social butterfly still capable of flight. Tanned young men with oiled hair and stiff shirts danced in the Palm Court with girls in gossamer gowns. Older women, no longer lithe enough to go naked beneath their dresses, hoped that their reinforcements would not show, kept their gloves on, and worked hard at being amusing. Old men with red cheeks, money in their pockets, and lechery on their minds smoked their cigars, talked of huntin' and the Raj, and watched for an opportunity to comfort a lady in distress. There were tears from the girls who didn't want to, tears from those who wished they hadn't, and tears from the ones whose escorts had passed out and couldn't. And then there were the girls who needed money.

My mother's choices of Grand Hotel escorts were, to say the least, eclectic. One among them was an Irishman named Patrick Herbert Mahon, who, said my mother, was a "very jolly chap and an excellent dancer." An older conquest, Emily Kaye, must have been equally impressed by Pat, who in the spring of 1924 took her from Eastbourne to a bungalow in the seaside village of Pevensey where he sawed her up and burned her head in the living-room fireplace. My mother thought the grizzly murder thrilling and ended her narrative with "Darling, imagine! It could have been me!"

It was at the Grand in 1924 that Dimps met the man whose baleful yet gilded influence would chart her course for close on fifteen years. To both my mother and me, he was our "Uncle Fred," Santa Claus in a dinner jacket. Part owner of a large Bradford department store known as "the Harrods of the North," Frederick Maufe, may have born the stigma of being in trade, but he knew the world, had a well-tailored shoulder to cry on, and could be so very helpful. Dimps's mother and her sister, May, having seemingly set aside their resentment of her previous behavior, were frequent visitors to the villa at Eastbourne, and at the Grand were often guests of Dimps's new and courtly acquaintance. Before long Uncle Fred became a friend of the family, and as such was accepted by my father. Indeed, he had no reason to do otherwise, and furthermore had little choice. He could not dictate what his wife could do or who she should see while he was absent in London. Besides, Fred Maufe was an old man, a father figure, whose friendship posed no threat; on the contrary it kept her amused and out of mischief.

If Uncle Fred had a fault, it had to be his readiness to help both husband and wife; yet there seemed no harm in allowing him the pleasure of picking up the tab for parties at the Grand or for theater seats in London. My father must have begun to have misgivings when the help extended to buying his wife expensive clothes and thereby pandering to the extravagance that had already been the cause of matrimonial friction. Inevitably there came a time when his efforts to curb Dimps's excesses were greeted with the answer, "If you won't buy it for me, Uncle Fred will." Two had become three: husband, wife, and friend; yet it was a triangle that, on the surface, was harmless enough. Fred, after all, was an old man who had had troubles with his own family and looked on the Humes as surrogate children. Nevertheless, as a friend who watched from the sidelines later remarked, "Uncle Maufe plied Dimps with checks and exotic clothes, but demanded his pound of flesh which was limited only by old age!"

With the actors on stage, the play progressed with the inevitability of Greek tragedy. Uncle Fred's price had to be met, and once paid, Dimps's responsibility to her husband was compromised. A protective wall of pretense had been erected between them, and from behind it she could hide transgressions more satisfying than feeding the fantasies of Uncle Fred. How much and how long my father suspected, I do not know, nor do I know whether the proof was secured by accident or entrapment. All that matters is that in the spring of 1931 he had the evidence. His problem was what to do with it. Rather than taking the contrite wife's way out and blaming the other man for leading her astray, Dimps castigated my father for not standing by her. Divorce was the logical course, but how would that play on Wall Street? The American bankers might frequent speakeasies and keep mistresses in Manhattan, but they did it quietly. How would the board of the Central Hanover Bank and Trust Company react to news that its swell young couple in London was breaking up under circumstances worthy of Michael Arlen?

My father concluded that his manhood and his honor were more important than expediency. In front of her mother, he told Dimps that the marriage would end just as soon as arrangements could be made to dispose of the Eastbourne and

Hans Place leases. True to his code he would do the honorable thing and take the uncontesting defendant's role, manufacturing the evidence of his own transgression: a room at the Dorchester Hotel, a primed prostitute, and a private detective to testify—the well-established charade ensuring that plaintiff and defendant were in and out of the Law Courts before a reporter could sharpen his pencil.

The marriage had begun without love, and after eleven years it would end the same way. There was to be no turning back, no weakening of resolve. Forty-eight years later, however, my mother cryptically suggested otherwise. "Always I have had deep regret," she wrote, "that I never said 'yes' when your father gave me two chances to start again."

Bridge-playing readers with memories geared to remembering which cards are out and which are not may recall my saying that I retained four infant memories, but described only three. The fourth is of a bedroom, a suitcase on a stand at the end of the large bed, and another case on the bed itself. The room is light and airy, sunlight streams through a tall window to the right of the bed. To the left in a corner of the facing wall, the door is open, and there is much coming and going through it, though the people are mere shapes, not eerily faceless, just lacking identity. There are ties on the bed. I pick one up; it has green stripes, and I hand it to a man who thanks me and lays it in the suitcase. That's all.

The man was my father, and the occasion the day of his departure.

Of one thing there can be no doubt. An era had ended; nothing would ever be the same again. A year later my father remarried, choosing the sister of one of those friends who had retreated to a safe distance during the latter years of his marriage to Dimps. Although he lost the Hanover Bank job in 1934 and would never again live the affluent life of the 1920s, he found a home and married happiness that transcended all material advantages. For Dimps, the future offered prospects for excitement and adventure to set her eyes sparkling and her senses tingling. Released from her marital fetters, she was free to play the field. Still young enough to be desirable, yet mature enough to attract men of substance, she was certain that she would quickly have the lions of London by their tails. Although her court-decreed alimony only amounted to seven hundred pounds a year, with care and a few economies it would do quite well while she took the time to carefully choose and bait her hooks. Besides, she still had the security that had given her the confidence to deceive my father; she still had Uncle Fred.

Perhaps as a symbol of her new freedom, in the summer of 1932 my mother abandoned "Dimps" in favor of a new nickname. Refreshed and repainted, "Poppet" was ready *pour le sport*.

3 🖋 *Poppet and Son*

FOR MY FATHER, picking up the pieces proved relatively simple. Although he had no parents to help him, he had many friends ready and eager to welcome him back into the club. The bad financial news from America initially brought no hint that his job was in peril, and no one at the bank had expressed disapproval at his discreetly handled divorce. The Hume future seemed bright enough; "Poppet" Noël Hume's prospects, on the other hand, were less clearly charted. Key ground rules had changed; with Hans Place gone and reduced to apartment living, she had lost her social place as a hostess. With her staff whittled down to one live-in housekeeper and the odd daily maid, the character of Poppet's parties changed from formal dinners to chic little gatherings of a few amusing people. She soon discovered a distinct difference between being a semiprofessional hostess for my father and his banker associates and relying for one's social life on being other people's guest.

No one could deny that my mother was an entertaining dinner companion. Her laughter, though brittle, was infectious; she had a vast store of hilarious stories about people in society (picked up from Lady North and others); and she could be counted on to be a good sport. No need for chaps to worry about whether or not they might be offending her sense of propriety. Poppet's talent for being one of the boys had its disadvantages. The wives of the boys were less enchanted, and remembering Iris Storm, they did not see her as the ideal dinner guest. From the curls of her bobbed hair to the tips of her manicured fingers, she was a competitor. Exercise and the contents of small jars from Elizabeth Arden enabled her to look twenty-three at thirty-three, a miracle she was able to perform through a decade of ups and downs that would have wrought havoc around the eyes of weaker women. But like Dorian Gray, the years had to go somewhere. Poppet's picture in the closet was me, and while for her time stood still, I kept on growing.

Keeping Ivor out of sight in an apartment was not easy; at Eastbourne, however, the problem was greatly reduced. Although the villa and its tennis court had been exchanged for a semidetached maisonette, it had two floors and a fair-sized garden, and, of course, there was always the beach. From her new base, my mother continued to shine at the tennis club, but was less frequently seen at the Grand Hotel. Short of close friends, she sought solace in the chilling bosom of her family, and while both Ahmoo Mann and sister May accepted invitations to visit, the "How could you?" and "I told you so" notes in their voices made them psychologically unhelpful. Their responses were not unexpected, however, and were brushed aside in the euphoria of an expected remarriage. I remember nothing about the suitor but his name, Leslie Atkins, and know only that he played tennis well and owned a fast car.

Driving from London to Eastbourne one day with Poppet as his passenger, and urged by her to show what he and the car could do, Leslie was roaring through the country roads near Guildford. Accelerating up a hill, he sped past a sign indicating a left intersection and was unaware of a horse and wagon coming toward him on a relatively narrow road. Swerving to avoid the wagon, he failed to see a man on a bicycle pedaling out from the intersection. Braking too late, Leslie hit him broadside; the car skidded and crashed into the bank, its passenger door flew open, and my mother was thrown clear. Leslie remained in the car bleeding from minor injuries and thanking providence that he was still alive. The bicyclist, however, was not.

I heard my mother's account of the accident several times, but I am hazy about its aftermath. There certainly was an inquest, but whether Atkins was sent to trial for manslaughter, I do not know. According to one version he was tried at Guildford assizes. But whether it was at the inquest or at the trial (if trial there was), my mother is credited with getting him acquitted. A friend of my father's recalled that "only Dimps's impassioned speech on Atkins's behalf saved him getting a prison sentence." Had the scenario been Michael Arlen's, Leslie would have emerged from the courtroom ashen but contrite and filled with love and gratitude. Instead, the car accident not only killed the bicyclist but was the death of the engagement—perhaps because my mother's impassioned defense made no reference to her own guilt in having goaded her fiancé into driving ever faster, or perhaps because she and not he had been at the wheel.

Never having had any filial relationship with my father, I can have felt no loss at his departure, nor any feeling of joy at the prospect of a replacement. Indeed, I remember the candidates less as people whom I saw often enough to like or dislike than as visitors who gave me things. There was Basil Stafford, who had made a modest fortune by inventing Ebe bath powder—small flower-shaped tablets which when placed in the tub fizzed about on the surface and turned the water a bluish green. To my childish delight, he tried them out in our bath at Eastbourne, but he scored his highest points when he gave me a digital watch. It didn't work, but by turning the standard winding and setting knob one could make the numbers appear in tiny windows in its silver-plated face. This was my introduction to high tech, and perhaps I owe my lifelong passion for gadgets to Basil's busted watch.

Of the suitors I saw or heard about, the next was the owner of a chain of London dry-cleaning establishments. I believe he was married and waiting for a divorce, but he never gave me anything and so cannot have been a very serious contender. Then there was Harvey Sangster, the rich owner of a famous motorcycle factory in Birmingham. He had a beard and looked interestingly piratical; more important, he gave me a copy of a fat book filled with the world's weirdest wonders, *Ripley's Believe It or Not.* I did. The drawings of redwoods with cars going through them, sea monsters, vampire bats, messages in bottles, Melanesian canoes, and shaded people with dinner plates in their lips and skewers through their noses first sparked my curiosity about the world beyond London's Kensington Gardens (on whose Round Pond my toy boat sank) and the beach at Eastbourne. Uncle Harvey's book had a profound influence, and I well remember him giving it to me saying, "That should keep you occupied!" (or words to that effect), and how my mother laughed as they went out and shut the drawing-room door.

The search for a new and wealthy father kept my mother busy through the 1930s—except on Thursdays. That was Uncle Fred's time, the day for running fingers through the faded feathers of the golden goose. Perhaps owing to servant problems at home I accompanied my mother on one such pilgrimage. Fred Maufe lived in a large, second-floor apartment in stolidly expensive St. John's Wood. I remember it as being dark—dark wood, dark wallpaper, a dark day. We had lunch at a very large table, just the three of us, and I recall being very small and isolated, perched on a chair too high for my legs to touch the ground and too low for me to be seen to "sit up properly." With the meal over, Uncle Fred took me to the bay window at one end of the long room and removed the cushions from its built-in seats that doubled as lidded storage space. Inside were numerous boxes of toy soldiers, each box crammed with soldiers, the legs of their horses, the trains of their cannon, and the shafts of their lances all tangled together, as though the carnage of Balaclava had been dumped into a few cardboard burial pits. "Be careful with them, young man. They're very old," I was told.

So play I did—but carefully. I untangled the cavalry, set aside the horses with broken legs, adjusted the heads of grenadiers decapitated in long-forgotten battles and reattached with matchsticks, collected up loose arms and pushed them back onto grateful shoulders, and reassembled the Coldstreamers' bandsmen. But by mid-afternoon the job was done, the army was in parade order, and all that remained in the boxes were chips of paint and broken feet. Playing with soldiers by oneself, particularly an old man's soldiers, has limited potential. And as the shadows of a winter's afternoon lengthened in the corners of the paneled dining room, I retreated to the window and sat watching what little life was to be seen in the street outside. There were iron railings on the other side and beyond them trees and a public garden where, on sunny days, nurses pushed perambulators and servants walked their employers' dogs. But on this dour afternoon there was no one to be seen. As dusk approached, fog inched its way around the trees until they disappeared into its gray shroud. An occasional car roared by, and a few horse-drawn delivery vans rumbled and clop-clopped down the street to break the monotony, but apart from those sounds and a loudly ticking clock, Uncle Fred's dining room was as silent and as chilled as a tomb. Eventually a lamplighter came down the street and put his fire to a light below my window; the gas flame, at first white and bluish, settled down to a warm yellow, turning the gray fog to the color of the nicotine in the old man's moustache. That transformation of the fog from gray to brownish yellow remains the most vivid image from my afternoon in St. John's Wood—that and the endless waiting for my mother to take me home. How much longer? When will she come? Isn't it time for tea? Although I cannot recall my waiting thoughts, those must have been among them, and it's a safe bet that I also asked myself, "What can she be doing that takes so long?" It's an equally safe bet that I had no conception of the answer.

In a characteristically candid comment, Dimps (as Uncle Fred continued to call her) told a friend that she looked on Thursdays as a burden to be born. Her duties, she said with a laugh, were not arduous. Nevertheless, Frederick Maufe took them seriously enough to pay an enormous price for such pleasures as he received—our London apartment, the house at Eastbourne, the account at Harrods, and the bills from Norman Hartnell and many another fashionable couturier. All this, as one friend put it, "to the general frenzy of his family." He also paid for my education.

At the age of six I went to school for the first time, at a private, family-run establishment in Eastbourne. I have no recollection of what they tried to teach me, and my short career there is worthy of note only in that it introduced me to the world of ceramics. I made a clay pea pod and placed therein a row of graduated clay peas. After it had been fired in the school's kiln, I painted it a bright green and presented it to my mother. Her response, however, is not on the "available" shelf in my memory.

In September 1934 I was packed off to boarding school—The Gables Preparatory School at Bexhill, a south coast resort only ten miles from Eastbourne. But it might as well have been a thousand miles from home, and like many another little boy from a one-son family, I found the discipline new and rather frightening. The Gables was no Dotheboys Hall, however, and the headmaster was not Wackford Squeers; but it was different, and dormitory living was not in the least like being tucked in by my nanny. Then, too, I was the boy in the brown boots. Nevertheless, I showed promise. It was at The Gables that I learned to spell the word "extraordinary," and glowed in the approbation of the be-beaded woman who tried to teach us English. Perhaps it was the first time that anyone had told me I had done well. I even won a prize for something or other, a green book on butterflies—the only time in my school life that I would step up to the platform to be acknowledged for my academic prowess. Athletic opportunities being limited by the fragility of my legs, I learned to box, and derived considerable satisfaction from thumping the heads of boys who made fun of my boots. I also was encouraged to develop a musical ear, but when this was slow to mature, I was relegated to the third triangle in the school band, where on Parents' Day (mine didn't come) I tinged away with a will in a spirited, if eccentric rendition of the *Marche Militaire.*

These academic and cultural accomplishments were not the only highlights of my terms at The Gables. The year 1935 was King George V's silver jubilee, and up and down the country, towns and villages mounted patriotic pageants in honor of the occasion. Bexhill put on a colorful show of imperial tableaux mounted by its Boy Scouts and Girl Guides, and rehearsed it on The Gables' school playing field. Seated on (and rolling about in) piles of new-mown grass at the field's perimeter, we watched their preparations with awe and wonder. The human mind accepts certain triggering commands, and whenever I smell freshly mown grass I am carried back to that spring, that field, and that jubilee pageant. It took second place only to the celebrations in London, which, thanks to "Thursdays," my mother and I were privileged to watch from a seat on the flag-decked stands erected in Piccadilly.

For almost the last time, the real-live counterparts of Uncle Fred's toy army were on parade. The route was lined with red-jacketed and bear-skinned guardsmen, and in the procession accompanying the gilded royal coach were the Household Cavalry, the bands of the Brigade of Guards, and the white-helmeted Royal Marines. There were hussars and artillerymen in blue uniforms with yellow plumes in their shakos, turbaned lancers from Bengal, Canadian Mounties—and several Indian princes riding rather disappointingly in open-roofed taxies ahead of the parade, apparently late to take their places at St. Paul's Cathedral, but getting a rousing cheer from the crowd just the same. The jubilee procession on May 6, 1935, was my first and last glimpse of the empire in all its splendor. Nevertheless, at the age of seven years and eight months, I became a lifelong imperialist. For the first time I understood what all those red bits on the world map meant. They were all ours, and from Adelaide to Zanzibar everybody loved us.

The pageantry of summer was followed at The Gables by preparations for the Christmas play, a traditional entertainment at virtually every boarding school in Britain, though the entertainment applied more to the participants than to those who had to sit through it on bottom-biting wooden seats in assembly halls and gyms. No program survives to recall the name of our play, but I believe it was extracted from a Christmas production devised by the playwright A. A. Milne in 1918 and titled *Make Believe.* At any rate, both involved a desert island and a cast of "Pirates, Dusky Maidens, Fireflies, etc." I was an assistant pirate and made the transformation with the aid of a bandanna and a beard created from burnt cork. For me, the best and most memorable part was not the production but the preparation for it. I was among those who helped paint the desert-island backdrop, a wonderful creation with a palm tree at stage left, a blue lagoon at center, a Jamaican tourist bureau–style strand at right, and the mandatory yellow sand in the foreground. When eventually our creation was bathed in theatrical floodlight, its colors glowed in a quite magical, tropical way. I could almost hear the waves tumbling onto the beach and the wind rustling through the fronds of our painted palms. Had I known that I would one day get paid for having such fun with a paintbrush, I almost certainly would have "Yo ho ho'ed" with even greater vigor.

In addition to my chorus role as a chanting buccaneer, I had a couple of lines to speak, and although I don't remember what they were, I recall my next theatrical encounter with arc-light clarity—as, perhaps, did everyone else who had to put up with me through the summer of '36. Amid piles of phonograph records in the sitting room at the Eastbourne house I had found one sold to raise money for needy American film producers. Behind the hiss characteristic of much-used records, a nasal American voice intoned, "The Cinematograph Trade Benevolent Fund presents . . . ," and then played bits of track from current movies. Playing it over and over, I learned most of the scenes by heart, including the opener in an accent achieved by gripping my nose betwixt finger and thumb. I managed a fairly soulful rendering of Elizabeth Bergner's never-to-be-forgotten (at least by me) line from *Escape Me Never:* "Maybe next time we live we'll have time for each other," followed by the sound effects of a train leaving the station. My tour de force, however, was a scene from Charles Laughton's 1935 *Mutiny on the Bounty*. Said Bligh: "A captain's a captain, and a seaman's a seaman, and a midshipman—Sir Joseph, or no Sir Joseph—is the lowest form of animal life in the British Navy." To which Mr. Christian added: "Now you know what a midshipman is." Both my Laughton and Clark Gable impressions were well reviewed by the cook and her husband, who enjoyed numerous encore performances. My mother and her friends, however, generally felt that once was enough, and sometimes I got no further than "The Cinematograph Trade Benev . . ." before she closed the show. Nevertheless, that scratched recording, coupled with my performance as a pirate, was sowing thespian seeds that would eventually leaf out if not bear fruit.

Deciding which childhood events played a significant part in charting one's lifelong course is a game to keep countless psychiatrists profitably employed. As a child grows older, his recollections become more numerous and their significance proportionately less profound. While one might expect that those stored on the reserve shelves and occasionally made available would be ones of some importance, I found this not to be so. Thus, for example, while going through the package of photographs sent to me after my mother's death, I came upon three taken in apparently successive years at the Eastbourne house. In one I appear with a grimly smiling nurse, in the next I am alone clutching a bear and a penguin, and in the third the cook's husband (who tripled as butler, gardener, and chauffeur) stands behind me. When I first looked through the pictures I remembered his role but not his name, and had my life depended on recalling it, I would have been out of luck. Several weeks later, however, while sorting the pictures into subject groups, I organized the Eastbourne shots and decided that the latest had to be the one with me and Quinn. Without the slightest conscious effort, his name had come back, a monumentally useless piece of information that had been shelved for half a century. But when I tried to recall the names of the nurse and the penguin, I got nothing.

Children who went to day schools had the advantage of making friends with whom to have fun through the holidays, but many who were sent away to boarding establishments were parted from them once the vacation months began. In my schooldays that was less true of boys who lived in the country. Upper-middle- and upper-class "county" families grew up on neighboring estates, and if the boys did not go to the same public school (as they often did), new term-time friends were simply exchanged for the old ones when the "hols" came around. For me, however, life was neither as stable nor as predictable. With the Christmas and spring breaks finding us housed in a succession of London apartments and the summers being spent at Eastbourne, I had few opportunities to make friends. Furthermore—and it was a big furthermore—my mother insisted that I should be kept away from such other children as I might encounter on the beach, in the conviction that they were not of our class and would be a bad influence on me.

My only approved—well, semi-approved—companion was Cousin Hugh, Aunt May's boy, whom I roundly detested. He was about five years older, large and red and usually looking as though he had been pulled through a bush—which is the way boys are supposed to look. Only I didn't. On one memorable trip to Ealing to visit Aunt May, I was dressed up in my Eton suit, an outfit comprising short striped trousers, an even shorter black jacket (popularly known as a "bum freezer"), and a white shirt upon which was anchored an enormously wide stiff collar. Worn outside the jacket, it was akin to casing one's neck in concrete and made lateral movement slow and hazardous. Furthermore, if it popped loose from its studs you were instantly transformed into one of those Burmese, ring-necked women from the pages of Mr. Ripley's book. Not my usual, everyday attire, this was reserved for special occasions. But in a manner of speaking, visiting Aunt May was a special occasion.

She and her husband, Reg, lived in a small but respectable house in Ealing with a large conservatory filled with Victorian-style green stuff and a garden featuring a concrete birdbath edged with rose bushes. They went to church, indulged in miscellaneous good works, and May was a power at the tennis club. She ran the house (and Reg) with admirable precision, and brought up her son on a no-nonsense regimen of love tempered with admonitions to succeed. And succeed he did; Cousin Hugh excelled both in the classroom and on the sports field. To their friends and neighbors, May, Reg, and Hugh were the ideal English family, solid, reliably rooted, the backbone of the nation. They also lived close to Grandma Mann, the only person to whom my mother could turn for psychological repairs. But because Glad and May both had a talent for saying what they thought and letting the venom land where it might, they vied with each other for their mother's ear. Consequently, life between the sisters was one of breaking up and making up, the latter role invariably falling to my mother, not through any love for May, but to minimize the damage she might do to her relationship with Grandma Mann.

The Eton-suited visit to Ealing was one such fence-repairing effort, but even in contrition there was competition. We had to demonstrate that while May and Reg plodded into middle-aged, middle-class mediocrity, we, in spite of a wrecked marriage and several changes of abode, had the world by its nose. This was not the ideal basis for sisterly reconciliation. Indeed, even our arrival at the door in our bright yellow Wolsley Hornet convertible (nicknamed the "buzz box" in the best Michael Arlen tradition) was a calculated reminder that May drove a boring Austin Seven. I have no idea what went on inside the house, but outside in the garden diplomacy broke down. A brawl developed, in the midst of which I threw one of Hugh's possessions (I forget what it was) over the fence into the next-door garden, where it crashed through the glass of a cold frame. When our mothers emerged, they found me in the grip of my much larger cousin, my nose bleeding, my Eton suit stained grass green, and my collar sprung. I would like to think that I inflicted serious below-the-waterline damage on the enemy, but in reality I think I got far the worst of it. I also got all the blame, Cousin Hugh shoveling it at me in a most unsportsmanlike manner. In the midst of the recriminations, the man next door discovered what had happened to his cold frame and shouted uncharitable things over the fence. My mother was livid. Three weeks later I was hauled back to Ealing and forced to apologize to Cousin Hugh. The worst part, however, was going next door on my own to express my regrets to the owner of the cold frame and to offer to pay for it out of my sixpence-a-week pocket money. Fortunately, the man was not at home; instead, his wife gave me a biscuit and assured me that boys will be boys.

This unfortunate and rather squalid affair would have no pertinence were it not that I was now old enough to move on from The Gables to the junior arm of the public school, where I would be expected to receive the rest of my education. I should explain that in England public schools are private schools, though in more recent generations the number of scholarship boys attending these bastions of privilege has drastically changed the cultural mix. To secure a place in the first rank of public schools one had to be "put down" at birth (meaning the placing of an application, not being shot), and like my grandfather and father before me, I was "put down" for Eton. However, the three great schools, Winchester, Harrow, and Eton (not necessarily in that order), catered to families who could afford the fees. We couldn't. Consequently, mother had to select another. Prompted by Grandma Mann, she chose Framlingham College in Suffolk, not for its scholastic reputation, but because Cousin Hugh was in the senior school and could be expected to keep a friendly family eye on me. Needless to say, the logic of that assumption was lost on both him and me. Nevertheless, it was on the strength of my cousin's proximity that at the age of nine I was enrolled as Framlingham's 5,307th pupil, put on the train to Suffolk, and launched into an academic life very different from the relatively small and benign world of The Gables.

Settling for "Hugh's school" instead of Eton must have been very hard for my mother. She had first tried a much smaller private academy, Cheam School near Epsom, which specialized in the small fry from noble families and which would later number Prince Charles among its alumni. I, however, was not destined to precede him—for reasons never divulged, but probably because, like Eton, its fees were too steep. Nevertheless, our inspection tour and interview with the headmaster played a part in shaping my future career interests.

While my mother talked in private with the headmaster in his study, I was parked in the adjoining library and allowed to play with a hand-cranked movie projector—my introduction to the celluloid world and to the educational potential of the motion picture. Although this was 1936, and picture palaces around the world were thrilling audiences with the adventures of Errol Flynn in *Captain Blood,* Gary Cooper's suffering in *The Plainsman,* and Charlie Chaplin's antics in *Modern Times,* no one could have been more enthralled than I was sitting in Cheam's darkened library watching the flickering exploits of *Felix the Cat.* I had sipped from the movies' magic cup and was forever addicted.

There were no picture palaces at Framlingham, however, and I would not have been allowed inside if there had been. Indeed, we small boys were not permitted to venture beyond the college gates unless accompanied by a parent or master. The town was small then and is not much larger today. Its principal distinctions are still its twelfth-century castle and late nineteenth-century college. The school proved to be an imposing red-brick pile stretching across the crest of a hill and flanked by groves of pine and other coniferous trees. At one end was the headmaster's quarters and at the other the chapel, the latter approached, rather curiously, by a broad corridor that served as a museum of geological specimens and relics from the Great War.

In the midsection of the main block stood the large dining hall, its walls covered with ethnological and antique weaponry, Zulu shields sharing space with Scottish broadswords, and flintlock muskets with Indian kukris and Turkish daggers. There was enough to create a museum of some distinction, but it had little to do with the educational ambience of the school, and when I returned for my second term, the dining hall had been re-paneled and the weapon collection had disappeared.

Before long someone discovered that the disenfranchised treasures were stored in a crypt beneath the chapel, its padlocked door in full view of one of the classrooms. The challenge, therefore, was to find a way of gaining secret access—though for what purpose I did not really understand. Nevertheless, anxious to be in on something, I went along with the conspirators. The chapel proved to stand on arched brick footings, and recessed under one of them was a small barred window leading to the crypt. Digging out the bars proved childishly easy, and for several weeks our gang had access to the treasures whenever we chose.

In case postwar Old Framlinghamians (or, for that matter, current Framlinghamians) should read this narrative and charge that no such arch exists beneath the chapel, I cannot deny the truth of it. At the same time, I urge them to look more carefully at the south-facing foundation, which, to an archaeologist's eye, will reveal a change in the bonding where the opening has been bricked up. Forty-five years later no one remained on the staff to know whether this was done when ammunition was stored under the chapel during the Second World War or to prevent further youthful escapades. Looking at the patched wall I wondered whether this was my enduring legacy to the Framlingham fabric and how small the likelihood that in a later age archaeologists will be able to correctly explain it.

Unfortunately, schoolboy secrets of that magnitude are not of long duration; before we knew it, ours was out, and a rival gang had taken possession of the crypt. In one of the resulting skirmishes I was cut by a defender wielding a claymore, and still bear the scar. I mention this exploit not for any dramatic effect but simply as a record of an early interest in antiques, an interest that transcended simply playing with weapons and extended to their age and their origins. After we were caught, my attempts to make that point were singularly unsuccessful. It was the first time that I was beaten with a cane, the weapon wielded with admirable precision by a gentleman of the cloth.

The Reverend Rupert Kneese (known to us as "Rupe") was the college chaplain and second master of the junior school, though I remember him only as my personal nemesis who occupied a rather grim and dark study, its mantelpiece and cupboards stocked with cups and trophies, memorials to youthful athletic prowess and the development of a strong right arm. His cane hung on a hook beside the fireplace, always visible, always reminding. I would encounter other masters and other canes before my schooldays were done, but none kept his weapon so prominently displayed. Instead, they were usually concealed in closets until the moment arrived. But not Rupe's. Today, of course, with parental and scholastic discipline compromised, the use of corporal punishment is seen as archaic and as barbaric as the thumbscrew or the rack. The cane was undeniably painful and could raise spectacular polychrome welts that ranged through black and blue to a noble purple. But contrary to the views of sociological reformers, these were not scars that lingered for life; they were badges of courage to be inspected and admired by one's chums. Small trickles of blood were seen not so much as evidence of magisterial sadism but as proof of stoic endurance—unless one emerged blubbing, which earned little sympathy and certainly no admiration.

In retrospect, it has always surprised me that the kind of thin, hook-handled cane that generated laughter when twirled by Charlie Chaplin could produce such lip-biting fear in the hand of Chaplain Kneese. The memory of the way it whistled as it cut through the air remains as vivid as the sound of falling bombs in 1940—and very similar. Nevertheless, I insist that rather than doing lasting harm, it nurtured a healthy respect for authority and prescribed rules of behavior. Much more damaging (at least to me) was Rupe's use of the Bible as an instrument of punishment. The penalty for failing to correctly learn one's Latin, or to divide one fool number into another, could be detention and the learning by heart of biblical chunks that then had to be correctly recited in the privacy of his study. The Beatitudes were never the same again, nor could I find it in my heart to rejoice and be exceedingly glad, or to believe that great would be my reward in heaven. Instead, I began to suspect that people who wore their collars back-to-front used the Book like a cane beside the fireplace.

Responding to my inquiries, the college's historian, L. "Bob" Gillett, has written that "almost every Old Boy who writes to me tries to vilify Kneese and I can see why, but history (at least mine) will reveal what a power he was for the good of the school." To which one can only add that the Lord works in mysterious ways.

Framlingham College, as I have explained, stands on rising ground overlooking a shallow vale beyond which tower the ruins of the great, flint-walled castle whose construction began at the end of the twelfth century. Home to Mary Tudor in 1553, it was dismantled in the seventeenth century and given to Pembroke College, Cambridge, with instructions to build a poor house within its walls. The resulting almshouses still stand and were used by the college as a backdrop for its annual Shakespearian productions. I saw but one, *Twelfth Night*, in 1938 in a high wind that blew most of the actors' words back where they came from. Amateur productions of the Bard's comedies tend to be tiresome even when audible, but when they appear to be mimed, small boys' minds can be forgiven for wandering. Against the setting of the old building, the actors in their Tudor costumes seemed to be part of the castle's past, ghosts stepping out from the pages of its history. Those images were to stay with me, and do still, as reminders that history, rather than being a catalog of dates, charters, and treaties, was a stage filled with real people. While everyone else in that audience was watching *Twelfth Night*, I was seeing what today has come to be known as "living history."

This was neither my first nor my most portentous visit to Framlingham Castle. I owed that to being a Boy Scout, for on more than one occasion our master took us tracking across the vale and around the castle's moat. The sight of the great walls and square towers rising to an enormous (or so it seemed) height above my head conjured up images that lingered long after lights out. I have no idea what Boy Scouts do today to be prepared, but in those days we learned a variety of useful accomplishments like whittling and tying knots. But tracking was the favorite. This involved sending two boys out into the countryside to leave a trail of arrows chalked on walls, bits of rag hanging on trees, and rude words scratched in the mud to enable the hounds to track the hares. On one such outing I was chosen to be a track layer. Being the boy in the boots, I was less athletic than the rest and so was better off putting out clues than racing after them. Our course took us out across the meadows to the castle and back along a stream, where we paused to try to catch stickleback fish in our scout hats. Lying on the stream bed I spotted a piece of flint that had a vaguely blade-shaped profile. I fished it out, took it back to the school, and later showed it to the scout master.

He told me that I had made admirable use of the scout's sharp eye, and that I might well have found an ancient British tool and a worthy addition to the scout hut's collection of bird bones, plaster casts of duck footprints, pressed leaves, and impaled bugs. I remember my pride in the blotchy label (I wrote it myself) which lay beside the rock stating that it had been found by me and presented by me. In the light of subsequent events, I very much doubt whether my discovery was, at best, anything more than a rock that had been hammered by someone using it for building stone. But as history daily demonstrates, the perception of truth is as potent a catalyst as truth itself. I was on record in the hut as having found an antiquity—an achievement with exploitable potential.

Every Sunday afternoon the entire junior school would line up in pairs to form a "crocodile" that would then proceed on a firmly regimented walk under the stern eye of a single master. One could converse with the boy with whom one was paired, but that was the only concession. There was to be no stopping to steal birds' eggs, no breaking ranks in pursuit of butterflies, no throwing sticks at boys in front. As I recall it, we went entirely by the clock; we never arrived anywhere. Suddenly the master would give the word, and round we would turn, and back we would march.

Masters stuck with the crocodile chore can have enjoyed it no more than did we; but they were lucky in that they took it in rotation. When I discovered that the scout master was to be in charge of the next Sunday's perambulation, I reminded him of my recent remarkable discovery, and suggested that I might better be employed returning to the scene of my triumph to search for more amazing relics—and he agreed. He actually agreed!

For the first time I was free to visit the castle on my own—not to go inside (that meant buying a ticket), but free to clamber about the dry moat and lie in the grass staring up at the towers and into the medieval sky of my imagination.

I had made no effort to hunt for prehistoric flints, and I knew very well that if I returned empty-handed there was little chance that I would be allowed this freedom again. So I took the only likely lump of flint I could find and beat it about with another stone in the hope that I could manufacture my own hand ax. I do not remember what, if anything, I accomplished, but I recall showing it to the scout master with considerable trepidation, and remember my sense of profound relief when he gave it barely a glance, said, "Well done, young feller" (or words to that effect), and hurried off to the masters' common room in search of tea.

I have no recollection of what formal education I was acquiring at Framlingham (other than getting a firm grip on the Beatitudes), and only a handful of anomalous moments have endured. The alleged weakness of my legs had kept me from playing games, and although I assume that I was well over the rickets and that my bones were as solid as the next boy's, I suffered two memorable setbacks while at Framlingham that were to keep me off the playing fields and in the cheering section.

One involved a fight outside the scout hut that ended in a pursuit through tall grass, though I don't remember whether I was the pursuer or the pursued. I only recall stumbling over something in the grass, getting up and attempting to keep going, finding that I couldn't, looking down, and discovering that my left knee was impaled on long and rusty nails protruding from a piece of wood. I recall feeling no pain until I saw the blood. The other setback involved the same knee and sent me to St. Thomas's Hospital in London to have its left cartilage removed.

The hospital was a vast and aging complex located on the Thames Embankment opposite the Houses of Parliament. Opened in 1870, with its staff nurses (called "sisters") dressed as austerely as in the days of Florence Nightingale, it was a scary place for a boy who had never been exposed to the world beyond the school gates. I remember the huge public ward with its rows of iron beds that seemed to stretch to infinity, and above all I remember one peg-legged man who stumped about the ward wearing the long blue coat of World War I patients in military hospitals. The nurses called him "Bluebottle," and so did I. He was to be my first adult friend. With me before I went down to the operating theater and there when I came back, Bluebottle made an indelible mark. We must have made a somewhat chuckle-worthy couple, he a rough, life-beaten, and at least middle-aged ex-serviceman, and me a rather weedy and tiresomely refined little lad. But from him I learned something of infinite value. Up to that time my only contacts with so-called ordinary people were the servants, who treated me with the deference afforded the property of their employer. From Bluebottle I learned that social stratification had nothing to do with worth or with kindness, and it is tempting (though probably incorrect) to think that he was instrumental in focusing my later archaeological interests on the village rather than on the manor.

My weeks in St. Thomas's Hospital (minor surgery was taken more seriously then than it is today) provided something else. They introduced me to the miracle of radio. A pair of black Bakelite earphones hung over each bed, and at night they remained so possessively clamped to my ears that they had to be forcibly removed. From its studios at Savoy Hill, the BBC filled the eager British airwaves with the kind of music and chatter it had featured in its first broadcast in July 1922, and which it had categorized as "unconsidered trifles of the lightest type." But no matter how trifling, I listened to it all with wondrous attention, convinced that when the announcer said "you," he really meant me. To this day

I continue to believe that radio is a more powerful and exciting medium than television, for it expects something more than a blank stare on the part of its audience. The wireless, as it was then called, made demands on its listeners; it made us think; it made us partners. The broadcasters gave us the sound of surf and the cry of gulls and out of them we fashioned our own tropical island. A piece of chain, two tin trays, and a pair of coconuts sent St. George out to slay the dragons lurking in the caverns of our imagination.

Although the memory of lying on a table with a gauze mask over my face and the sickly sweet smell of chloroform being dripped on it has little to commend it, thanks to Bluebottle and the BBC, my stay in St. Thomas's belongs in my ledger's credit column—though I have a lingering suspicion that the knee surgery wasn't really needed. We hear a lot these days about unnecessary surgery and are led to believe that it is a new and venal phenomenon. But it was ever thus— as I would soon discover to my cost.

I have no record of how the Framlingham masters assessed my scholastic prowess, but it was a matter of no interest to my mother, and I do not recall any time in my school and college career when she commented on it. I do know, however, that years later one of the last reports carried the headmaster's overall assessment "Could do better," and it is safe to assume that the same conclusion was reached term in and term out. Consequently, end-of-term exams were approached with neither confidence nor enthusiasm; in fact, they were enough to give me an upset stomach.

"What sort of a tummy ache?" the junior school matron wanted to know. "Show me where it hurts."

"Sort of here and to the right," I replied.

Now it is true that I did have an upset stomach, but the "here and to the right" bit had been provided by the school-smart lad who occupied the dormitory bed next to mine. "Tell her the pain's on the right and she'll put you in the sick bay," he had said. And he was right. But then things began to get out of hand. Although in the exam-escaping safety of the sick bay my nervous stomach quickly solved its problem, the doctor had been sent for, and I was stuck with my story.

"Hurts on the right, does it, young feller?"

"Yes, sir." I could hardly say it didn't. But I should have. Before the day was out I was carted away to the Ispwich Hospital and was still there when the rest of the college went home for its spring vacation. The card at the end of my bed read "Acute Appendicitis"—and I had a large, sewn-up hole to prove it. And the pain to the right was now genuine.

Holidays were eagerly looked forward to by most of my confreres, and plans for great adventures were endlessly analyzed, details from parental letters read aloud and vicariously enjoyed by boys who were not going to Davos or Cannes or hiking in the Peak District. For me, however, there were no plans, no letters, no surprises. It was the villa at Eastbourne in the summer, and the London apartment in Kensington's St. Mary Abbott's Court for the Christmas and Easter hols. Either way, the directives were simple enough. "Amuse yourself, Ivor. But do it quietly. Be a darling, and don't make a mess."

We had moved to the relatively new art deco–esque apartment building in 1937. Everything about it was modern, and so, of course, were we—with the exception of the elderly and motherly "Nanny" Bolton, who represented the amalgamated staff: housekeeper and pourer of oil over the troubled heads of unpaid tradesmen, cook, lady's maid, parlor maid, and nanny to a rapidly growing lad more in need of a friend than a nurse. Although I became deeply fond of Mrs. Bolton, short walks with her to the grocer or to the fishmonger in Kensington High Street were modest adventures having relatively low excitement value. On two memorable occasions, however, with Mrs. Bolton's tacit concurrence— "I'm not looking, Master Ivor"—I was able to escape on my own.

There used to be a small movie house in the High Street, a rather sleazy emporium entered by a small door between two shops (I believe it was destroyed in the war), and it was there for the first time that I struck out on my own. Using nine pence of my by then shilling-a-week pocket money, I invested in a seat to see Richard Dix in a film called *The Tunnel.* It was a tremendous advance on *Felix the Cat,* and the inevitable moment when the sub-Atlantic tunnel sprang a leak took an early place in my lexicon of great cinematic moments. Alas, like Dracula when the sun goes down, the 1936 movie rises again and again on late-night television to remind me that there is a difference between being a film fan and a film critic.

Although this was my first solo as a paying customer, it was not my first visit to a cinema. That had taken place at Eastbourne when my mother took me to see something innocuous and English starring Jack Buchanan. But like most movie theater programs in those days, this turned out to be a double bill. The British main feature was supported by a Hollywood B picture titled *Big Brown Eyes.* Today this gangster epic rates a grudging half star on the very late show. Nevertheless, it managed to scare me witless, and at the point when two hoods entered an elevator, I had to be removed. Whether I yelled, burst into tears, or chewed on the hat of the lady in the next row, I have no idea. But I remember the scene and, inexplicably, the name of the film.

I have a nasty feeling that some readers (but not you) might consider the chronicle of my early moviegoing to be trivia unworthy of pursuit. But as I explained at the outset, the isolated and sometimes seemingly irrelevant events and recollections of my early childhood seem to have played a role in heralding if not guiding the course of my later life.

Although my trip to the High Street movie theater was never (to my knowledge) revealed to my mother, my second solo flight from my Kensington cage could not be concealed, for I returned visibly damaged. An entire city block had been torn down behind our apartment building, presumably with the intent of constructing something that never got off the ground. In some areas the old buildings had been demolished to their foundations, but in others roofed cellars survived, with their doors gone, the openings black against the daylight. Since all the windows in our sixth floor (or was it fifth floor?) apartment looked out onto this example of man's unfinished handiwork, I had plenty of opportunity to wonder what went on down there. From time to time, ragged derelicts could be seen tottering amid the rubble, and everywhere there were cats—also garbage. But in the spring and summer, weeds and even small trees managed to grow, turning winter's desolation into something less forbidding, even inviting. The low mounds of greening rubble became the crags behind which highwaymen waited to rob fat travelers (which was probably true had a fat traveler been fool enough to venture there), and the black holes of cellar doorways became entrances to pirates' caves.

With the hindsight of old age, it seems inevitable that I should be drawn to that abandoned demolition site. Careful surveillance had detected a moveable board in the fencing though which I had seen an old man emerge. So where he came out I went in. My high-rise fantasies became reality—to the extent that, armed with a toy pistol, I would lurk amid the rubble waiting for fat travelers. Eventually I settled for a thin cat, and while in hot but still booted pursuit of it, I tripped and landed on my nose—which bled.

An agitated and clucking Nanny Bolton was still cleaning me up when mother returned. "Ivor, how could you! How could you! Go to your room. And Ivor! Don't you ever do that again! Only urchins play in the dirt!"

For a fatherless boy, going to one's room was the only punishment, and although at Eastbourne it could mean not going to the beach, in London its impact was minimal. I spent most of my time there anyway, for when my mother and her friends were at home I would be told that "grown-up talk's not for little boys' ears" and urged to run along. In our relatively small apartment "running along" was limited to my room or the kitchen—which was off-limits when Nanny B. was cooking and not much fun when she wasn't.

I knew nobody in the block, having been told never to talk to strangers, but somehow (perhaps through Mrs. Bolton's gossiping) a middle-aged and childless couple on the floor below knew me. In the summer of 1938, the first year that we did not rent the Eastbourne house, they offered to take me with them on a caravan vacation in Devonshire. It was the most exciting prospect of my childhood, and I well remember adding the Morrisons to my prayers, and pleading with God not to let me die before the big day came. That rather melancholy notion, which seems to have surfaced for the first time in the precaravaning weeks, has remained firmly entrenched throughout my life—prompting the writing of several wills and now this book.

THE MORRISONS' KINDNESS was such that they deserved a well-thumbed place in the scrapbook of my memory alongside my friend Bluebottle, but perhaps because they neither had wooden legs nor wore long blue coats, they are nowhere to be found. Even their name remained lost for decades, popping out only as I began to write about them. Fortunately, however, the lasting significance of my caravan adventure rested not on them but on where they took me.

The caravan was not of the horse-drawn, gypsy variety. In 1930s terms it was as up-to-date and as streamlined as they came, though by modern American trailer standards its interior was simple and very small. On a wet day two adults and a boy were at least one boy too many, and whenever the rain stopped, and often when it didn't, I set out adventuring. The caravan was parked in a wooded driveway near the central Devon village of Eggesford, which then comprised little but the railroad station, the Fox and Hounds hotel, and a short string of Victorian cottages. However, it was not the village that called to me, but the deep, dark green woods on our side of the track. They had once been part of the estate of the earls of Portsmouth, and the driveway had wound its way through a mile of woods and parkland to Eggesford House. The huge property had been sold as several parcels in 1914, and one of them was now owned by friends of the Morrisons—hence our presence.

Although at a very early age I had been taken on a picnic to London's Richmond Park and had been mislaid amid its ferns, a walk alone in the woods was something new and wonderful to me. One morning, after it had rained hard in the night, the sky was leaden and a heavy mist turned shadows gray under the dripping trees. Forests, which in the sunlight were filled with happy elves and merry men, had become the lair of monsters and of bandage-trailing mummies, a place where gnarled hands of the buried dead reached up to grip a boy by the ankle. My previous explorations had never taken me beyond the woods, but on this wet morning I struck out in a new direction and was relieved to reach the edge of a large meadow before the goblins got me. The mist still hung over the field, softening the silhouettes of the distant members of a herd of grazing cows and separating from its foundation the sprawling, towered, and crenellated ruin of Eggesford House.

So unexpected and yet so in tune with my imaginings was this sight that in subsequent telling I would claim that I believed I was seeing a ghost castle. In truth, I have no recollection now of what I thought. My fear, if fear there was, evidently was insufficient to send me fleeing back into the woods. Instead, I adventured on and quickly discovered that this was no apparition, no castle in the air, but as solid a touchable, climbable, and even enterable ruin of a mansion as any devotee of English literature could hope to find. It could have been Rebecca's Mandelay after the fire, Mr. Rochester's Thornfield, or Miss Havisham's Satis House. At one end a great medieval tower stood intact, linked to the body of the house by a ribbon of rubble, while the core of the battlemented mansion rose even higher, capped by clusters of Jacobean brick chimneys. Although the rear of the house had collapsed, the heart of it remained more or less intact. Glass survived in some of its windows, and though rotting, the floors of the first-floor rooms could still take the weight of a boy—albeit a rash intruding fool of a boy.

Framlingham Castle and the rubbled building site behind St. Mary Abbott's Court had introduced me to the romance of ruins, but my discovery of Eggesford House turned it into a lifelong passion. Here was the quintessential ruin, part castle, part great mansion, the right backdrop for tales of derring-do from the pens of Sir Walter Scott and Rafael Sabatini; in short, the reality behind the fiction upon which every empire-building British boy was fed.

Each remaining day of that summer's vacation, in sunshine and more often in rain, I returned to Eggesford House to drink its magic and board its time machine. Through the ensuing years I would return to it in my sleep, sometimes with pleasure but as often in nightmares; I would doodle its tower and chimneys in moments of boredom; and I would see my long-suffering wife wince when, as often happened, a dinner guest would ask, "How did you first get interested in archaeology?" She knew all too well that the answer would begin: "I think it was in the summer of 1938 when . . ."

It was inevitable, therefore, that one day we should return to the source, and we did so in the late summer of 1966. From a distance the ruin remained almost exactly as I remembered it. Cows still grazed in the meadow; the tower still stood, so did the Jacobean chimneys. But as we got closer I saw that much had changed. Where I had remembered glass in the window frames, now there was neither glass nor frames; floors and ceilings had gone, leaving only the shell in a state of what the French call *dégringolade*—a wonderfully expressive word, but for which one has very little use. Perhaps to a painter of romantic ruins, the walls had grown even more picturesque than before; but my own first reaction was one of anger, not at the cruelty of time, but at having been duped. The only armored knights and cavaliers who had walked the courts of Eggesford House had been of my own creation. Machine-cut nails had held its woodwork together; its bricks and plaster were relatively modern.

Subsequent research revealed that the mansion had been built in 1830 by the Honourable Newton Wallop Fellowes, later the fifth Earl of Portsmouth. It was a product of the early nineteenth century's medieval revival architecture designed to recapture the imaginary days of knights-errant and damsels in various brands of distress.

Psychologists may claim to detect an unhealthy connection between my sheltered, rather solitary home life and my growing affection for the past. There's no denying that had ours been a two-parent household, or one where I was seen as something more than a thrice-yearly visitor to be endured, I would have been exposed to a much wider range of ideas and activities. It is probably also true that something could have been done to overcome my conviction that my boots, like divers', were soled with lead. Instead, at home or at school when it was said that Ivor can't do this or that, I made no effort to prove otherwise. Unable to participate in the games that developed the team spirit headmasters always extolled on sports days, or to share the alleged satisfaction of being a supporting player in the game of life or a precious grain of sand in God's grand design, I preferred to be both captain and team, and to own the beach.

I have little recollection of newspapers or of concerning myself with the big stories of the '30s. Mussolini's invasion of Abyssinia in October 1935 was for me just a red box shared between a platoon of leaden Italians in sand-colored uniforms, and as many black Ethiopians in white robes. Nine months later, the Spanish Civil War broke out, and although I recall seeing pictures of bombed buildings and fleeing peasants in the pages of *Picture Post* (the British version of *Life* magazine), I don't think I knew or cared whose side our team favored.

While the Morrisons and I were vacationing in tranquil Devonshire, the European pot was beginning to boil again. Hitler intended to free the Sudeten Germans from alleged Czech tyranny, and the French and British were treaty-bound to stop him. But neither had the will to do so, and on September 15, Prime Minister Neville Chamberlain went, umbrella in hand, to negotiate with Hitler. At the same time, perhaps to kid him that we meant business, trenches were dug in the London parks, sandbags went up around public buildings, and thirty-eight million gas masks were supplied to regional centers throughout the country. We seem to have been stronger on those than anything else. A plan was hastily concocted to evacuate London's children, and although the "Where to?" was only vaguely answered, 83 percent of parents filled out the application. My name was not among them because I was leaving the city anyway to return to the supposed safety of rural Framlingham. Had I not been, my mother could have been faced with a knotty dilemma: whether to continue to keep me from being contaminated by the despised working class or to sign me up and be rid of me at government expense.

I must have already been back in Suffolk to begin the Michaelmas term when the German time bomb was defused. On the evening of September 30 (my birthday), Chamberlain made a regal appearance at a window of 10 Downing Street to promise "peace with honour . . . peace for our time."

On the Kensington home front all continued relatively well. My mother had yet to land me a new father; but the by then long-established relationship with Uncle Fred, allowing my mother all the fun of the field for six and a half days a week, had more to commend it than settling down to be somebody's wife. The Christmas of 1938 was memorable for its short trip to the circus and for my being given my very own movie projector and two five-minute versions of Charlie Chaplin films. With a hand-stamping printing set I manufactured tickets and printed programs that I planted conspicuously around the apartment, and with long-suffering Nanny Bolton as sole customer, I presented my double bill—again and again.

The following spring, as Czechoslovakia fell apart and Hitler threatened Poland, large supplies of black and green roller-blind material were unloaded at Framlingham and hastily attached to all the window frames to hide our lights from Hitler's bombers. At about the same time we lined up to be fitted from the stock of gas masks that had briefly been thought superfluous.

They were singularly unattractive things, composed of a black rubber mask with its own sickly black rubber smell, a single oval plastic window, and a short, disk-shaped snout full of charcoal. Only if you blew out when they told you to breathe normally did the thing have any appeal. The air exiting beside one's ears could be made to emit satisfyingly vulgar noises.

In spite of all the rumors and warlike posturing, March ended and April began without further dramatics, and we all went home for the Easter vacation. Although through much of that month Britain busied herself trying to reach a mutual defense agreement with Stalin, in the smaller but hardly less Machiavellian world of St. Mary Abbott's Court a negotiation no less delicate suddenly went sour. Driving into the country in our "buzz box," my mother explained that we were going to spend the weekend with "Uncle" Harvey at his cottage near Long Wittenham in Berkshire. How would I feel about having him for a father? she wanted to know. I don't remember how I replied, but I suspect that I provided the right answer, albeit tinged with caution. "He'd be okay, I suppose." He had been pleasant enough to me, but he had a beard, wore tweed sports jackets, and was rather intimidatingly loud. By my mother's standards of social acceptability, the ideal husband should do either "something in the City" or nothing in the country. Consequently, she preferred to vaguely describe Harvey as a company director rather than to admit (as she privately put it) that he was "in motorbikes." Nevertheless, his business made a machine with a famous name and, with war clouds gathering, could be expected to remain profitably busy. As my mother explained, Uncle Harvey would be a good provider, and we had to look to the future. His cottage certainly was a winner, its thatched roof and rustic exterior belying its spacious and richly furnished interior. Close-cropped lawns sloped down to the bank of the river Thames, where boating and fishing could be mine for the asking. The prospect of trading our boxlike apartment for such a home was almost too good to believe.

In the space of twenty-four hours something went hideously wrong. All of a sudden we were packing, throwing suitcases into the back of the car, and heading home to London. Uncle Harvey's incumbency as Father Elect had been abruptly terminated—why, I never discovered. I returned to Framlingham for the summer term, from which is implanted only one trivial picture in my memory: lying on my rug (each boy had one) watching a cricket match while playing with a red plastic doughnut-shaped toy, which, when one pulled a cord from its side, uttered the memorable words "That's Shell, that was!"

There was something more exciting ahead, however. Rather than going straight home at the term's end, our junior scout troop was to spend two weeks camping at a site several miles away owned by Mrs. E. M. Pretty, a lady with land, money, and archaeological curiosity. In the summer of the previous year, and with help from the county museum, she had opened three burial mounds in a group of eleven located on a bluff about half a mile from the river Deben.

Although all three tumuli had been disturbed by earlier treasure hunters, sufficient evidence of late Roman or Anglo-Saxon burials survived to make the project interesting, and to encourage Mrs. Pretty to resume digging in 1939, this time into the largest of the mounds.

By the time we pitched camp on her estate, the new excavation was well advanced and on its way into the annals of archaeological history. Keeping the lid on an archaeological find of any importance is not easily done, and when word got out that the excavators were guardedly asking museums for information on Viking ships, an Anglo-Saxon authority, C. W. Phillips, visited the site to find out what was afoot. What he saw was the partially exposed bow of an eighty-foot ship, the largest of its kind ever discovered in Britain. Recognizing its importance, Phillips prevailed on Mrs. Pretty to halt the digging while he sought help from the British Museum and the Office of Works. Meanwhile, he hastily recruited some of the most experienced archaeologists in Britain to continue the project, and on July 10 took over its direction himself. The result would be described by the British Museum as "the richest treasure ever dug from British soil." But when we set out on a field trip to visit the dig, we knew only that it was going on at a place called Sutton Hoo—"hoo," we were told, being an Anglo-Saxon term meaning the spur of a hill.

When we got there we found a long slice through the mound and in it something resembling a giant, attenuated, and upturned toast rack. Although all the ship's wood had long since rotted, its iron nails survived, and thanks to brilliant excavating, the sand matrix in which they lay had been sculptured to reconstruct the hull's ribs. The ship had contained the funerary kit, but not the bones, of a seventh-century East Anglian king who some authorities speculate was drowned at sea. Although its wood-supported, tentlike burial chamber had soon collapsed under the weight of sand mounded on top of it, the contents had remained undisturbed. I have a vague recollection of a dark area amidships, but whether that was the partially removed burial deposit or an awning erected over it, I cannot say. I also remember somebody handing me a bucket and asking me to empty it into a wheelbarrow. In hazy retrospect I like to think of this incident as my initiation into the world of professional archaeology, though at the time it made little impression. On the contrary, nothing much seemed to be going on, prompting the conclusion that if this was what archaeology was all about, it was slightly less exciting than watching apples grow. Audrey Baines was another child visitor, who had been brought there by her uncle, who happened to be a friend of Mrs. Pretty, and, like me, she was unimpressed.

Had anyone emerged from the hole to tell us that we were witnesses to one of the most important discoveries of the twentieth century, better-focused images might have entered my memory bank. I suspect, therefore, that our presence was not appreciated and that Phillips and his team wanted the work kept secret until the silver and gold were safely out of the ground. That was accomplished on July 29, and the man in charge of the delicate task was William F. Grimes, who, had he looked up, would have wanted us gone. Fate ordained that almost exactly ten years later our paths would again converge, at which time his wish would remain the same.

On August 14 the Sutton Hoo discovery became public knowledge. A coroner's inquest was held that day to determine whether or not the treasure could be seized by the Crown under the twelfth-century law of treasure trove. The Sutton Hoo artifacts were declared not to be treasure trove, and therefore belonged to Mrs. Pretty, not only because the tumulus lay on her land but because— regardless of the big-name archaeologists on hand—it was her excavation. Nine days later the British Museum announced that Mrs. Pretty had given everything to the museum in what would be described as "one of the most remarkable and splendid gifts that has ever been made to the national archaeological collections."

I was home in Kensington when Nanny Bolton showed me the back page of the *Times* and its pictures of the ship and some of its artifacts. "Fancy you being right there, Master Ivor!" she declared. "What a thrill that must have been!"

Only then did the importance of Sutton Hoo get through to me, forcing me to focus on its already fading memory. In reality, of course, I kept the memory not because I was impressed by what I had seen but because I flattered myself that I had been one of the very few British boys privileged to have seen something so important as to be proclaimed by the *Times*.

It was also one of the last bits of good news to reach the British public for quite some while. On the same day that Mrs. Pretty's gift was announced, Germany's foreign minister, Joachim von Ribbentrop, signed a treaty with the hated Bolsheviks designed to keep Russia neutral if Hitler went to war. Soon Hitler's first Wehrmacht divisions demonstrated their new blitzkrieg tactic by plunging across the Polish frontier, and Luftwaffe bombers emptied their bays over Warsaw.

A few days earlier, a bombshell of scarcely less tonnage had exploded in the Noël Hume household.

Uncle Fred was dead.

5 ❧ Displaced Persons

THE BRITISH REMEMBER September 3, 1939, as universally as Americans recall where they were on the day Pearl Harbor was attacked or John Kennedy was shot. My mother being away for the weekend, Nanny Bolton and I were alone in the Kensington apartment listening, like millions of others, to the prime minister as he told us that his government's ultimatum given to the Germans at nine o'clock that morning had expired at eleven o'clock without any response, and that in consequence Britain was now in a state of war with Germany.

Chamberlain had barely finished speaking before the air raid sirens began wailing to herald the approach of Nazi squadrons. Minutes later our telephone rang. It was the hall porter instructing all tenants to collect their gas masks and proceed in an orderly fashion to the safety of the basement. A new authoritarian breed had been born; yesterday's hired hand had become master of the herd. With the outbreak of war, the Emergency Powers (Defense) Bill, signed into law ten days earlier, immediately imposed seemingly endless restrictions on the public. Nanny Bolton resented being told what to do by the porter, and in any case we couldn't find our gas masks. By the time we had located them and dragged over the steps needed to fish them down from the top of the kitchen cupboard, the steady note of the siren's "all clear" made the trek to the basement unnecessary. The Nazi bombers turned out to be a single passenger plane carrying the French attaché going the other way. Thus did the summer's phoney peace surrender to an equally phoney war. Six months were to pass before a single civilian would be killed by a German bomb, one that fell almost as far from London as it was possible to get, landing in the Orkney Islands north of Scotland. Nevertheless, fear of what the enemy planes might do was real enough. Reports of what was happening to Warsaw told of bent-winged Stuka dive bombers screaming out of the sky, elevating destruction, terror, and death to an unprecedented level of efficiency. What the public, and perhaps even the government, failed to recognize was that without airfields in Holland, Belgium, or France, the Stukas lacked the range to attack British cities.

Nevertheless, preparations of the most somber kind were quietly being made, not the least of them the requisitioning of thousands of papier-mâché coffins. Hospitals were cleared of all but the deathly ill, and on September 1 the blackout began. After-dark church services were banned for fear of light leaks from large windows; cars were forbidden to use their headlights—a decree that in September increased fatal road accidents by 100 percent—and the proposed evacuation of four million children from the London slums, along with the mothers of those under five, got under way, while schools were closed for any who remained behind.

The clash of classes resulting from the arrival of the London poor on the doorsteps of the country wealthy caused wounds that would fester to the war's end and contribute to Britain's subsequent glide to the left. The owners of large houses wanted nothing to do with supposedly lice-ridden city urchins, and those that did take them in left them in the charge of servants no less resentful than their employers. The majority of evacuees, however, were billeted on the rural poor, who already had large families in little houses.

In addition to the one and a half million children and parents who had been evacuated in September under the government program, two million other people left London under their own steam—Mother and I among them. However, our flight had less to do with Hitler's phantom bombers than with our inability to pay the rent. Uncle Fred's death had pulled the rug out from under us, along with the furniture, Nanny Bolton, and just about everything else we thought we owned. He had promised (so my mother claimed) to leave her well provided for, and that assurance had remained in mind as she headed for St. John's Wood on Thursday afternoons through so many years. But the instant Uncle Fred died, his bank closed his account and obeyed his resentful family's instruction to accept no outstanding bills chalked up in my mother's name. At first, she thought this no more than a temporary annoyance typical of Fred's vicious children, and felt sure that she could stall our creditors until the will was probated. After all, she had accounts at Harrods, Fortnum's, and innumerable butchers, bakers, and handsome hatmakers that went back to the glory days of Hans Place. But for both big stores and little, times had changed.

"Don't you know there's a war on?" became the tradesman's standard response when challenged for not doing what was expected of him—and not extending credit to haughty ladies rose high on his list of things not to do. The will (as I have hinted) contained no provision for Poppet. My father's dream job had long ago fallen victim to the American Depression. Consequently, he had made no alimony payments in several years, and his ability to help now was minimal. In short, we were suddenly close to destitute. There would be no return to the safety of rural Framlingham. Like the kids who stayed in London, I had no school to go to when the Michaelmas term began.

I have no recollection of our last days at St. Mary Abbott's Court or what drew us to where we went, but wherever it was, it marked the beginning of an odyssey that would rechart the course of my life. The years of luxury living were over; instead we were to join the ranks of the evacuated, the soon to be bombed out, and the homeless whom the government categorized as "displaced persons," but differing in that most of them were of the so-called working class and so could expect sympathy from others more fortunate, if no richer. But we were fish of another kind, exotic, but out of water.

Everything we owned was packed into several enormous and heavy cabin trunks that took a pride of straining porters to move, a matter of small concern when traveling first class on a Cunard liner, but a problem when presenting a third-class ticket at a railway station preparing for war. Besides the expensive trunks, we also sported large and no less expensive suitcases, two of them specially made for the trunk of the Willys-Knight touring car. Like the trunks, these were plastered with shipping labels whose first-class identifications and references to "A Deck" cabin were taken for granted in our old world but seen as snobbish affectation in our new—though not by my mother. She called it "keeping up appearances," and later when the labels began to peel, she would carefully glue them back. In the same way, as the war dragged on and her couturier-designed clothes became too old to wear, she salvaged the labels of Worth, Hartnell, Molyneux, and suchlike famous names and sewed them into her personally improved versions of the drab "Utility" clothing that took the fun out of fashion throughout the later war years. Even Aunt May, who had no difficulty enumerating her sister's shortcomings, admitted that Glad was "very good with her needle." Perhaps unwisely, however, instead of using it to create camouflage to help us blend into our environment, she used it to keep herself conspicuously different.

The chosen haven proved to be the village of Angmering on the Sussex coast at a point between Worthing and Bognor Regis, a place with better beaches than houses. Most of the latter had been run up during the 1930s and looked like it. Several, however, belonged to well-known music hall comedians and cabaret artists, and it may have been someone in this circle who had suggested we move there. Ever since kings made friends of jesters, members of the entertainment profession have been accepted into the circles of people who consider themselves their betters. Thus, my mother, who made much of knowing the "right people" (or people who knew the right people), was equally happy to discuss her encounters with café celebrities. If one of them lived at Angmering, he had not revealed himself when, from somewhere, my mother found the money to send me off to a new boarding school, this one relatively nearby at seaside Bognor Regis.

Bognor, according to the guidebooks, is famed for its "dryness, brightness, and mildness of climate." But in the winter of 1939 I found it to be gray, grim, cold, and damp; so, likewise, was the school. I don't recall that I learned anything there—other than the usual stuff about the number of sheep in New Zealand and the tonnage of coal from the pits of Wales, but for some inexplicable reason I acquired the nickname of "the professor" and a reputation for being a swot. It was the first and last time. If I had disliked the Sunday walks along the country lanes at Framlingham, I positively loathed the two-by-two crocodile marches along the sea front at Bognor, where biting winter winds blew off the Channel, and waves slapping against the stonework doused us in fine salt spray. In retrospect, the sea air was wildly good for us, and had we been better at reading tea leaves, we would have known that we were enjoying a luxury soon to be denied the British public until the war's end. Six months later barbed wire and land mines would ensure that no civilians could get near the beaches.

It was at Bognor that I first tasted the reality of war, not in news from over the Channel but across a playroom tabletop. Several of us had collections of British lead soldiers, most of them more traditional than contemporary. But opposing us across the table stood the German army, its soldiers in modern olive green uniforms, some with automatic weapons, others in lifelike postures tossing stick grenades and charging with bayonets fixed, all about five inches tall and incredibly lifelike. They belonged to a rather swarthy, black-haired, but quiet and pleasant boy named Klaus whose family had left Germany to avoid persecution.

Tabletop maneuvering had been interrupted one Sunday afternoon by the inevitable promenade walk, a time admirably suited to the misuse of idle minds. A plot hatched in the course of it was executed soon after the toy soldier war resumed. The British side accused Klaus of an illegal troop movement, and when he denied it, someone shouted, "Nazi pig Jew!" at which signal the conspirators attacked him with fists and shoes. Although I was not one of them, I am ashamed to say that I did nothing to help him. A few months later this shameful incident would be magnified to national proportions. In the summer of 1940 thousands of professedly anti-Nazi Germans who had fled to England after Hitler came to power were rounded up and shipped to the Isle of Man in the middle of the Irish Sea, the government considering as suspect anyone not holding a British passport. Consequently, German Jews whose dread of Hitler was such that they had given up everything to escape him now found themselves concentrated in internment camps and classified as "Class B Enemy Aliens."

But at Christmas 1939 the atmosphere had been different. Local government-generated paranoia had subsided; cars were allowed to use shielded headlamps and so ran over fewer pedestrians; and although food rationing was about to begin, the public welcomed it as a means of ensuring everyone a fair share. With the impregnable steel and concrete Maginot Line substituting for the previous war's mud and sandbags, and the Jerries stuffing themselves with sauerkraut behind the safety of their Siegfried Line, it seemed that a harmless stalemate could persist indefinitely. For the time being it was enough to sing about hanging out the washing on the Siegfried Line without worrying too much about how to do it.

For me, however, the status quo had not been static. The new home being established at Angmering when I was dispatched to Bognor Regis had been abandoned in favor of a hotel room at another resort a few miles to the east at West Worthing. With it came a new candidate for Father.

I don't know what prompted the move to West Worthing or whence came the trainee parent. But there we were, my mother occupying a hotel room of average size rendered minute by the number and bulk of the trunks and suitcases parked around it, and me in a boy-sized room on the floor above. The rest of the hotel's residents were elderly, and in spite of jolly Christmas decorations, became animated only when someone usurped their table in the dining room or their chair in the lounge. In the credit column, however, was Bill Williams, a captain in the Royal Sussex Regiment and Dad Elect. He was about forty, had lost most of his hair, but sported a splendidly debonair military moustache. Of all the candidates, he was the only one who treated me as something more than a necessary evil. To be fair to the others, I was now twelve years old and at an age when a father and his son can enjoy being together. For the first time in my life, mine was a truly family Christmas. Instead of being kept out of sight and having my festivities orchestrated by a nanny, mother and me and Bill made three.

Although I was unaware of it, however, a ghostly fourth presence hovered over the holiday: Captain Williams had a wife.

In mid-January I returned to the Dickensian private school at Bognor and resumed my rather unproductive studies.

The beginning of food rationing in January, and insistent government demands for belt tightening of every kind, were warnings that in spite of the stalemate in France, things were getting tougher. But not to me; I recall only the nightly blackout and voices in the street yelling, "Put that light out!"

At about the time that the Bognor school's spring term ended, so did the phoney war. On April 9, 1940, Hitler invaded Denmark and Norway, and like pulling a thread in a knitted sweater, a succession of sharp tugs quickly unraveled the Franco-British defense of Europe. Within two months the badly mauled BEF (British Expeditionary Force) had its back to the sea at Dunkirk, and the French were in flight in all directions.

I had expected to return to the West Worthing hotel for the Easter vacation, but my mother had already moved on. Bill Williams's unit had been ordered north to guard an airfield in Cambridgeshire, and she had gone with him. I had a ticket to follow. Our new home was one in a row of modest, semidetached houses a couple of miles from the base, but not actually part of any village. In short, they were nowhere, which made life difficult for families without transportation—and we were one of them, the "buzz box" having gone with everything else before we left London in '39. It was at this nameless place, therefore, that I borrowed a neighbor's bicycle and learned to ride it, ending the first lesson by pitching headfirst into a bed of stinging nettles. I was severely, if temporarily damaged, and the condition of the bicycle was not enhanced. Worse, I got no sympathy from my mother, who berated the neighbor for lending me the bike, and me for damaging clothing we couldn't afford to replace.

Even with the bicycle mastered, the new life took some getting used to; so did accepting the "fact" that at last I had a stepfather. Shortly before my arrival my mother had gone through what she described as "a form of marriage," and now signed herself as Mrs. Williams. There was even a photograph taken on the day of the wedding, a picture whose negative remained in her pocketbook until she died nearly forty years later. Whether they went as far as having a church wedding, I never learned; but henceforth the army knew us as Williams's dependents—and paid accordingly.

I have often wondered whether I really thought Bill and my mother were legally married, but I'm sure I knew nothing of the army allowances. Nevertheless, there was a danger that somewhere, sometime, I might say the wrong thing. From everyone's point of view, therefore, I would be better out of the way. The question was, where? In preparation for the impending German invasion southeastern coastal towns were being partially evacuated, so there was no sending me back to Bognor. The ideal answer was to export me to Canada.

The idea of sending British children to safety in Canada was by no means new. At the time of the Munich Crisis, John Baines of Wimbledon had made plans to send his daughter, Audrey, to Vancouver if war should break out. But when it did, and the liner *Athenia* was torpedoed with the loss of twelve hundred lives, he changed his mind. In so doing he changed his daughter's future—and probably mine, too. Regardless of the *Athenia*'s fate, a small but steady stream of British children were shipped to Canada and to the United States.

Unlike the government-sponsored program to evacuate millions of working-class children from the cities, the Canadian evacuation scheme favored the children of the professional and upper-middle classes, and of parents who could pay the fares. The children also required Canadian sponsors, and although we had none, my mother discovered that by knowing the right people, a sponsor could be assigned. Following her long-established policy of not wasting time on underlings, she secured an appointment with Lord Rosebery, who headed the selection committee, and she appeared for it smartly suited with her shoulders swathed in the silver fox furs that were the uniform of the "best people" in the prewar era. What happened in the interview, I never knew. But Canada was not in my future.

Although 1939's mass exodus of city children had gone into reverse by the year's end, new evacuations were ordered in June 1940 when it became clear that Britain was to be a battleground. The owners of large houses in rural areas who had managed to evade their responsibilities the first time now had a second chance to be kind to slum children. There was much to be said, therefore, for magnanimously offering to take in a quota of one's own choosing, and to do so by advertising in the better newspapers and in society magazines. A middle-aged brother and sister named Chubb did just that, and Mother, being a reader of such magazines, found the ad.

Early in August I arrived at Maidstone railway station in Kent to be greeted by a thin, graying, and severe-featured but gold-braided naval person who told me I could call him "Sir." To others he was Lieutenant Commander Chubb, RN, who did something important at Chatham Naval Dockyard. He told me that in spite of his duties he was able to spend several days a month at his home near the village of Linton, which he shared with his unmarried sister.

"Don't let her scare you," he told me. "But she may take time to get to like you. She's not used to boys around the house. She's the oldest of us," he added, "and we've always called her Boot."

"Why is that, sir?"

"Because she's got a face like one."

Although she did indeed have a face that was both long and leathery, such familiarity was not for the evacuee. To me she remained Miss Chubb. She turned out to be far less formidable than she looked, and as long as I obeyed her instructions, "Don't slouch about, and don't be a nuisance," we got along pretty well. In fact, in the difficult weeks ahead, I grew quite fond of her. A few days before my stay there was to end, she asked me whether I knew why her brother called her "Boot."

I confessed that I did.

"One never gets used to being ugly," she said, and quickly left the room. For an instant I had seen a quite different Miss Chubb, and over the years when I have said something deliberately or inadvertently hurtful, I have remembered the pain her nickname caused her, and have felt the more guilty because of it.

If Miss Chubb's shortcomings were visible for the world to chuckle over, her brother's were concealed and far from amusing. On the night of my arrival I awoke to find the light turned on and the gallant commander standing in the doorway stark naked. He told me that he had come to have a chat, and he hoped that I wouldn't be afraid if he sat on the bed, and that I could recognize the beauty of the unencumbered human body. I recall nothing in the least beautiful about this pale and bony Priapian apparition. On the contrary, in basic mufti, Lieutenant Commander Chubb, RN, looked small and ridiculous. How, and even if I could have kept him at bay, I do not know. Fortunately, he had barely sat down before his sister arrived. Her gray hair flowing down her back over a voluminous white nightgown, she swept in like the wrath of an emancipated god. The body beautiful fled, never to return.

"If he tries that again," Miss Chubb had snapped, "tell him you'll go to the police." Fortunately, the developing war was to keep the commander at Chatham, and on the rare occasions that he was at home he had very little to say to me. Thus, throughout August and September Miss Chubb and I had the large and rambling house to ourselves. My time was passed in assisting with the domestic chores—digging an air-raid shelter and working in the vegetable garden, where I spent less time weeding than watching the sky.

While the officially organized evacuation schemes had taken children out of the danger areas, mine had dumped me into the eye of the maelstrom. The

Battle of Britain began on June 10 when the Luftwaffe attempted to chew up fighter airfields and to blind our all-important radar stations. The Chubbs' house at Linton was squarely in the middle of Britain's Group 11, and on the German flight line to its sector airfield at Biggin Hill. Day after day the Luftwaffe formations came over, thin-bodied Dornier 17 bombers that the spotters nicknamed "Flying Pencils" and their chunkier cousin, the Heinkel 111, flying like flocks of disciplined blackbirds and surrounded by fighter escorts of Messerschmitt 109s. White contrails streamed behind the formations, and around them the cotton-ball explosions of ack-ack shells made pretty patterns in the air force blue sky. Then up would go the British Spitfires and Hurricanes to spoil the symmetry, the tidy German fighter screen breaking up as the dog fights began. Within minutes the original straight streamers of the contrails turned into a cat's cradle of loops and streaks; and the air was filled with the rattle of machine-gun and cannon fire and the whine of diving aircraft. From time to time the vapor trails became black smoke as a stricken plane spiraled downward, and the white mushroom of a pilot's parachute drifted lazily overhead.

Bits of shrapnel and occasional bullets rattled down onto our roof, and later, in a night attack in September or early October, a cylinder of incendiary bombs known as a "breadbasket" landed just beyond the garden and decanted part of its contents through our hedge, none of the bombs igniting. I was bitterly disappointed at not being allowed to keep one as a souvenir, for by this time I had become an avid, even fiendish collector. Standing at the top of Linton Hill, the house provided a fine view to the north and west, enabling me to get a good idea of where crashing planes would hit. Armed with a kitchen knife and a pair of pliers, and mounted on Boot's bicycle, I would try to beat the police or army to the wreckage. My room rapidly became a museum of aircraft artifacts; some, like my long ribbons of 7.9 mm machine-gun bullets and shorter lengths of the much larger 20 mm cannon shells were highly dangerous exhibits. However, that cannot have occurred to me, for I recall taking apart several British 0.303 bullets from a downed Spitfire and trying to make their spaghetti-like rods of cordite into fireworks. My greatest prize, however, was most of the painted swastika from the tail of a Messerschmitt 109.

In spite of the daily excitement of the air battles and the prospect of fresh loot, life at Linton was lonely, and would have been worse had I not been able to make friends with New Zealand soldiers who were camped across the road in Linton Park. They taught me to handle and clean rifles, sometimes allowed me to ride in their armored vehicles, and let me share a camaraderie that I'd never experienced at school. One even drove me to the wreck of a Spitfire that had crashed in the park and helped me salvage bits of perforated aluminum from the tangled fuselage. The best bits had already been retrieved by the air force and trucked away for reuse.

Not all my treasures were products of the Battle of Britain; one was a relic of a much older conflict, or so I was told by the farmer who found it in his plowed field. It looked like a rusted pair of pliers, but in reality was a pincer-type mold for casting lead bullets. The farmer gave it to me and said that it could have been lost in the seventeenth century during a Civil War skirmish between Royalists and Roundheads. But for all he or I knew, the mold could just as well have dated from the eighteenth or even the nineteenth century; nevertheless, it sparked my interest in a period of English history about which I had previously known nothing.

In weak moments, when one sets logic aside and dares to tiptoe through the woods where wizards dwell, it's tempting to speculate that the pattern of life is in some way preordained, and that from the start, fate has one by the hand. In such a scenario the allegedly Civil War–period bullet mold presaged the culmination of my archaeological career forty-five years later. Framlingham flints notwithstanding, the Linton mold was my first genuine archaeological artifact, and three more seventeenth-century bullet molds would be among finds from my last excavation at Martin's Hundred in Virginia. Coincidence?

Of course.

In October the Chubbs decided to close the house and evacuate their evacuee. Under the circumstances it was not the most chivalrous of decisions, for there was no certainty that the train would ever reach London, and no provision had been made for anyone to meet me if it did. Furthermore, the blitzkrieg on London had begun. On October 15, the night of the full moon, four hundred bombers unloaded more than a thousand high-explosive bombs (and an untold number of incendiaries) on the capital, killing 430 civilians and shutting down five main railroad stations and damaging four others.

Rescue workers were still digging through acres of rubble beside the tracks as my train from Maidstone inched its way into London. Bill Williams had been transferred from Cambridgeshire to a unit stationed near the industrial city of Coventry, and naturally, as his "wife," my mother had gone with him. So I was to be dumped on Aunt May in Ealing. I have little recollection of how I got there; I only remember the starting and stopping journey as we crept into the outskirts of the city. I suppose I should have been scared by the sight of the carnage, but I wasn't. The train would roll forward a few hundred yards and then stop to show me a new picture of rubble piled in interesting shapes, curtains in the window of a house with no back, bathtubs suspended by their pipes, a mirror-fronted wardrobe standing undamaged in a room that had lost everything else but the stub of its floor. The people clambering through the ruins, struggling to save lives, seemed unreal, and certainly no concern of mine. I ought to have been appalled by the destruction and fearful that at any minute the train would be bombed. But as I say, I recall feeling nothing.

The train journey ended prematurely at a small and badly damaged suburban station where we had to get off and travel the rest of the way on the subway. Although Ealing lies about nine miles west of the heart of London and boasted no military targets, bombs were falling there with fair regularity and continued to do so throughout the Blitz. Because Uncle Reg Horsley's office had been evacuated to Reading, Aunt May had gone there too, leaving an aging maid alone in the London house, and it was to her that I went. Grandma "Ahmoo" Mann was also still in Ealing, but she was not strong enough to look after a thirteen-year-old boy with nothing to do. So May's maid and I kept each other company, playing cribbage on the dining room table through the evenings until the sirens wailed, and then huddling together under it as the guns banged away and, from time to time, the bombs screamed down. The floor shuddered under us, and crockery fell out of the cupboards in the kitchen, but that was all.

In one respect my mother had been equally lucky. In Coventry on the night of the great raid of November 14, she had escaped unscathed. But shortly afterward, Bill Williams moved yet again, this time to Bedford. At one of his postings he had been responsible for the mess accounts, which, when audited, seemed to be in less than parade order. Although no charges were placed, and my mother was sure that he had not been responsible for whatever was amiss, Bill was now transferred to one of the least attractive posts the army had to offer. Italy had entered the war in June, raising British concern that Italian armies in Abyssinia, Eritrea, and Somaliland would jeopardize British bases on the Red Sea and in Kenya. So in December Bill Williams was seconded to the King's African Rifles at Mombasa.

With her husband gone, Mrs. Williams returned to the only available haven: her mother's house in Gordon Road at Ealing, where I joined her. The family reunion was not a happy one. Ahmoo Mann's Victorian views of how ladies should behave generated much sighing and head shaking. Ahmoo made her points with quiet and regal dignity. Although I was not present at any of her lectures, I have no doubt that she had much to say about the morality and honesty of the "Mrs. Williams" charade, and did not accept the explanation that there would be a proper wedding as soon as Bill was free and the war won. If proof of his sincerity was wanted, my mother later insisted to me, had he not assigned his army family allowance to us?

The money was important, indeed vitally so, but my mother was genuinely in love with Bill Williams, and although he had no income other than his army pay, I am sure she would have married him. "If only he'd been free before he sailed," she often told me, "by now you'd have a real father." Christmas 1940 was a grim affair, emotionally and physically chilling: my mother in turns tearful at her loss and railing against the War Office that had treated Bill so cruelly, Ahmoo icy in her disapproval, and me in a house short of coal and kindling where I spent much of my time rolling up old newspapers and making them into slow-burning fuel to keep the few lumps of coal alight.

In 1936 a German munitions worker had assembled a thermite incendiary bomb numbered AZ8312, a magnesium alloy cylinder just under 2 inches in diameter and $9\frac{3}{4}$ inches long, with 4-inch-long, green-painted sheet-iron fins, an object of perverse beauty to students of art deco design. On the night of December 29, more than a hundred Luftwaffe planes dropped thousands of them on the city, some like AZ8312 falling harmlessly into the Thames (where ten years later I would find it), but the majority raining down in the immediate vicinity of St. Paul's Cathedral, creating so many fires that photographs taken in Queen Victoria Street at 9:40 p.m. appear to have been shot in broad daylight. From the house at Ealing we could see the city burning. What appeared to be a thick bank of clouds was really smoke that hung on the skyline, its underside orange red, glowing momentarily brighter here and there as high explosive bombs struck into the inferno.

It was a Sunday night, and most of the city buildings were locked up and without fire watchers to smother the incendiary bombs and douse their initially small and manageable fires. By the time anyone saw the flames and broke into the buildings, it was too late. Early in the raid a lucky bomb ruptured the principal two-foot water main feeding the city hydrants and quickly reduced pressure to virtually nil. Since it was a full moon, the tide in the Thames dropped so low that fire pumps couldn't reach the water, and firefighting boats were kept so far from shore that they were of little help. To make matters worse, a high wind was blowing that increased to fifty miles per hour, gaining strength from the fires and ensuring (as in the Great Fire of 1666) that much of the mischief was caused by sparks blown from one roof to another.

In my previous weeks of under-the-table nights I had grown accustomed to the characteristic pulsating growl of the Luftwaffe engines and to the banging of the antiaircraft guns, and rather than being afraid I grasped any opportunity to watch the searchlights raking the sky, hoping to glimpse a silver raider caught in their crossed beams. For my mother, however, whose recollections of Coventry were still fresh, the Blitz was no game, and to her the holocaust of December 29, though distant, was a harbinger of worse to come. If proof was needed, it allegedly hung from a railway bridge behind the houses on the other side of the street. Along with large bombs that dove into the ground before exploding, sending most of their force upward, the Germans were also dropping magnetic sea mines on parachutes which detonated on contact and thus spread their explosive force laterally, doing infinitely more damage. Rumor had it that one of these mines had been found, its parachute caught on a lamp post on the bridge, the cylinder with its fifteen hundred pounds of explosive swinging below only a foot or two from the track. Had the line not been blocked further down, the next train along would have blown itself, the bridge, and much of Gordon Road to blazes. True or not, fear of what might happen next, coupled with Grandma Mann's cold disapproval, was enough to make us pack up and head for the country, responding to a newspaper ad offering "peace and quiet" to paying guests at a farm deep in the safety of rural Somersetshire.

We set out by train in the bitter cold of January 4, 1941, and reached Shepton Mallet at dusk; by the time we secured a taxi (whose driver declined to take most of our luggage) and reached our rural sanctuary, it was pitch-dark. An elderly man holding an oil lamp greeted us at the door and showed us to a large but bleak room which I was to share with my mother. "Supper's serving," the man told us. "We eat early here."

Rural Somerset might be offering peace and quiet, but its idea of hospitality left virtually everything to be desired. Nevertheless, my mother made up for the man's dourness with her own expressions of delight at having arrived. Our entrance into the dining room was equally upbeat, but no better received. Six or eight grim and haggard people sat around the table, their faces parchment yellow in the oil-fed lamplight. When my mother told them how wonderful it was to feel safe at last, one of them laughed.

"Peace and quiet, is it?" said another. "Just wait a while and you'll see."

Shepton Mallet lies about sixteen miles due south of Bristol, a city that had endured its first great German raid the night before. British scientists, knowing that the enemy planes were guided along radio beams, had learned that the beams could be bent and the squadrons diverted. To prevent the Luftwaffe from unloading its cargoes onto this strategic western port, the British Army had set decoy fires in the country well clear of the city to simulate the lead bombers' incendiary markers. The place chosen to light the fires was in fields adjacent to our haven of peace and quiet.

The night of our arrival marked the second devastating raid on Bristol, and once again the decoys were fired, and again a worthwhile number of bombardiers took the bait. The Somerset fields shuddered under the explosions, and we lay awake waiting for the next stick to surprise us. The raid did not last long, but it was enough to convince my mother that the grim Shepton Mallet farmhouse was not as advertised. Nevertheless, she had a quite astonishing ability to make the best of bad luck, and like Tennessee Williams's Blanche Dubois, we were learning to rely on "the kindness of strangers." From somewhere there emerged a rather insignificant but pleasant salesman who not only had a car but gas to run it. He took us to lunch in the town and then drove us into Bristol to view the damage. In retrospect it was an extraordinary thing to do at a time when every billboard carried posters asking, "Is Your Journey Really Necessary?" Not only was it unnecessary, it was also unhelpful to the weary firefighters still struggling to extinguish the last of the flames and pull through the rubble in search of casualties. It was, nevertheless, an unforgettable sight: the car bumping over unretrieved hoses and skirting its way around bricks and timber that littered the roads. At one corner near the city center a theater or cinema was still smoking yet draped with icicles from the water used to fight the flames that had destroyed it.

At the day's end the salesman took us back to the farm and, as far as I know, was never seen again. Hour by hour we waited for the first pulsing sound of the returning German bombers. But they never came. Nevertheless, the next day we boarded another train bound for somewhere safer—a seaside resort on the north coast of Wales about the same distance from the port of Liverpool as Shepton Mallet had been from Bristol.

Seaside resorts can be grim in winter at the best of times, but in an off-season destined to last more than five years, and with no colored lights along the promenade to brighten the cheeks of boardinghouse keepers, it would be hard to imagine anywhere more depressing. My recollections of the town of Rhyl are of gray streets and gray stone houses with gray slate roofs under perennially gray skies. Why we chose such a place, I have no idea. Perhaps it was because it seemed to be about as far as one could get from Hitler's attention and still be in touch with civilization. Certainly my mother, whose métier was bright lights and smart people, had no affinity for the industrial north, nor for the "Bed &

Breakfast" emporia of working-class landladies; yet it was under such a roof that we now found ourselves.

When we arrived in a taxi from the station, the woman and her husband received us like royalty. Although the heaviest trunks were to follow later, our impressive array of far-traveled baggage was carried indoors as it might have been by obsequious Indian servants in the high days of the Raj. The proprietors knew a "lady" when they heard one, and gave thanks unto their Welsh gods that a golden goose had miraculously fallen into their laps. If they smiled a lot and got the butcher to come across with little bits under the counter, perhaps we could be expected to keep the boardinghouse business going until the real people could come again. Had they known the truth, our hosts would almost certainly have pitched both our baggage and us straight back into the street. The goose was barren.

Bill Williams's transfer from the Royal Sussex Regiment to the colonial King's African Rifles had resulted in some unpracticed War Office bookkeeping, which in turn caused a delay in reestablishing and redirecting his marital allowance. Consequently, the funds on which my mother was relying had not arrived. Although Bill had left her with as much cash as he could raise, nearly a year of doing his best to keep Poppet in the manner to which she needed to be accustomed had seriously depleted his funds. The debacle at Shepton Mallet and the cost of shifting ourselves and all that luggage around the country had brought us to penury.

Style carried us through the first couple of weeks, for although our landlady expected her guests to pay by the week, my mother's willingness to smile upon such an ordinary person made the ordinary person reluctant to mention so crass a subject as rent. Besides, it would have been unpatriotic to be unkind to a lady who had just seen her husband go off to war. Realizing that the time would quickly come when the landlady's husband would demand that there be an end to this grace and favor, my mother played the only card left. She made up a small parcel of her jewelry and mailed it to a "little man" in the City—a pawnbroker who specialized in helping nice people through nasty predicaments.

Several weeks elapsed before the War Office checks began to arrive, and the little man in the City notwithstanding, the Indians broke through our wagons. The back rent was requested, and when it was not forthcoming, our hosts' attitude changed abruptly. Yesterday's obsequious deference turned mean and scornful, revealing the smoldering class hatred so long hidden behind the mask of servility. Although we weathered the storm and were able to pay up before we were thrown out, the old "Yes, thank you, Mrs. Williams; right away, Mrs. Williams" never returned. Instead, each rent request came with the half smile of one who knew that the screws were on, and hoped they hurt.

The gray winter months saw the European war stalemated, but on March 30 the German Afrika Corps under Rommel swept eastward. Other German forces tore through Yugoslavia and were into Greece before British troops could come to the rescue. And between April 8 and 12 back came the waves of bombers, striking at Coventry, Birmingham, and Bristol. They had come within sight and sound of us at Rhyl on March 13 and 21, when 250 planes struck at Liverpool and the Merseyside shipyards, prompting my mother to conclude that once again it was time to move on.

6 🪶 *Yo-Yo Years*

M Y MOTHER WAS A MISTRESS of the heart-rending and guilt-stirring letter. Recipients were known to pale at the sight of them, and sometimes,
on the grounds of ill health, to destroy them unopened. Of sterner stuff, however, was Renée Redfern, a yachting acquaintance from the good years, who
responded to my mother's plea by offering us temporary shelter at her summer
home near Salcombe in Devonshire. If any further encouragement was needed,
the Luftwaffe provided it. On May 1, 1941, Göring sent over the first of eight
hundred bombers to begin seven consecutive night raids on Liverpool. As far as
I know, not a single bomb fell anywhere near Rhyl, but my mother had become
convinced that fate was out to get her: first at Coventry, then London, next Bristol, and now Liverpool. I doubt whether we checked the map to note that the
distances between Shepton Mallet and Bristol, and between Rhyl and Liverpool, were almost exactly the same as between Salcombe and Plymouth—where
more than a thousand civilians had been killed in the previous two weeks.

In the prewar decade Salcombe had become second only to Cowes as an
anchorage for blazered yachtsmen. Its narrow Fore Street, laid out when fishermen walked between the ferry slip and the chandler's shop and boatbuilders
steered an often unsteady course between their yards and the Anchor Inn, had
been invaded by the roaring sports cars of wealthy weekenders. The terraces of
its Marine Hotel and Ferry Inn catered to smart women displaying their wide
white trousers and polka-dot scarves and desirous of drowning themselves in
nothing more saline than gin. To the relief of the old salts sitting on the quay, all
that had ended with the war, and being on the way to nowhere (and ten miles
from the buffers at the end of the railway line), Salcombe had become again the
quiet fishing village it had been through more than four hundred years before
the city sailors found it.

Renée Redfern's husband, John, had bought the house she called The

Cottage in the tiny hamlet of Coombe shortly before the war began. It was a thatch-roofed, casement-windowed, two-story house of the kind that estate agents like to advertise as "a residence of great charm." Its manicured lawns, rock garden, and herbaceous borders flanked a stream that dutifully cascaded over rocks to calm even the most ragged nerves. Inside, the house was furnished in the handsome "Old English" style promoted by the Parker Knowell company. Lamp shades and sconces with their alternating parchment and red silk panels were in tasteful harmony with the rest. On the coffee tables the magazines fanned out to expose just the banners of their titles: *Field, Country Life, The Tatler, Vogue, The Queen,* and so forth. The newspapers, too, were no less neatly folded to show the name of each, and woe betide a boy who took one and didn't put it back precisely in its place.

Behind the cottage stood a pair of real cottages of some antiquity, occupied by Gill the gardener and his wife, who cooked. There being only two guest rooms in the Redfern house, one assigned to my mother and the other kept for weekend visitors, I was relegated to the Gills' cottage. But that was no hardship, for I quickly became deeply attached to them. My mother, whose nerves had suffered mightily during the deadly months at Rhyl, quickly returned to her old, gay self and reveled in her assignment to look after and run the house in Renée's absences—which were frequent. In truth, Renée had only given her the "job" to prevent her from feeling that we were receiving charity. The house needed no manager, and from time to time I would hear Mrs. Gill angrily telling her husband just that.

For me, however, the joys of returning to something approaching the good, prewar life were less recognized and appreciated. In spite of the freedom to walk the fields and to clamber over the crags and wave-swept granite rocks of Bolt Head, I was becoming bored with my own company. The carefully erected barrier that had separated me from children not of our class now made it difficult for me to find common ground with the few children I encountered in the neighboring villages. Besides, the "neighboring" was not exactly close, there being a four-mile walk through narrow lanes to Malborough in one direction, and no less distance to Salcombe in the other. My principal friend, therefore, was Gill the gardener, who was easily coerced into stopping what he was supposed to be doing to indulge in the ancient Devonian pursuit of "yarning." Gill could yarn by the hour, telling tales of Armada gold washed ashore in Bigbury Bay, of wreckers waving lanterns to lure ships onto the Bolt Head rocks, and of a tunnel reputed to run from the cliffs to the churchyard at Malborough to spirit away the loot. Then, too, there was the man-made cave at South Sands with a great storage pit at the end of it where other wreckers hid their spoils until they could be moved by rowboat up the harbor estuary to Salcombe.

"Oi remember, when Oi was jest a lad, goin' into that tunnel with me candle," Gill told me, "and right at the end there was this ship's ladder goin' down. Right old, it was."

The South Sands tunnel was no yarn. I soon found its entrance, but although equipped with a candle, I couldn't keep it alight, and so was forced to retreat. But now I knew that Gill's yarning was not just making stuff up. If the South Sands tunnel was real, then all the rest of his tales had to be true—or so I reasoned. A few days later, in preparation for my next expedition, I persuaded him to lend me an old bicycle lamp that operated, not on batteries, but on acetylene gas, generated by dripping water onto pellets of calcium carbide. The lamp had a reservoir at the top and a screw-on canister for the carbide below. When the water cock was turned on, the gas went up a pipe where one lit it like an oil lamp. It was, as I say, an old-fashioned device, but much brighter than the light provided by a regular flashlight battery, and it did a splendid job of illuminating the tunnel. Its walls and roof were covered with phosphorescent lichens that continued to glow eerily in the dark after the lamplight had passed them by, and behind them I could see the marks of the tunnelers' picks—just as Gill had said I would. A few yards in, the shaft took a slight turn and then straightened again, and there at the end of it was the pit, and going down into it an iron ship's ladder, though probably not a very old one. From the start, the acetylene lamp had been leaking, hissing and bubbling around the junction of container and housing. Just as I was about to descend the four or five rungs to the pit's sandy floor, the lamp fell apart. I dropped it and was left in the darkness save for the green glow of the lichens. Although the tunnel was no more than fifteen to twenty yards long, groping my way out was a terrifying experience. I well remember that the entrance was large, black, and forbidding. When I went back, in 1966, the blackness was as stygian as I remembered it, only the largeness had dwindled in proportion to my own growth. The iron ladder was still there, and although there was no sign of my lamp, I saw for the first time what I would have seen had it not gone out. The tunnel did not end at the pit as old Gill had said. Like the shaft-protected tunnels in Egyptian tombs, the passage went on beyond it to I know not where.

The South Sands adventure was important, because it introduced me to the excitement of quasi-archaeological discovery and, coupled with Gill's yarns, stimulated my growing fascination with the sixteenth, seventeenth, and eighteenth centuries. At the same time, however, I was being exposed to counterbalancing tales that stoked more traditional archaeological fires—these from an elderly but still raven-haired Greek lady, a reputed witch, who lived alone in a nearby Coombe cottage and who found in me a wide-eyed and appreciative audience. She introduced me to the Aegean world of *The Iliad,* to Schliemann's Troy, to Mycenae, to Halicarnassus, to the bulls of Minos, and also to her husband—dead some twenty years.

"Listen! Do you hear him? He's upstairs. You'll hear him close the door."

And I really thought I did.

She told me how her will power could bring him back to sit with her at night beside the fire. "Ghosts, like wireless waves, are all around us," she explained. "All we have to do is tune them in."

At the end of one of my visits this unusual lady gave me five ancient Greek coins that were to become the nucleus of my second museum; my first (the Noël Hume Museum of Battle of Britain Treasures) had been left behind with the Chubbs at Linton. The thrill of being able to hold coins that were thousands of years old reminded me of the essay my class had to compose so long ago at The Gables: A Day in the Life of a Penny. Where had it been? Whose hands had held it last? Looking at the Greek coins with their portraits of helmeted gods and the prows of warships, I asked myself how like me, or how different from me, had their ancient owners been? Although professional archaeologists and historians ask rather similar questions posed in seemingly more erudite ways, I confess that throughout my career I have continued to ask them just as I did when I held those first Greek coins. Furthermore, I remain reluctant to deny the possibility that their donor, who could teach her dead husband to shut doors, might also have been able to clutch the coins in her gnarled hand and "see" what I could only guess at.

Although I had no previous interest in the Greeks and so had no visual images of my own to play with, my months at Coombe provided another, quite different route to the ancient world. In its library I found both Robert Graves's *I Claudius* and his *Claudius the God and His Wife Messalina,* and for the first time I plunged into the Augustan Age of first-century Rome. I was blinded by the glare of the sun on white marble walls of temples and palaces; I lay on couches eating grapes; I marched with the legions into British triumphs and German disasters; I was with Gaius Caligula gathering seashells on the coast of Gaul; I stood at Claudius's shoulder as the Sibyl foretold his future, hoping all the while that in some way Ancient Rome would have a place in mine. I began to build cardboard models of the pictures that Graves had left in my imagination, models that, with the addition of a proscenium frame, quickly turned into theatrical sets. If the omens were taken at face value, and if indeed Rome was to figure in my future, I would find it on the stage or from behind a movie camera. At least that was how Renée Redfern read the tea leaves.

It was she, too, who first became concerned about my education. I had not seen the inside of a classroom since April 1940; but although I was bored, I did not see school as the ideal answer to my problem. Perhaps if I had had brothers or sisters I would have recognized the need to compete; instead, I had no sense that I was the loser. Nevertheless, in the crucial learning years between fourteen and fifteen, I was missing the all-important, foundation-laying semesters linking what little I already knew (but could scarcely remember) with what I had yet to learn. My mother, more interested in sports than books, had given the matter no thought, and when Renée insisted that something be done, she said she supposed that I would just have to go to the local "board" school at Malborough.

This is not to say that my mother lacked interest in my knowing what needed to be known. It was just that to her, knowing how to behave was more important than algebra or the date that William Rufus got shot. She taught me to tip my soup plate away from me, not to hold a knife like a pen, to cut toast into small pieces before buttering it, to stick stamps on envelopes half an inch from and square to the corners, and never to pronounce the "l" in golf. Most important, one must never forget that a gentleman is born and not made. No matter how shabby his clothes or eccentric his behavior, he remains a gentleman. Much of this would be useful when taking one's rightful place in society—provided one had the money not to have to work and didn't mind being liberally ignorant. It also presupposed that one *had* a rightful place.

Renée Redfern earned my eternal gratitude, first by recognizing that my future depended not on class but on a sound education, and then by ensuring that I could get it. Although living apart from her husband, John, Renée was able to persuade him that I was a good prospect in the process of going down the drain, and that saving me would be a noble thing to do. He agreed.

John Redfern's reason for agreeing to pay for the education of a boy he had never met had its genesis in a London nightclub. His flying-officer son was among the eighty revelers and musicians killed in the Café de Paris on March 8, 1941, when a bomb crashed through the roof and exploded on the dance floor, and John's memorial to him took two forms: He published a special edition of poet Alice Duer Miller's moving *White Cliffs*—and he sent me to school.

The trick, however, was to find a good school that would take a boy who had missed a crucial year of his education. Most required a passing score on an entrance exam, and it was a safe bet that I would fail. By some means never revealed to me, the headmaster of St. Lawrence College at Ramsgate accepted the challenge. Like all other schools along the invasion coast, this one had been evacuated, to the safety of Northamptonshire in the English Midlands. That would have been a sensible move even if the government had not insisted, for by November 1941 Ramsgate had been bombed forty-one times, seventy-one civilians had been killed, and 8,500 homes damaged.

The war was not going well. The fall of Greece and Crete, coupled with the Italian control of Sicily and the Germans strafing Malta, had virtually closed the Mediterranean to British shipping. Consequently, letters from Bill Williams in East Africa had to travel round the Cape of Good Hope and were painfully slow in reaching Salcombe. Week by week, my mother waited in anguish for news of him, and every three days she sent letters out, each sealed on the back with a bold, lipsticked kiss. The responses, when they came, slowly grew less affectionate and more informative (within the limitations of army censorship), and I remember my mother worrying lest Bill had been wounded and was keeping that from her.

One letter contained numerous photographs of a nonstrategic nature: views of Mombasa, Nairobi, Bill as white hunter with his large rifle beside a delicate but very dead gazelle, and most interesting—at least to me—prints from the contents of a camera Bill had taken from a captured Italian. There were shots of villages, a Mussolini monument, a downed British biplane, and a smiling trio: two soldiers and a darkish lady naked to the waist, each nipple gripped 'twixt thumb and trigger finger. When I naively expressed surprise that the soldiers should have posed like that, my mother laughed. "Darling, they're Italians," she replied, as though that explained everything. Although the captured pictures no longer survive, that of Bill and his gazelle does, and on reflection his seems the greater obscenity.

In September I left Coombe bound for St. Lawrence College, via London, and my first meeting with Renée's husband and my benefactor, "Uncle John." It was, at best, a stiff meeting, he not knowing what to say to me nor I to him. He wanted to know what I hoped to accomplish in life, and I'm sure I gave him a hopelessly inadequate answer. Even if I had had career aspirations (which I did not), I am certain they would have been buried deep beneath my apprehension at becoming a new boy at a school I had yet to see. Although my trunk and tuck box (the traditional wooden chest containing a schoolboy's luxuries) were being sent independently, getting around London and finding the train to Northampton were gut-twisting challenges for one whose previous experience of urban life had been limited largely to prewar walks in Kensington Gardens with Nanny Bolton and to the two solo exploits described earlier. At fourteen I had a lot of growing up to do.

Across the nation, owners of large estates and big houses faced the unpleasant prospect of being "requisitioned," of seeing their homes turned into government offices, military barracks, hospitals or hostels, and the trauma of trying to get adequate compensation for the damage once the war was won—*if* the war was won. Wise owners did what had to be done before they were forced to do it, seeking out government-approved tenants who would wreak the least havoc. Sir Hereward and Lady Wake of Courteenhall did just that, bravely accepting St. Lawrence College as their occupant, and moving into the groom's apartment over the stables for the duration of the war. Although most of the Wakes' furniture was taken out, their magnificent collection of portraits by Van Dyck, Daniel Mytens, and other masters remained behind, as did the contents of their library. But in spite of the fact that the drawing room became a dormitory and saw many a pillow fight and thrown shoe, and the hall became a classroom and the dining room the dining hall for the entire school, not one painting was damaged and not a single book was lost in the four years that St. Lawrence was there. Luck played no small part in this admirable record, yet most of the credit belonged to the school's headmaster, the Reverend Peter Perfect.

In his clerical collar, mortarboard, and flying black gown Perfect paralleled the formidable Reverend Kneese, but in all else he was a man apart; a commanding presence but imbued with tolerance and a gentle understanding—not of willful disobedience, but of academic shortcomings. He put the welfare of his charges above all else; their successes were his joy and their failures his pain. Not surprisingly, his key staff members were of a similar disposition. Because the school's enrollment had been drastically reduced by its move to Courteenhall, its structure comprised a junior school and only two senior "houses"—that division necessary to create the internal rivalry needed to build esprit de corps and to provide opposing teams in hockey, cricket, and football. I was assigned to Cameron House, whose senior master was a rotund and elderly bachelor named Reggie Shaw who meant it when he said, "This is going to hurt me as much as it'll hurt you." The latter half of that cliché was true, as I would discover on several painful but well-deserved occasions.

Being a new boy anywhere, at any time, is not easy, but for me it was particularly difficult. The loss of five median semesters (called "terms" in England) had left me in parlous shape to absorb subjects dependent on the accumulation of knowledge, and that meant languages and the various branches of mathematics. Although I was starting at the bottom class in the senior school, much of what I needed to know was being taught in the junior school and therefore lost to me. On the other hand, geography, history, English literature, scripture, art, indeed any subject graspable from a standing start, caused me no problems. Consequently, I lunged wholeheartedly into the subjects I could handle and therefore liked, and lazily admitted defeat in those that I couldn't and didn't. The harassed St. Lawrence staff had no time to provide backup tuition, and at home no one gave a damn.

Renée Redfern had listened to the call for women to do their bit in beating Hitler and had joined the MTC—the Military Transport Corps, an elite unit of volunteer women who provided their own uniforms, supplied their own cars, and served as drivers for generals and such tiptop people. It also meant closing the house at Coombe. At first Renée had planned to let my mother continue to live there while paying a nominal rent, but gradually they had fallen out.

Mother claimed that the problems stemmed from Renée's almost neurotic passion for tidiness. "As soon as you stood up," Mother told me, "Renée'd be puffing up the cushions in the chair behind you." There was no denying that Renée Redfern was house-proud; but my mother, who made a fetish of dressing-table order, was not an untidy person. Whatever the cause, their friendship cooled, and by the time I went home for the 1942 Christmas holiday, home was no longer at Coombe. Furthermore, we were no longer dependents of Captain William Williams, or the recipients of his marital allowance. I never discovered what happened, and to my knowledge my mother never mentioned him again, though as I have noted, she was still carrying his picture when she died nearly forty years later.

I returned instead to a different house in Salcombe, an old fisherman's cottage hugging the estuary close by the ferry slip, named with embarrassing cuteness The Little Grey Home in the West. We were sharing it with a lieutenant commander in the Royal Naval Volunteer Reserve, Alexander Anderson, a fiercely black-bearded seaman with a patch over one eye (blinded by an errant firework when he was a boy), a character straight from the pages of a Rafael Sabatini novel. He commanded a naval rescue launch that plucked downed pilots out of the sea and picked up survivors from ships sunk by enemy action along the coast. Alex was the new "father" candidate, and he and my mother seemed totally compatible. Nevertheless, I was aware that I was in the way and found myself looking forward to going back to school.

St. Lawrence placed strong emphasis on traditional Church of England values, as one might expect from a college with a clergyman as its head. I found the Sunday services and daily school prayers boring and a dissipation of time that could be much better spent. Consequently, when called upon to try out for the choir I deliberately sang off-key. I needn't have worried; I did anyway. While these activities, along with seasonal sports, kept most of the boys busy on Wednesday and Saturday half holidays, I preferred to go off on my own and to try to snare rabbits in the Courteenhall park, and on the rare occasion that I caught one, to make a fire and roast it. This was a forbidden activity, but made more exciting for that reason. There was something immensely satisfying about cooking on a fire even if it only involved boiling a revolting dried soup mix in a blackened tin can. Unfortunately, one tended to return with one's best suit smelling incriminatingly of wood smoke, thus prompting the prefectorial question, "Where have you been, boy?" and the inevitable consequences.

On occasion we were allowed to bicycle the five miles to Northampton, a rather grim industrial town noted for the manufacture of boots and shoes. Nevertheless, it had two museums (one with a memorable mummy) and several secondhand bookshops. Old books became my passion, and because I received only a shilling a week in pocket money, I sold my toys and the contents of my tuck box to raise funds to buy more. Eighteenth-century volumes of the *Gentleman's Magazine* and the *Annual Register* could be bought for sixpence each, and reading them from cover to cover I found myself becoming immersed in the arts and letters of the period. Since many of the topics related to matters antiquarian, my interest in archaeology found a new stimulus, albeit from a rather archaic point of view.

One of my book-buying excursions yielded a quarto-sized volume bound in thick boards covered with black leather embracing heavy, coarse paper pages, printed in a bold Gothic style, and published at some date in the 1630s. I do not recall its title, only that it was a commentary on the Bible—not one of my favorite subjects. What had attracted me to the book was its appearance of antiquity. On dipping into it, however, I found that it had much to say about the misleading passages and euphemisms in the King James version. Thus, for example, the word "feet" in the line "with twain he shall cover his feet" really meant penis. There were numerous other hidden references to parts of the male and female anatomies and to sexual activity which I did not fully understand, but which I was sure amounted to a deliberate cover-up.

The master who taught us scripture was the college curate and rejoiced in the barely believable name of Vicary. He was young, earnest, and normally very good with the boys, but he did not take kindly to my primed questions. Feet were feet, and he wasn't interested in prurient alternatives. Shortly after acquiring the Black Book, I came upon another that peaked my theological curiosity. It was a modern work that set out to demonstrate that the miracles described in the New Testament either had logical explanations or simply didn't happen. The rolling away of the stone was dismissed as the product of an earth tremor. "The Bible tells us, so we must believe," was Vicary's constant response to the inexplicable. Lacking any homegrown grounding in faith, I found all this very unsatisfactory, and began to try to learn how other religions grappled with history and the hereafter. I read the Koran, and books on Buddhism and Shintoism, and also (though I can't remember why) *Mein Kampf.* The result was a maturing cynicism toward all who peddle faith in preference to proof. Although that critical outlook has served me well as an archaeologist, I'm sure it has denied me much of the contentment and optimism that most people draw from their religious beliefs.

The early months of 1942 were among the grimmest of the war. Although the Russians had halted Hitler short of Moscow, and America had entered the war, few people had any sense that the tide really was turning. Indeed, the British civilian population was beginning to lose confidence that a military victory was possible and to look to God to save the day. Since Dunkirk he had not been particularly active on our behalf, and his sending us another wretchedly cold winter had not helped morale.

When the spring term ended in late March there were not many signs of seasonal improvement. Getting home to Salcombe involved two train journeys, the first easy enough, for the majority of us traveled together to London's Euston Station, where most were met by happy parents. For boys going further afield, first there was the long wait for a taxi and then the even longer wait for the next train out of stations whose timetables were regularly interfered with by Luftwaffe vandalism. My train west to Devonshire left from Paddington Station, in the best of times a grim and smoke-begrimed terminus situated in Praed Street, one of London's least attractive, and inhabited, so my mother warned, almost exclusively by working-class tarts. In March 1942 it was also full of troops, as were the trains, every seat occupied and the corridors filled with standees and kit bags—rendering a journey to the john something akin to an assault course.

Rail travel's principal joy—the pleasure of watching the English countryside slide by—had gone for the duration, the carriage windows covered with a shatterproof scrim save for a small diamond-shaped aperture in the middle. I forget whether the carriage lights were yellow or blue, but I remember that they were not bright enough to read by, and that once the sun went down we sat in shadowy gloom. Progress was painfully slow, the steam train huffing forward for a few miles or yards, then stopping and jerking the carriages backward with a clanking of chains and buffers and a hiss of escaping steam. While we waited for we knew not what, other trains would clatter by us, hauling flat cars carrying strange lumps under large tarpaulins, and giving us an "I'm all right Jack" toot on their whistles as they passed.

This journey was the slowest ever, and by the time it ended at Kingsbridge, I was something like five hours late, and it was past eleven at night. My mother had written telling me that she would arrange for me to be met, but she had omitted to say by whom or with what. Half a dozen people alighted and made their way through the blacked-out Kingsbridge station to waiting cars. Standing in the darkness clutching my suitcase, I watched the last red tail lights disappear. Behind me the booking office and waiting room were in darkness. So was the town.

When we lived at Coombe I had several times taken the bus from Malborough to Kingsbridge, and so knew the four-mile road at least that far. The remaining two and a bit to Salcombe would be new. Although all road signs had been removed in 1940 to irritate invaders, I remembered that to get there all I had to do was to turn left a mile short of Malborough. After standing alone in the station yard for half an hour in case my mother had been waiting in Salcombe to hear that the train had arrived before coming to fetch me, I decided that I must either freeze or start walking. So I set out, suitcase in hand, certain that before I had gone a mile someone would drive by and give me a lift. But nobody did.

The station stood close to the edge of town, and I was soon out in a countryside as silent as a cemetery and where winter was enjoying its last hurrah. The night was clear and the moon near full, turning the frosted fields and hedgerows an eerie bluish white. Here and there a gaunt tree stood black against the frigid meadows, and in the hedges sheltering birds occasionally shifted feet and rustled in their pillows of dead leaves as they watched me pass. I remembered the old Greek lady and her ghostly husband, and the words of the Devon folk song "Widecombe Fair" and how across the moor in the night, with a rattling of bones, the ghosts of Tom Pierce's gray mare and the seven old men on its back would gallop by. The song was a favorite around Boy Scout camp fires and was sung with much tremolo and wind whistling, and laughing shouts of "There they go!" But as I trudged along that empty ribbon, I wasn't laughing. It took only an occasional cloud to cross the moon or a gust of wind to stir the brittle hedges for me to imagine the dead of centuries watching, beckoning. I had gone about a mile when something really did move behind the bushes and seemed to be following me. But when I stopped, it stopped. I could hear heavy breathing; then a monstrous head rose above the hedge, an eye glittered in the moonlight, steam came from its nostrils, and I was scared witless. Then it spake unto me. "Mooo!" it said.

"And the same to you," I replied, in a voice I'm sure still trembled with fright.

Having recovered myself, my fear of ghosts and goblins melted away in the face of bovine reality. Instead, I began—perhaps for the first time ever—to consider my life and where, if anywhere, I seemed to be heading. There was plenty of time for self-analysis; my suitcase was getting heavier and with each hill my progress became slower. My first concern was that something dreadful might have happened to my mother to prevent her from coming to collect me. But the more I thought about it, the less likely that appeared. After all, if she couldn't come, naval officer Alex was capable of taking command and ordering a taxi.

Throughout my early childhood, my friends, confidants, and jailers had been nurses, real or titular, with my mother playing only a cameo role. Her appearances had been irregular yet welcome additions to my day. What she thought of me, or really I of her, was never defined. It didn't have to be. I called her "Mummy" because that was what little boys were supposed to do, and she called me "Darling" because that was what she called all her friends. Once the war started and Fred was dead, we were thrown together as we had never been before, and yet to a very real extent we were strangers with barely more than our names in common. That conclusion hit me at about the time that the spire of Malborough church came in sight. It was a never-to-be-forgotten moment of revelation. The black-out and the lateness of the hour left the village in darkness, and I do not recall that so much as a dog barked. The reality of the silent night allied itself with my growing conviction that when I reached The Little Grey Home in the West no welcome would be waiting. Never before or since have I felt so alone.

At about two o'clock in the morning I turned out of Fore Street and into the pitch-black passage leading to the house. I knocked on the door. When nothing happened, and fearing that there might be no one there, I pounded on it. That brought results.

The door opened a crack and a pajamaed and disheveled Alex peered out. "Who's there? Oh, it's you. What the hell d'you think you're doing making that racket? D'you want to wake the whole bloody town?"

From upstairs my mother called asking who I was. "It's Ivor," he told her.

"At this time of night?"

Perhaps suspecting that I might be disappointed by my reception, Alex muttered: "When you didn't make it on time, we thought you'd missed the train. So we weren't expecting you till tomorrow."

So there I was, home for the holidays. The Little Grey Home was as I remembered it three months earlier, but life inside it had changed appreciably. Alex Anderson was no longer the smart Naval Reserve officer; now he was Alex, an increasingly scruffy fisherman. I never learned precisely when or why the transformation had occurred, but it seemed that his air-sea rescue craft had been moved from Salcombe up the coast to Dartmouth, a larger but less attractive and less socially popular estuarine port. Rather than move, my mother had beguiled Alex into trading his RNVR blue for the often evil-smelling uniform of a commercial fisherman. With money scraped up from somewhere, each bought half a share in a fishing boat of the kind used for trawling and hauling crab and lobster pots.

The business had gotten off to a shaky start, primarily because the boat's motor wouldn't. Weeks slipped past while it was being fixed and the bargain boat made seaworthy—at a cost far greater than budgeted. To add to the partners' problems, on one of its first days out, an expensive trawl became snagged on an underwater obstruction and had to be cut loose, adding yet another item to the red-ink column. Meanwhile, Alex shifted from midday social drinking to anytime reinforcement, which in turn led to uncorked vituperation within The Little Grey Home. But there were lighter moments, the most memorable my mother's attempt to teach me "proper behavior" by example.

A local boy aged about ten and a girl slightly younger were playing in the alley outside our kitchen window, play that turned acrimonious when the boy seized something that belonged to the little girl. Her plaintive, pleading voice drifted through the open window.

"Oh, please give it back. Oh, please, please, give it back."

"There, Ivor," said my mother, "there's a well-brought-up little girl. 'Please' and 'thank you' are the most important words in the English language. You can take a lesson from that little girl."

Outside, the standoff continued. "Please, oh please give it back."

"Such a horrid boy, and such a nice little girl."

"Oh, please! It's mine. It's mine. You *bugger!*"

"They're just village children," snapped my mother, abruptly shutting the window. End of lesson.

My mother was right about "please" and "thank you," but I also had other more practical lessons to learn. Alex taught me to row, to mend nets, put out trot lines, and gaff conger eels. Occasionally he would let me steer the boat down to Salcombe estuary, past the ruined castle, out through the channel between the rocks under Bolt Head, out into the swelling sea. More often, however, I would take the dinghy and row down to the castle and put out my own lines to catch pollock and mackerel, a solitary pursuit but it got me away from the house.

Early in the morning of April 26, 1936, in a thick fog, the largest sailing ship still in service had slammed into the Ham Stone rock two hundred yards from the cliffs near Bolt Head. The Finnish four-masted barque *Herzogen Cecilie*, bound from Australia to Falmouth with a cargo of grain, remained impaled for seven weeks before being lifted clear and hauled into Starehole Bay at the entrance to Salcombe Harbor. For three years she remained a slowly disintegrating tourist attraction until, in 1939, without warning she suddenly capsized and sank. On still, sunny days, at the slack of the low tide, one could lean over the side of a boat and see her weed-growing shape resting in the sand. "Aqualung" diving gear had yet to be invented, but I longed to be able to go down and see what the fish could see so much better. More than thirty years later I would do just that, and the thrill was just as great as I knew it would be. But even while sitting on the sea bed off Bermuda beside the wreck of the *Sea Venture*, one of the world's most historic undersea documents, my thoughts went back to Salcombe and the thrill of glimpsing the noble *Herzogen Cecilie* resting in her blue green grave.

In 1942, just as there was no scuba gear, there were no outboard motors to hustle small boats up and down the estuary. You got there through arm power and, if you were smart, with help from the tide. It was a mile and three quarters from Salcombe to Starehole Bay, the last half mile in open and often dangerous water that could pitch a small boat onto the rocks or draw a tiring rower out to sea. A tidal bar at the mouth of the estuary added another peril to idiots in small boats who did not know when and where to steer over it. I did it only once, and then on impulse on a calm day while fishing below the castle. Getting out to the wreck site had been no problem, but as the tide turned, the wind freshened, and while trying to get out of the bay I found myself being pushed toward the rocks below Sharp Tor. To my vast relief, a passing fishing boat took me in tow and hauled me rather ignominiously home. The penalty for that foolishness: the loss of dinghy privileges. On other occasions, however, a stopover in Starehole Bay became Alex's compensation for my helping him haul his pots, though none was needed, for going out with him was my vacation high point.

Nevertheless, a loose boy about the home was not to Alex's liking, and understandably, he didn't appreciate being told "Hush, Ivor'll hear you." On more than one occasion I heard him answer, "I'll be damned if I'll hush in my own house!" Just whose house it really was, I never discovered, but clearly it wasn't mine. On Alex's good days, however, and while working on the boat, he and I got along pretty well, and his change from navy officer to fisherman made my vacations more interesting—at least at the beginning.

Besides opportunities for messing about in boats, living at Salcombe offered another delight. The town had its own movie house, albeit somewhat dilapidated and with projectors that were inclined to eat the films and so frequently broke down. The programs came on small reels and were spliced together by the projectionist to minimize the number of changes from one machine to the other. Consequently, leaders had to be removed on arrival and replaced before the reels were sent out again. In doing so, and while repairing rips in the film, several frames of picture would be trimmed off and thrown away. Instead, the Salcombe projectionist saved them for me. After seating each frame in a hand-crafted cardboard mount, and building my own projector out of old flashlight parts and binocular lenses, I went into the slide-show business, reinforcing my fascination with films and filmmaking that had begun with my Eastbourne renderings from *Mutiny on the Bounty*.

Back at Courteenhall that interest translated into writing miniplays, the parts read by any of my colleagues whom I could corral and who lacked the ingenuity to have something better to do. From those small beginnings, I would later go on to direct and act in two more or less full-blown productions performed before the entire school as well as people from the village. The first was a patriotic piece of my own about vile Nazis in France, and the second a truncated version of Lord Dunsany's 1921 play *If*. I shudder to think what the villagers made of either them or of our excruciating performances; but twenty years later when I returned to Courteenhall and was introduced to people who had worked at the school, a very old lady said, "I remember you! You were the boy who put on those wonderful plays." I don't think I have ever been more flattered.

Having kept no diaries through my years at St. Lawrence, I find one term and one vacation have tended to blur into another. Although I no longer wore the hated boots, I was still categorized as frail and "excused games"—which suited me just fine. I was already developing the not particularly praiseworthy attitude that if I couldn't do something really well, I didn't want to do it at all. Consequently, I had neither scholastic nor sports trophies to mark my progress. Instead, the highlights tended to be unorthodox bordering on the prohibited. I became a pyrotechnician obsessed with the desire to build a rocket that would actually leave the ground. Mine never did. They would smoulder, fizzle, burn, occasionally explode, and once went several yards sideways; but never up. I made my own gunpowder using saltpeter, ostensibly purchased for curing badger skins, sticks of medicinal sulphur, and charcoal made from twigs burned in my illicit cooking fires.

In testing the mix in the Cameron common room on the top floor of Courteenhall House—firing a small quantity by means of a spark from a flashlight battery—I ignited my whole supply, spread on a newspaper on top of the radio. There was no explosion, only a choking, sulphurous smoke which we absorbed with wet towels. Damage was limited to the radio, but I could very well have set the house on fire. Fortunately, no prefect or master came along. But the scare was enough that thereafter I left firework manufacturing to the professionals.

Another window on the same floor looked across the park to the village church. From it one morning just as the sun was rising, I noticed a curious phenomenon, a dark pattern resembling the ground plan of a long building etched on the surface of grass wet and shining with dew. At that time I knew nothing about crop and shadow marks that enable archaeological sites to be recorded by aerial photography, nor have I since heard that the density or durability of dew plays any part in defining underground features. Nevertheless, the ground where I saw the pattern turned out to be in the vicinity of the medieval Courteenhall manor house which had been pulled down when the eighteenth-century mansion was built. It is equally curious that though I often looked for it, I never again saw the pattern on the ground. But I did find an artifact.

The college cricket pitch was located near the site, and nonplaying boys were required to sit around the perimeter and give encouragement. Although doing anything that could be construed as damaging the parkland was strictly forbidden, I used a cricket game as a cover for my first excavation. Seated on a blanket to the rear of the spectators, equipped with a penknife and a spoon, I began to dig a hole where I thought the house to be, interrupting my work to join in occasional shouts of "Well played, sir!" or to offer sympathetic applause to a bowled batsman. In reality, my excavation was so small that no self-respecting Courteenhall rabbit would have adopted it, but it did yield the artifact: a worn lead pencil of the kind used through the centuries on schoolboys' slates. In that simple object I encountered the thrill of archaeological discovery that had totally escaped me at Sutton Hoo. Whose hand had last held the pencil and what had he written with it—Latin declensions, a mathematical problem, something rude about a schoolmaster? I had reached out to the past and touched it.

At about this time, my reading turned to Sir Arthur Conan Doyle and the wonders of Sherlock Holmes's investigative logic. I have heard that until relatively recently recruits to London's Metropolitan Police were required to read the Sherlock Holmes stories as part of their training. Even today aspiring archaeologists might do a lot worse. They taught me to look beyond an object's identity to the way in which it had been used.

Other lessons learned from Conan Doyle were less useful. Although he is remembered almost exclusively for his Sherlock Holmes stories, he was a prolific writer on a multitude of subjects that ran an erratic gamut from a six-volume history of the First World War to *The Evidence for Fairies.* Among his short stories were several set in the Roman period, and at least one of which he entered through a quasi-archaeological door. Conan Doyle's narrator had the knack of sleeping with an artifact under his pillow, and in his dreams reliving the events in which that object had figured. Like the psychic lady at Coombe, the reader was allowed to assume that for people whose brains were capable of being tuned to the right station, this really was possible. Perhaps Conan Doyle himself believed it, for he joined the British Society for Psychical Research in 1893 and, throwing his famed logic to the wind, became a vocal supporter of spiritualism. He certainly convinced me enough to seek out a spiritualism chapel in Northampton, and one Sunday afternoon I attended its service.

I had expected amazing revelations, phantom figures materializing out of the floor, or at the very least floating lumps of ectoplasm. Instead, a handful of very ordinary people were gathered in a bare-boarded and dingy room to repeat Christian-style prayers led by a little man in a worn brown suit and to sing hymns accompanied by a fat woman on a harmonium. With all that finished with, the brown-suited man called on the spirit world to respond to the needs of his congregation, and then asked us to focus in silence on our departed loved ones. Not having any, I found the process extremely boring. After what seemed like a decade, a middle-aged woman in the row beside me provided the only moment of drama when she suddenly shouted, "I can hear him! It's him! It's John, my husband!" Then moments later, "No, no, it's not him."

The woman's wrong number evoked no excitement. Tired of listening to congregational heavy breathing, I slipped away and bicycled back to Courteenhall, a disappointed but not much wiser lad.

The idea that some kind of communication with the past might be possible continued to fascinate me. Indeed, I told myself that although nothing had happened in that drab Northampton chapel, there had been no fakery and the congregation was not noticeably laced with nuts. These unorthodox interests found little encouragement from the hard-pressed staff of St. Lawrence. There, was, however, one master who took an interest in my researches into comparative religions and spiritualism, and he, oddly enough, was a mathematics teacher. We shared a common enthusiasm for billiards, and over the table I told him my stuff and he told me his. A new world order was coming, he said, a new Utopia wherein all peoples of the earth would be united. There would be no more kings, no more rich, and no more poor. Esperanto would be the universal language, and we should all start learning it. So I did. But my enthusiasm didn't last, nor did the communistic master who was there one term and gone the next. Nevertheless, the utopian left his mark on me, for before his pool-table lectures I had never considered the possibility that anyone would promote an alternative to the established British way of life. Gentlemen were born to lead and workers to work, and that was that. It was true that the unnatural circumstances created by wartime had pushed the classes into abrasive juxtaposition—as our Rhyl experience had demonstrated. Even at St. Lawrence we were taking in some rough-edged day boys from Northampton (known disparagingly as "oiks"), but my mother assured me that all that forced fraternization would disappear once the war was won and everything went back to normal.

Winning the war seemed no more imminent in 1943 than it had in '42. The Battle of the Atlantic raged on, Nazi submarine wolf packs chewing on the convoys, their successes translated into ever-increasing home-front belt tightening. Shortages of everything became the rule, and rationing got leaner. I well recall the horror of the boy sitting next to me at lunch in the splendid, picture-hung dining room at Courteenhall when he found an eye in his helping of sheep's-head stew.

Food shortages aside, at Courteenhall we remained relatively insulated from the war. It was only when we left its tranquil park to return home for the holidays that we became aware of the price that England was paying for her freedom. As the train approached London there seemed to be hardly a suburban street without a gap in its terraced houses, sometimes cleaned up and smoothed over, but more often a still-jagged scar flanked by neighbors with windows boarded over and tarpaulins over holes in their roofs. In the narrow garden behind each house, a tumulus-like lump protruded from the earth—the so-called Anderson air-raid shelter. Though they were better suited for growing mushrooms than housing people, families lucky enough to have them were supposed to hide there until the "all clear" sounded. But as the war dragged on, many had decided that they were in greater danger of catching pneumonia than of being bombed, and so the shelters stood abandoned, the earth sliding from their rusting roofs, their sandbags rotting and broken. No doubt the melancholy appearance of London's approaches seemed less so when the sun shone, but my recollections are not of sunlight but of gray, drizzling days and of grim, whey-faced people.

Most of us approached the end of term with barely concealed jubilation, and when we gathered for the last assembly to sing "Lord, dismiss us with thy blessing," we gave it all we had. For me, however, emotions were mixed. I did not enjoy being a mediocre scholar and was glad the term and its exams were over, but at the same time the prospect of returning as an intruder into a "grown-ups only" house held no pleasure. But in the summer of 1943, things were different. My mother had written to say that she and Alex had given up The Little Grey Home and had bought the *Jessie L,* a seagoing yacht complete with saloon and staterooms. For the first time that I could remember, I was to have a summer to brag about.

I imagined a sleek white vessel rich in shining brass and gold trim, of the kind aboard which the king used to review his fleet at Spithead. I could see her lying at her moorings in the Salcombe estuary with small pleasure boats coming out to row around her and admire her lines, and people on the terrace of the Marine Hotel using their binoculars to catch a glimpse of the lucky owners. But, like so many of my mother's claims, the reality was distinctly different.

The *Jessie L* was not a pleasure yacht, she was not white but black, what brass she possessed was green with corrosion, and she did not ride proudly in the estuary. She was an ancient Bristol Channel pilot cutter, and she lay chained to the shore in a muddy cove across the harbor from Salcombe. Afloat at high tide, at the ebb she sat down in the mud like a beached whale kept upright by wooden legs bolted to both sides. She had masts but no sails, and her engine's capabilities were questioned but never put to the test. You went below via the stern cockpit or through a forward hatch into the combination sail locker and two crewmen's bunks—which were to be my quarters. The promised "staterooms" turned out to be singular, a tiny, one-bunk skipper's cabin—occupied by my mother. Alex was assigned the remaining bunk in the companionway beside the head, whose hand-operated pump only worked when the tide was high. A bathtub for which water was boiled in a kettle, a small galley, and a saloon about seven feet wide and twelve long made up the rest of the *Jessie L*'s amenities, plus a locker containing an auxiliary motor that provided electricity while spewing gasoline fumes from stem to stern. On damp days it refused to work at all. There being no shortage of such days, oil lamps provided most of the light and paraffin heaters the warmth. With the hatches closed, condensation gathered along the head beams and dripped down your neck. Our primary source of fresh water, however, was the water man, a semirecluse who lived aboard his tank boat and made a thin living servicing the few seagoing vessels that still lay in the estuary.

Although few city slum families can have lived in such congestion or under worse conditions, my mother gallantly fought to maintain her standards. Society magazines were laid out à la Renée Redfern, table napkins were correctly folded and the cushion puffed up, and even if she was going nowhere, my mother would take an hour to get ready. Alas, the high-society façade that had first intrigued and attracted Alex Anderson became a growing irritant in the confines of the *Jessie L*. And there was something else: the Americans were arriving. The harborside Salcombe hotels were filling with American naval and army officers who commanded the local respect that had been Alex's as long as he wore the king's uniform. But now, like Emil Jannings in Fritz Lang's *The Blue Angel*, whose infatuation with a cabaret singer led him from respected schoolmaster to despised lavatory attendant, Alex had given up his commission and his house in exchange for a mud-bound hulk and the perennial aroma of fish. Such solace as he could find came from bottles, and for days at a time he would not move from his bunk, lying there alternately weeping and raging, and cursing my mother for having stolen his honor and his dignity. She, in turn, accused him of rape.

After being caught in the crossfire throughout one particularly unpleasant morning I decided that I had had enough. While the barbs flew I went up on deck and over the side—the tide was out—and started walking. I had no plan, no destination, I would just keep walking. Eventually I would be missed. Then they'd be sorry.

I climbed the hill to East Portlemouth, went through the village, and struck out across the fields heading east. By the time I had gone two miles I became aware that I was missing lunch. But having no money I had no choice but to keep going. So on I went up over the headland and along the coast past Gammon Head and Lannacombe Bay, and over the bluff by Shoelodge Reed to Hallsands. Perhaps I had meant to get there all along. I had certainly heard of it, for it figured in many of the yarns spun by Salcombe fishermen.

The village of Hallsands nestled in a forty-foot-wide ribbon below the granite cliffs, protected from the waves by a stone seawall and beyond it by a natural shelf of submerged shingle. About thirty homes flanked a narrow street wide enough only for pack ponies, many of the houses hugging the cliff so tightly that it provided them with their back walls, and all stood with their foundations chipped into a rocky shelf. No one knew how long there had been a fishing village at Hallsands, but the majority of the houses, as well as the London Inn (Hallsands's only place of entertainment), had been there through the nineteenth century and probably long before.

In 1896, during expansion of the naval dockyard at Plymouth, a dredging contractor had been granted a license to remove shingle along the coast in front of the village, the pebbles to be used in making concrete. Government experts had concluded that the 650,000 tons of shingle extracted was sea deposited and would quickly be replaced. But they were wrong. The stones had been laid down during the Ice Age and couldn't be renewed. With the barrier removed and the sea-bottom contours changed, wave action caused the remaining shingle beach to slide away from the Hallsands seawalls, and in the winter of 1903–4 they were breached a dozen times with a loss of two houses and the access road. The government's Board of Trade accepted no blame, but paid for a new seawall—which lasted until the night of January 26, 1917. Unusually high tides coupled with an easterly gale broke through the wall and sucked the foundations out from under several houses, hurling waves so high against the cliff that it thundered down onto the roofs of others, causing them to collapse. The storm lasted four days, and by the time the wind dropped and the seas abated, only one house was left, the home of the innkeeper's daughter. She was still there when I reached what was left of the village in 1943, and she would remain there living alone and still defying the sea until she died in 1964.

Newspapers had described Hallsands as the "ghost village," but no lives had been lost in the great storm, though over the years many of its fishermen had been claimed by the sea. The ruins stood gray and gaunt against the cliffs. Some of the interior walls still retained bits of their plaster and even a few scraps of wall-paper. It was a gray day; wind whistled through empty windows, and agitated seagulls shrieked overhead, their cries battling to be heard above the pulsating rumble of the waves as they pounded the remaining shingle. My impression of the Eggesford House ruins had been of romantic grandeur, but these stone walls wore an eerie mantle of melancholy squalor. Yet in their way, they were no less evocative and the lives of their onetime inhabitants no less interesting.

On that miserable day at Hallsands, I doubt that I had such thoughts. I was cold, damp from the wind-blown sea spray, and damnably hungry. I was also beginning to feel sorry for myself and doubting whether my grand gesture had been worth it. Furthermore, it was a long walk back to the *Jessie L,* but much further to nowhere in particular.

"Ah, Ivor. You can start laying the table," said my mother as I opened the cockpit door.

If she and Alex had been scouring the countryside while going mad with worry, they did a remarkable job of concealing it.

"Guess where I've been?"

"I have no idea," my mother answered.

"Hallsands."

"That's nice, darling. Don't forget the butter knife."

WITH THE WAR OVER in Africa and British and American armies pushing though Sicily up into a capitulating Italy, southern England became a vast military camp. Its ports, harbors, and estuaries were crowded with supply vessels and landing craft of every description, all waiting and rehearsing for the second front to open. Salcombe was almost exclusively American. Troops camped on the farms and manned concrete bunkers overlooking the harbor, and navy personnel charged about in landing craft, slamming their bows onto sandy beaches to disgorge splendidly equipped and fed young marines who assaulted the rocks with grim determination. As far as I can recall, British troops were thin on the ground, less well equipped, and certainly less well fed. One English contingent manned a large gun tucked into the cliff near Sharp Tor concealed under an extensive camouflaging cover of netting and bits of brown and green burlap. After years of inactivity, our gun's day finally came. A German U-boat surfaced off Bolt Head to charge its batteries or empty its slops. The gunners took aim and fired—just once, whereupon the netting collapsed. By the time the crew got themselves untangled, the U-boat had gone.

I was at school at the time and only heard the story later. But the event characterized the slightly surrealistic war that was being waged from Salcombe. On two occasions it became more serious. On the first a German fighter bomber supposed to be harassing shipping in the Channel decided to unload on the boats in our harbor. It dropped but one bomb, hitting its target squarely amidships. As military objectives went, it was not much of a score, but for us aboard the *Jessie L,* it was a minor disaster. The bomb killed the water man and sank his boat. The second plane found me peering into an antique shop-window at the south end of Fore Street. A Focke-Wulf suddenly flashed low overhead, a dark shadow against the sunlight, allowing no more than a glimpse of the black crosses under its wings before it was gone. Its pilot fired one machine gun burst down the street and another about a mile or so to the north, killing a farmer pushing a plow near Batson Creek. I believe that he and the water man were Salcombe's only civilian losses to enemy action. Nevertheless, there was plenty of other action to keep the locals on their toes. Opportunities to be run down by speeding Jeeps or to be pinned to the wall by trucks traversing streets better suited to donkey carts were legion. Then, too, there were surprises on the water. On a foggy night in the winter of 1944 a navy landing craft plowed into the stern of the *Jessie L.* The subsequent inquiry failed to determine what the craft was doing under way in the middle of the night or why there was no one on board!

Alex Anderson's fishing business never prospered. His quick trips across the harbor to the post office or to fetch supplies invariably ended in a bar and a shouting match when he got back. Time that should have been used to keep the fishing boat and its gear in trim was spent in his bunk waiting for spare parts or for the weather to "fine away"—anything rather than going to sea. Parcels to the pawnshop became more frequent, though the quality of the collateral declined as redemption dates came and went, and the "little man in the City" took his cut. But salvation (of a sort) was at hand—courtesy of the American navy just before dawn on Monday mornings.

About this time, storekeepers aboard the American vessels decided to dispose of their unwanted food supplies. I do not recall the exact rationale (perhaps I never knew it), but it seemed that stocks of desirable foodstuffs would not be replenished if supplies of less interesting stuff remained aboard. Consequently, the leftovers were tossed over the sides into the harbor. On days when the early morning tides were rising, the lighter cans and cartons floated upstream and washed ashore in the bays and inlets, from which I and others would rescue them. Alex, however, developed a more reliable technique. Having worked out deals with cooks and quartermasters, he would ferry them back and forth to the shore and supply them with crabs and lobsters. In exchange, Alex would take the fishing boat alongside at the moment of dumping, accepting everything that was being discarded—cans of butter, peanut butter, beans, powered eggs, frankfurters, luncheon meat, dried milk, virtually anything that came in a can, and, to further sweeten the deal, cartons of cigarettes and an occasional fresh steak. By this means, the standard of living aboard the *Jessie L* dramatically improved. At the same time, however, our financial picture darkened. Such profits as were to be made from the crab and lobster pots depended on shipping the catch to the London market. Trading it for canned goods enriched nothing but the larder. The only recourse, therefore, was to sell some of the food ashore, an illegal and risky business that could have put Alex in jail and seen the Americans court-martialed. Besides, such deals invariably were made in the pubs, and so by the time Alex returned, the cash had been transformed into bottled booze. These clandestine sales, however, made no appreciable inroad into our hoarded stores, which grew so large and so fast that Alex lowered most of the *Jessie L*'s ballast over the side and replaced it with American canned goods.

It was at Salcombe that I again tasted the thrill of the hunt and the satisfaction of finding—anything. Day after day I escaped from the *Jessie L* and with the dinghy scoured the tidal beaches for American jetsam: cartons of K-rations, overshoes, jackets, ammunition belts, helmet liners, anything even remotely interesting and American. The most intriguing of my prizes was an open canvas pouch containing several soggy maps of the north coast of France, one of them featuring a stretch from the mouth of the Somme to Le Havre with Fécamp and several villages carefully marked by hand in red ink. This was in April 1944, less than two months before D-day. It turned out, of course, that the landings were all to the south of Le Havre and that it was the British Second Army and not the Americans who went ashore closest to that port.

I have often wondered whether my beached maps were evidence of incredibly sloppy security or were a small part of a cunning ruse to spread false rumors about the invasion beaches. If that was the intent, mine accomplished nothing. Alex confiscated the maps and returned them to an American MP.

On my way back to school for the summer term I stayed overnight in London so that I could go through the annual ordeal of reporting my progress to "Uncle" John Redfern. I owed my education and my future to this man, who had no reason to know or like me, but who continued to support me out of love for his estranged wife. Nevertheless, regardless of my debt, I looked upon these visits with all the enthusiasm of a dental appointment. En route to Uncle John's Kingsway office I stopped at Foyle's in Charing Cross Road, then among the world's best-known secondhand bookshops. There, in the archaeology section, I found a copy of Gaston Maspero's *Dawn of Civilization* and bought it, not so much because I was developing a keen interest in Egyptology but because the book was rich in illustrations of people with flat faces and oversized eyes doing interesting things.

I was still clutching the book when Uncle John's secretary ushered me into his office. After the usual rather strained pleasantries about the weather and comfort (or lack of it) in my train journey from Devon, the conversation went something like this:

"Well, Ivor, and how old are you now?"

"Sixteen and a half, sir."

"Time you were planning a career. Have you given some thought to that?"

"Er, well, yes, sir," I lied.

"And? What are you going to do with yourself?"

"Ah, yes," I replied, frantically trying to think of something intelligent. Then I looked down at my book. "I want to be an archaeologist, sir."

Uncle John's neck reddened. "I'm not asking you to choose a hobby," he snapped. "Young man, archaeology's an avocation, not a profession!"

I left with the strong sense that John Redfern did not list me among his wiser investments. It was, in fact, our last meeting, though in 1954 when I sent him an advance copy of my first book, *Archaeology in Britain,* he wrote saying:

> I was so interested to see you had stuck to Archaeology, after my instill-ing into you for so long that there never could be any money in it, but you at that time did not worry about money; it was only the interest in the Art for which you had a flair!

He went on to hope that the book's royalties would keep me well provided for from year to year. I had neglected to mention that I had sold the copyright for a measly hundred pounds. Nevertheless, John Redfern was right. At the age of sixteen I lived from day to day and term to term without giving much, if any, thought to my future and how I would earn a living. Although Maspero's book stoked my interest in Egyptology, my enthusiasm for archaeology was more visceral than educated. I had read about Howard Carter and his discovery of Tutankhamen's tomb; about Belzoni, the circus strongman, who had been the first to enter the great, rock-hewn temple at Abu Simbel; and of Schliemann and the treasures of Troy, adventurers all—and lucky. Of such were a schoolboy's dreams woven. But John Redfern's recollection notwithstanding, I had no seri-ous plan to become an archaeologist, or anything else for that matter. Aboard the *Jessie L* future plans were not the sort of thing that came up, and schools in those days did not go in for career counseling. I suppose they thought that boys from good homes took their fathers' advice.

Once the Allied armies landed in France, at Courteenhall our interest in the progress of the war sharpened. Maps went up in the common rooms and daily we moved our pin-posted flags forward. We drew lots for the pictures in the school's newspapers and pasted them in scrapbooks. I was already a none-too-athletic member of the Army Cadet Force, and now I resolved to shine in this if in little else. At first we drilled with wooden rifles, to the general merriment of onlookers who preferred sports to war games. Later, after the Home Guard had been fully equipped, the War Office got down to arming the cadets—though arming was perhaps too strong a word. They sent us a motley collection of rifles, Canadian Rosses from the First World War and short-barreled Martini-Henrys that had been standard issue in the Boer War, but no ammunition for either. We had uniforms but had to provide our own helmets. Mine, for reasons I forget, was World War I German; but I was destined to remember wearing it every time I looked in the mirror. While realistically hurling myself to the ground and assuming the firing position, the helmet slipped down over my nose and snapped off half a front tooth—which my mother found far more distressing than any poor end-of-term report.

When Operation Overlord finally began, I was back at Courteenhall. Several days earlier Salcombe had awakened to find its guests gone. Although every landing barge and support boat had disappeared in the night, they had left the estuary awash with garbage: cartons, crates, tarps, parts of uniforms, anything not needed aboard when the invasion began. As was true in every coastal town and village, the exodus was greeted by some with relief and by others with tears. For the crew of the *Jessie L*, the D-day departure of the Americans meant the death of the golden goose and the need to make more frugal use of its eggs hidden in the bilge below the saloon floor. The only salvation lay in returning to serious commercial fishing, but Alex was neither mentally nor physically prepared to do so. Shortly before St. Lawrence's summer vacation was to begin, my mother wrote to say that Alex had tried to kill her and that, fearing for her life, she had left him and moved to a boardinghouse ashore. I was to join her there.

Although vacations aboard the *Jessie L* had been grim, they had had their compensations, notably the opportunity to use Alex's dinghy to go fishing or beachcombing for Americana. But the summer of '44 had no compensations, unless one includes the opportunity to help a large and grim woman make funeral wreaths in a tiny house that reeked of stale vegetables. There being no room in the pension where my mother now lodged, I was boarded out across the street in a room over the greengrocer and florist's shop. Alex had left town and had sold the *Jessie L* to help pay off his debts, and presumably had given my mother some of the proceeds as a settlement dissolving their fishing partnership. We were back to square one and worse off than at Rhyl in the winter of '41, for then my mother could rely on monthly checks as Bill Williams's wife. Now there was nothing, and nobody. For the first time I realized how great a financial burden I was to her, and that rather than being a welcome companion I was an embarrassing encumbrance. The semblance of youth was Poppet's only remaining asset, and the last thing she needed was a son pushing seventeen and six feet tall.

Shortly after I returned to Courteenhall in September, the school was visited by a young officer who was introduced to the assembled cadet force by our rarely seen honorary commander and St. Lawrence's benefactor, Major General Sir Hereward Wake, who turned out in his full, red-tabbed uniform—which impressed us no end, as indeed it was intended to do. The officer was a recruiter for the Indian Army. The war was nearly won in Europe, he told us, but if we signed up now we would be just in time to teach the yellow Jap a lesson he would remember for generations. Under a special program designed for Britain's future leaders, volunteers could sidestep regular British Army conscription and go straight into officer training. It was a unique opportunity for young men like us to take our place in history alongside the heroes who had made the Empire the envy of every nation. The recruiter neglected to mention that we stood more than a sporting chance of making our mark by getting killed. The Japanese had learned that the best way to disorganize Indian troops was to pick off their British officers. Consequently, the army was getting through subalterns at an embarrassing rate. Hence, this appeal to the cradle.

Two of us signed on. My fellow volunteer, Peter (I think his name was) Barnard, was academically sounder. In those days, passing School Certificate was the minimal form of graduation. To go on to university, one had to do better by passing Matriculation. Both called for a balance between humanities and math and sciences, but no amount of brilliance in one arm could substitute for failure in the other. Twice I sat for the School Certificate and twice I blew it, doing better than necessary in English, English literature, history, geography, scripture, and art, but staring blankly at my logarithms and having not the faintest idea what "X" had to do with seven apples costing a shilling and six pears at eight pence. Barnard knew the answers to stuff like that, and so was better officer material. However, I was assured that if I secured my Cadet Force War Certificate "A" and could pass the relatively easy Indian Army selection board exam in London, I would be off and running.

Well, not exactly running. My always weak legs coupled with renewed cartilage trouble in my left knee still kept me out of any really taxing exercise, yet getting my "Cert A" depended on completing several physical tests, including a five-mile march in a given time and successfully climbing a twenty-foot rope, something I had never before attempted. I managed the march with time to spare, but the rope was a different matter. Slung over an ancient tree in the park in front of the mansion, it hung intimidatingly between me and a career as a tiger shootin', polo-playin' defender of the Raj. We were allowed three attempts to scale the rope, but having no experience of twisting it between my legs and gripping it with my feet, twice I barely got off the ground. So, on my last try I simply grabbed it and went up hand over hand, propelled by a strength I did not know I possessed. Almost before I knew it, I was at the top. Getting down without help from one's legs was easier but equally unorthodox. The friction left the palms of both hands a bleeding mess, but I barely felt the pain. I had done it! The gnarled and venerable tree became a careerlong reminder that all things are possible if one tries hard enough. It was distressing, therefore, to return to Courteenhall in the mid-1960s to find that my limb had fallen in an ice storm, and later that the whole tree had been cut down. Worse, when reading my precious certificate for the first time in forty years, I discovered that I had failed the climbing test!

Nevertheless, I had passed in enough other categories, and on November 28, 1944, I proudly sewed the red star badge of War Certificate "A" to my uniform. Shortly thereafter I went to London to sit for the Indian Army entrance examination to be held at the once handsome Marylebone Hotel, but then occupied by legions of military clerks. Most of the testing was of the "pick an answer" commonsense variety:

> Army vehicles are painted in zigzag patterns of brown and green because:
> a) It looks nice.
> b) The War Office has large supplies of those colors.
> c) They help conceal them from the enemy.

The math questions promised to be trickier, and I approached them with misgiving, but fortunately something else approached to disrupt the course of scholarship.

That something was in the shape of the new V-2 rocket which, unlike the V-1, or "doodlebug," struck without warning. On the morning of my exam one fell sufficiently close for the testing to be halted. As far as I recall, testing was never resumed, for if it had been, I cannot imagine that I would have passed. But I did.

For the first time in my school career I had accomplished something admirable. A prefect in my last term, I was now an embryo leader off to win the war. Barnard, my fellow volunteer, and I were invited to tea by the usually aloof and fearsome Sir Hereward Wake, presumably to give us useful military pointers—though I don't recall that he did. His first bit of advice, however, has remained firmly planted. The invitation was for 4:30 and with hair combed and necks clean, we were there smartly on the dot.

"Boys," said Sir Hereward, "when you are invited anywhere there is only one thing worse than being confoundedly late, and that is being either early or precisely on time. A considerate guest allows his host exactly five minutes' grace." It was sound advice and I have done my best to adhere religiously to it.

Thanks to Uncle John Redfern I had spent two crucial years at St. Lawrence. Although very little of what I was formally taught was destined to be of much practical use to me, I think it likely that the interests stirred there had a far greater influence on my future career than was the case with most of my classmates. My seedling enthusiasm for archaeology, though firmly rooted, was destined to lie dormant for several years, but my desire to write (albeit for the theater) was buoyantly alive—in spite of my commitment to soldiering. My last term at Courteenhall taught me one more lesson, and like the others it was not part of the curriculum. Perhaps running out of zeal for teaching as the term wound down, the history master tossed his ball into our court, and selected several of us to take one teaching period and instruct the class on any historical event we cared to pick. I had been reading William Prescott's *Conquest of Peru* and had been fascinated by the way that, in a matter of months, a handful of scruffy and vicious Spaniards had been able to destroy a civilization that had taken centuries to develop. While the rest of the boys took their task as just another assignment and gave standard pedagogic interpretations of familiar events of English history, I went for the wide-screen adventure of the brothers Pizarro in their march from the sea over the Andes to Cuzco. I spent hours drawing war-style progress maps and painting watercolor pictures of the murder of Atahualpa and of caravans of ransom gold winding their way across the mountains. Today, such visual aids are commonplace, but for us pictures had played no part in history classes. With Prescott's graphic descriptions to help me, I built my presentation into a "you-are-there" drama. It was my first assay into the art of lecturing, and the resulting applause coupled with a 10-out-of-10 rating convinced me that here, for a change, was something at least marginally academic that I could do satisfyingly well. It was a tiny beginning that one day would lead to the platform of Washington's Constitution Hall and to writing a book on the lecturer's craft, which unfortunately was never published. More prophetically, however, it pointed westward and to a combination of archaeology, history, and theater.

In mid-December I said goodbye to Courteenhall and to the schooldays that adults insisted were the best of one's life. Henceforth, the army would be responsible for my education. But first there was a medical hitch. The St. Lawrence doctor had concluded that I needed to have the remaining cartilage removed from my left knee. I forget why. Nevertheless, Christmas of 1944 was spent in a military hospital at Byfleet, and it was not until February that Peter Barnard and I were reunited and reported for duty at Maidstone Barracks, the home of the Royal West Kents' and our temporary regiment, the Queen's. There we were to undergo our basic training, and with that behind us we would become fully fledged officer cadets completing our textbook training on the long round-the-Cape voyage to India. Not until we got there were we to be formally inducted into the Indian Army. Nevertheless, from the day of our arrival at Maidstone our company of seventeen-year-olds was known as "them Indian wallahs" and treated as semisuperior cannon fodder. At our first parade our company sergeant explained our status in a speech that went something like this:

"My name is Sergeant Burton. You will call me Sergeant. Is that clear?"

"Yes, Sergeant!" some of us replied. The rest answered "Yes, sir."

"Who said 'sir'? Some of you young gentlemen got cloth ears? I want you to listen very carefully to what I'm tellin' you, 'cos I ain't goin' to say it again. Corporals is called corporals, sergeants is called sergeants, and sergeant majors and hofficers is called 'sir.' 'Owever, when I speak to you I shall address you as 'sir,' not because you deserves it, not because I wants to, but because my hofficer says so. And when an hofficer says so, that's an order, and an order is obeyed. Do I make myself clear? Speak up, I can't 'ear yer!"

With the exception of being called "sir," basic training differed not a wit from that of any ordinary recruits. Apart from being supplied with Urdu textbooks and being told that we would have to be proficient in that language by the time we got off the boat, our instruction had no Indian overtones. It was pretty much the same training we had already had in the St. Lawrence Cadet Force, except that we now had blank ammunition for proper rifles, and Bren machine guns to take apart and reassemble without leaving bits out.

Unfortunately, the bits out of my leg were proving to be a problem, and marching, running, and throwing oneself into ditches while instructors tossed practice grenades over the hedges exacerbated it. Soon I was finding myself left behind when the company went off on maneuvers. Fear that I would not complete the course and would be held back to the next became a constant nightmare. I had gone in with Barnard and had envisaged our going to war together as brother officers. The prospect of that link being broken loomed ever larger. In the meantime, armed with weekend passes we returned for a triumphal visit to Courteenhall—wearing officer cadets' white bars to which we were not entitled.

Another weekend leave took a group of us up to London and a visit to a West End theater that catered to the cultural needs of servicemen. Throughout the Blitz and the flying bombs, its shows had gone on, earning it the proud slogan that from 1932 to 1945 "We Never Closed!" Because my knowledge of the real theater was limited to Shakespeare and a production of *Where the Rainbow Ends,* the Windmill Theater's show came as something of a shock insofar as it featured ladies who had left their costumes in the dressing room.

Although I was old enough to get myself shot by the evil Nip, I knew very little about life and nothing about women. In the cloistered isolation of St. Lawrence, girls were never discussed—with the exception of a rumored unpleasantness involving a senior boy and a female farm worker. Those who had sisters made a point of despising them, and love, as portrayed in novels or in BBC radio plays was considered sissy. At school you learned to play backbone-building games like rugger, hockey, cricket, but certainly not dancing—as I was embarrassingly reminded on V-E night.

At a free dance hastily organized for the armed forces I found myself hauled onto the floor by a bun-faced ATS (Auxiliary Territorial Service) girl who, after a few moments of being marched on by my army boots, asked, "'Ave you ever done this before, luv?"

I confessed that I hadn't.

"Then I wouldn't try it again."

And I never have.

The end of the war in Europe on May 8 was welcomed in London with memorable joy, thousands upon thousands of young people jamming Trafalgar Square, Piccadilly, and the Mall in front of Buckingham Palace. At Maidstone, however, the jubilation was more low key, and I remember half a dozen of us making rather forced whoopee as we walked back through empty streets to the barracks. Like London, Maidstone and the county of Kent had been in the forefront of the air war since 1940. Although across the nation the cost in sons, fathers, and husbands had not been as appalling as in the First World War, few

English families had escaped being hurt in one way or another. Consequently, for the middle-aged and old, V-E Day was greeted with relief and gratitude, but also with weariness and somber reflection on the price that had been paid. Besides, the end had been spun out like a mad melodrama. For years we had listened to singers on the radio and at camp concerts telling us what to look forward to "When They Sound the Last All Clear," but when its final wailing note died away on March 5 (three days before the first American troops crossed the Rhine), nobody realized that it *was* the last.

A few days after V-E Day a bad cold turned to pneumonia, and I found myself in the barracks sick bay, where I would remain for two weeks. By the time I emerged, my company of "Indian wallahs" had completed their basic training and gone, apparently having sailed for the Far East. Although I never heard what happened to Peter Barnard, it was unlikely that he got to India in time to see action before the Japanese turned in their swords. For my part, the army gave me the choice of staying in and applying for a commission in some noninfantry sphere like the Pay Corps (hardly my line) or getting out. I chose the latter, thus bringing to an end what must rank among the least impressive military careers on record.

Sent to London to be demobilized, my orders brought me full circle, ending my war within sight of where it began. The clearing house for returning servicemen had been set up in the Olympia exhibition hall across the road from our apartment in St. Mary Abbott's Court, where Nanny Bolton and I had listened to Chamberlain's declaration nearly six years earlier. The vast building that I remembered only as the temporary home of Bertram Mills Circus was now partitioned into pygmy-sized booths designed to process thousands of home-hungry men and women as quickly and painlessly as possible. But when I arrived, there was virtually nobody there but clerks waiting for the rush. In almost surrealistic silence, I made my way from booth to booth filling out forms and selecting from a narrow range of options: shirt, bone cuff links, tie, suit, socks, shoes, raincoat, and hat, a civilian kit almost as uniform as the khaki it was replacing.

I emerged from Olympia into a bright June day feeling slightly ridiculous in my blue trilby hat with my uniform in a paper parcel under my arm, a seventeen-year-old ex-serviceman without home or job, and only a schoolboy's concept of life and labor—one to be enjoyed and the other left to the working classes.

Like my father before me, I had escaped from an impossible home life by going into the war as soon as I was old enough, and like him I had come out of it without the slightest idea of where my future lay. But unlike him, I had no wealthy and titled friends to open doors. My mother had made it clear that returning to Salcombe was not a good idea, and so, having nowhere else to go, I went back to Ealing and to Grandma Mann, who agreed to house me for a few weeks until I decided what to do with myself. To the family's surprise, Harold, the prodigal brother, had returned after twenty years in America. Black sheep though he had been (at least in the eyes of his mother and Aunt May), he was now received as a shining example of a Mann who had made good—probably because my mother had long since replaced him as the family's chief disappointment. Harold, who through hard work had risen to be "chief engineer" for Henry Ford, would be just the person to set me on the right road.

In my imagination he had become a swashbuckling, Douglas Fairbanks–style hero forever leaping from balconies to stay one jump ahead of a venal Establishment. But the Uncle Harold who opened the door of his rented Ealing apartment was short, fat, red-faced, and balding. His eyes were moist like those of an aging spaniel, and his speech slurred, alternating between an authoritative bark and an almost tearful mumble.

"By God, boy, I wish I were in your shoes! A young guy like you with all your years ahead of you. Just put your mind to it, and you can do anything you want, any goddam thing you want! You may not think it to look at me now, but I was like you once. And I was at a crossroads, just the way you are. Yes sir, just the way you are. And you know what I did?"

He told the story that I had heard before: taking the cargo boat to Mexico, where he bought a white hat, a pearl-handled pistol, and a white horse, and rode it into the lobby of the best hotel in Tampico.

I had heard the Tampico story before, and had no doubt that it was true. My mother had a picture of the horse. So in spite of Uncle Harold's disappointing appearance, I listened with awe; though at first I was less than sure I wanted to take his advice.

"Hop a boat. Go to Mexico. It's the land of the future, no doubt about it. Gold, oil, agriculture; it's all there for the taking. The living's cheap, and the climate's okay once you get used to it. And the peasants'll do anything for you, just so long as you let 'em know who's boss. Take my word for it, there's one hell of an opportunity waiting in Mexico for a young feller like you. But first you've gotta learn the lingo."

Had I been a little older and wiser, I might have taken time to wonder why, if Mexico was waiting for an English Cortez, Uncle Harold had moved on to the United States. Instead, I bought a copy of *Teach Yourself Spanish*.

8 Overture and Beginners

> When the lights go on again
> All over the world,
> There'll be times for things
> Like wedding rings . . .

T HE HAUNTING, YEARNING SONGS of the war promised a return to the old values once the dark years were behind us. Britain had risen to Churchill's challenge and had given of her blood to preserve the British way of life, yet only a tiny minority (my mother and a few others) wanted a return to the *status quo ante bellum*. When servicemen joined Vera Lynn in singing "The Homecoming Waltz," they were looking to a new day and a new way, and in July 1945 they made that painfully, almost cruelly clear at the ballot box. The Sergeant Burtons were through with saying "sir" to callow schoolboys. The Labour Party swept to victory with a 150-seat majority.

Labour offered them full employment, housing, social security, a national health service, nationalization of the coal mines—a welfare state. This was what the boys from "over there" wanted when the lights went on again.

Unfortunately, they couldn't have chosen a worse time to ask for it. But at least the growing stream of men emerging into the sunshine of "Civvy Street" in their trilby hats and "demob" suits had trades and skills to offer. I had nothing.

Even Grandma Mann agreed that Uncle Harold's Mexican solution was worthless, the product of a sick old man in search of his youth. He died a few months later.

I do not recall that it ever occurred to me to seek any career advice from my father. Although my mother wrote to him fairly frequently asking for back alimony, she had made it very clear to me that he felt no responsibility toward either of us. He was married, had a new son, and that was that. So I turned to the only father figure in sight, the Reverend Peter Perfect, headmaster of St. Lawrence.

The school had a reputation for producing stellar performers in two spheres:

the church and the stage. Not being cut out for the cloth, the latter seemed my only possibility. Remembering my Courteenhall productions, Perfect contacted Old Lawrentian and veteran character actor Ralph Truman, who said he'd take a look at me and see what could be done. To my eternal gratitude Truman did so, though I'm sure for the sake of the old school and not for any talent he detected in me. I had taken no acting lessons and had been no closer to a professional stage than the back stalls at the Windmill. Nevertheless, Ralph Truman got me two interviews, the first on the stage of the most prestigious and venerable of all British theaters: The Theatre Royal, Drury Lane.

What carrying a bucket at Sutton Hoo should have been to an aspiring archaeologist, treading the hallowed boards of Drury Lane was to a would-be actor. The theater had been closed since being bomb damaged early in the war, its vast stage subsequently converted into the headquarters for the drama division of ENSA (Entertainments National Service Association, the British parallel to the USO), which packaged plays and players and shipped them out to battle boredom in military camps around the world. Many later-to-be-heard-from British actors honed their talents on ENSA stages and in front of audiences who would rather have had a visit from the Windmill Girls but who were grateful nonetheless. It was to ENSA rather than to the Theatre Royal that I was directed, and to an interview with the division's director, Henry Oscar. A gnomelike man with enormous ears, Oscar sat behind his desk in an office built from theatrical scenery and asked me why I wanted to be an actor. The words came from deep in his chest (which is where actors' voices are supposed to reside), but they gave no suggestion that he was likely to be at all interested in my answer. He was simply going through the motions because Ralph Truman had asked him to.

In the eyes of Grandma Mann, "going on the stage" was on a par with whoring; my mother, on the other hand, couldn't have been happier for me, and agreed that I should return to Salcombe until the call came. But, of course, none did—until Ralph Truman tried again. This time he got me an interview with actor-manager Guy Verney at the Connaught Theatre, Worthing. Among the few good things to come out of the war was the maturing of the British film industry under the benevolent yet monopolistic J. Arthur Rank Organization. Because the movie business needed fresh young faces, Rank invested in two theaters where the faces could learn to act, the more successful and prestigious of the two being the Connaught. So the chance to work there was one that any young actor would jump at.

Although London's West End was the heart of English theatrical life, being the home of close to thirty showcase theaters and considerably more agents, most of the employed actors and stage staff eked out a precarious living in the provinces. Between the wars most big cities boasted one or more relatively commodious theaters, one for music hall (vaudeville) bills and another for touring productions of plays and reviews hoping for a London stage or cashing in after a successful West End run. In addition to these rented theaters, most of which were owned by London impresarios, there were more than two hundred repertory theaters run by descendants of the Victorian actor-managers, who used them as frames for their own talents and egos. At the same time, however, they provided young actors on the way up with chances to develop their craft, and old ones on the way down with a place to decline with dignity. Except in large cities such as Birmingham, Bristol, and Liverpool, few repertory theaters could rely on a sufficiently large audience to mount a repertory program in the true sense of the word, that is, rotating several productions and keeping them in the repertoire long enough for the cast to make the best of them. Instead, the managements used a company of about ten people to mount a new production every week, a horrendous schedule for both players and stage staff. Most directors (in England then known as producers) estimated that it took about eighty hours to properly rehearse a three-act play, but the repertory actors were lucky if they got fifteen. Those with leading parts could expect to do little more than learn the lines and remember the moves before the ASM (assistant stage manager) called, "Overture and beginners, please!"

The Connaught Theatre, thanks to its Rank Organization backing, was better off than most. When the ASM called "Overture!" there was a live orchestra to play it, and although the shows did change weekly, the permanent company was frequently augmented with lead players sent down from London for a single production, and who therefore had had time to learn their parts before the first rehearsal. There was no question that if Guy Verney gave me a job, I would be starting at the top.

On the morning I left for London I developed a toothache, and by the time I got there my face was beginning to swell. I was to stay overnight at the Imperial, a large and cheap hotel in Bloomsbury that specialized in traveling salesmen, before taking another train to Worthing. In the morning, my jaw was ablaze and my cheek looked as though I were chewing a cannon ball. At breakfast a waiter seated me at a table with a middle-aged and balding salesman who commiserated with my plight. I told him that I was an actor on my way to an important interview.

"I wanted to be an actor once myself," said the salesman. "I used to think I had the right looks for it."

He told me that he had some pills in his room that would take the pain out of my tooth. I was to give him a few minutes and then come on up.

When I opened his door the room looked empty. Then the door shut. Behind it stood the salesman stripped to his socks. Commander Chubb, RN, had risen again.

When I told him to get the hell out of the way, he snarled, "Come off it, sonny! You actors are all the same. So don't you gimme none o' that!" I don't remember whether I kicked him or stamped on his foot, but I left him folded and cursing.

As I boarded the train for Worthing, I was wondering what the hell I was getting into. And the abscess on my tooth was giving me fits.

Nevertheless, it may have been the tooth that got me the job. Guy Verney never asked me to read *Hamlet* or do my Captain Bligh imitation; he simply gave me a three-month contract as assistant stage manager and sent me to a dentist. I was to report for rehearsals in mid-December for the Overture Players' Christmas production of *Alice in Wonderland;* my roles: the frog footman and the Knave of Hearts.

In electing a Labour government, Britain may have renounced imperialism and the class-structured society, but its theater still clung to the old values. A few leftist playwrights railed at the establishment, claiming that the stage belonged to the People and should be a pulpit for new and preferably revolutionary ideas, but managements from the West End to Penzance were content to produce middle-class plays for middle-class audiences. Trifles by Noël Coward, Terence Rattigan, or Ben Travers filled houses. Ibsen, Strindberg, Chekhov, Shaw, or Shakespeare generally didn't. The theater provided escape from the reality of clothing coupons and postwar food rationing. Audiences wanted sunshine outside the French windows and happy young men bounding through them crying, "Tennis, anyone?"

When I joined the Overture Players the resident company was already at work on *Alice in Wonderland,* the management having relieved the cast of appearing in one production while rehearsing the big Christmas show. Instead, the Connaught offered a two-player saga called *Happy and Glorious,* starring Guy Verney and a fine actress, Sheila Burrell. Although this freed the *Alice* cast, it was hell for the stage management, which had to handle at least a dozen set changes in the course of a play that covered the characters' adult lives. At each performance I sat in the wings watching the amazing transformations as back-cloths, doorways, windows, trees, came down on ropes from the flies above, and as swift and silent stagehands wheeled platforms, steps, and even rocks into position. A pile of fourteen-foot-high wood-framed canvas flats could be miraculously transformed into three walls of a bedroom, the back of each flat having a cord attached to its top right corner and a cleat to the left. With a deft flick of the wrist, the stagehands sent the rope snaking up and over the cleat of the next flat to the right, pulled it tight, tied it over two lower cleats, attached a wooden brace to hooks in the frame, and anchored the bottoms to the stage with iron weights or sandbags. It was a process so fast that it barely took longer to accomplish than it has taken to read my description. From his panel in the prompt corner the electrician pulled levers and threw switches in innumerable permutations controlling the floats (footlights), overhead floods and spots, stand-supported lamps in the wings, and more anchored to the balcony in the auditorium. Along the side walls taut hemp ropes attached to pulleys and counterweights disappeared into the darkness above, tracing their way across the huge wooden grid that spanned the stage close to the roof. To the ropes were attached the "flying" scenery and painted cloths which, with a quick tug on the right rope, could glide up out of sight above the proscenium arch to hang like ancient banners in a cathedral's clerestory.

Here, for me, was the magic of the stage: the mechanics of illusion. In the weeks that followed, I spent hours practicing the flick of the wrist that sent the flats' anchoring cords over cleats that were sometimes sixteen or eighteen feet from the ground. I learned how to snap the tied lines, and to tell from the sound whether they were tight enough. I learned the subtle "natural" lighting effects achieved by the skillful balancing of amber and "surprise pink" gelatin sheets in front of the lamps in the floats and overhead battens. Most satisfying of all, I learned to paint scenery.

The Connaught, as I have said, was well equipped. Whereas, in most British theaters, sets had to be painted on the stage itself or brought in from a studio elsewhere, we had our own paint frame anchored to the back wall. It was a huge timber structure that rose and fell on counterweights passing the artist's gantry, which was suspended sufficiently high above the stage for work on new sets to go on while the actors were performing in the old ones below. The company's elderly scenic artist, George Flowers, had been among the best in the business, having worked for years on the staff of Drury Lane. He taught me to boil size, to mix paint, and to use the snap lines, which were tacked, wire-taut, to both ends of the frame, coated with chalk or charcoal, and then snapped to apply white or black guidelines across fifteen or twenty flats. In this way the horizontal lines of cornices, chair rails, skirting boards, or baronial paneling could be drawn in a single flick of the string. He also taught me how to hold a four-foot straight edge and deftly paint lines along the chalk and charcoal marks.

George was considered a grouch who had little time for the kinds of young people he considered to be only playing at theater. But for anyone who really wanted to learn and who was prepared to work (and very dirty work it was), the old man was unstintingly generous with his knowledge. He taught me the subtleties of light and shade, how to use tonal variations to create apparent depth in stonework or a picture rail. He showed me how to suggest age in a painted wall-papered room by gluing small pieces of paper to the flat before applying the color and then tearing it to create the effect of peeling wallpaper. But George's tours de force were his backcloths, for which he would let me do no more than flat in the blue for his sky or the green for a field. Like some lunatic Leonardo working in silence above the heads of the choir, week after week he would paint enormous and beautiful pastoral and garden scenes, destroying the last with the paint of the next.

I had taken lodgings in a gray house whose equally gray proprietor catered to the peculiar hours of theater folk, and was fortunate to share them with Robin Bailey, the company's leading man, who was to go on to a distinguished career on West End stages and in television. In exchange for my reading other parts to help Robin learn his lines, he did his best to teach me to say mine. However, my professional debut was not one to go down in theatrical legend. Concealed within a vast papier-mâché frog's head, I was called upon to do little more than announce an invitation from the Queen to the Duchess to play croquet.

All the parts were cast within the resident company, with the exception of Alice, who was to be played by a strapping infant prodigy sent down by the London office who rejoiced in the star-quality name of Deirdre Doone. Nobody knew anything about her (I have never since seen her name in a program) and so received her with wary politeness. A young lady who held her talent in high esteem, she had not only memorized her own long role but everyone else's as well. Although the old pros considered her pushy and precocious, forty years later I still remember her with admiration and gratitude.

We opened on December 26, Boxing Day, to a packed and enthusiastic house. I remembered my lines, and in my role as Knave of Hearts I even managed to get a few laughs and a good round of applause at the end. I was sure I was off and flying. The second night, however, when the curtain rose on my frog footman scene, my mind went as blank as the blackness inside the frog's head. Not a word could I remember, and muffled within the head I had no hope of hearing the prompter. Then Alice, who was standing beside me through the scene, fed me my lines until my stage fright passed and I was back on track. It was the most terrifying moment of my public life, and thereafter I have remained forever fearful that it would happen again and that there would be no Deirdre Doone to rescue me. Throughout my career as a speaker, I have never risen to give a speech or mount a lecture platform without crossing my fingers and silently calling on her to see me through.

In a large company, ASMs were rarely assigned parts of any consequence, and in the next four productions I played an assistant butler with one line in *Charley's Aunt;* a bright but unimportant young man (type casting) in *French without Tears;* a butler with about six lines in *Promise,* a French play set in Paris where it should have stayed; and "Frenchy," an assistant burglar in *The Bishop Misbehaves.* My most convincing portrayal of "Frenchy," however, turned out not to be on the Connaught's stage but a few doors up the street in the Worthing police station.

One morning in the midst of rehearsals, the company manager came backstage with a sergeant who looked around at the cast and then asked me whether I would mind assisting the police by standing in an identification lineup. It sounded like an amusing experience. Standing against the wall in a long, brightly lit room with nine or ten other quasi volunteers, we watched the police bring in their suspect. He was a scruffy, fair-haired fellow of medium height in his mid-thirties who did not look much like any of us—which may have been the idea. Just for a lark, therefore, I put on my best "crook" look, a slouching of the shoulders, a villainous scowl, and a deliberate avoidance of looking the first female picker-outer in the eye. She walked slowly down the line, hesitated in front of me, then passed on. At the end the sergeant asked, "Well, madam, did you see him?"

"Oh, yes."

"Then please point him out."

The woman came back down the line and stopped. "That's him. That's the man I saw." She nodded at me. "I'd know him anywhere."

"You're quite sure, madam?"

"I'll swear to it," she answered, looking at me with triumph in her eye.

Score one for my acting, I thought as I reset my "Frenchy" scowl for the next witness. She was an older woman, and more deliberate than the first. She stood in front of each candidate, looking us up and down, pausing to consider what she had seen, then shaking her head—until she got to me. "This is him," she said firmly. A small chill ran down my spine. I had read about mistaken identity and innocent people getting hanged for murders they had not committed. The police had not told us what crime their suspect was believed to have committed. Suppose it was murder? The joke had gone far enough. No more acting. From here on I would be my innocent, angelic self.

The third witness was also a woman. I don't remember what she looked like or how old she was—only that she also picked me.

The fourth, and last, did not. Instead, after much hesitation she selected the official candidate. Shaken, I returned to the rehearsal still wondering what might have happened had all four witnesses voted for me. It taught me an unforgettable lesson that I have remembered throughout my career as a reconstructer of the past, namely, that honest witnesses testifying in good faith may be no more reliable than three in four women from Worthing.

Meanwhile, back on the Connaught stage, another chance encounter was to play its part in paving the way ahead. The production of the neither wildly funny nor very frightening comedy-thriller *The Bishop Misbehaves* marked the Worthing debut of a fresh-from-the-army comic actor named Clive Cable. He was a small man with thick and wavy black hair who only needed a square moustache to be mistaken for Charlie Chaplin. Waiting in our dressing room for our entrance in the third act, he told me of his hopes to one day manage his own company and promised that if he did there would be a place in it for me.

Our friendship, however, had little immediate chance to ripen. In March, at the end of my three months, my contract was not renewed, and for the first time I tasted the bitter wine of being an out-of-work actor. The misery of it was muted by the generosity of a duck and a dormouse, or more precisely by the young actresses who had played them in *Alice in Wonderland*. Irene, the duck, had wealthy parents and lived in a handsome apartment in London's fashionable Sloane Street. Though both she and dormouse Betty were fresh from a convent school, they enjoyed the company of actors and provided several of us with welcome shelter, as well as feeding us most handsomely from the food halls of nearby Harrods, all of it charged to Irene's mother's account.

For a couple of months we lived the kind of bohemian Belgravian life that Michael Arlen had written about in the '20s, roaming the pubs and artist's hangouts of Chelsea, joining wild and usually drunken parties in apartments and studios of people we barely knew, and somehow gaining admission to the notoriously lesbian Gateway Club to watch the other half live. In the space of eight weeks I had managed to become deliciously or disgustingly decadent—depending on one's point of view. Fortunately, I was rescued from further depravity by an agent who offered me a job as stage manager, scenic designer, and occasional actor (my resumé claimed competence in all three) with White Heather Productions at the John Gay Theatre at Barnstaple, in North Devonshire. The opportunity came just in time; Irene's mother had discovered what was afoot in Sloane Street, had barred her daughter from using the Harrods account, and shortly afterward had closed the apartment.

The Barnstaple theater (named after John Gay, the author of *The Beggar's Opera*) was about as far from the Connaught as imagination could conceive. Indeed, until relatively recently it had been an abandoned iron foundry and ten years later would become a garage. Its tiny stage had no space above it to fly anything, and its wings allowed scarcely enough room for players awaiting their cues, let alone the placement of lights and stage equipment. Scenery was painted, not on a frame above the stage, but usually one flat at a time in a shed beside the auditorium. Owned by an old-school husband-and-wife team, J. B. Vignoles and Joyce Heather, White Heather Productions skated on the cold, thin edge of bankruptcy, trying to wrest an audience out of a sleepy market town that preferred to get its laughs and thrills from a seat at the pictures. By the time the cast and management salaries had been covered, and rent, entertainment tax, and author's royalties paid, there was little left over for a rainy day, and in the lives of small, postwar repertory companies, it rained as often as it shone. One popular, money-saving device was to announce that in the interests of community relations the management was prepared to put on new plays by local authors. Translated, this meant that we were prepared to perform your play provided you contributed to the cost of its production, while paying you a royalty only in the highly unlikely event that the box office showed a profit.

The quality of amateur playwriting in North Devon was questionable at best, and it took only two or three local duds to lose the loyal and regular audience on which the company's existence depended. One such gem was to open on the night of my arrival, a stirring drama entitled *To What Red Hell* (borrowing a line from Oscar Wilde's *Ballad of Reading Gaol*), its plot a familiar tale of a man falsely accused (I forget of what) and unjustly condemned.

"Thank heavens you're here! We were expecting you yesterday," said Joyce Heather, as soon as I stepped inside the theater. "Have you ever done an Irish priest?"

I confessed that I hadn't.

"Well, you'll have to tonight," she snapped.

Three hours later, after a single rehearsal, I was on stage in cassock and black hat, Sure and begorrahing my way through the condemned man's last rites, from a script hidden in my prop Bible. Neither my frog footman nor my "Frenchy" had prepared me for doing Irish priests, and I am sure my performance turned a moving moment into broad farce and threatened the local author (who was present at most performances) with cardiac arrest. But nobody laughed. The Barnstaple audiences, small though they were, treated their weekly night at the theater as a solemn ritual akin to a religious experience. They were intensely loyal, laughed only when they were supposed to, were moved to oo! and aah! at sentiment, and blew their noses through the sad bits.

Working in an impoverished repertory company differed little from the theater as Dickens knew it a century earlier. As performers we ranged from the once sublime to the perennially ridiculous. To the former category belonged an aged character actor who never tired of recalling having seen Sir Henry Irving in *The Bells* at the Lyceum. With barely a hint of encouragement he would roar his impressions of Irving, or stop in mid-rehearsal, shade his eyes, peer out into the dark auditorium and tell the producer, "That's not the way we used to do it, laddie. When I was with Matheson Lang . . ."

Back would come a pained voice from the stalls. "Thank you, Claude. I'm sure you're right. But I'm producing this play and the late Matheson Lang is no longer with us . . ."

"More's the pity, laddie," the old actor would rumble as he walked back to his place on the set. "Moooore's the pity."

In small, mini-salaried companies like ours, the old school cohabited with the no school at all and resulted in a sometimes ludicrous imbalance. With the cast for next week's show still trying to get the hang of the one they were playing this week, producers had little time for coaching and were lucky if they got the cast word-perfect in time for the dress rehearsal. One producer, for whom I would later work in an old theater in the East End of London, was content to sit in the gallery and occasionally shout, "I can't 'ear yer dear!" at his young and inexperienced players. A cast that knew its lines and could be heard at the back of the hall was all that Barnstaple-style audiences asked for—which was just as well.

My Barnstaple landlady, Mrs. Belinger, was a stalwart theatergoer. She was present at every opening night, often accompanied by Avis Parsons, her blind sister. Country women who, as far as I knew, had never traveled more than fifty miles from their town, they looked on the theater as their window on the world, though in retrospect it must have been a pretty weird view. They also were among the most warmhearted of people; they treated me like a son, feeding me three meals a day (making the best rabbit pies known to man), doing my laundry, helping me learn my lines, and when I fell in love for the first time, helping me keep the job and the pain of it in perspective. This last was a neat trick. For several months I shared a room with fellow actor John Hess, who was no less smitten with Dot, the company's ingenue. Calling us both "her boys," Mrs. Belinger managed to keep us at the same time both good friends and rivals. In truth, the rivalry never got much beyond disputes over which of us would get to sit next to Dorothy in the back of a car driving home from Lynton on a Monday night.

Once a month we trucked last week's show sixteen miles to the coastal village of Lynton for a single performance in the village hall, a performance attended largely by the "Wood Family"—theatrical gallows humor for the rows of empty wooden seats. On a particularly dismal evening I recall peering between the curtains to count the house and finding that five minutes before we were due to begin, we had an audience of one. After a quick debate, our business manager went out and asked the man whether, if no one else showed up, he would be distraught if we canceled the performance.

"It be up to you, sir," he replied. "Oi'm just 'ere to close up when you'm through."

The incident was characteristic of the uphill struggle faced by provincial theatrical companies as they tried to stay alive. Some companies even less affluent than ours had no permanent theater and relied solely on these one-night stands. Known as "fit-up" troupes, they were the final inheritors of the medieval mummers' patched mantle, and were considered the very dregs of the thespian barrel. But once a month we came very close to them. Hauling all our equipment across the country to Lynton and trying to make last week's Barnstaple set fit on the new and inadequate stage, to rig temporary lighting, and to apply makeup in dressing rooms without mirrors, was a miserable experience for all concerned. Two hours later, with the show over and the thin applause no longer ringing in our ears, we had to pack costumes, sets, lights, and ourselves back into the trucks and cars and return to Barnstaple before our landladies locked their doors and went to bed.

Why, one might ask, would we go to all that trouble for so little? The answer lay not in the Lynton box office but in a rebate of entertainment tax for companies making cultural contributions. And that's what we were doing, although the cultural contributions might have been questioned: Edgar Wallace's *The Case of the Frightened Lady; The Red Umbrella*, by nobody anybody's ever heard of; *Smilin' thro' "That Grand Romantic Drama"!* by nobody at all (hence no royalties to pay); or Cicely Hamilton's *Diana of Dobsons*, "a story of youth, struggling to find its happiness and laughter in the difficult places of life." From my stack of yellowing programs, only one production had an educational ring to it, and that's because it was a period piece by another local author. Advance blurb for *Chance and Mrs. Buffington* called it a "gay and witty play" in which "Rodney Buffington stakes his wife on a game of cards—and loses her!" The decorative costumes and white wigs of the reign of "Farmer George," added the management with a nudge and a wink, "enhance the gaiety of this sparkling comedy."

Sparkling, my foot! It provided only one moment of hilarity, and that wasn't in the script. The previous week's settings for *Diana of Dobsons*, a girl's dormitory, a hotel at Pontresina, and the Thames Embankment, had taxed both my artistry and our supply of scenery. Consequently, Mrs. Buffington's boudoir (it was that kind of play) got somewhat shortchanged. Since this was a "Regency comedy," I had whipped up a soufflé of white paneling and patched up several battered pillars into Adam style. When, on the first night, I tried to make my entrance in the pithy role of Sir Bertram Peascod, an old door thickened by countless layers of paint declined to open. Struggling with it, I could hear my cue repeated several times from the other side. In panic I put my shoulder to the door; the entire set shuddered, there was a tremendous thud, and the door flew open propelling me on stage—and over a fallen pillar which now lay guts-upward like a beached canoe.

In July 1946 White Heather Productions split in two and sent half of us off to Leighton Buzzard, another small provincial town, this one in central England and with no apparent yearning for live theater. We performed in the Corn Exchange, which boasted a stage and some minimal equipment, but the conditions were not far removed from "fit-up" at Lynton. In the five-week season I stage-managed and served as electrician for all five productions (with only one ASM), designed and painted the sets for each of them, and played parts in two. By the time we got back to Barnstaple I was a nervous wreck. For the record, I should add that in a theatrical career spanning four years, I played four policemen, one burglar, three butlers, nine miscellaneous young men (known as juveniles), one French professor, two clerics, one demon king—and the frog.

9 ✦ *Things That Went Bump*

THE FALL OF 1946 saw the end of the John Gay Theatre, and me out of a job and far from any sources of new employment. Postwar austerity was squeezing the small theater companies on which so many actors relied for a thin living. And mighty thin it could be. I was paid four pounds for a week of seven working days. In American currency that would have been about nine dollars and sixty cents. Fortunately, however, my weekly board with the Belingers (with its three meals, laundry, and mothering) cost me only one pound, five shillings, or three dollars. Knowing that in London I could barely feed myself for so little, let alone rent a room, I stayed on in Barnstaple hoping that letters to agents would be persuasive enough to win me work.

They weren't. The months since the fall of '45 had brought a flood of ex-servicemen and women back into the ranks of the theatrical unemployed, many of them talented people with far more experience than some of us who had slipped in through the back door when the pool was so much smaller. Although no figures are available to document the ratio of jobs to applicants in the autumn of 1946, estimates for 1951 show that 80 percent of the profession could find no work in the legitimate theater—this before the full impact of television was felt. The small provincial repertory companies were not the only victims, however. The second-rate touring companies, which before the war could enjoy bookings the year round, were finding transportation costs and theater rents prohibitive. Even the summer, pier-end concert parties were dying, their demise blamed in part on the cinemas, but more on a public that had outgrown an entertainment form that had changed little since 1914.

Finding myself in deepening debt to the Belingers, I wrote to Clive Cable, the friend from Worthing who dreamed of launching his own repertory company. He answered that his dream had faded, but that he did have a new idea. If I could get myself to London, he would put me up in his house at Hammersmith while we worked on it. Without knowing anything more than that, I said good-bye to Barnstaple and headed for Hammersmith.

Clive and his wife, Betty, lived with their two children in the basement of a house the rest of which they rented as unfurnished apartments. They let me have the front room of the vacant one on the first floor, furnished with absolutely nothing but a bed they had brought up from below. But at least it was a roof, and it was free. Clive's idea, however, turned out to be even less appealing.

"Have you ever thought of a double act?" he asked.

"You mean, on the music halls?"

"Yes."

"Like Nervo and Knox, Flannigan and Allen, that sort of thing?"

Clive must have detected a note of wariness in my reply. "Well, yes. But more sophisticated," he assured me, "much more sophisticated." Ours would be a comedy team with a difference. He would be the Chaplin-style comic, the universal, put-upon little man, and I would be his toff (upper-class) straight man. "It'll be a song and patter act," Clive explained.

"But I don't sing."

"You don't really have to. Just follow along. I'll be leading," he added, "and playing the instrument."

"What instrument?"

"A one-string fiddle."

I thought he was joking. But he wasn't. He had taught himself to play the thing well enough to scrape a few accompanying notes out of it. "It doesn't have to be good. The worse it is, the funnier it'll be," he contended.

I was not convinced, but took heart from Betty's assurance that it would sound better on a stage than in their tiny basement living room. However, nothing could convince me that I liked the name Clive had chosen for our act.

"We're going to call ourselves Cock & Roach. How do you like it?"

I couldn't think of a thing to say.

"I promise you, it's an inspiration," Clive insisted. "You're tall. You're the toff, the swell, Cock o' the walk, you see. And I'm Roach, the little feller who always gets stepped on."

"Look, really," I stammered, "I don't think I can do this. I'm not a comic, I can't sing, I . . ."

"Don't worry. All you have to do is play it straight. Be yourself. Leave the rest to me. We've got nearly three weeks before the audition."

"Audition! What audition?"

We were to try out for the manager of one of the most historic of all British variety theaters, Collins's Music Hall in Islington, a district in London's East End and one of the roughest and toughest in the city. English music halls had developed in the 1850s out of taverns that provided their customers with live entertainment supervised by a "chairman" to announce the acts and keep the beer-swilling audience in line. The music halls switched the priorities, providing proper stages for the shows and pushing the bars to the back of the auditorium. Most of them eventually removed the serving of drinks to rooms out of sight and sound of the stage, but not the Collins, Islington. The audience could still lubricate its throat from the back of the pit and shout its opinion of the acts. I remember sitting on the underground on our way from Hammersmith to Islington, my knees knocking as loudly as the rattling of the train. At the theater, a spotty youth showed us into an equally unattractive dressing room that smelled of sweat and stale greasepaint. An old man was sitting in front of his mirror, kneading Leishner No. 5 into the lines around his mouth and eyes with his forefinger, and from time to time gargling from a small bottle of whiskey. I don't recall what he did, but whatever it was he did it before us, and returned grumbling that the management didn't know a solid act when it saw one.

We were to do our stuff with an ancient frontcloth as backing, behind which other hopefuls were thumping about. Only a single overhead work light lit the stage, and in the auditorium the lights remained up as cleaning women clattered around with their mops and pails. At the back, the manager (or whoever was rating the talent) chatted with the bartender as we struggled through our routine. In front of an appreciative Cable family audience, some of the lines had seemed passably funny, but here they rolled out into the dark footlights and lay there dying. My memory has shown a modicum of mercy by allowing me to forget every word, presumably concluding that keeping alive the humiliation of it all is punishment enough.

"Thank you. Thank you very much," called a voice from the back. "Who's next?"

The music hall career of Cock & Roach ended with those words. Like our whiskey-gargling dressing-room companion, Clive's first reaction was to blame the management for its lack of lighting, courtesy, and perception. But by the time we got home he conceded that the act just wasn't good enough. Three choices were open to us: we could spend more time trying to improve it, we could go our independent ways and rejoin the queues in the agent's waiting rooms, or we could think up another brilliant cooperative scheme. We chose the last. And this time it was my idea.

If it was true that live theater was losing its audiences to the cinema, why not go into the cinema business? The J. Arthur Rank Organization might have a monopoly on Britain's town movie theaters, but nobody had cornered the village halls. Out in the countryside there had to be a vast, untapped audience yearning for quality entertainment. It would be cinema "fit-up," but with the assured quality that came with the can. All we had to do was rent a film a week and show it in each of six village halls. Even if at the start the audiences amounted to no more than fifty or sixty a performance, at two shillings a head we should easily cover our operating cost by Thursday, leaving the potentially big nights of Friday and Saturday for pure profit. Clive and I would handle the setup and projection, Betty would manage the box office, and the Cable boy and girl would be ushers. First, however, we needed a vehicle, a screen, and a pair of 16 mm projectors. Although only Clive could provide the capital (I hadn't enough for a small lunch), my labor would earn me a share of the profits. Thus, out of the debacle in Islington emerged London Mobile Cinemas.

After much debate and more haggling, Clive invested in a stately prewar Ford sedan big enough to take the five of us and all our equipment. Projectors, even secondhand projectors, turned out to be more expensive than we had expected, so we settled for one. Theater audiences didn't mind an interval, so why should a cinema be any different? Our first films were old and therefore cheaply rented, opening with Grace Moore in the American *You Were Never Lovelier,* followed by Robert Morley in *The Great Leslie Stuart,* both musicals, chosen on the grounds that if the villagers went away humming, they would be back next week. If all went well through the first month, we would be able to try something classier, hence a tentative booking of Laurence Olivier's *Henry the Fifth.*

I have neglected to mention the proposed location of our first lucky villages. That, too, was my inspiration. We would base ourselves at Barnstaple (where I could return to Mrs. Belinger and her rabbit pies) and make our selection from among the numerous small villages eastward toward Lynton and west in the direction of Bideford. It was a long way from London and projector spare parts, but I knew the territory and there was no denying that North Devonshire was just about as rural (and therefore as culturally bereft) as one could get.

On a bitterly cold December 31, 1946, we loaded the old Ford and, with a panel bearing our slogan "Stairway to the Stars" attached to one door, we headed west. There was little traffic on the road. Gasoline was still severely rationed and relatively few people had kept their cars through the war or were able to buy them now. Besides, no one traveled far on that icy New Year's Eve. We planned to break the journey at Salisbury, find a cheap hotel, and reach Barnstaple by late afternoon the next day. But we had started late, and with snow on the roads, progress was much slower than we estimated. Consequently, it was well past midnight by the time London Mobile Cinemas drove into Salisbury's deserted town square. Not a reveler was to be seen or even heard. Apart from the street lamps, the town was dark and fast asleep—and we were virtually out of gas.

No gas station would open before morning, and no cheap hotel would welcome us at that time of night, even if we knew where to look for one. And light snow was falling and sticking to the car's windows. All we could do was to huddle down and hope we wouldn't be discovered frozen to death in the morning.

Of the several low points in my life, New Year's night 1947 is about the deepest. But it turned out to be only the herald of more to come. Within a day of reaching Barnstaple we discovered that my great scheme was breached by a flaw a mile wide. Villages might be eager for movies, but some had no halls, and others that did, lacked the key ingredient that Messrs. Bell and Howell, the projector manufacturers, demanded, to wit: electricity. You couldn't run a movie projector on lamp oil! Although we found two adequately equipped halls, the shows drew tiny audiences, owing in part to a lack of advance publicity, but more to their proximity to Barnstaple and its two movie houses. The search for electrified village halls drew us farther and farther away, so far in fact that our gasoline ration would not cover the mileage. There was nothing for it but to leave Barnstaple (and Mrs. Belinger's haven) and find a new hub closer to the chosen halls. We found it on a snow-covered hillside near the town of Coombe Martin.

The house, named Blurridge, was a two-story, stuccoed structure of late Victorian vintage with a row of older brick outbuildings behind it. In the summer the place was rented to vacationing families, two at a time, and so was partitioned down the middle across a glass-walled conservatory. We rented the north side at a modest price, its modesty perhaps due to the fact that the electrical generator was not working. Otherwise the place was fully furnished, and to help out, the real estate agent promised to provide several oil lamps and the fuel to burn in them.

With our new base secured, we spent the day distributing leaflets to village shops announcing that London Mobile Cinemas would be offering *You Were Never Lovelier* at their very own hall. With that done, we began to set up for our first show. We had already discovered that the projector was disconcertingly noisy, and while that would not have mattered were it shut in a booth, out in the hall it was objectionable to anyone sitting within twenty feet of it. That problem had been solved when the owner of the vacant John Gay Theatre let

Clive borrow an old curtain left behind after the repertory company closed. The curtain was heavy, hemmed with lead weights, and ideal for the job. But the weather, in Britain's worse winter in fifty years, was anything but ideal, and by show time only about thirty people showed up.

Nothing was going right. The search for halls had eaten alarmingly into our gasoline ration, and our original estimates had failed to recognize that the entertainment tax had to be paid on the gross and not on the profits. But even though the car later slid into a ditch and broke its axle, it was Blurridge that did us in.

After our first show, we arrived at the house around 10:30 on a pitch-black night and in light but wind-blown snow. As we stood shivering in the muddy yard while Clive, with the aid of a dying flashlight, fumbled with the door key, the building seemed singularly inhospitable. Inside, it was not much better. The place smelled stale and damp, and the bright blue paint in the hallway was stained and flaking. To understand what was to happen there, one needs to know the layout of the building, or rather the half of it to which we had access.

The hall was really a largish reception area entered through the exterior door. To the right a staircase ascended to a short gallery, off which were three doors: a bathroom, the master bedroom (to be occupied by Clive and his family), and adjacent to it, at the end of the gallery, another much smaller room which was to be mine. Downstairs, leading out of the hall, was one large sitting room, and to the right of it a passage provided access into a stone-flagged room reached by three descending steps. It may have been a buttery when the house was first built, but now it had been converted into a rather awkward kitchen. Beyond it, the passage was boarded across, but in daylight one could see by peering between the cracks that it became a conservatory, with a couple of dirty shelves on which stood several very dead plants. Daylight also revealed that the sitting room was painted a ghastly pink, which was not out of character with the room's fussy Victorian furnishings, which included more than their fair share of framed religious texts of the "Bless This House" variety. Although the best room in the house, its atmosphere was that of a museum's period exhibit—a sitting room not to be sat in. So we didn't. Instead, what little time we had in the house we spent in the hall, its dreary flaking blue paint notwithstanding.

The agent had been true to his word and had left half a dozen or more oil lamps in the kitchen, but I forget what, if anything, he had done to provide heat. I do recall, however, that we were so cold that we had to keep our overcoats on when we first sat down to our supper of baked beans. We had barely done so when the oil lamp on the table guttered and went out.

There is something disconcerting about being plunged into darkness in a strange environment, and it seemed an eternity before Clive found his flashlight and his matches. When he did, I was dispatched to the kitchen to fetch another lamp. About ten minutes later, that lamp behaved like the first. Its flame skittered back and forth over the wick, smoked, flickered, and went out. Both lamps were full and neither had anything visibly wrong with their wicks. Another trip to the kitchen brought a third lamp, but a few minutes later that, too, died. It may have been at this point that one of us suggested that the house was haunted, but I do know that by the time we went up to bed that notion had been firmly planted. It is highly likely that the seed, once sown, colored our interpretation of everything that was yet to happen.

The weather remained true to the forecast, snow flurries continued all day and contributed to the number of people able to resist the temptation to turn out to see *You Were Never Lovelier.* By this time Clive and Betty Cable were beginning to doubt whether they could afford to nurse London Mobile Cinemas through so slow a start. Though both were by nature warm and optimistic people, the strain was beginning to show, and that second night in the house we all went up to bed in a melancholy mood. No sooner had we settled down than we heard a distant door slam somewhere in the empty half of the house. A few moments later we heard another, closer at hand. I heard Clive get up, and when I opened my door I found him standing in the gallery listening. As we stood there in the light from his flashlight, more doors banged. Then a silence, and finally from below us in the darkness, the click of the pink room's door handle turning, another pause, and the sound of the door closing.

We waited in breathless silence for what might happen next. But nothing did. I do not recall whether Clive heard the click that preceded the closing. Perhaps I had been mistaken in thinking that I had. Set that click aside, and there is nothing surprising about doors banging on a windy night—except that it is odd that they should all have chosen to shut within the same few minutes on a night no more blustery than the last.

The third night was equally windy, but the snow had stopped. The audience had been larger (though not large enough) and we all looked to the future with slightly more confidence. Some time after we had turned in, Clive came to my door. "There's something you ought to see," he said.

I followed him into his room. "Up there," he said. "Over the window."

Betty and the children were staring at a white light spreading from the window across the ceiling. The room had two windows, one beside the Cables' bed with its curtains drawn back, and the other with curtains closed at the far end of the room. The light had a yellowish cast, its color and position on the ceiling just what one would expect from a city street lamp, except that none of it illuminated the window itself. As we watched, the glow faded and shrank, then finally disappeared. Almost immediately we heard a violent banging against the glass of the other curtained window, the kind of sound that could be made by a frightened bird or a windblown tree limb.

Bird it may have been, but tree limb it wasn't. Inspection in the morning found no tree anywhere near the window and nothing on the ground below it. The next night would be our last.

My bedroom was L-shaped, the door at the top of the L, a small window opposite it at the right angle, and the bed occupying so much of the foot that there was barely twelve inches of space between the bed frame and wall. Beyond the bed and close by the window stood a dark-wood chest of drawers. On this night, as I had on the past three, I hauled the John Gay Theatre's old curtain upstairs and threw it onto the bed to help keep me warm. That done, I climbed in over the foot of the bed, crawling crablike up it while still holding a lighted candle in a metal stick. Once there, I blew out the candle, set it down in the narrow space between bed and wall, and eventually fell asleep.

Although the night was dark, I awoke to find some light filtering through the window, just enough to let me see the end of the bed—and something standing between it and the chest of drawers. It looked like a silhouetted doorknob about the size of a large man's head, and below its projecting collar a dark shape extended downward beyond the path of the window light. The thing did not move. It had no features; it was simply a darker darkness interrupting the passage of light, which otherwise would have picked out the details of the chest and which reflected off the pale wall behind.

At first I thought I was mistaken. I closed my eyes and looked again. But it was still there. To get past it I would have to crawl back down the bed and push it out of the way. In retrospect, I cannot imagine why I didn't yell for Clive. Instead, I shut my eyes again, vowing to count to ten. If the thing was still there at the end, I would throw the candlestick at it, then leap down the bed and bolt for the door.

I counted the ten, and then another for good measure. But when I opened my eyes the shape hadn't moved. So I reached down with my left hand fumbling beside the bed for the candlestick, found it, hurled it, and tried to follow it. But being right-handed, my aim was atrocious. So was my progress. I had misjudged the size and weight of the theater curtain and, lunging down the bed, ended up on my face tangled in its weights and draw lines. The crash of the candlestick into the wall brought the Cables to my rescue. But by then I knew that there was nothing at the end of my bed except a chest of drawers.

Was the thing merely the product of an imagination excited by the events of the previous nights? I have no way of knowing. Nevertheless, the next morning Clive decided that we had had enough. We would return to Barnstaple and consider what to do next. Before leaving Coombe Martin, we stopped at the real estate office, the rest of us waiting in the car while Clive turned in the key to the agent—who expressed no surprise.

Over the next few days the weather grew worse; we no longer had reachable bookings yet the film rents had to be paid. Then came the broken axle and the demise of London Mobile Cinemas. Clive and his family returned to London, and to my regret I never saw them again. After staying on flat broke in Barnstaple for a few days, I returned briefly to my mother in Salcombe and then, with borrowed funds, went back to London and to a rented garret room in Earls Court.

For years after the strange affair of the house on the windswept hill, I have wondered how much of what happened was the product of imagination or of a shared hallucination. Was what I saw on the last night merely a trick of the light? Was there something wrong with the lamp wicks? Did the wind blow the doors, and was that only a bird that beat on the window? And what about the light that we all saw? Nineteen years later I went back to Coombe Martin to find out.

The particular real estate agency was gone, but in another the young girl behind the desk said that her father, the butcher, knew all about the surrounding area and might be able to help. During the short life of London Mobile Cinemas we had never approached the house from the town side, but always came at it up a narrow lane from the west. Consequently, I had no idea of how to find it. Finding the butcher was no problem, however, for his line of Saturday morning customers stretched out into the street. Joining the queue, I slowly worked my way up to the counter, and visibly surprised him when I explained that I wanted information rather than beef. Nevertheless, he listened patiently to my explanation (which was more than could be said for the line behind me), then said, "Ah. That'll be Blurridge. You go back to the church, turn right, and it's up the hill on the left. You can't miss it."

I thanked him, and then could not resist adding that there had been talk years ago that the place was haunted. The butcher smiled. "Aye, that'd be the house."

Blurridge was easily found, but it bore little resemblance to the grim pile I remembered. The muddy and iced yard was now a pleasant garden, and in the September sunlight the neat, white-painted house looked warm and inviting. An elderly dachshund yapped at me as I stood at the gate, bringing out its owner. Her name was Bea Watson. She and Fred, her husband and an ex-RAF officer, had bought the house five years earlier and were making their own improvements, among them the removal of the conservatory. Mrs. Watson explained that a previous owner had done away with the buttery, tearing down the wall between it and the pink sitting room to create one large living space. However, while rewiring, her husband had had to go under the floor and found older stone paving about three feet below. They had concluded that the present house, which had been built in the late nineteenth century, overlay a much earlier building. She added that they believed that the wing that extended out to the south of the house (where the door banging had started) was about four hundred years old.

I hesitated to explain my interest, and hedged by referring only to "some perhaps imagined experiences," but she insisted that I be more specific. I told her the whole story. In return she invited me inside. I found it hard to believe that the comfortably furnished home was the same house in which I had once sat shivering with cold and apprehension. Nevertheless, traces of its past survived; though painted more than once since 1947, hints of the blue in the hall and of the pink in the living room could still be seen. Mrs. Watson admitted that from time to time the kitchen door in the old wing would spring open, prompting the family to jokingly call, "Come in!"

Around nine o'clock one summer evening Mrs. Watson had seen a light on the ceiling above a window—but in the passage over the conservatory and not in the Cables' room. Her husband had dismissed it as the product of a car's headlights shining up the hill. I thought it inappropriate to ask why, if that was the simple explanation, the light had been seen only once. Mrs. Watson also recalled how one afternoon the old dachshund had run down the garden toward a gate barking furiously, then suddenly stopped dead. With hackles high he sat and howled, then slunk trembling back to the house with his tail between his legs. Neither Bea Watson nor her husband could offer any explanation, and the dog had behaved normally thereafter.

In subsequent correspondence with Mrs. Watson she remembered taking in a family of summer boarders who planned to stay for two weeks, but who, after the second morning, asked whether their daughter could have another room. When told none was available, they apologetically canceled their holiday. In the same letter, written in 1985, Bea Watson described her children's fear of "our" bedrooms.

> When they slept over that side of the house it was in the room at the top of the stairs. Nigel, our youngest son's bed was nearest the door. He recalls how he was petrified of facing the door during the night. When we used those bedrooms Pamela slept in the little one [mine]. She was only a toddler when we found she always seemed to have nightmares in that little room. She used to wake up screaming and pointing to the wall.

Again and again over the years I have asked myself the same questions: were both the Watson family's experiences and ours merely the products of overactive imaginations, ill-fitting doors, car headlights, dirty oil lamps, and an old dog who made an embarrassing mistake, or had something happened at Blurridge (a corruption of Blow Ridge, Bea Watson explained) that had left an indelible mark?

10 🖎 *Curtain Down*

B ACK IN LONDON IN February 1947 there was nothing to do but cook baked beans on a small electric ring in my garret and to make the rounds of the theatrical agents, while keeping a wary eye on the soles of my shoes, which daily grew thinner—as did I. The agents were spread all over London's West End from Piccadilly to Holborn, and just getting from one to another took time, time that all too often translated into a familiar "Nothing today, sorry. What a shame you weren't here half an hour ago. We just filled a spot that'd have been right up your alley. Try again tomorrow."

There were quality agents with elevators up to their suites and thick carpets in their waiting rooms, and there were small-time operators with neither elevators nor carpets who did business from garrets no more prepossessing than mine. But no matter whether one was riding in a Regent Street elevator or climbing a stone-stepped staircase in Cambridge Circus or a creaking wooden stair in Long Acre, the people you met waiting at the top invariably were the same timid, arrogant, hopeful, fearful lot. And their greetings rarely differed.

"David, dear boy! Marvelous to see you. But where's your little friend, the one with the poodle? Don't tell me he's working."

"He got the juvenile lead in *Buttons and Bows*."

"I don't want to know!"

For me, whose forte was stage management rather than acting, the opportunities were scarcer than for most supplicants. But eventually the waiting paid off, after a fashion: assistant stage manager at the Arts Theatre in Great Newport Street. It was a big step down from stage manager, but this was a West End theater, albeit a fringe one, and I could afford to eat.

Unlike most London theaters, which were run by nonperforming managements, the Arts was run, and well run, by actor-manager Alec Clunes, whose adventurous policy provided a month-long showcase for new plays that frequently were successful enough to transfer to bigger houses. My first production was not one of them, nor was my first performance on the West End stage a moment to remember. As "Second Man" I had no lines. The play was *Maya*, a translation of a French play by Simon Gantillon, who had conceived the not altogether novel idea of seeing a prostitute as the eternal woman. Banned by the Lord Chamberlain (the British theatrical censor) in 1927, *Maya* was said to have "been the pet play of pirate theatres for years," but our production was not well received. Wrote one reviewer: "Except for the sight of a serious and clever West End actress standing stripped to the waist with her back to the audience, there is nothing very unusual in the production." Another described her performance as "desperately aiming at the South of France but deriving eradicably from South Kensington."

For me, however, *Maya* left a scar that would not be erased until thirty years later, and it is the manner of the erasure that merits its place in this tale. Were that not so, the pain and humiliation of it would be better forgotten.

In the large *Maya* cast was a titian-haired actress of quite extraordinary beauty. I'll call her Nicolette Barrett. One afternoon following the matinee, I found her weeping in her dressing room, and in what I am sure was an embarrassed and gauche way, I did what I could to comfort her, though I had no idea why she was crying. She did not confide in me, but we had touched, and I was lost. Nicky was eight or ten years older than me. She had been part of Laurence Olivier's Old Vic company and had given a critically acclaimed performance in his great production of *King Lear.* Though not a star, she was a recognized West End actress with an established career; she knew all the right people, and according to one actor who offered a fatherly warning, she had slept with half of them. I, on the other hand, was a humble ASM with little but baked beans in my future. Nevertheless, Nicky was kind and affectionate, and from the loneliness of my garret, I responded with all the guileless love of a dog for its mistress.

Obsessed by the fear that I would lose her after *Maya* closed, I suggested that we should go away together for a weekend in the country. She accepted, and so we did, booking separate rooms at a hotel I couldn't afford near Amersham. Sitting in the train I became increasingly conscious of the difference between us. Here was to be no juvenile groping in the back seat of a car driving through the night on the Devon moors. This was a woman of apparently legendary experience, whereas I had none, being still encumbered with the legacy of my monastic years in a boys' school where girls were scarcely mentioned. Suffice it to say, the weekend was a disaster.

My total, naked love for Nicky Barrett was something that I would never experience again. Although in my waking hours I knew that that was just as well, in my sleep she kept coming back, her beauty as magical as ever. Time after time, year in and year out, I would wake in the same mood of frustrated despair that had made me so tiresome to work with in that summer of 1947. Eventually Nicky married and left England to live in France, but now and again we would write to each other, as old friends do. Improbable though it may sound, one day in 1980 she wrote to say that she was coming to Williamsburg to visit a writer friend who had a visiting fellowship at the College of William and Mary. He would arrange a dinner party for us.

My wife, Audrey, knew that Nicky and I wrote to each other, but I had never told her that across thirty years my early morning black moods were the product of Nicky's nocturnal visits. I suspect, however, that we both went to the dinner party with some apprehension. I know that as I rang the apartment's door bell, my heart was in my throat.

The door was opened by a very small woman whom I took to be our host's wife. Beneath thinning and bleached hair, and from a face lined by the years and too many summers in the sun, a voice I knew said, "Hello, Noël, it's been a long time."

It had, indeed. Throughout the evening I searched for some trace, a smile, a mannerism, something to show me that this was my titian-headed goddess. Only the voice remained, and what it had to say made it painfully clear that this aging woman and I had absolutely nothing in common. After that embarrassing evening, Nicky never again intruded into my dreams. It was as though a sudden power outage had wiped her image from my memory bank.

After six months at the Arts, I thought I knew enough about the workings of the theater to begin a career as a playwright. While appearing in my second nonstarring role there ("A Footman" in a ponderous German comedy *Trapeze in the Vatican*), I wrote a play for Nicky Barrett that owed too much to the theme of *Maya*. Alec Clunes was gracious enough to read it and to write telling me that I had talent as a writer of dialogue and showed promise once I found a more original plot. Buoyed by this qualified praise, and in collaboration with the actor Stephen Darlot, with whom I shared a dressing room during the run of *Trapeze*, we wrote a melodrama titled *One-Way Street*, a play of sufficient merit to get a well-known agent, Eric Glass, to agree to try to sell it. He couldn't. Fishing it down from the shelf nearly forty years later I was surprised to find: "The scene is the interior of one in a group of huts that make up the camp of a party of archaeologists in the jungle of Guatemala." I had not remembered that my archaeological interests were stirring in 1947. However, it is clear from the dialogue that my notions of archaeological techniques and ethics were still at a Hollywood level. A prefatory note explained, "Each year expeditions set out to bring back the perhaps mythical wealth said to lie buried in the Mayan ruins of Guatemala." Some of these, we explained, "are dispatched by reputable societies and some by hare-brained adventurers. Of the latter, many fail to come back. What becomes of them no one ever knows or really cares."

Theatrical managements had a rather similar view of the play. Coauthor Steve Darlot left the Arts to take a small part in Michael Redgrave's production of *Macbeth,* and when he found that there was an opening for a spare thane and all-purpose understudy, he arranged for me to audition. In nervous haste, and armed with an 1897 copy of the Bard's complete works, I learned Romeo's first speech from the balcony scene. From the bare stage of the Piccadilly Theatre I could see Michael Redgrave and a couple of other people sitting in the darkened stalls waiting for me to begin. Thanks to Steve, this was a one-on-one opportunity. There was no competition for the part; it was mine—if I could convince Redgrave that I could act. I stood in the wings mumbling the lines for what seemed like hours waiting for the call to begin. My hands, damp with terror, stuck to the rice-paper-thin pages of act 2, scene 2.

"Right, Mr. Hume. When you're ready!"

Remembering the acting style advocated by old Claude at Barnstaple, I resolved to make an Irving-style impression, rolling the words out resolutely, round like an orange, echoing to the farthest seats of the gods.

"He jests at scars, that never felt a wound. But, soft! [Shade eyes with hand as though searching for a rescue ship.] What light through yonder window breaks? It is the east [takes in whistling breath], and Juliet is the sun! Arise fair sun, and . . ."

"Yes, thank you very much, Mr. Hume. An interesting interpretation."

And that was as close as I ever got to appearing in a major West End production. I still have the copy of *The Complete Works,* and of its 1,264 pages two are stained brown where sweating fingers once clung to them as the lines of act 2, scene 2, were fruitlessly learned. Those dirty marks are the legacy of an unforgettable moment—yet only I am able to explain them. For an archaeologist that is a sobering and frustrating thought, for virtually everything he finds has a comparable human story to tell, provided he has the wit to hear it.

Steve Darlot had been a tank officer in a mechanized horse regiment and so was a member of the Cavalry Club in Piccadilly; and it was there, inspired by liberal supplies of the then fashionable pink gin, that we met to review and edit the latest slabs of our play. The club provided me with my first taste of the kind of world my mother had prepared me to appreciate. A richly carpeted marble staircase, life-sized portraits of officers who had built and defended the Empire, deep and complacent leather chairs in the smoking room, and a staff attentive to every member's smallest need. This was the England of Galsworthy, of Kipling, and of Henty, a far cry from the ranks of the theatrical unemployed.

Even before my engagement at the Arts ended, I was in deep housing trouble, so deep that one night I had nowhere to sleep but in the bed on the set of *Trapeze in the Vatican*. With Steve's assistance, however, I obtained a room at 7 Bentinck Street, one of London's more elegant addresses, where an elderly lady, Mrs. Winter, rented rooms to "gentlemen in the City" at extraordinarily reasonable prices. For three pounds a week, I received not only breakfast but a second-floor view onto a street of noble brick houses, with handsome stone steps, shining brass doorknobs and letter boxes, and finialed iron railings obscuring the entrances to the servants' basements, where Mrs. Winter herself resided.

A large woman, too large for her own good, she suffered from phlebitis and hobbled about, her bulging legs swathed in bandages. In constant pain, she was rarely joyous, had no time for dust or laziness, and on those Fridays when I was unable to pay the rent ran a close second to the Last Judgment. But she was kind to me, quite remarkably so for a landlady who needed the money; and when she raised the rent for her other rooms, mine remained the same. No. 7 Bentinck Street became my version of Steve Darlot's club, a comforting corner of the velvet life and of the way things ought to have been. It also was an addiction that I could not, would not give up; and when, for a few weeks or months at a time, I found work in the provinces, I kept the room on. But paying rent in two places made it impossible to save anything for the next bout of unemployment.

The winter of 1948 was as cold as my prospects. A month of stage management at Hayes, in Middlesex, a couple of weeks here and there in tiny, fringe theaters in London kept me going, though not in high gear. My sets for *Two Gentlemen of Verona*, performed in a Knightsbridge basement, earned me nothing but coffee and several sandwiches. Not until April did the endless up and down the agents' stairs pay off. At a princely ten pounds a week I secured the job of stage director at the New Market Theatre, Aylesbury, a fair-sized town about forty miles northwest of central London.

Under the management of Bill Stephens, one of the kindest men I ever met, the Aylesbury theater was close enough to London to draw on established names to augment the resident repertory company. A short, cherubic man in his early fifties, Bill had been a music hall and seaside concert-party performer. Compere, singer of comic songs, and a fine pianist, his infectious optimism was guaranteed to charm seagulls on a wet day. But a sunny disposition was not enough. To be a star comedian, he needed some quirk of character, some gimmick, an indefinable magic that simply wasn't there. Bill Stephens had known it from the beginning, and so he dreamed of owning his own theater and orchestrating the talents of others. The New Market Theatre was the fulfillment of that dream, and although he recognized that starting anything in the tight-belted postwar years was a risk, Bill felt sure that his slogan, "The New Market trend is to bring a friend," would soon pay off. Besides, his years in the light entertainment business had built him a wide circle of famous pals willing to help out—particularly when they needed the work.

Not content to give Aylesbury's relatively unsophisticated public safe and standard entertainment, Bill convinced himself that if he could couple his "name" friends with new productions, his theater was close enough to London's West End to be what Boston is to Broadway. And he had evidence to prove he was right. After a week at Aylesbury, a creaky American melodrama, *Seven Keys to Baldpate*, starring Michael Howard, a comedian of modest fame, had been rewritten, retitled, and largely recast, and sent out on a national tour prior to its West End debut. With one such winner in the bag, others were sure to follow.

The sad truth, however, was that in spite of the major surgery, Bill Stephen's investment in the *Baldpate* tour died somewhere in the hinterland. The London impresarios who gave Bill encouragement had to have known (as the recasting of *Baldpate* demonstrated) that although the New Market players could give potential backers a free look at how a show might play, there was no way that their production could be considered ready for the road.

On weekends, in an effort to gain local support for his theater, Bill put on charity concerts for worthy causes like the Bucks Constabulary Widows' and Orphans' Fund, again drawing on his old music hall friends for the talent. Although show people are generous in their contributions to charities, market-town residents still believed that the only Sunday shows should be in churches, and so audiences were small and Bill's expenses massive. Those, coupled with the *Baldpate* failure, brought the New Market Theatre to its knees. At a crisis meeting of the company Bill explained that he was temporarily unable to pay our salaries.

"I'm not going to beg any of you to stay, but I can promise that one way or another, you will eventually be paid. This is a wonderful theater, and if we can hold on a little longer I know we can build an equally wonderful audience. The bad weather's over. Petrol rationing's coming off, and we've got some marvelous plays lined up. And best of all, we've got friends. All we need is time, and a little luck."

We were about to rehearse George Bernard Shaw's *Candida,* in which I had been given the most challenging part I had yet attempted. Without exception, we applauded and vowed to stay until we starved. But martyrdom was not enough. The male lead was to be played by another imported "name" who knew nothing of the crisis. When he arrived for the first rehearsal and learned that the company was working for love, he telephoned Equity (the actors' union) and reported that we and the management were in violation of his contract. His damage done, our star departed. A resident character actor took over the lead, and rehearsals went on while Bill Stephens reasoned with the union. But neither Bill's optimism nor the company's desire to keep going cut any ice with Equity. Pay your cast or close down, it said.

Bill Stephens did what had to be done—as a faded copy of the *Candida* program recalls. Scrawled across one corner is my notation: "May 24, 1948. This show never opened."

While rehearsing *Candida* we had been playing a thriller titled *Grand National Night,* and before the Saturday evening's performance Bill went in front of the curtain to announce to a half-filled house that more "unforeseen circumstances" had forced the cancellation of next week's show. A few "oohs" of disappointment greeted the news. Bill held up his hands and smiled. "But don't worry, we'll be open again very soon, better and stronger than ever."

Backstage nobody believed him.

Bill had asked whether I would stay on for a couple of days to take inventory and close the theater down, and having nothing else to do I readily agreed. When I arrived after breakfast on the Sunday morning, I was surprised to hear the sounds of the piano from the orchestra pit. The auditorium was in darkness save for the lamp over the instrument's music rack, its light creating a dim aura around Bill's hunched figure. He did not hear me as he sat playing the sad wartime songs of parting—"Give Me Something to Remember You By," "We'll Meet Again." Almost inaudibly, he was singing the words.

> . . . Don't know where, don't know when;
> But we'll meet again,
> Some sunny day.

Tears were rolling down his cheeks. I hesitated, not knowing what to do or say. I had never seen a man cry, and that it should be this man, this invariably happy man, came as a shock I would never forget. Nor would I forget my own inability to help. Instead, I tried to creep away. But he saw me, and stopped playing.

"Noël," he said, "I don't suppose you can understand. You're young. But this was my life."

There was something else I didn't understand. I was witnessing not only the misery of a broken dream but the end of an era. Across the country, one by one, the provincial repertory companies were hearing their stage managers give their last instructions, "Curtain down!" the cue for the cast to take its final bow before the stagehands struck the set.

Back in Bentinck Street and helped by a loan from my Aylesbury stage manager, Louise Bartmann, I tramped the streets haunting the agents for three months, living almost exclusively on Mrs. Winter's breakfasts, growing thin, pale, and perhaps interesting in the process. The ritual was briefly broken in June when I designed and painted the setting for a comedy at the Chepstown Theatre Club. The critics thought the play needed some laughter to brighten it up, but the cast being unable to generate any, it shriveled and died.

In mid-September I landed the job of scenic designer for another husband-and-wife management, this time almost as far from the West End as it was possible to get without actually falling off England's Atlantic extremity: the Pavilion Theatre at Penzance. It was, and remains, a large and rather hideous building facing the promenade, flanked by a pair of ill-proportioned towers, its principal feature a glass-walled tearoom stretching the full width of the front. Closed during the winter months, the tearoom's windows grew opaque with sea salt, while those of us who had to use the room for rehearsals gently froze. Behind this bleak frontage the theater was relatively comfortable, in a style best defined as 1930s art cheapo. The stage was shallow and had no space for flying large scenery. Most of the flats, windows, balustrades, and so forth were stored beneath the stage, making passage from one side to the other more than a little difficult for the cast, some of whose dressing rooms were on one side and some on the other.

As scenic designer I also found myself responsible for the company's costumes, and with the help of an equally new assistant stage manager, Delia Paton, I spent my second afternoon on the job cataloging the contents of several wicker baskets filled with aging costumes. Worn countless times by people of the wrong sizes, the dresses and doublets were patched and split, and cotton hose ended in feet as hard as boards. Capulet caps and Mistress Shore gowns had lost half their sequins, while ruffs caked with old greasepaint seemed to have been slept in by mice. The lifting of each creaking basket lid released a sickening smell of damp, making the cataloging process in the small room to the right of the stage a memorably unpleasant chore. At about four in the afternoon I suggested that we should quit and go up into the town for tea—which we did.

Barely had Delia poured the first cup than we heard the clanging of fire-engine bells as the brigade raced through Penzance en route to some unfortunate's blaze.

"Let's hope it isn't the theater," I said.

But it was. When we returned we found the engines in the parking lot and the firemen dragging their hoses out of the stage door. The fire had been confined to the costume room, but had destroyed the floor and the contents of three of the baskets, and the water had done for the rest. The senior fireman made it clear that he thought it our fault. The fire, he said, had started inside one of the baskets, in which case a careless smoker had to be the culprit. Our response that neither of us had either cigarettes or matches, and that we both were so broke that we could not afford to smoke if we had wanted to, left the irritated officer without a suspect. Another fireman suggested that a glass jar standing on the small windowsill might have served as a burning glass focusing the sun's rays onto the front of one of the baskets. That seemed a rather unconvincing explanation, for the sun's angle was wrong and the afternoon intermittently cloudy.

That night, when the cast returned for the evening performance, I learned that several members believed the theater to be the home of a poltergeist. Since poltergeist activity is commonly claimed to be associated with children or adolescents, there was speculation that the malicious spirit had its host in a pimply and rather simple youth employed on the electrical staff.

About three weeks later, returning to the empty theater at about the same time we had left on the day of the fire, I smelled burning emanating from somewhere to the right of the stage. There were two rooms on that side, a large girls' dressing room and the gutted costume store. The latter had two doors, one opening into the dressing room and the other onto the stage-side corridor. Finding nothing amiss in the dressing room, I opened the corridor door to the store and found a blue haze of smoke spread across the charred joists rising to about six inches above floor level. There was no sign of flame or any other evidence of the fire's source, and so I decided that rather than put in a false alarm to the fire brigade, I had best call the manager on the house phone. By the time I got back to the room the smoke had gone, and the only lingering smell came from the charred floor timbers.

There could be no denying that some very odd things happened at the Pavilion Theatre, but whether some were real and others not is hard to say. Theatrical people are notoriously superstitious, and anything allegedly supernatural can be relied on to be embellished to attract attention or create a dramatic effect. Thus, for example, the manager was said to have had his coattails sharply tugged while leaving the bar after turning the lights out. He also reportedly received numerous phone calls from backstage when he alone was in the locked building. Stage crewmen playing cards one Saturday night were said to have watched a milk bottle move down the table. Throughout the autumn, however, apart from the fire and smoke, my experiences were limited to finding lights on and a door unlocked after securing the building for the night—and to a missing hammer that unaccountably reappeared on the stage in the second act of a play whose props did not call for it.

The 1948 season ended on December 27 with what was billed as a "Grand Pantomime based on The Sweetest story of all," to wit: *Cinderella*. Mercifully, the theater closed during the week before Christmas while the company rehearsed, and while I and an assistant frantically painted five vast backcloths and the rest of seven sets that ranged from "The Green by Hardup Hall," to Prince Goldenheart's castle ballroom. In addition, I was to play the King of the Demons, or as irreverent members of the cast called him, "Kemon Ding."

In the immediate postwar years, English theatrical versions of familiar fairy stories retained an almost superstitiously preserved format dating back to the mid-nineteenth century—providing psychology students with material for innumerable theses. The Principal Boy was a girl (often of advanced age) who wound up winning the hand of the heroine; the Dame was a man liable to be married to or wooed by another man, the wicked baron; and the Fairy Queen and Demon King, the sparring representatives of good and evil, watched over all this superficially good, clean fun.

Tradition required that the gossamer-clad Fairy Queen always entered and exited at stage right, while the Demon King entered in a puff of smoke at stage center, preferably through a trap door. There being no trap, I was to enter by stepping through the curtains while covered by the smoke. To exit I was to leap off stage left in another puff of smoke, the leap giving the impression of flight. Or so it was planned.

Attired in red doublet, black cloak, and a rubber bathing cap equipped with cardboard ears and horns of my own design, I was supposed to scare the stuffing out of every child in the audience with my demonic laugh and a speech that ended with my demand to

> Let the fairies work in vain,
> I am king and I shall reign.
> Holding sway in woe and pain,
> Till the world be mine again.

Big cackle, puff of smoke, and balletic leap into the wings to be caught by assistant stage manager.

The electrician, unfortunately, had either his wires or his cues backward, and on opening night heralded my entrance by igniting the stage-left flash powder first—to the puzzled surprise of both audience and Kemon Ding. By the time I was halfway though my thunder and lightning doggerel, most of the house realized what had happened and gleefully waited to see what would happen when I departed. Demon King leaps off left; puff of smoke stage center; roar of laughter from supposedly terrified children out front.

Still smarting from the laugh that accompanied my first exit, I was enraged to stand in the wing as the opening scene progressed and see the backdrop wiggling. Before the dress rehearsal I had explained to the cast that the big opening scene on "The Green by Hardup Hall" made use of the full stage, its countryside backcloth being so close to the real wall that no room remained for anyone to pass behind it. Consequently, dancers entering from stage left had to be in place before the show started. Certain that the wiggling was caused by someone squeezing along behind it, I waited to pour a stream of Demon King invective in the ear of whoever emerged. But nobody did. The edge of the cloth shivered, and that was that.

The possible poltergeist made one more appearance. The show's first half was to end with the entrance of the magic coach that would carry Cinderella to the ball, a spectacular moment of enchantment and audience bedazzlement. Our fairy coach was made out of a small pony cart, embellished with plywood panels and with its downstage wheels covered with pink-painted disks fitted with sockets for several dozen lightbulbs. Illuminated by a shaft of limelight aimed from a booth above the audience, the effect would be, if not spectacular, at least pleasantly pretty. To provide this level of illumination, a special electrical line had been run into the projection booth, a line whose terminals were firmly secured to the lamp housing by means of a U-clamp bolted at both ends. Came the big moment. Out trundled the coach trailing its electrical cable, its lights modestly atwinkle, but from the projection booth came nothing. In the subsequent post-mortem, the electrician apologetically explained that just as he was to power up the limelight, the line fell out of its clamp and dropped to the floor.

Had he missed his cue and offered this incredible explanation to hide his mistake? He had been sharp enough at rehearsals. Did a draft create the slow ripple behind the backcloth? It was never repeated. Indeed, to my knowledge, until *Cinderella* closed on January 8, 1949, nothing more could be blamed on the poltergeist. Whether it left when we did, whether it again made its presence felt when another company moved in, and whether it existed at all are questions for which I have no answer. And thirty-six years later, my inquiring letters to the Pavilion's manager and the captain of the Penzance Fire Brigade went unanswered.

That a production as surefire as a traditional pantomime could only draw an audience for eleven days and nineteen performances further dramatized the declining appeal of live theater in provincial Britain in the postwar years.

My thespian career, too, was over. I had begun it as a frog footman and ended as a demon king. Although the realization would take several months to take hold, I had painted my last backcloth and lit my last set. Things were tough and getting worse. I knew that. But I was convinced that I had learned at first-hand what I needed to become a successful playwright. To prove it, I still had my letter from Alec Clunes, the letter I'd read a hundred times:

> I should like you to know that both my readers and myself regard [your play] as considerable evidence of promise and we should like to encourage you to send us anything else that you may write. . . . As an exercise in play-writing based on "Maya" it is very good indeed. . . . Go on writing, you've got something to give to this.

All I needed was time.

BEING PENNILESS and out of work anywhere, at any time, is not a good idea, but being broke and jobless in London in January had nothing whatever to commend it. Openings for stage staff were nonexistent. The Christmas shows were still running, and few repertory companies or touring productions would be hiring before March. Always too impoverished to afford union dues, I had failed to join Equity, and now found that film companies were no longer willing to hire nonunion bit-part players. For the same reason, I had failed to keep up my National Insurance payments and so had insufficient stamps on my card to draw the dole. Nevertheless, I still had my warm and comfortable room in Bentinck Street and a generous degree of forbearance on the part of Mrs. Winter.

Throughout the Penzance autumn I had earned eight pounds a week, of which sixteen shillings went to the agent who got me the job, two pounds, fifteen shillings for Penzance lodging, and three pounds to Mrs. Winter for an empty room. It took only minimal math to realize that this left less than two pounds for meals, laundry, insurance, and everything else. Even an apprentice financial counselor would instantly light on Bentinck Street as an unaffordable expense, yet without it I would have returned to London with nowhere to live and with no phone number on the agents' books. Psychologically, however, the good address contributed to my problems. It perpetuated and nourished the Victorian beliefs taught me by my mother. A gentleman is a gentleman and must never forget it, no matter how impoverished his circumstances. Never must he compromise his ideals, for by these he retains the respect of the working classes. His employment, therefore, can only be in the professions, never in trade.

In postwar Britain none of this made sense. Nevertheless, I saw Bentinck Street and my tenuous membership in the theatrical profession as being true to the creed, and could not bring myself to break ranks by seeking a job in trade.

Each morning, therefore, I read the employment ads in the *Daily Telegraph* (it came with the breakfast) in case some international company was offering the kind of socially acceptable job that the Central Hanover Bank had given my father in those stock-soaring days before the Crash. The truth, however, was that had such a job been offered, I had grown too shabby to win it.

My old girlfriend from Aylesbury, Bobby Bartmann, came twice to my financial rescue, once tactfully lending me money in the guise of buying my radio—which she then let me borrow. In spite of this and other such kindnesses from friends, my situation was growing desperate as my health unraveled. Something, therefore, had to be done, and done quickly. Among my assets was a letter from the Aylesbury impresario Bill Stephens:

> First of all let me thank you for your extreme loyalty and your part in making The New Market Theatre an artistic success.
>
> No words of mine can ever repay you for these things. If ever I can help in any way in the future you have only to call on me.

Perhaps by now, I thought, Bill's situation might have improved and a new company could be in the offing. In any case, a letter could do no harm.

By return, he telephoned to say that he was, indeed, thinking about starting a new company, and if I would come up and stay with him for a few days, we could work on it together. He mentioned that he was thinking of opening thirteen miles away at Leighton Buzzard, where I had stage-managed eighteen months earlier. The news was almost too good to be true, and I promptly took the next train north.

I found Bill looking older than I remembered, but buoyant as ever, and bubbling with plans to turn his Aylesbury dreams into reality in the Leighton Buzzard Corn Exchange. Neither of us mentioned the obvious truth that the building was an assembly hall, and a bleak one at that, and not to be compared with his beloved New Market Theatre. Instead, we read plays and discussed casting and equipment while I built a cardboard model of the Corn Exchange stage. Meanwhile, Bill's wife, Kathy, fed me nourishing foods which I suspect they could ill afford. After two weeks as their guest, I was told by Bill that we had completed all the preparation that was needed until he had his backers on the hook, and that he would be in touch with me just as soon as he had any news. So back I went to London, and never heard from Bill Stephens again. In retrospect, I suspect that the Leighton Buzzard plan was no more than a charade allowing him to pay his debt to me in the only currency bankruptcy allowed—in soup, and cake, and kindness.

My two weeks in the country had done wonders for my health. Bill had made it clear that I should not turn down other opportunities while waiting for Leighton Buzzard to materialize. But the other opportunities were elusive. At about this time my mother wrote to my father asking whether he could help me find a career outside the theater, thus orchestrating our first meeting since I handed him his ties on the day he left us at Hans Place.

Through the intervening seventeen years my father's fortunes would have been as uncertain as my own had it not been for a loving wife and son to support him and provide a castle of confidence behind whose drawbridge he could shelter. A much-loved figure at his club and around the Stock Exchange, my father waited Micawber-like for something to turn up. His honesty and his social graces had earned him his American job, and these attributes remained his trademark through the lean years, a trademark recognized and appreciated by the directors of a company that owned an iron foundry in Wolverhampton and planned to make a fortune out of scrap metal salvaged from the battlefields of Europe. My father had been made a partner, and since 1947 had run the London office, a task that involved surprisingly little—which was just as well since he knew nothing about scrap iron or foundries.

My first meeting with my father was awkward at best. He made it clear that while he felt an obligation to do what he could for me, he had no intention of allowing my mother to use me as a lever to intrude into his family life. Furthermore, he considered the theater a frivolous and potentially disastrous occupation, and would not help me unless I renounced it. If I agreed to do so, he could offer me an apprenticeship in the Wolverhampton ironworks. It would mean starting at the bottom, but given time I would learn the business and move into management.

I had never been to Wolverhampton, but I had seen enough pictures of industrial towns and their grim-faced inhabitants to know that this was an offer I had to refuse. I suspect that my father was more relieved than surprised when I did so. Shortly afterward the company's other directors were arrested in Austria and jailed for black marketeering, and once again he was no more gainfully employed than was I.

Had Bobby Bartmann taken the radio I sold her, my future, whatever it was, would have been very different, and I would not be writing this book. Instead, she left it with me, which gave me the opportunity to hear a talk on the BBC by Robin Green, a London auxiliary fireman who had fallen into the Thames on the night in December 1940 when the City burned, and surfaced clutching a broken clay tobacco pipe. He was describing his recent ramblings along the river's foreshore, where at low tide he could pick up coins, jewelry, cutlery, and countless other relics from the two thousand years of London's history. He mentioned, too, that he had deposited part of his collection at the City of London's Guildhall Museum.

If Robin Green could do it, so could I! Besides, what better way could there be of passing time than spending it treasure hunting? Time was my principal asset. Much of it was spent writing plays that ran out of plot somewhere in the second act. To try to improve my understanding of human character and behavior, I became a familiar face in the public galleries of the Old Bailey and the Law Courts. For the aspiring novelist or playwright there can be no better education. Furthermore, the Old Bailey trials offered the best free show in town. The Law Courts' dockets, on the other hand, tended to be less dramatic and often downright boring, dealing as they often did with tangled commercial and monetary skullduggery. But they, too, had much to teach a young writer about the way people react under stress.

Through the spring and early summer of 1949, my fruitless rounds of the theatrical agents were interspersed with hours in the courts and, when the tide was down, walking the muddy strands between Queenhithe Dock and Cannon Street Bridge on the river's north bank, and between Southwark and London bridges on the south. In spite of the bombing, these sections of the waterfront had changed little since Gustave Doré drew them and Dickens and Mayhew wrote about them in the mid-nineteenth century. The Victorian, six-story brick warehouses along Upper Thames Street still smelled of spices, could still swing their wooden cranes out over the river to off-load bales of furs from Hudson's Bay, chests of tea from India, cotton from Egypt, and nutmeg and mace from the Molucca islands, the exotic aroma of the spices sweetening the stench of river mud. On winter afternoons, as yellow fog crept in from the water to girdle the buildings, one could still hear the occasional dray-drawn cart clattering over cobbles, the creaking of ropes, and high above, the echoing cough of an ailing warehouseman. But in the limited visibility allowed by the fog, the alleyways were deserted save for the occasional brown rat scuttling home, hugging the warehouse wall. In such a setting, a barking dog easily conjured up the cudgel-carrying shadow of Bill Sikes, and a woman's hurrying footsteps could only be those of the fleeing Nancy. Although Thames Street ghosts might take

Dickensian shape, they were also the incarnation of a terrible reality described in 1851 by Henry Mayhew.

> There is another class who may be termed river-finders, although their occupation is connected only with the shore; they are commonly known by the name of "mud-larks," from being compelled, in order to obtain the articles they seek, to wade sometimes up to their middle through the mud left on the shore by the retiring tide. . . . They may be seen of all ages, from mere childhood to positive decrepitude, crawling among the barges at the various wharfs along the river.

By the mid-twentieth century, except in the recessed docks, the Thames foreshore had become less muddy than in Mayhew's day, and although soft spots remained where one could sink to the knees, much of the frontage was strewn with brick rubble and the trash of centuries, built up here and there with platforms of chalk known as "hards" on which the barges rested. Exercising a modicum of caution, a latter-day river-finder could walk the shore without getting mud above the welts of his shoes. The danger lay in becoming too engrossed in the hunt, getting trapped by a rapidly rising tide, and, while wading to safety, floundering into rather than skirting the tricky bits, as more than once I discovered to my cost.

For at least a year, Robin Green and his cohorts made mud-larking a weekend sport, and being first in, they had found more and better objects than would be discovered until the advent of the unsportsmanlike metal detector. Nevertheless, I had more time to devote to the river than did Green, and three and four days a week, passing policemen would find me waiting for the tide to uncover the first yards of shore, and see me still there as the last of it went under once again.

Beneath the relatively stable rubble surface stretched many feet of mud accumulated through the centuries, and suspended in the mud were countless objects, whether deliberately thrown there, dumped down the privy shoots that overhung the water as late as the nineteenth century, lost overboard from capsized boats, or, more recently, tossed from London, Southwark, and Blackfriars' bridges. There were coins for luck, finger rings for love denied, a typewriter— evidence, perhaps, of incrimination—and maybe, in the case of a portable bus stop sign, of inebriation. Most of my treasures were smaller than that, and a good day's haul would fit neatly into a can for throat lozenges. Among them were pewter badges from the caps of medieval pilgrims, marbles of uncertain age, Elizabethan children's pottery dogs, Georgian dollhouse plates and cups in pewter, lead seals from seventeenth- and eighteenth-century textiles. The variety seemed inexhaustible: buttons in brass and pewter, tobacco pipes, wig curlers, glass seals from wine bottles, and the most obvious prizes—coins, coins of every age from the Roman consul Agrippa who died in 12 BC through to lucky pennies donated to the river days or even minutes before I retrieved them. Like a magic cookie jar, the river seemed never to tire of sneaking its treasures to the surface.

As the tide receded, leaving a patch of black mud glistening between the brickbats, you could see the shapes of coins, seals, buckles. and so forth, their forms visible yet softened by a thin film of silt. One by one you'd winkle them out until the patch was barren. Tomorrow the patch might yield nothing, or the next day, or the next, but the day after that there'd be more coins, more buttons, more toys. In one area of no more than two square yards, and over a period of eighteen months, I found thirty-three coins dating between 1673 and 1700, but never more than one at a time—a single silver sixpence, three halfpennies, and twenty-nine farthings. When I got greedy and attacked the patch with a trowel and a sieve, it gave me nothing; yet a week later, there'd be another coin, and the next day another.

Treasure hunting has to be among man's oldest addictions, and something for nothing one of his greatest joys. But neither mud-larking nor listening in the courts to other people's problems did anything to alleviate mine. Hopes that theatrical companies planning summer seasons would be scrambling for my services dimmed as April slipped into May, and save for the lifesaving interlude with Bill and Kathy Stephens, not so much as an interview had come my way. All the time, however, I kept on writing, pounding my typewriter until the shredded ribbon barely marked the paper. In one of my brief associations with frayed fringe theaters (I forget which one) I had met Pamela Grieve, a forceful lady in her thirties with the somewhat alarming appearance of an ATS drill sergeant. In the spring of 1949, we got together to write the kind of mindless farce that West End audiences loved and that we were convinced the few surviving repertory managements would perform for years to come.

In essence *House to Haunt* was a 1920s Edgar Wallace thriller played for laughs, and though set in the contemporary postwar era, its characters had not made it past 1939. Nevertheless, the writing of it meant a weekly visit to Pam's apartment in South Kensington, where we would compare notes—and where she would feed me.

Pam was undeniably a sensible person, even if she gave her sound advice as though issuing company orders. I should stop fooling about and take a proper job that would keep me while we both struggled to make our way as playwrights. "Keep on the way you're going and you won't be capable of writing anything," she said. And I knew she was right.

To preserve the peace between us, I looked more carefully through the *Daily Telegraph*'s employment opportunities, and lighted on an ad for a young man of engaging appearance willing to enter a training program for marketing paper. Since the company was located adjacent to my river haunt by Southwark Bridge, I thought the omens might favor me. Fortunately, they didn't. It took the interviewer just long enough to discover that I was "one of them theatricals" to convince himself that I had no future in paper.

Had I been straight out of school, or just out of the army, a perceptive recruiter might have recognized my promise; but with my most recent employment experience defined as Demon King, my strong points were hard to pin down. In any case, I had no more desire to become a paper salesman than to be a tea boy in an iron foundry. When I left the office I found the tide falling and so returned to the river and its marvelous ability to enable me to blot out reality and focus solely on whether something splendid awaited me beneath this brickbat or wedged between those lumps of chalk.

Although Mrs. Winter's breakfasts stoked me up for my morning trek through the West End to the Old Bailey or on to Queenhithe, the long walk back without lunch or prospects of supper became increasingly exhausting. Luckily, I had been able to gain access to a small patch of shore beside Billingsgate fish market, a stretch not previously milked by Robin Green, and there I found numerous coins, including several fine examples that must have been tossed by the Romans from their first London Bridge. But more desirable to me at this time were the much more recent coins, half crowns, shillings, and sixpences from the reigns of Victoria to George V, and all still legal tender. A sixpence promised a bus ride home, and half a crown a dinner. That some of them landed with a dull leadlike thud when inadvertently dropped had, I decided, more to do with my imperfect hearing than the quality of the silver. Handed over to a harried bus conductor collecting fares in the rush hour, a river half crown readily turned into a ticket, and two shillings in change acceptable to even the fussiest café cashier.

As one tiptoes through the graveyard of one's life, it is tempting to assume a posture of cautious reverence, but that squalid episode marked the low point of mine, and no veil can hide its ugliness. Although to explain is not to excuse,

I can only say that when one is hungry, principles are easily swallowed. How many of the coins were genuine and how many were duds, I have no idea. It is certain that forgeries there were on the Billingsgate foreshore, for several that had been detected by honest fishmongers and been deliberately mutilated before being thrown into the river. Fortunately for my conscience (if not for my health), the supply quickly ran out, with no replacements creeping to the surface to replenish the stock. Thus did the river god save me from a life of larceny.

After several weeks of collecting a wide range of objects I could not identify, I followed again in Robin Green's footsteps and took my treasures to the City of London's Guildhall Museum, where I was kindly received by its keeper (another word for curator), Adrian Oswald. This would prove to be one of my life's most felicitous encounters. Short, balding, and round-faced with a somewhat untidy moustache, he was an immensely engaging man who invariably wore a dusty blue suit and managed to deposit extraordinary quantities of cigarette ash down his waistcoat. I found him in a small, cluttered office tucked beneath the stairs of the Guildhall Library, a room he shared with his assistant. Cramped though it was, Adrian explained, the little room was a notable improvement over his previous quarters, which had doubled as a cloakroom for the library's staff. From such small favors the Guildhall Museum drew its life force, and it had been forever thus.

Since I was destined to spend the next seven years under its roof, the history and geography of the place were important to me and so have a place in these pages.

In 1826 the Court of Common Council had ordered the library committee "to consider the propriety of providing a suitable place for the reception of such antiquities relating to the City of London and suburbs, as may be procured or presented to this Corporation." Shortly thereafter, a room was set aside to house artifacts salvaged from public works excavations in the City, and in 1872 when the library opened its handsome new building abutting the fifteenth-century Guildhall, the museum moved to larger quarters, albeit in the basement.

As at most London museums, the autumn of 1939 had seen the Guildhall collections packed up and shipped away to safety in the country, specifically to the Russell family home at Swallowfield Park in Berkshire. When the collections returned in 1946, they found their basement museum usurped by the library, whose staff had no intention of shifting its valuable books to make way for a collection of old pots. Part of Guildhall's 1411–25 crypt had been assigned to the museum in 1910, and in it large relics such as Roman stone sarcophagi and bits of pillars were displayed. Although the crypts had survived the 1940 fire that consumed all but the building's outer walls, the large architectural and funereal artifacts were still there. Several of the sarcophagi had been damaged and had become repositories for garbage left behind when the crypt was used as a kitchen for civic banquets, sharing the space with several large iron stoves that, when not in use, served as residences for rats. In short, the Guildhall Museum had fallen on very hard times.

Some of the museum's returned collections were stored in sagging cardboard boxes in Adrian Oswald's office, but the bulk were housed in top-floor rooms in the Guildhall's late eighteenth-century front, which miraculously had survived the fire. At the same attic level, the museum also had the use of a large room that served as a laboratory—though any scientist would have had difficulty recognizing it as such. The roof leaked, and its artifact-washing sinks had only cold-water pipes, which froze in winter. Three space heaters were expected to both dry the washed artifacts and warm the room, and any boiling of lye or other chemicals was done on an ancient gas ring otherwise used to heat the tea kettle. At one end of the room an interior door bore the stenciled instruction "Messengers Only," to which someone had prefixed "Heavenly"; the door, which once led to the attic of the adjacent art gallery, now opened into space. The gallery had gone in the 1940 fire and so, across the yard, had the Church of St. Lawrence Jewry. The collapse of its steeple had expelled the sparks that helped ignite the Great Hall's roof. From the lab door one had a spectacular view over the gutted church and across the battered city to St. Paul's Cathedral, but that was about all that could be said for the museum's sole working facility.

Thanks to Adrian Oswald's persistence, the museum did sport a temporary exhibit gallery, a wide corridor-like room known as the Bridge which before the war had been the office shared by the young Oswald and his superior, the museum clerk, Quentin Waddington. In those days, and indeed in the postwar years, the head of the library took the dual title of librarian and curator, though none who held it had any museum experience. As the title museum clerk suggests, Waddington's role was seen as that of a scribe who was required to do little more than enter new acquisitions in a ledger as a library clerk would accession books.

The museum and archaeological professions have enjoyed (or tolerated) more than their fair share of eccentrics, and Quentin Waddington was one of them. He was sixty-eight when Adrian first met him, still vigorously coupling the pedantry of an ex-schoolmaster with the drive of a zealot. Forever frustrated by the museum's lack of space and money, Waddington devoted part of his time to what Adrian described as "interminable cataloging," while sharing the rest between writing a weekly column on London antiquities for the *Evening News* and making regular sorties onto City construction sites in search of new acquisitions. Adrian accompanied him on these expeditions and remembered them well:

He was about 5 feet 10 inches in height, but looked less as his very broad shoulders were somewhat bowed. He had white hair a little thin on top, broad forehead, a somewhat narrow face with a prominent nose. . . . Once or twice a week he would issue forth walking at high speed carrying a large wicker bag (he got them from fishmongers in Leadenhall Market) and descended on any active building site, returning with what he could get from foreman or worker, never spending more than a pound and usually reckoning in shillings (I think he frequently used his own slender resources). Often he could gain no access to the site owing to hostility, mainly from foremen keen to get on with the job, and so had to meet workmen in their lunch break round the corner.

Unfortunately for the City's museum, Waddington was not the only customer for what the workmen found. Years before, he had had a formidable rival in G. F. Lawrence, known to every London navvy as "Stoney Jack." In the 1920s Lawrence had held the post of inspector of excavations on behalf of the competing London Museum, which was located uptown at Lancaster House and was far better known and financed than the poverty-stricken Guildhall Museum. For a while Lawrence coupled his museum responsibilities with running a shop that specialized in London antiquities, a duality that could hardly avoid raising the specter of conflicting interests, a problem that may have been in the minds of the museum's trustees in 1926 when they abolished the job and sent Stoney Jack into early retirement.

Adrian Oswald's father, Felix, after a distinguished career as a geologist (he mapped the geology of Armenia in 1898), later focused his analytical attention on the Roman-period pottery called *terra sigillata,* and thus became a legendary figure in the history of Roman archaeology in Britain. Felix Oswald was the pioneer in cataloging potters' names stamped on the red-gloss pottery, and his researches remain a cornerstone for the dating of Roman sites. While still a boy of sixteen or seventeen, Adrian had assisted his father in this work, yet at first he did not gravitate to a career in archaeology. Instead, he took a post in Uganda as an assistant district commissioner, probably inspired by his father's work in 1910 in southwest Kenya, where he found the Miocene fossil deposits later made famous by the Leakey family's discovery of early humanoid remains. Adrian's African career was less spectacular. Racked by malaria and without a job, he went home in 1932 to a Britain in the grip of the Depression. One temporary job followed another, until, with no prior experience, he landed a contract with the Ancient Monuments department of the Ministry of Works to excavate a Roman villa at Norton Disney in Lincolnshire. With that behind him, and aided by his father's illustrious name, he earned a thin living as a lecturer at the University College of Nottingham (no audience, no pay), before being taken on by Waddington at the princely salary of five pounds a week.

After serving in the army throughout the war, Oswald returned to find life in the Guildhall Museum even worse than before. The museum existed only in name and in the presence of Waddington, who, though retitled assistant curator, had little to do and declined to start it until he had completed the *Times* crossword puzzle, which on tough days took him until 4:30 in the afternoon. For Adrian such lethargy was vastly frustrating, as was Waddington's lack of interest in seeing the collections as catalysts toward reconstructing the life of Roman and later London. Had Waddington not dropped dead while walking home from the train station in 1948, Adrian claimed that he would have resigned and gone back into the army. Instead, he stayed to take possession of the shoes he had, in fact, been wearing for three years.

If Adrian had indeed rejoined the army before I turned up with my boxes of river treasures, my future would have been very different. Instead, I like to think that he saw in me the mirror of his own youth, and in my penury the memory of silent lecture rooms and empty pockets. From the museum's slender resources (and I suspect from his own funds) Adrian helped me by buying some of my artifacts for the museum. There was precedent for so doing, for the Library Committee had recently authorized the purchase of the entire Robin Green collection at a figure which, to me, seemed astronomical. Nevertheless, I was pathetically grateful for the few shillings that Adrian was able to give me.

The acres of vacant lots created by the Luftwaffe's bombs offered unparalleled opportunities for archaeological study as well as for inspired city planning. Both were missed, though limited test excavations were conducted under the aegis of a committee named the Roman and Medieval London Excavation Council, which was formed in 1947 and funded largely by private donations amounting to about £2,600 a year, which, alas, did not go very far. Although the work was to focus within the area administered by the Corporation of London, the latter's enthusiasm for its past could be measured by the size of its contribution: by the end of 1948, it had donated only a miserly £250 to the excavation council's war chest of £6,000 9s. 9d.

Some idea of what was then thought important in London archaeology was revealed by the council's first title: the Roman London Excavation Committee. Under pressure from Adrian Oswald and several others, the designation was expanded to take in the medieval period—while still hurrying past the most recent four centuries of the city's history.

The council's praiseworthy goal was to dig at least one trench through the ground beneath every bombed site before any new buildings went up. In reality, it completed only a tiny part of this mission because the work was done by no more than half a dozen paid laborers and a handful of student volunteers, one of whom was Audrey Baines. William F. Grimes, who had conducted the Sutton Hoo excavations, was now both keeper of the London Museum and director of the council's excavations. In the intervening years, Grimes had risen from the ranks of the muddy to wear the uniform of a museum chieftain: white shirt, black suit, shining shoes, and white handkerchief neatly displayed in the breast pocket, and it was thusly attired that he directed his London excavations. It was not, needless to say, what is today termed "hands-on" direction, and much time was wasted "waiting for Grimes." Nor did his excavations pay much attention to reading the artifacts to determine where they belonged in time. By arrangement with the Guildhall Museum, the bags of unwashed material were to be delivered there for processing and analysis by the council's honorary secretary, Adrian Oswald. But in the absence of anyone to wash or repair Grimes's artifacts, most of them were stored away on attic shelves exactly as they came into the museum. How to properly interpret what the trenches were revealing, and how to write even interim reports, remained a puzzle.

At this same time, the enormous task of rebuilding the City was beginning, which meant that for the first time since 1939 there were to be construction sites from which artifacts should be salvaged, a responsibility that Adrian had inherited from Waddington. The first of them, however, was not in the City proper, but across the river in the Borough of Southwark and theoretically the responsibility of the London County Council. But because the LCC had only one quasi archaeologist (his training was in architecture) to watch over the whole of Greater London, and because Southwark had been part of the Roman and medieval city, Adrian had agreed to keep an eye on the project.

The site for the Bankside Power Station, he quickly discovered, demanded more than an eye. Vast gangs of laborers and massed machinery tore into an area of several city blocks. Almost as soon as they started, they uncovered two medieval boats and pilings for adjacent jetties, all of which were torn out before they could be properly studied and recorded. Even as this project was beginning, another opened up to the west of the City in Farringdon Street. More threatened.

From bringing in my river artifacts, I had progressed to spending several hours a week up in the lab washing some of Grimes's artifacts, and so it came as no great surprise when Adrian asked whether I would be willing to help him monitor the progress at Bankside and, no less important, to help haul home the artifacts—which we often did in coal sacks on our backs, the city fathers having provided its museum with no transportation. In the days of Waddington and Stoney Jack, the Guildhall and London museums had begged and bought only the obviously good stuff, such as the well-preserved metal objects from the silt beside the river and the relatively intact pottery from sewers and cesspits. The objects stood alone, speaking for themselves, robbed of any association one to another or of any time sequence. In 1949 antiquarian collecting and archaeology had ceased to be synonymous, and Adrian Oswald was by experience (if not by formal training) an archaeologist. The pretty object was no longer king; where it came from was as important to him as what it was or how complete it remained. A hundred related fragments were more valuable than a dozen complete pots from nowhere in particular—and a lot more difficult to transport.

The hours of pot washing had done little to dent the enormous load of accumulated artifacts from Grimes's excavations, but for me no time was more rewardingly spent—thanks to Adrian's willingness to teach me to recognize the wares of different periods, and to know whether I was washing a shard from the base of a cooking pot or the rim of a ewer. Before long I was seeing beyond the fragments to the whole vessel and thence to the world in which they were made and used. At the same time, Adrian taught me the basic rules of archaeological reasoning. They were (and still remain) as follows:

1. The ground is made up from an accumulation of layers, each deposited at some time after (but never before) the manufacture date of the most recent artifact it contains.
2. You peel the layers back one at a time, the last in being the first to come out.

Was it really possible, I asked myself, that archaeology could be rooted in nothing more mystic than common sense? If so, why could I not become an archaeologist?

My childhood benefactor John Redfern had given me the answer. Archaeology was an avocation not a profession. And Adrian Oswald reiterated it. There were virtually no jobs for archaeologists as such, and most people who earned a living in the antiquarian field did it as members of the staffs of museums. So how could I get a job in a museum?

The approved route was first to study for the diploma of the Museums Association. But a visit to the association's offices was not encouraging. If I had a university degree I could be enrolled for the diploma course. Alternatively, I would be eligible if I already had a museum job. Although Joseph Heller had yet to define Catch-22, it already had me firmly in its grip. The Museums Association interviewer suggested that since my interest was in archaeology, I should try for a diploma at the University of London's Institute of Archaeology. So I did—and got much the same answer. For me, as John Redfern had foretold, archaeology could be no more than a hobby, or so it seemed in the summer of 1949.

Through those months I was spending more and more time helping Adrian Oswald and less and less making the rounds of the theatrical agents, and worse, I was paying too little attention to Pam Grieve and the play that was to make our fortunes. The river still beckoned, however, for its trove continued to enable Oswald to pay me small sums for the work I was doing. In retrospect, my behavior was totally irresponsible, content as I was to live from day to day while going ever deeper into debt to the long-suffering Mrs. Winter.

Although Adrian Oswald had been brought up by a father whose later life's work focused solely on the Roman period, his own interests had been unexpectedly thrust into another time period by a chance discovery on a London building site in the summer of 1939. Workmen digging foundation holes for an extension to Barclays Bank in Gracechurch Street broke into a cellar containing a hoard of glassware and other artifacts dating from the first half of the seventeenth century. It was the most dramatic discovery of its period since a jeweler's stock had been found in Cheapside in 1912. Most of the glass was shattered and of little interest to the laborers as marketable loot, and so Adrian was able to salvage most of it and get it back to the museum for repair and study. But war would soon break out, and before he could do either, the fragments were packed up and sent into hiding along with the rest of the collections. Upon his return late in 1945, Adrian set to work on the collection now known as the Gracechurch Street Hoard, and thus focused his interest on the seventeenth century.

Two years later, one of the first of the Roman and Medieval London Excavation Council's sites straddled the City's medieval ditch at Cripplegate, a ditch kept relatively clean through the Middle Ages but a repository for Londoners' garbage in the seventeenth century. The layers from which Grimes's workmen retrieved this refuse provided a valuable chronological sequence—if only one had the wit to date the most recent artifact that each contained. Up to this time, however, no archaeologist had shown any interest in systematizing the dating of such recent trash, and although museums contained fine Elizabethan and Stuart objects, their curators lacked enthusiasm for broken kitchen crockery, shattered bottles, or old clay pipes. Yet these were signposts on which archaeologists would have to rely if they were to know where they were in time as they dug down into the City ditch.

As Adrian Oswald explained it to me, just as on Roman sites his father's work on *terra sigillata* potters' marks made it possible to determine the approximate date when a new shape became popular or a new manufacturer got started, so by associating initials molded on tobacco pipes with those of pipe makers named in parish and other records, it should be possible to provide the same kind of information for the seventeenth, eighteenth, and nineteenth centuries. From the hundreds littering the Thames foreshore, I had already discovered that pipe bowls exhibited a distinct evolution in both size and shape. But for such knowledge to be archaeologically useful one had to know when those changes took place.

Although Oswald would be the first to publish a scholarly paper on the evolution of the English tobacco pipe, and thus to emulate his father as an archaeological trailblazer, he was by no means the first to recognize that clay pipes had something to tell us. In August 1935, across the Atlantic in Virginia, excavations were in progress on the site of seventeenth-century Jamestown, and there (like Oswald a decade later) the archaeologist J. Summerfield Day was speculating that "if research will result in the identification of the manufacturers of these pipes . . . a fair idea of the date of occupancy of the site where they were found will be gained."

Excavations at Jamestown had been in progress off and on from 1934 to 1942, yet there had been little, if any, cross-fertilization between the American and British archaeologists, presumably because nobody in Britain was specializing in that period. Be that as it may, Adrian Oswald's study of clay pipes developed independently of the American. Summerfield Day had passed out of the Jamestown picture to be replaced by Jean Carl "Pinky" Harrington, who was developing a revolutionary theory that in England at first generated more merriment than serious attention. Besides studying the evolution of bowl shapes, he was measuring the diameters of the holes through the pipes' clay stems. Like Oswald, Harrington was fated to play a key role in charting my future—but not just yet.

Through the medieval centuries the London suburb on the south bank of the Thames known as the Bankside had been what Tijuana became to Southern California, a center for every brand of dissipation. London's across-the-river red-light district known as the "stews" brought welcome revenue to the bishops of Winchester, whose land they occupied and who regulated their hours of business. Brothels doubled as taverns and vice versa, and for those who preferred gambling to gamboling there were cockpits and bearbaiting. The theaters came later: the Rose, Swan, Hope, and Globe. By the beginning of the seventeenth century, however, fun gave way to industry, and the area became a center for brewing, foundry work, dyers, glassmakers, and potters. It was the legacy of these last that was being so richly revealed in August 1949 as bomb-created ruins were dug out to make way for the Bankside Power Station.

Two vast holes were scraped out with mechanical draglines, the sides then riveted with steel pilings, locking one into another and pounded into the clay subsoil with a steam-powered pile driver. It was in the two-foot space behind the steel wall that Adrian and I cut into the remaining banks of earth and rubbish to salvage the debris from seventeenth- and eighteenth-century delftware and brown stoneware manufacturing, a hitherto forgotten facet of the site's history. With the pile driver crashing over our heads and the sound of every blow reverberating through the growing steel wall, Adrian shouted his lessons on stratigraphy and the art of archaeological recording. All too frequently our undercutting of the bank to save the artifacts—coupled with vibration from the pounding—caused the dirt wall to cave in on top of us. Fortunately, the pile driving stopped at five o'clock, and after that, as our hearing returned, I was able to ask specific questions about the pottery we were finding and bundling into old cement bags and any other containers we could find around the site.

By the end of the month I must have learned enough to be left to watch and record on my own, for the Guildhall records contain my illustrated report on the project in which I was confidently identifying the wares and describing the saggers in which the delftwares and stonewares had been fired, as well as the contents of a cesspit containing three complete leather shoes and "a number of clay pipes of the period 1600–1630." In later years I would chasten students for being so imprecise. Never say "a number" or "several"! If you count six or sixty, say so! Nevertheless, in spite of its shortcomings and being written by an unpaid volunteer, the report stands as the first relatively detailed record of a post-medieval site to enter the City's archives.

While the distant Bankside site was holding our attention, another blossomed almost in sight of the museum. Spared from the fires that raged around it in 1940, Selborne House in Ironmonger Lane survived unscathed until October 6, 1944, when a flying bomb demolished all but its façade. In September 1949 its owners, the international accounting firm of Peat, Marwick, Mitchell and Company, began to rebuild, and once again it became the museum's responsibility to salvage what it could. But now there was a difference. Adrian Oswald was no longer Waddington's fish basket carrier, and no longer was it his mission to buy or scrounge disassociated goodies from the workmen. With the written cooperation of owners, architects, and builder, he had the authority to be present on the site as the work progressed, to save both information and artifacts. The other side of the coin, however, was that he had no money, no tools, and no one to help him but me—who might at any moment depart to stage-manage a distant repertory company, or be called away to assist in the production of *House to Haunt.*

That No. 11 Ironmonger Lane might yield something important had been hinted at in 1888, during demolition work at the adjacent Church of St. Olave Jewry which had revealed a Roman mosaic pavement sixteen feet below the street, as well as a stone wall whose footing had not been reached when digging ceased at a depth of twenty-four feet. Although much damaged by burials in what had once been part of the St. Olave churchyard, the site quickly yielded parts of the mosaic and introduced me to Roman archaeology—again under the tutoring hands of Adrian Oswald.

As Roman pavements go, this one wasn't up to much, nor was it of the "best" period, dating as it did to the third century AD when the shadows were lengthening at the fringes of the empire. All that survived of the floor was a section of its coarse, red-brick border and parts of four roundels containing rosettes in red, blue, yellow, and white tesserae, these last not in white marble but crumbling chalk, and the whole floor laid directly on the dirt without any cement bed to secure it. Subsequent ground pressure, coupled with the digging of graves and trash pits through it, had given the mosaic a surface of humps and valleys that did nothing for its stability. Nevertheless, we had found part of a Roman house of some importance, and I was even more firmly on the archaeological hook.

My visits to the theatrical agents were becoming increasingly sporadic and half-hearted, for I had no desire to abandon the adventure of delving into a real lost world in favor of creating new make-believe ones from paint and canvas. Besides, as my mother had so often instructed me, appearances are what count. This certainly was true when seeking jobs in the theater, and my appearance was rapidly deteriorating as the result of wear and tear on the London building sites. Having neither the clothing nor the inclination to emerge from 7 Bentinck Street and walk through the City looking like a laborer, I wore the black shoes and business suit given me by a grateful government. Already old and shiny-elbowed, brown earth and gray cement dust quickly rendered them shabbier still.

Although my father may have felt that he had done all he could for me when I turned down his offer to find me a job in darkest Wolverhampton, his door had remained, if not open, then slightly ajar. When I later told him that I was working as a volunteer at the Guildhall Museum, he saw this as a step in the right direction, for he was above all else a son of the City. Though it had done little to earn his affection, he remained confident that through his contacts there one day something wonderful would turn up. In the meantime, he worked to establish himself as the City's unpaid public relations advocate, and eventually became secretary to the City of London Society. In short, fate had set us on somewhat parallel courses, and on several occasions during the autumn of 1949 I visited his office in Bishopsgate to report progress and to receive help in placating Mrs. Winter. Awkward at first, my relationship with my father grew steadily closer, though the only surviving documentation says otherwise. In a vitriolic letter written a year later, my mother reminded him that "it was not very long ago when you were running [Ivor] down over the way he was living, and you asked me to stop his calling at your office because it let you down." I was becoming a protohippy twenty years too soon.

Had I been inclined to take stock, I would (or should) have concluded that my situation had deteriorated rather than improved. Banking on *House to Haunt* to bale me out was as realistic as winning the Irish Sweepstakes. I had been out of work in the theater so long that getting in again was now most unlikely, and with no stamps on my National Insurance card, I could get no public assistance. On the other hand, I had Adrian Oswald's friendship, and I was working long hours at something I immensely enjoyed. Although a much harder and dirtier job than being a shop assistant, and in its protracted pottery washing, a task not unlike that of a restaurant dishwasher, the work had an aura of romance and professionalism about it that made it acceptable within the limits of my mother's doctrine of what a gentleman might or might not do. But I was still broke, still went to bed hungry, and had an embarrassingly large hole in the sole of my right shoe.

"Suppose," said Adrian. "Just suppose it were possible to get you a job at the museum as my field assistant. Would you be interested?"

"Well . . ."

"Think about it. I know you're intent on a career in the theater. But this could be temporary, just until something turns up. You could be a big help," Adrian added. It was characteristic of the man that he would throw me a lifeline disguised as doing him a favor.

"Just until . . . ?"

"Something turns up."

· Dimps ready for the hunt, September 1920.

37 Hans Place, ca. 1930; destroyed 1942.

Left: Plaster-legged at Eastbourne, 1929.

Below: On the road to riches, the 1927 model Willys-Knight. Advertised as "85,000 miles—no repairs," but broke down in Richmond Park in 1929.

Deceptively happy group: Aunt May, Cousin Hugh, nurse, and Ivor. Eastbourne, ca. 1929.

Quinn, Jimmie, and Ivor with tie improperly tied, ca. 1935.

Aged four at Eastbourne with warder and assorted friends.

Poppet and Bill Williams on their "wedding day," 1940.

Poppet and son in a maritime moment, Cambridge, 1940.

The Eggesford House ruin as it had deteriorated by 1966.

Renée Redfern at Salcombe, 1942.

The last record of the mighty hunter Bill Williams, Kenya, 1941.

Black sheep and white horse, fortune-seeking Uncle Harold Mann, Tampico, Mexico, ca. 1930.

Above: Theater job-hunting portrait by John Vickers, 1946.

Right: Demon King, December 1948. Note soft focus at chin due to exhalation of demonic smoke.

Audrey Baines digging for the London Museum, spring 1949.

Mudlarks on the Thames: Peter Clark, Audrey Baines, and Donald Bailey, 1950.

Above: Uncovering the fourth-century Roman pavement in Ironmonger Lane, supervised by Adrian Oswald, September 1949. (Photo by William Gordon Davis)

Right: The Walbrook site, autumn 1949. Intrepid archaeologist bending into cliff to right. (Photo by William Gordon Davis)

The Guildhall Irregulars: Audrey, Skip Allen, Johnny Johnson, and INH, summer 1950.

Right: Excavating the amphora pit, Walbrook, January 1950. (Press photographer unidentified)

Below: A cold and wet day on the Upchurch Marshes with Donald Bailey and Peter Clark, 1951.

Wedding day, September 30, 1950. (Photo by William Gordon Davis)

Above: Audrey on her lunch break at the St. Mary Axe charnel pit, 1951.

Right: Pa and stepmother Joan at a friend's wedding, ca. 1965.

Above: Audrey with tortoises, big and little, 1955.

Right: Tigillinus leaving for Virginia, February 1957. (Photo by William Gordon Davis)

Picnic at the Rosewell ruin: John Dunton, Audrey, INH, and Anne Parrish, fall 1956.

The iconic stratification model as completed in April 1957. (The Colonial Williamsburg Foundation)

Audrey in her lab with President Nixon, 1985. (The Colonial Williamsburg Foundation)

Sir David and Betty Burnett at home in Tandridge Hall, ca. 1985. David, though chairman of Hays' Wharf, a company that owned part of the Thames foreshore, was not above accompanying me as a latter-day mudlark.

Burial detail at Carter's Grove, *from left:* archaeologist John Hamant, INH, the Reverend Richard May, coffin builder Woodrow Abbot, archaeological foreman Nate Smith, and Granny, 1983. (The Colonial Williamsburg Foundation)

The reconstructed Traveler's Room in the Colonial Williamsburg archaeological exhibit, 1975. (The Colonial Williamsburg Foundation)

Audrey in for scale below Cleopatra at Dendera, Egypt, 1974.

Left: Teddy Tucker studying clay pipes from the *Warwick,* ca. 1980.

Below: Diving on the *Sea Venture* wreck with Smokey Wingood, 1978. (Allan J. Wingood)

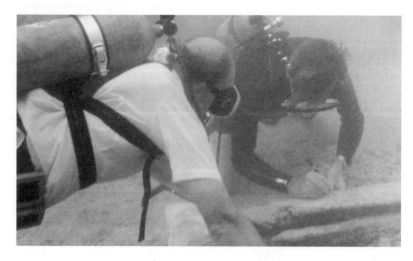

Received by Her Majesty Queen Elizabeth II at Buckingham Palace, October 1992.
(British Ceremonial Arts Ltd.)

Above: Audrey and Smokey Wingood measuring *Sea Venture* pottery, 1980.

Right: Upstaged by a mermaid at the National Geographic Society, 1994.
(National Geographic Society)

The Lost Colony team in the reconstructed fort on Roanoke Island during a visit by the Harringtons, October 1992. *From left:* Martha Williams, Bill Kelso, Virginia Harrington, Eric Klingelhofer, Pinky Harrington, David Hazzard (with bear), Carter Hudgins, INH (with duck), Nate Smith, Audrey (with backup bear), Nick Luccketti, and Jamie May.

Left: Carol feigning the fun of fishing, Salcombe, 1995.

Below: All that survives of the Winthrop Rockefeller Archaeology Museum.

This museum is also a tribute to
Ivor and Audrey Noël Hume

As Colonial Williamsburg's
chief archaeologist and curator of
archaeological collections, respectively,
from 1957 to 1993,
Noël and Audrey played leading roles in the
growth of historical archaeology in America
and in the remarkable discovery and
subsequent interpretation of
Wolstenholme Towne,
the site that you are about to visit

R ETURNING FROM FORAGING beside the river one damp, gray day in October 1949, I chanced upon an extraordinary procession making its way
down College Hill toward the Church of St. Michael, Paternoster Royal. Led by
trumpeters in medieval garb and the banners and staff bearers of the Worshipful
Company of Mercers, marched a miscellany of clerics and black-coated dignitaries. Joining the thin crowd of roadside spectators, I asked who they were.

"It's a bunch of them archi . . . watcha call 'ems, them antique diggers," a
man explained. "They're going to dig up Dick Whittington."

"Whatever for?" asked a woman who had overheard the explanation. But
neither the man nor anyone else who joined in the resulting conversation had
any idea.

The answer, as the next day's newspapers revealed, was publicity—for the
Roman and Medieval London Excavation Council. St. Michael's Church had
been built in 1409 at the expense of London's most famous mayor, Richard
Whittington, who, as every pantomime-going child knew, came to London
penniless believing its streets to be paved with gold, found they weren't, yet
made a fortune as a mercer and four times became mayor of the city. He was
buried in St. Michael's Church in 1423, but the exact location of his grave was
lost when the building burned in the Great Fire of 1666. The church was rebuilt
to the design of Sir Christopher Wren in 1694, and survived the 1940 Blitz only
to fall victim to a belated bomb in 1944.

Whittington, though never penniless, was undeniably a worthy fellow and
an inspiration to upwardly mobile urchins of the fifteenth century, but it was
pantomime Dick and his apocryphal cat upon whom Grimes and his troops were
advancing on that glum October day. In recognition of Whittington's latter-day
fame, the Church of St. Michael included among its treasures a rather revolting self-mummified cat that had been found during the prewar renovations.

Whether the idea was to inter it with Dick's bones or to put his bones in a case with the cat was anybody's guess.

The history of St. Michael's believed that Whittington's remains lay buried on the south side of the chancel of the medieval church, and so that was where the congregation gathered in the existing newly repaired building to hear prayers read and watch (as newsreel cameras whirred and flashbulbs popped) the Master of the Mercers' Company turn the first ceremonial sod. As a mere bystander in the street outside, I naively supposed that the RMLE Council regularly launched its excavations with such civic pomp, and that getting a bit in the paper was part of the job. I would later discover to my cost that I had it all wrong. What was sauce for the goose was not transferable.

"Already a trickle of rebuilding has begun on the waste spaces which, thanks to the last war, abound in many of our ancient cities," Adrian Oswald wrote in August 1949. "Soon it will become a flood and with contractors pressed by time the opportunity for careful and detailed excavation will be gone forever." Adrian's article in *Antiquity* magazine ended with the warning, "Now is the time for archaeologists to prepare the organization for dealing with the flood of rebuilding which will shortly burst the sluice gates."

Archaeologists knew him to be right, but archaeologists without money or civic mandates could do relatively little. In London, in November, the floodgates flew open, and as its contribution to stemming the tide the City Corporation agreed to invest five pounds, seventeen shillings a week—in me. On the 25th, the librarian, Raymond Smith, wrote offering me the vaguely defined position of "temporary whole-time assistant in the Museum of the Corporation of London," a post I officially assumed on December 5, thus becoming gainfully employed for the first time in ten months.

Adrian's prophesied flood began in a large bomb-stripped city block behind the Mansion House and extended from St. Swithin's Lane in the east to the street named for the Walbrook River to the west. By the late fourteenth century the river had become "stopped up by divers filth and dung" and was deemed a public nuisance, so that in 1440 part of its course was covered over. Toward the end of the next century it had disappeared altogether.

The "divers filth and dung" had been accumulating in the Walbrook bed since Roman times, compressing into a rich peatlike mass whose organic content had remarkable preservative qualities—as the City's builders' laborers well knew. Whenever a construction project had cut into the Walbrook's black organic strata, treasures could be expected to emerge—treasures readily converted into beer money by the likes of Stoney Jack Lawrence. However, the last great Walbrook bonanza had been before his time, and dated from 1872 when the National Safe Deposit building was under construction west of the Mansion House. Although Roman coins, jewelry, and other relics were sold to several collectors, the secretary of the London and Middlesex Archaeological Society, John E. Price, did his best to record what was being found, and described it in the book he published a year later. The frustrations he had experienced as he struggled to save what he could came bitterly to the surface in his closing paragraph:

> We institute researches abroad, sometimes on doubtful sites, and criti-cally examine every shovel-full of earth, often with no certain prospect of reward; but in a comparatively small space situate at home, and illustra-tive alike of the origin and progressive growth of the empire, sufficient interest has never yet been manifested to induce a properly organized in-vestigation of any given site.

In 1949, seventy-seven years later, Price's plea still echoed.

The about-to-be-developed Walbrook site for St. Swithin's House lay slightly to the east of the assumed course of the stream; nevertheless, Adrian Oswald had good reason to believe that its floodplain would be included. In any case, for the first time in more than seventy-five years, archaeologists would have an opportunity to take a careful look at the heart of Roman London. With luck, he said, we could expect to find the remains of homes, shops, warehouses, and even a temple. Although such low-lying and wet ground seemed an unlikely place to build a temple, the London Museum's collections offered evidence that one might indeed be there. Among its most prized treasures were the marble upper torso and head of a river god, a two-foot-tall but headless statue of a male figure holding a cornucopia, and a rectangular relief showing the Persian god Mithras slaying a sacred bull, all three "Said to have been found in the City, near the middle of the Walbrook, at a depth of about 20 ft."

In the seventy-seven years since John Price had scrambled about in the huge hole that was to seat the National Safe Deposit building, archaeological knowl-edge and techniques had greatly improved. What had not changed for the bet-ter, however, were the conditions under which the information would have to be retrieved. On the contrary, they had become infinitely worse. Whereas in 1872 the digging had been done by hand, with the potential for every shovelful of dirt to be examined before being carted away, now in postwar London mechanical excavators stood ready to claw out in one bite as much ground as a man could dig in a morning. On the other hand, the men behind the machines had changed not at all. Some would be helpful and others not; some were interested in history but more were not; some could be bribed and others could not.

"A building site under observation," Adrian explained, "is like a baby; it cannot be left for long without something going wrong and all depends on adequate preparation and tireless nursing, as to whether the child repays the trouble."

Adrian Oswald practiced what he preached. He would have made a first-rate teacher, for he had a rare facility to instruct without pontificating, and when he wooed the workmen he could teach them about Roman London as easily as though talking about Saturday's football matches. He was, as one laborer put it, "an all right gent." But the building site game was not won by charming and educating only the laborers; the preparation and nursing began at the top by securing the support of the landowners, then their architects, and finally the various levels of supervision on the site. These last were led by the architects' agent and the builders' clerk of the works, the latter being in overall charge of the project. Under him came the site foreman, responsible for progress and discipline and in charge of the subforemen known as gangers, who, as the name suggests, were in charge of work gangs: excavators, timbermen (who installed supporting wood framing), concrete pourers, bricklayers, and so on. Then, too, there were the new kingpins who could make or more often break an archaeological opportunity—operators of the grab, dragline, and bulldozer. Each man had a primary goal of his own: to ensure that nothing and nobody interfered with the progress of the job. Since the desire of an archaeologist was to do just that, and the builders knew it, his first and sometimes insurmountable task was to convince them otherwise, while his second was to discipline himself not to do so.

Winning the support of the landowners was the least difficult step, particularly when they were reminded that the antiquities were theirs—as indeed they were. Later, of course, one hoped that the owners would recognize the wisdom of presenting or loaning them to the Guildhall Museum; but at the outset, the ploy was to suggest that the museum's site observers were white knights doing them a free service by ensuring that their property was neither smashed nor stolen. A letter from the owners to the architects and clerk of the works instructing them to cooperate was not, by itself, enough, however. The site supervisors were sure that the owners would not expect such cooperation to go to lengths that cost money; and in the eyes of an unsympathetic foreman, asking a laborer to use his shovel rather than a pick as he dug through a pit full of Roman pottery could be construed as slowing progress. In short, the diplomacy of building-site archaeology was as delicate and disaster prone as walking a high wire.

Mercifully, that was not to be my responsibility. Adrian knew several contractors and foremen from before the war, and with the aid of a little beer money and a seemingly endless supply of cigarettes, he had many friends in low places. Besides, diplomacy called for an appearance that inspired confidence and respect. Adrian spoke with authority, looked like a schoolmaster, and had a balding head, whereas I spoke with no authority, looked like an out-of-work actor, and had a surfeit of hair. Nevertheless, regardless of my negative qualifications, fate decreed that within a week of my appointment I found myself both digger and diplomat. Adrian Oswald caught pneumonia and disappeared, never to return. Before the year's end he had resigned and accepted the curatorship of archaeology at Birmingham, thus dashing my hopes of continuing to learn from so able a friend and teacher. Almost simultaneously, his ex-dentist assistant, G. W. Lawrence, concluded that he preferred studying teeth to catalog cards, and he, too, resigned. Consequently, there was no hyperbole in the Guildhall Library's annual report when it stated that "the working of the department was thrown into a state of near-chaos [when] the Museum was deprived at one stroke of its two main supports."

In the midst of the crisis I had no time to question whether Adrian's new and better job materialized like a pantomime fairy while he lay on his sickbed or whether he had known for some time that he was leaving and engineered my appointment as a last kindness to me and as a sop to the City. Caring deeply as he did about the coming slaughter on the building sites, he may have sent me as a conscience-clearing, if thinly armored, St. George into the battle against the advancing mechanical dragons.

Shortly before the blow fell, the Library Committee had enlarged the museum staff by adding a typist, an attendant, and a curatorial assistant, Lysbeth Webb, who also fell sick in December and temporarily left the ship. Thus, I found myself the museum's sole professional, responsible not only for maintaining the exhibits and the collections but also for keeping my finger in the building-site dike. Had I been older and wiser I would almost certainly have quit before I began; but at twenty-two, towel tossing was not something I even considered. Besides, I knew too little to know how little I knew.

In spite of my growing commitment to Adrian Oswald and his building sites, I had continued to walk the Thames foreshore, and on a Saturday in October I was there once again. It was a particularly dismal morning; fog still hung over the water, obscuring the bridges and deadening the noise of city traffic. Now and again an invisible tug approaching Southwark Bridge would blow its hooter, emitting a melancholy "whoop whoap!" while closer at hand dew dripping from a gantry would thud onto the taut tarpaulin of a beached barge. Although in my many hours beside the water I had never encountered Robin Green and his cohorts, I had seen occasional silent figures prowling the shore, all middle-aged and elderly men, but as if by mutual consent we avoided each other, never intruding on each other's turf, and never offering more than a grunted "Mornin'" as we passed. On this particular morning the fog was thick and visibility no more than a few yards. No clean-air legislation had yet been enacted, and the autumn fogs were still free to grip the City by the throat as they had in Dickens's day. Out of the yellow pall emerged a stooping, gaunt, and eerie figure, a brown shape almost the color of the fog itself. Bent in the characteristic attitude of a mudlark, and focusing on the shore with all the concentration of a sandpiper, this apparition failed to see me until it was almost on top of me. So surprised were both it and I that we were jolted into an exchange more voluble than a "Mornin'." Draped in a long brown raincoat, this ghost of mudlarks past identified himself as Johnny Johnson, a thin-faced and bespectacled man in his fifties, and an amateur antiquary from Wembley in northwest London. We talked for a few minutes about our finds (they had been few that morning), and I mentioned my work on Bankside.

"If you ever need any help," he said, "just let me know."

I thanked him and took his phone number, meaning to ask Oswald whether additional volunteers would be either useful or acceptable. Then I forgot about Johnny Johnson until I exchanged my own volunteer's cap for the professional's hat and could decide for myself whether the Guildhall Museum needed more free help. I called Johnson and told him that huge holes had been dug into the Walbrook site and that with work halted over the weekend I had permission to salvage and record what I could. Would he be willing to give me a hand on Sunday?

He said he would, and he'd meet me there as soon after nine as he could make it.

I had recruited my first volunteer.

The Walbrook building site embraced several properties, the largest of them the bombed hall of the Worshipful Company of Salters, as well as the City-owned side street named Bond Court, but all had been purchased by the land developer Rudolph Palumbo. Alone among the owners who sold to Palumbo, the Salters retained ownership of such antiquities as might be discovered on their property. The decision was wise, for it ensured that a measure of concern would be shown for the salvage of what was legally theirs. At the same time, however, it posed horrible problems, since the boundaries of the Salters' property disappeared into the huge construction hole. Once spectacular discoveries began to be made, Palumbo, too, became interested in knowing who owned what, and would appear on the site asking, "Is this mine?"

The answer, as a rule, was yes, for as Adrian Oswald had foretold, the Walbrook with its metal-preserving silt lay along the western edge of the site, while Salters' Hall had stood to the east, fronting on St. Swithin's Lane. The assault had begun in both areas simultaneously, but while the Salters' ruins were dug out with a dragline bucket, digging along Walbrook was mostly done by hand, sinking large square holes along a frontage of about 180 feet into which concrete footings were poured. It was in these holes that the most substantial Roman building remains were to be found; indeed, so substantial that the concrete floor of one of them defied workmen with pneumatic drills for the best part of a day.

On the Sunday that Johnny Johnson was to assist me in my first solo research as the Guildhall's temporary full-time assistant, I awoke to find it raining. But knowing that what I failed to record that day would be gone tomorrow, I set out for the City, hoping that by the time I got there the rain would have stopped, and it had—more or less. The fat authoritative drops had diminished to a furtive bone-chilling drizzle which did its wetting work while pretending to be clearing. A thin, gray mist hung over the silent streets and bombed sites. Even before the war, few but caretakers lived within the famous square mile, and after it the ruined acres ensured that their number was even smaller. On the Walbrook site, the foremen's and surveyors' office sheds were locked tight; the huge iron tubs known as skips, into which the laborers shoveled their dirt, sat empty in pools of mud, while the machines to lift them stood idle, their cabs locked, oily water dripping from their hooks and cables. The watchman to whom I was supposed to report was nowhere to be found—nor was Johnny Johnson.

The only choices for shelter were a yet-to-be-demolished cellar under the Salters' Hall (but which, upon inspection, proved to be in service as a plumbing-free workmen's lavatory), or in the space between scaffolding supporting the platform on which stood the surveyors' drafting shed. I chose the latter and sat there listening to the water dripping from the steel poles, waiting for the drizzle to stop and Johnson to arrive. Neither happened. Instead, I had ample time to take stock and to ask myself: What the hell am I doing here?

Cold and wet, alone in a silent, desolate landscape, wearing an aging duffle coat caked with mud, I huddled under the leaking platform like a skid-row derelict. If the future looked at all like the present, it was anything but bright. Yet I had a job, albeit temporary and woefully paid. Furthermore, a door against which I had been vainly pushing for more than eighteen months had opened. On November 19 the *Times* had carried a long column from its archaeological correspondent, William Thompson Hill, describing the Walbrook discoveries being made "on behalf of the Guildhall Museum under the direction of Mr. Adrian Oswald and Mr. Noel Hume."

"Archaeology is engaged in a fight with the grab," wrote Thompson Hill. "Enormous buckets are suspended impatiently over the heads of the diggers. As soon as they desist the mechanical digger begins again. In the fog of a London November it is this week possible to see the undisturbed layers of occupation since the earlier years of the first century A.D." That report and others like it prompted the BBC to call the museum to ask whether one of us would be willing to talk about the discoveries on its nationally heard radio program *Current Affairs for Schools*. With characteristic generosity, and knowing how useful the proffered eight guineas would be, Adrian told the BBC that I would be the spokesman, thus opening the door to much future work on radio and television, as both a writer and a speaker. But on that December Sunday morning I could see no farther than the rain drop on the end of my nose.

Finally realizing that no help was forthcoming that day and that the weather would not clear, I left my shelter and sallied forth onto the site. London stands on a bed of yellow gravel, and to the east of the site the vast hole had been dug some thirty feet into it. At the edges, and thrusting down like long black fingers, were several deep refuse pits varying in date from the first century AD to late medieval times (some even later still), and it was these pits that offered the best reward to so-called rescue archaeologists.

On this wet day, although freshly exposed pits were visible in the sides of the hole, their bottoms (where the good stuff generally lay) were as much as fifteen feet below the existing land surface and about the same distance from the bed of the excavation—reachable only with the aid of a tall ladder. Several were available, but with no one to steady them I decided that my archaeological career might be unacceptably short. Instead, I contented myself by rounding up such artifacts as were littered around the top of the hole or being exposed as the rain washed away the soil at its edges.

In this sector of the site the Thames Valley gravel was capped with several feet of clay, and it was on and into this, after the Claudian invasion of AD 43, that the Romans had built Londinium. Whether there had been any earlier, Iron Age settlement on either of the two hills was one of the many questions archaeologists had long been asking—questions that might be answered by the careful excavations conducted by W. F. Grimes but hardly as a result of hasty building-site salvage.

In the summer of 1949, Grimes's platoon had sunk a forty-foot-long test trench beneath a courtyard of Salters' Hall, an area undisturbed by bombing and where, if he was lucky, its stratigraphic sequence stretched downward undisturbed by previous basement construction. But he wasn't lucky. After digging down through seven feet of brick rubble he came to two cellars apparently filled in the 1920s when the company built itself a new hall. Grimes would later describe the ground into which the cellars had been cut as "tantalizingly featureless." Ironically, when I came on the site, the courtyard fill through which Grimes had so carefully and fruitlessly dug by hand had been swept away by the builders, who, for reasons known only to themselves, had elected to halt at the Roman levels. With the paid help of the kind the RMLE Council could muster, we might have learned more in two days than Grimes had in months of deep trenching. But by this time he had gone about Dick Whittington's business, and without help I was unable to devote my time and energies to laterally excavating one area when so much else on the site demanded my attention—as did the still-continuing work in Ironmonger Lane and at the Bankside Power Station. Consequently, not until the mechanical grabs began to extend their great hole eastward did I see what Grimes had not: the walls and tesselated floors of a substantial Roman building. Destroyed by fire, clay daub from its walls and ceilings lay in red lumps on the floors, a clearly identifying marker for the remains of a burned structure whose wattle and pargeted clay paralleled our modern lath and plaster.

Laymen educated by movie-set designers may be forgiven for imagining Roman cities as white and gleaming with stone and marble under a sea of red tile roofs, their rooms stuccoed and painted with multicolored murals. But, like every city from then until now, there was another side. Much of Londinium had been walled with humble wattle and daub, and roofed only with thatch. Both sides of the architectural coin were to be found on the Walbrook site. To the west and close to the river, stone walls still stood high enough to retain the edges of floral and geometric murals that may well have rivaled those of Pompeii. Tantalizing fragments of the plaster could be salvaged from the skips before they were whisked away and dumped into waiting trucks; here a six-inch slab decorated with a spray of flowers and part of a bird, there a scrap with half a hand holding something. Parts of cement floors mixed with crushed tile, smoothed until the pink surface glistened like wet marble, would be uncovered only to be instantly attacked with jackhammers and wrecking balls. To the east of the site, however, no such measures were needed. Lightly built and combustible structures had reverted to nature as they burned, the daub settling into a bed of red, characterless clay.

London burned twice in the first century of its existence: deliberately torched in AD 61 by the vengeance-seeking warriors of Boudicca, queen of the Iceni, in her ultimately doomed attempt to rid Britain of the Romans, and again (presumably by accident) in about AD 120 in the reign of the emperor Hadrian. Both fires were to be seen as successive red stripes, sometimes several feet thick, in the sides of the Walbrook excavations—which brings me back to that sodden Sunday in November.

Along much of the western edge of the great excavation hole the burned red clay lay bared, and it was there while rounding up miscellaneous burned potsherds that I came upon a small gully cut by the rain. In it the dissolving pink clay colored the water to a hue that a little imagination might describe as blood red, particularly when it trickled through the eye sockets and mouth of a human skull.

Save for a papier-mâché prop left over from *Hamlet,* I had never before seen a skull, and to come upon it under these circumstances was, to say the least, a surprise. It also presented a problem, for as I looked more closely I could see other bones protruding from the red clay. Part of the skeleton had already fallen victim to the grab, but bones of its torso survived in remarkably good condition. They rested in a layer suggesting that here was a victim of Boudicca's revenge, but who was to say that they were not of much more recent date and buried in a hole that simply cut the burned clay? Should I try to find a policeman or call for a coroner's inquest? What was my responsibility as an officer of the Corporation of London? I had no idea. So I dug around the bones looking for associated artifacts, found none, then paced off enough measurements to enable me to roughly plot the skeleton's position on the site map, secreted the skull in my canvas knapsack, and hurried it rather furtively back to the lab.

Adrian Oswald's lightning training had not included dealing with human remains, and from an archaeological point of view I had done nothing right. Working in the rain, I had taken no photographs, made no drawings, made no record of osteological data. Nevertheless, the experience had an indelible impact. I had come face to face with a Londoner who knew the answers to many of our questions; a person who had shivered as I was shivering, who wondered, as I did, what the future held; a person who had laughed and loved, feared and fretted—a person whose emotions had differed little from my own. As I scraped the wet clay from around the bones, my earlier doubts disappeared. I knew exactly what I was doing there—and where I was going. My future lay in trying to share that emotional involvement with the public, to try to build bridges across time. In retrospect I am convinced that all the disparate events I have described in previous chapters were leading me to that Sunday at Walbrook and to this commitment.

Few if any scholars, then or now (with the possible exception of Adrian Oswald), would allow that occasional childhood brushes with archaeology or several years in the theater could be an adequate grounding for an archaeologist or a museum curator. Yet, as I was soon to learn, in December 1949 a talent for communication was precisely what the Corporation of London thought it needed.

Within days of Oswald's departure I received word that Librarian and Curator Raymond Smith wished to see me. In the halls of the Guildhall Library, where even "Good mornings" were uttered in whispers, the summons was akin to a novitiate being called for a quiet word with the Pope. The librarian's office doubled as the committee room and thus was as intimidating in its Victorian Gothic grandeur as was Smith himself. Tall, white-haired, and stiff-collared, he wore his black coat and striped trousers as a knight would armor. Then and later, I found him anxious to put me at my ease and liberal in his praise for my efforts. Indeed, in his annual report he would write of my "devoted services [without which] all work in the Museum would have come to a complete standstill, and much material relating to Roman and Mediaeval London would have been lost." But on this, my first official encounter with Raymond Smith, I had no idea why I had been summoned or what to expect.

"In Mr. Oswald's absence," he began, "there are several things you need to know. The Guildhall Museum is in danger of closing and it's up to you to ensure that that does not happen."

I listened in a state of semishock as Smith explained how the library's unavoidable takeover of the museum's prewar basement space was destined to continue for the foreseeable future. There were several members of his staff, he told me, as well as of the Library Committee who felt that even the narrow Bridge room where Oswald had mounted his first Bygone London exhibition in

1948 should be surrendered to the library as a reading room. Smith went on to note that powerful (but unnamed) forces were at work to get the committee to vote to amalgamate all the City's archaeological collections by transferring the Guildhall's holdings to the London Museum. Such a move, Smith said, made good sense in many ways. The London Museum's City-related collections were as large as, if not larger than, ours. Its archaeological credentials were impeccable and its director a distinguished scholar. Although closed since the war, it was about to move from its old home at Lancaster House to open in new quarters at Kensington Palace. In short, the Guildhall Museum's present hard times coincided with the London Museum's renaissance. Such an amalgamation, Smith added, had everything in its favor—save for the fact that as the City of London's librarian and curator he had no desire to preside over the demise of his museum.

But what could I do? Surely the museum's future (if it was to have one) lay in far more august hands than those of its muddy, temporary full-time assistant?

"You must court the press," Smith told me. "The public must be aware— more important, the Library Committee must be aware—that through its work on the building sites the museum is serving a vital function. If the museum's activities are recognized, no one is going to risk the criticism that its closure would generate in the press."

Smith went on to note that it had been Oswald's policy to make a few recent discoveries available for inspection at the monthly Library Committee meetings. "You must continue to do so," he said. "But show them more. Let them see quantity as well as quality. But not potsherds. They don't understand potsherds. Let them see whole pots. Mend them if you have to."

If my "Yes, sir," sounded hesitant, it was because pottery restoration was something else that Adrian Oswald's short course had not included. His lessons on the importance of courting friends in the press, however, had been well taught and carefully learned. He had often told me how his predecessor Quentin Waddington's weekly column in the *Evening Standard* had made his name usefully familiar in his dealings with builders and landowners, and how it had given him a measure of protection against library superiors who might otherwise have more openly and successfully challenged his somewhat unorthodox work habits. Adrian also introduced me to two valuable allies, William Thompson Hill of the *Times* and William Gordon Davis, a freelance photographer specializing in historical work for the *Illustrated London News*. The latter's coverage of our work on the Roman mosaic at Ironmonger Lane had already given me access to

Britain's most prestigious weekly outlet for archaeological news. Where went the *Times* and the *Illustrated London News,* so went the Associated Press, the national dailies, and most importantly for Raymond Smith's purposes, the London evening papers: the *Star, News,* and *Standard.* A story in any of those could be relied on to generate a call from the BBC, whose various radio magazine programs from *Woman's Hour* to *Radio Newsreel* had a taste for treasure. Thus, once the Walbrook ball was rolling it generated its own momentum without any help from me. Raymond Smith's year-end report to the Library Committee summarized these public relations successes:

> The Walbrook site has received a great deal of publicity from the daily press and the British Broadcasting Corporation. The papers that have published pictures of the excavations include *The Illustrated London News,* the *Sphere, The Times,* and sundry evening and foreign newspapers.
>
> The Museum Assistant gave a talk on these Walbrook excavations on the B.B.C. Home Service on the 21st December, 1949. This was relayed on the Overseas Services, and published in *The Listener.* Other B.B.C. references to the work have appeared in Schools' Programmes, Radio News Reels, and the normal News Bulletins.

With so much accomplished in three weeks, I felt that I had more than earned my salary. Indeed, I had visions of a grateful City (perhaps even a nation) bestowing something nice upon me. I had no idea—as Raymond Smith must have done—that in so faithfully doing his bidding, I was cutting my own throat.

The Guildhall Museum needed publicity to enhance its prestige, but Grimes and the RMLE Council also needed publicity, to encourage donations and keep digging. Although Smith was a member of the council and sometimes its acting chairman, he had set the two institutions on a collision course, knowing that if a sacrificial goat should be needed, I would wear the horns. Years later, when I asked Adrian what he knew of this, he answered only that Smith "taught me ways of intrigue that stood me very well at Birmingham."

In the race for publicity Grimes had bet on Whittington and lost. Through the grim winter months his loyal workmen dug in the cold emptiness of St. Michael's Church, slowly working their way down through ground riddled with graves, each new interment having played havoc with the last. When eventually it became clear that none of the bones unearthed from the south transept could be identified as Dick's, Grimes opened another excavation in the north transept, and there quickly found himself in an eighteenth-century family vault.

Had Whittington been found, the council would have enjoyed enormous publicity from the yellow press—creating public interest that might have been translated into financial support. But without the right bones, there was nothing to photograph, nothing to report. Meanwhile, up the hill on the Walbrook building site, each day brought new discoveries and fresh columns in the papers. Drawn by the publicity, crowds lined the street straining to catch a glimpse of something being found. Reporters and cameramen slipped past the guards ordered to keep them out, infuriating the foreman when he discovered them lurking behind the skips or down in the holes plying their trade. A headline in the *Evening News* read "Mr. Condon Gets Down To Earth."

> Thirty-eight year old Labourer Tommy Condon of Ceniden-road, Hailsham, dug his spade into the earth 28 feet below road level at Walbrook, City, where excavations are going on for a large new office building.
>
> Suddenly his spade "bit." He moved it about and lifted the skull and bones of a human skeleton.
>
> Gingerly Tommy lifted the skull and turned it around on his spade. "It had about 24 teeth," he told me, "beautifully preserved."
>
> The curator of Guildhall Museum, Mr. B. Hume, who has been carrying out archaeological excavations on the site was summoned. . . .

I doubt if even Raymond Smith found merit in this level of reporting. Who was this B. Hume (alias Ivor Newton Hume and Ivor Newton) whose pronouncements were so regularly in the papers and whose voice (in December alone) was heard on national radio on at least four occasions? What was his background? Who knew him? Where had he trained?

I had materialized like a pantomime demon to spoil Grimes's Christmas. He had every right to be furious. And he was. What can generously be termed a certain coolness had existed between the Guildhall and London museums long before I arrived, a situation not helped by the disappearance, allegedly while in the Guildhall Museum's possession, of one of Grimes's most important artifacts—a Saxon pendant found on the floor of the Roman city wall bastion at Cripplegate. Had the relationship between Grimes and Oswald been closer, my efforts might have been channeled to complement those of the RMLE Council while I learned from Grimes as I had from Oswald. Smith could have made that happen—were it in his interests to do so. But for the time being at least, I was more useful as a rival whose youth and inexperience could be regretted and, when expedient, condemned.

Three months later Adrian Oswald sent me fatherly advice from Birmingham:

> I met Grimes over the week-end, and he brought up the subject of Hume himself. He is out to clip your wings if he can, says you're a menace. That of course would go for anyone in his field, but I am afraid that he will do what damage he can in archaeological circles. The press reports with their inaccuracies give him a handle. He won't compromise now, and all you can do is to continue and to make sure of Corporation support.

But that was next year. As 1949 came to an end I was naively unaware that I was a thorn in anyone's flesh. Working seven days a week on the building sites, I had time only to worry about my inability to be in at least three places at once, and how to sprout several extra pairs of hands.

13 ⟨⟨⟨ *Dead Birds and Stupid Statements*

Dᴇᴄᴇᴍʙᴇʀ's ᴘʀᴇss ᴀᴛᴛᴇɴᴛɪᴏɴ had accomplished precisely what Raymond Smith wanted. His museum was now squarely in the public eye, and so were its archaeological rescue efforts.

For me, the publicity had already had one salutary result. By the first week in January 1950, Johnny Johnson was no longer my sole volunteer helper. Londoners who had read the newspaper stories or had heard reports on the wireless were calling the museum and offering their services—among them the girl who had also failed to be impressed by the Sutton Hoo ship. By this time Audrey Baines had earned a history BA at Bristol University and had spent the summer of 1947 excavating a Roman villa at nearby King's Weston. Back in London, she had worked for several months as a volunteer for the RMLE Council on a bombed site in Queen Victoria Street before enrolling for the diploma course at London University's Institute of Archaeology. Her father had died at the early age of fifty-eight the previous October, his death hastened, she believed, by lung damage caused by the gas attack that had sidelined him in the First World War. Without his hand to steer her, Audrey's ship was on an uncertain course. She thought she wanted to become an archaeologist, but was unsure how to make a living at it. Nevertheless, she knew that the institute's diploma was an essential prerequisite, and thus became a student of the twentieth-century's most colorful figure in British archaeology, Eric Mortimer Wheeler. He was Grimes's predecessor as director of the London Museum and, among many other duties and achievements, from 1944 to 1948 had been director general of India's Archaeological Survey. Back in London with nothing more taxing in the offing than teaching Roman Britain to Audrey Baines and two other girls at the institute, Wheeler unexpectedly accepted a short-term advisory trip to India. With characteristic aplomb he departed, dumping his class on his friend and colleague Rupert Bruce-Mitford, then assistant keeper in the Department of British Antiquities at the British Museum. An expert on Saxon rather than Roman Britain, Bruce-Mitford's name was associated with one great discovery, which, naturally enough, was to feature prominently in his instruction: the Sutton Hoo ship burial.

Not even the opportunity to touch the Sutton Hoo treasures was enough to excite Audrey to the mysteries of Saxon England, and finding the British Museum lectures no substitute for the dynamic Wheeler, she rashly dropped out of the institute's course and came to work for me. I have not the slightest doubt that had her father lived, he would have talked her out of such folly. Instead, she brought to my Guildhall Irregulars the credentials and experience that I so conspicuously lacked—though never once did she draw that to my attention.

Although the rest of the team fluctuated in size as would-be warriors wilted in the face of mud and hard labor, a core half dozen strong remained on call through the years that followed. First aboard after Johnny Johnson came a middle-aged Cockney with an unlikely name: Charles LeFevre, a meatpacker from Bermondsey, then Cynthia and Diana, two well-bred young ladies whose surnames I ungallantly forget. They were quickly joined by two young men barely out of their teens, Peter Clark, an apprentice printer, and Donald Bailey, then a library assistant but destined to go on to a distinguished career at the British Museum as a specialist in Roman lamps. The last of the long-term faithful was H. E. "Skip" Allen, an ex-major in the wartime Home Guard, every inch a soldier, and invariably attired in hacking jacket and army khaki shirt and tie—the kindest and most hardworking and reliable of men. Later loyalists included the architect Peter DeBrandt; Peter Drury, a medical illustrator; Douglas Walton, a timber broker; and in a more exotic vein, Rufus, Lord Noel-Buxton, known to the press as the "Wading Peer." He had tried to wade across the Thames to prove the location of a Roman ford.

All but one of these stalwarts was available only at weekends, and so it was left to Audrey Baines to become my seven-days-a-week right hand. In moments of crisis, I could call on the services of Edward Doyle, the attendant assigned to the museum; but although Ed did us yeoman service, wearing the same blue uniform in which he had to do duty in the sober halls of Guildhall, his contributions were usually limited to where mud and water were not. But even three pairs of hands, trying to minimize the loss of historical information being wrought on four or five sites at the same time, were ludicrously inadequate. Professional archaeologists like Grimes and Oswald well knew that salvaging relics was no longer the name of the game. What were needed were carefully recorded, datable contexts in which the objects lay. That meant archaeologically disciplined digging—not just grabbing what the construction gangs turned up. Raymond Smith, however, was not an archaeologist, and to him the museum's prestige rested on the artifacts it possessed and could acquire, and it made no difference whether they came as sixpenny purchases from the laborers who had found them or as the products of our relatively careful digging. What mattered was that the objects should be complete enough to impress the monthly meetings of the Library Committee. As people in any period rarely throw anything away until it is broken, providing a supply of unbroken antiquities was much easier said than done.

Audrey Baines had taken part of the Institute of Archaeology's course in object conservation, while I, as an ex–stage manager, had gained considerable experience of modeling in plaster of Paris props such as cups, plates, vases, and bottles that could be dashed to the floor twice nightly. Armed with that experience, we quickly transformed the museum's attic laboratory into an antiquities factory. An old gramophone turntable became our potter's wheel, and with the aid of vertically mounted metal templates, supplies of plaster, and molds fashioned from potters' clay, we converted ceramic fragments into whole pots. Dust from the lab floor (never in short supply) was mixed with paint and shellac to simulate coarse earthenware, and we used oil colors and varnish to reproduce the red gloss of Roman Samian ware and the greens of medieval jugs. Missing handles and other details we copied from examples already in the museum's collection. But being babes in the ceramic woods, we sometimes copied from the wrong pots—as I discovered to my dismay several years later. Showing a visitor from another museum around our pottery storeroom, I drew his attention to a particularly choice specimen.

"Now here's something that'll interest you," I said, reaching to the back of a shelf. "It's an ordinary thirteenth-century baluster jug which normally has no lip. But as you see, this one has an elaborate bridged spout. I've never seen another like . . ." Then I realized that the jug was mine—and so was the spout.

My embarrassment at the moment of realization was on a par with dreams in which I deliver a speech to a packed audience and suddenly discover that I am sans trousers. Nevertheless, it taught me a valuable lesson about the ethics of restoring or reconstructing anything from jugs to houses. But in the winter of 1950 I had neither the experience nor the time to worry over such niceties. All that mattered was that the Library Committee's display be ready on time. On the building sites, by four in the afternoon the light was going, construction work was ceasing, and the workmen preparing to go home. But for Audrey and me, it meant wearily returning to the lab to wash what we had found, convert muddy sketches to clean drawings, and mend yesterday's now dried pottery, hoping that enough shards would fit together to make a committee-worthy exhibit.

When I began, the museum owned no shovels, picks, or buckets, nor any means of getting what we found back to the lab. Lacking so much as a bicycle, the muddy treasures (and their equally filthy finders) traversed the City on London Transport buses—to the disgust of bowler-hatted fellow passengers. Often, however, the finds were too plentiful to be carried in a knapsack or a bucket, and came from sites not served by the buses. The Bankside Power Station was one of them, and on many an occasion I would have to walk the miles with a coal sack of artifacts on my back. It was on such a trek that I was picked up by the police—as a likely candidate for yet another identification lineup. Remembering my performance at Worthing, I decided to appear neither villainous nor angelic, but to try for a look that was pleasantly bland—all the more necessary, since the sack between my feet must have looked like a bag of loot. I need not have worried. The suspect was promptly picked out by three witnesses.

"Thank you, gentlemen. That'll be all," said the officer in charge. "Stop by the desk on your way out."

So I picked up my sack, collected a shilling for my trouble, and headed, heart pounding, back to the lab. The incident deserves a place in the annals of the City police force as the only occasion when it had one more person in a lineup than it counted. Ground clearance that morning at the Bankside site had hauled out a human skeleton. Rather than letting the bones be trucked away in the pretense that nobody had noticed them, I had decided to take them back to the lab in the hope that osteological information might be forthcoming.

Although through the winter of 1950 the Bankside project continued to yield pottery, glass, clay tobacco pipes, and numerous other artifacts of the seventeenth, eighteenth, and nineteenth centuries, it was the St. Swithin's House site on Walbrook that most demanded our attention. Lying as it did at the very heart of Roman London, this area and this period were of premier interest to both archaeologists and the public—and therefore to the press.

As Adrian Oswald had predicted, the hand-dug foundation pits alongside the Walbrook Street cut through the floodplain of the ancient stream, exposing the layer of rich-smelling black peat which preserved virtually everything buried in it. In the late first and second centuries, the Walbrook valley had been the workplace of tanners whose scrap leather, emanating metal-protecting tannic acid, was liberally distributed through the stream's mud. Whereas most British archaeological sites yield up iron as lumps of shapeless brown rust and copper alloys reduced to green and purple corrosion, after nearly two thousand years in the ground, the Walbrook's iron came out virtually ready for use—knives still sharp, chains that rattled, and nails ready to drive. Copper alloys emerged not just brassy but positively golden—which had its disadvantages. Workmen who found coins of the yellow metal called orichalcum were convinced that they were gold, and so declined to exchange them for the pennies I could offer.

The foundation pits being dug beside the Walbrook Street were about fifteen feet square and ten or fifteen feet deep, requiring that their sides be supported by temporary wooden walls installed in four- to five-foot increments. Skilled gangs of "timbermen" did the work, first setting heavy lumber framing in place and then driving short planks called "polling boards" down behind it to support the earth sides. Because our only chance to study its layers was the time between the diggers stopping digging and the timbermen ramming home the boards, the recording process was erratic and imprecise. More often than not, salvaging artifacts protruding from the sides took precedence over trying to draw sections. Because the laborers knew that if they found the antiquities before I did, there would be beer money in it (if not from me, from wealthier lunchtime customers in neighboring pubs), some of them proved more competitive than helpful. This was particularly true when the metal objects were small and easily marketed.

Although Adrian Oswald had demonstrated the art of digging into the exposed dirt walls at Bankside, at Walbrook such sorties were frowned on lest the undercutting cause the sides to cave in. Nevertheless, in one instance (and one instance only) I ignored the ground rules, beguiled by a thin and delicately woven brass chain, half an inch of which dangled tantalizingly from the stiff black wall of peat—as had been pointed out to me by one of the timbermen as he left for lunch. Through the work break I chased the chain inch by inch back into the side, and after tunneling more than a foot I was relieved when it began to turn back on itself. At twenty-one inches the chain ended in a magnificent trumpet-shaped brooch (fibula), its safety pin–style spring as supple and ready for use as it had been when first worn in the early second century AD.

The artifacts that came from the Walbrook peat had no immediate relationship one to another. What made them archaeologically important was their immaculate state of preservation, and that extended to other materials besides iron and copper. Alas, damaged beyond recall in transit to the skip was a small brown bird; though squashed flat and its skin black, its matted feathers were still recognizable. No ornithologist, I took it to be a sparrow, and was moved by the sight of this frail and tiny thing to a degree matched by no other discovery in more than thirty years of digging. The presence of perhaps identical birds hopping about the construction site in search of crumbs from the workmen's sandwiches was a graphic reminder that were it not for the scourge of mankind, the natural face of the land would have changed little in the centuries between the sparrows. I am often prompted to wonder why, if God so loved the world, he did not do away with mankind before it got out of hand.

An elderly man who stopped me as I left the Walbrook site one afternoon may have been asking the same question. He was well dressed in an old-fashioned City way: bowler hat, striped trousers under a dark overcoat, black tie with a stiff, winged collar. But he had taken liquor with his lunch, and staggered as he seized me by the arm.

"Young man," he mumbled, "d'you know why we're in such trouble today?"

I forget my reply.

"It's because they cut down the flower of our manhood, cut it down in the Great War. All our fine young men, a whole generation." His voice was getting louder. People were staring. I broke free and rather churlishly hurried away as the old man shouted after me. "Why! Why would God take all those fine young men? Answer me that!"

Silly old sod, I thought, cursing him for the embarrassment he had caused me. I was young and insensitive, and knew little about the impact of the First World War. But the encounter was so unexpected, so bizarre, and the man's last shouted question so filled with despair that I hear it still. Why did he pick me to ask that question? Was it perhaps because I resembled a son whose bones lay in the Flanders mud?

The first skeleton I had found on the Walbrook site had made me think about and care about the life and feelings of the person whose bones they were. My encounter with that old man in the street outside introduced me to the impact of death on the living. John Donne told us that "the death of one good man diminishes us all," but good or bad makes no difference. The death of any human memory erases the history of every inanimate object that has contributed to it. A pebble brought back from a honeymoon may lie in a dresser drawer throughout a married lifetime, yet in the twilight of widowhood it recalls the moonlight, lapping waves, sand between the toes, and whispered words of love. It is the pebble that he picked up as he spoke them, yet at the instant of her death that magic pebble becomes just another rock.

These are not, I fear, very scientific thoughts and can expect to score few points among archaeologists, who are taught to think of human bones in terms of measured millimeters rather than a widow's tears, and the pebble only as a geological specimen whose source may be evidence of travel. They—we—are right to do so. Knowledge is acquired from facts, not fancies. But it is also a fact that the most important contributions to a human life are emotions, opinions, memories, hopes, that have no afterlife of their own. Like a treasured pebble or the regret represented by the shards of a dropped cup, their importance cannot be quantified or otherwise analyzed. Yet for archaeologists to ignore their existence or deny their importance is to forget what archaeology is supposed to be about: *the scientific study of material remains of past human life and activities.* The words are Webster's; only the italics are mine. For me, therefore, the excavated artifacts have always been seen first as fragments of life and only afterward as potsherds to be scientifically studied. Thus, the discovery of an intact leather sandal in the Walbrook peat made me think first of the Roman Londoner who wore it before considering it in terms of leather-working technology.

It is hard to say whether, for me, an open-toed sandal was more inspiring than a complete boot, but for the press a boot was a winner—perhaps because it smacked of what were still referred to as the working classes. Our boot had been preserved intact in the wet mud of a timber-lined well, and was almost certainly the first to be carefully excavated from Roman London.

By comparison with some of the treasures we had been finding in the Walbrook silt, the well's contents were not all that exciting, the boot being its most spectacular object. The rest included an iron bucket handle, part of a cow's skull, a bronze bracelet, fragments of jet, a spindle whorl, and a miscellany of potsherds. However, at the bottom, and sealed within a layer of chalk (apparently used to filter water rising through the natural gravel), lay a brightly shining orichalcum coin of the emperor Postumus, a renegade army officer who, in AD 258, set up his own Roman empire based in Gaul where he reigned for ten years. Because his coin was almost certainly placed in the well as an offering when it was first dug, it followed that our boot could not have been thrown away before AD 258.

In those days archaeological conservation in English museums was fairly primitive. Although the Institute of Archaeology had a laboratory and taught conservation, it focused predominantly on treating metals and restoring pottery. What we desperately lacked were reliable techniques for preserving organic materials such as leather and wood.

The government's Ministry of Works had responsibility for preserving artifacts recovered from properties owned by the nation, and to that end had a small lab attached to its Ancient Monuments Division. Though always willing to offer advice, its staff seemed to know no more about preserving leather than we did. On one visit I found a technician experimentally heating a shoe sole over a stove in an oil-filled frying pan. I admired the resulting suppleness of the child's shoe.

"Thanks," said the sad-faced technician, "but it started out as an adult's."

The problem of how to save wood was very much on my mind in January 1950 as we dug down into our well and found its oaken walls waterlogged but otherwise splendidly preserved. If we could take them apart, treat the wood, and reassemble it as an exhibit, the Guildhall Museum would have one of the most impressive examples of Roman handiwork that Londoners could hope to see. Thanks to herculean efforts on the part of Skip Allen and others of the Guildhall Irregulars, by late February we had the timbers safely apart and dumped (pending conservation) in a yard beside Guildhall, where Audrey and I reassembled a section of it for the benefit of photographer Bill Davis. His pictures would figure prominently in the next week's *Illustrated London News,* to the general satisfaction of Raymond Smith and his Library Committee.

Recovering the well timbers greatly increased public interest in the race to save what we could before the new London totally destroyed the old. To a certain extent, the publicity began to create an awareness that this was something that the nation, and London's government in particular, needed to take into account. Unfortunately, that awareness did not pay real dividends until several years after Audrey and I had given up the struggle. In the short run, however, Londoners in increasing numbers were becoming interested in what we were doing. And it wasn't just Londoners. On February 16, in the wake of the well salvage, a film crew from *Gaumont British News* spent a day on the Walbrook site and in the lab, shooting footage that would be seen in cinemas from the Orkneys to Land's End. The publicity door was pushed even wider when I left 7 Bentinck Street, and Mrs. Winter's protective wing, to share an apartment with Rene Cutforth, a distinguished radio war correspondent with an active interest in archaeology—and ready access to the BBC's daily news magazine *Radio Newsreel.*

There is an old theatrical adage that it doesn't matter what the press says as long as it gets the actor's name right. In archaeology, it's not the archaeologist's name that matters. What really matters is that the reporters get the archaeological facts straight, for in many instances theirs is the only record that ever gets printed. I would slowly learn that if accuracy is what one wants, the best way to get it is to hand the reporter a press release or a fact sheet and to discuss nothing that is not covered by them. I would learn, too, that it helps to keep the press at bay until one has something definitive to say—in a setting of one's own choosing. But even if I had had the maturity to realize any of that, putting it into practice in the hurly-burly of a building site would have taxed the skill of the most astute politician.

Although the contractor's gatekeepers had been told to keep the press off the site, at any moment I could expect to look up and find a reporter peering over my shoulder or shouting questions down at me as I worked in the pits. Knowing that we were likely to make our more spectacular finds on Sundays when construction was halted, reporters seemed to materialize as miraculously as Macbeth's midnight hags. They were there on March 5, a date that Audrey's diary defined simply as the "Amphora Day."

The *Daily Telegraph* correctly described the discovery of a Roman garbage pit as "the most important find yet made at the site."

From the pit's bottom protruded the neck of a first-century Roman amphora or wine jar. Had the contractors' mechanical dragline cut three feet closer, the jar would have been shattered. Instead, three feet, two inches long, it lay intact across the pit, crushing under it sixteen kitchen pots and breaking a large, two-handled flagon whose neck and handles lay to one side of the amphora and the body to the other. Some of the cooking pots had shattered as they landed, before the amphora fell on top of them. So many had been whole when they reached the pit that they all looked more like the product of wanton destruction than of domestic spring cleaning.

I was convinced—and still am—that what we had found was evidence of one of the most dramatic moments in London's history, the day in AD 61 when Boudicca's vengeance-seeking hordes swept down on the undefended city. Provoked beyond endurance, the East Anglian Britons rebelled against their Roman conquerors, sacking Colchester, London, and St. Albans (Verulamium) before being defeated by the better disciplined, better equipped, and better maneuvered Roman legions under Suetonius Paulinus. But before he caught up with Boudicca's army somewhere in Northamptonshire, she had slaughtered seventy thousand Roman and Roman-supporting inhabitants of the three towns. The historian Tacitus summarized the carnage like this: "The halter and the gibbet, slaughter and desolation, fire and sword, were the marks of savage valor." A later Roman chronicler, Dion Cassius, whose style might have earned him a job in

Grub Street, was more detailed: "Those who were taken captive by the Britons were subjected to every known form of outrage. They hung up naked the noblest and most distinguished women and then cut off their breasts and sewed them to their mouths, in order to make the victims appear to be eating them; afterwards they impaled the women on sharp skewers run lengthwise through the entire body. All this they did," Dion added, "to the accompaniment of sacrifices, banquets and wanton behavior."

Were our shattered pots the product of one such banquet and its wanton behavior? We would never be sure. But there was little doubt that whatever the circumstances, the crash of breaking pottery was soon followed by the flames of burning buildings, for it was their debris that filled the pit and covered the ground around it.

Given more time, we would first have cleared around the pit and dug down into it from the top to carefully expose and record the position of every potsherd. In theory, too, we should have kept a thorough photographic record. But I had neither the equipment nor the experience to do it. Until I met Adrian Oswald my photographic prowess had been limited to poking the lever on my mother's Box Brownie and getting scolded for wasting a snap. The museum's camera was somewhat more sophisticated, but it was of prewar vintage, used 118-gauge film (rather than 120 or the increasingly popular 35 mm), and had several small light-leaking holes in its bellows which were covered with surgical tape. Returning one day from the Bankside site, Adrian had dropped the camera in the street; so when I inherited it, the back, too, had to be secured and sealed with tape. Consequently, the ratio of fogged film was high.

With Oswald gone, I was getting my photography lessons from William Thompson Hill, the *Times* correspondent. A splendid photographer who preferred to take his own pictures, he always arrived bowed under the weight of a huge wooden tripod and a massive glass-plate camera. Though as nice as he could be, he had little but scorn for the museum's camera with its fancy variable shutter. "Quite unnecessary," he told me. "All you need is a lens cap. Just take it off and put it back." True to his counsel, Thompson Hill's camera had no shutter. He simply pulled the cover off its lens, counted the seconds needed for the exposure—"Timbucktoo one, Timbucktoo two, Timbucktoo three"—and put it back. He explained that, spoken clearly and roundly, the word Timbucktoo took close enough to one second. I would learn later that the American Civil War photographer Mathew Brady had used the same method, though intoning "Mississippi" rather than "Timbucktoo" to span the seconds.

Although Thompson Hill's advice on exposure was of little use to me in trying to handle the museum's shutter-operated monster, his thoughts on composition and the use of natural light have stood me in good stead over the years. Indeed, it was a measure of my respect for his teaching that as soon as I could afford to buy a camera of my own I invested in one that used glass negatives— albeit with a variable shutter. However, in the winter of 1950 the museum's camera was all I had. Not only did we lack a light meter, we had no tripod, and no money to spend on development and printing. For that we relied on my fellow mudlark and first volunteer, Johnny Johnson, who processed the films in his bathroom and provided me with prints made on bits of scrap photographic paper cut in extraordinary shapes. Poorly fixed, the images often turned brown after a few days and occasionally disappeared altogether. Those that survived were glum testimony to the photographer's incompetence and his equipment's shortcomings. With film too expensive to waste on bracketing exposures in the hope that one would turn out to be right, too-dark shots were brightened only by the white streaks from the light-leaking camera, while the pale ones revealed my inability to hold it steady. The few photographs I took in the excitement of "Amphora Day" were of atrocious quality, and thus it was left to the press photographers to record the emergence of one of the few intact and closely datable amphorae to survive from first-century London.

"Two-Pot Luck Found on Bombed Site," trumpeted the *Daily Herald;* "2 Roman Wine Vessels Dug Up In City," announced the *Daily Telegraph.* The *Times,* whose reporter was not there, was less flamboyant, limiting its account to two paragraphs under a sober headline, "Two Walbrook Amphorae." I was soon to wish that the other papers had let it go at that. Instead, the *Herald* quoted me as saying, "I believe that there are only four others in existence like this perfect one." I still find it hard to believe I said that, but if I did, it had to be one of the stupidest claims on record, there being four amphorae of the Walbrook type in the Guildhall Museum alone. I wanted to believe *that* was what I had said, but the *Daily Telegraph*'s account, though not quoting me directly, reads singularly like the *Herald*'s: "There are believed to be only four similar amphorae in existence," it stated, adding, "One is in the British Museum."

The curators of every museum that owned such an amphora must have been close to apoplexy when they read this nonsense, not the least explosive being Grimes at the London Museum—which was home to at least three! A week later I received a letter from a man in the south of France claiming to have found a Roman shipwreck containing a cargo of these amphorae. How many would we like to buy?

From his new post in Birmingham, Adrian warned, "I do suggest that you insist with the *Telegraph* that you vet their reports and their captions to photographs." But as he very well knew, this was easier said than done. Weekly magazines might have time for such niceties, but not daily newspapers. To be news the story had to be in tomorrow morning's edition and had to go swiftly up the line from the reporter's typewriter. Were he to agree to let the source check his copy before it went to print, he would soon be out of a job—and with a few more "Pot Luck" stories like that, so might I.

14   *A Bit o' the Old Roman*

WITHIN DAYS OF finding the "amphora pit," the publicity propelled us into revamping Adrian Oswald's small Bygone London exhibit in the Guildhall Library's Bridge to enable lunchtime Londoners see what we were finding. But both Audrey and I well knew that showmanship was not enough. The specter of Grimes's disapproval hung heavy over us, and only a demonstration of academic responsibility could hope to change his mind. So along with the digging, the pot washing, the mending, and the restoring, we worked at nights to write publishable reports on the Walbrook pits, a project that called for the drawing of more than a hundred pottery and glass vessels.

While writing the academic and deadly dull report on the pits, at Raymond Smith's suggestion I also wrote the text for a small popular booklet titled *Discoveries on Walbrook 1949–50*, which allowed me to give credit to my Guildhall Irregulars. To my surprise, it was published with a preface by Smith publicly putting his imprimatur on our rescue efforts. Considering the number of would-be assassins lurking in the woods to nail me, Smith's stand was medal-worthy. At the time, however, I was more interested in converting his favor into equipment and a vehicle to carry it around the city. But expressions of confidence were one thing and money to back it quite another. Weary Irregulars pushing borrowed wheelbarrows through the empty city as the shadows lengthened on a Saturday afternoon would have become a familiar sight had there been anyone around to watch us.

On one occasion, several days of rain had turned the construction holes on the Walbrook site into something akin to Passchendaele in the autumn of 1917, and mud, brick dust, and cement caked our clothes and smeared our faces. Homeward bound, escorting an equally filthy wheelbarrow piled with soggy bags of artifacts, we turned out of Gresham Street into Guildhall Yard. Our procession found itself face to face with all the majesty of the City. Under a striped, mock-medieval awning a red carpet waited to welcome the Lord Mayor, the mace bearer, sword bearer, sheriffs, and aldermen of the City, as well several gold-uniformed state trumpeters of the king's Household Cavalry. On either side, the stately greeters stood. Only the frog footman was missing.

For a moment we hesitated, then marched on across the yard, up the red carpet, and into the building—and nobody said a word. The City police and Guildhall beadles had recognized us and concluded, as I had, that the sooner we were in and out of sight the better.

The beadles were responsible, among other things, for the building's security, for acting as guides to the hall ("Would the little girl like to sit in the Lord Mayor's chair?"), and for liaison with contractors for civic functions. They had their common room directly under our laboratory and became our valued friends and confidants—as well as a source of nutrition. At a time when food was rationed and you had to stand in line for an hour in Smithfield Market to buy a pound of horse meat, a Guildhall "do" meant a momentarily exotic leap in our standard of living. Food left over became the perquisites of the beadles, who always remembered their friends upstairs, and the annual Lord Mayor's Banquet could be relied on for several weeks' worth of nourishing turtle soup.

At the St. Swithin's House (Walbrook) site, Adrian Oswald had originally secured the support of the Company of Salters through its engaging and able clerk W. R. Nichols, who remained steadfast throughout the project, later commissioning a report to be preserved in the company's archives. Rudolph Palumbo, the other ground landlord, limited his interest to a catalog of those artifacts that were his. Nevertheless, together their cooperation ensured access to the site no matter what the clerk of the works or the senior foreman might have thought about it. And they thought a lot. Ruling the Walbrook foundation crews with a huge and horny hand was an Irish foreman named Connolly, who remains for me the Simon Legree of the construction trade. He had worked in India during the war and had learned to treat labor like galley oarsmen. Back in Britain he saw no reason to change his style. In me he saw a pale shadow of the Indian Army officer class he despised, and which had gotten in his bloody way at every turn. A bull of a man who always wore a brown trilby and a brown suit—perhaps he saw it as a uniform—he no doubt was an excellent foreman, being myopically dedicated to letting nothing and nobody stand in the way of the job. My Guildhall Irregulars, and above all, the paparazzi press, were unconscionable obstructions, and the fact that I was there with the blessing of the owners must have gnawed at Connolly's leathery soul.

"Look out, mate!" The sudden shout from the edge of the timbered hole made me look up just in time to avoid a shower of wet cement. From the huge crane in the site's center swung hoppers of cement whose bottoms opened by remote control to decant the contents into the foundation pits. Some of the cement invariably remained in the hopper's mouth, and could be shaken loose by the crane operator from high above in his control cab. In those days no one wore hard hats, and had even a couple of ounces of wet cement falling from 150 feet slapped me on the head I would, as they say, have known all about it. At the time I dismissed it as an accident and thanked my stars that someone had seen it coming. But several days later, one of the laborers (perhaps the one who had shouted the warning) told me, "That weren't no accident."

Maybe it was, and maybe it wasn't, but I had little doubt that the man in the brown suit would have shed no tears to see me carted away. The view was mutual. Knowing that effective foremen were considered by contractors to be pearls of great price, I had every expectation of facing him on other sites when this one was behind us. But I never did. Rumor had it that he went back to India or Pakistan, failed to realize that the day of the white bully had passed, and was enthusiastically beaten to death with pick handles.

I would receive a second cement message on another City site a couple of years later, this time while working within the confines of another timber-lined Roman well. Once again the foreman saw archaeology as a disruption and wished me gone, but on this occasion the cement came down, not in drops, but in a large, wet lump that landed with a formidable splat! several feet from the well. Apart from these "accidents," only twice did I come close to becoming the late City archaeologist. The first time was my own fault, having misjudged the space between the back of a crane and the wall of Walbrook's St. Michael's Church. As the St. Swithin's House construction holes expanded, the perimeter of high ground grew ever smaller, until at the north there remained a strip only about thirty feet wide—thirty feet occupied by the mobile crane and its rotating cab. While I was trying to get past the idle machine, the driver put it in gear and rotated, trapping me between it and the church. Fortunately, his maximum swing left a space of about nine inches in which I was plastered up the wall like a cartoon cat. Pinned there, waiting to find out whether the cab had further to go, gave me ample opportunity to question whether building-site archaeology was a sensible way to make a living. Had I been a portly person, the question could have been academic. My second opportunity to (as bad novelists say) dice with death would come much later.

Buoyed by the excitement of discovery and, to a degree, by the danger, and not a little by the press attention, I was giving no thought to the future—as Pam Grieve, my playwright partner, was at pains to point out. *House to Haunt* still needed polishing, but I told her that I had no time to do it. "But you can find time to write for the BBC," she angrily replied. Pam was right, for by this time I was contributing to anything from *Schools Broadcasting* to *Woman's Hour*. And that, in a way, was the problem. My longing to write for the theater was being satisfied by the BBC's radio opportunities. Worse, the magic of the theater was fading as the advantages of regular eating took hold. After a couple of stormy meetings and several recriminatory telephone calls, Pam agreed that we should send out copies of the imperfect play to agents in the hope that one would agree to handle it. We'd leave polishing until we found someone who cared enough to want it done.

In rare moments of reflection I recognized that I was no better prepared for a career in archaeology and museums than I had been for the theater. To be a successful Romanist (and that is what anybody who was anybody was), one needed fluent Latin and German—just for starters. My Latin was thin to the point of emaciation, and I held Grandpa Mann's "Ushen gushen gerfleishen" views of German. Besides, to make a mark in a well-trodden field calls for expertise beyond that of the recognized experts. The trick, therefore, was (and still is) to focus on an area that has hitherto received little attention. Then at least one has a sporting chance of making an uncontested yet legitimate name for oneself.

I have described how the Walbrook building site had exposed the red welts of the two devastating fires that swept London in the Roman era. Higher up in the layers was a third, that of the Great Fire of 1666, equally red, but composed of brick rubble rather than scorched clay daub. To the east of the site it overlay an Elizabethan floor of green and yellow glazed tiles. Just as anything found under the Boudiccan fire level dated before AD 61 and anything over it was later, so the 1666 debris cut the seventeenth century in half.

Adrian Oswald's work on clay pipes, his excavation of the Gracechurch Street Hoard, and our joint digging on the Bankside Power Station site had convinced me not only that "later stuff" was just as interesting as what a laborer friend called "a bit o' the old Roman" but also that very few archaeologists (with the exception of the Americans at Jamestown) knew anything about it. They seemed content to leave the artifacts of Tudor and later centuries to the curators of art museums, who in turn were interested only in objects that were both whole and visually appealing. The broken and commonplace had no supporters; yet, as Adrian had taught me, these were the tools to give post-medieval history a new dimension.

Recognizing the value of *terra sigillata* potters' names in dating the Roman ground, I looked for similar controls for pre- and post-1666 London. Adrian led the way with his marks on clay pipes, and I tried to follow by studying the evolution of another no less common object—the glass wine bottle. Though never marked with the names of makers, a small percentage bore glass seal impressions on their shoulders giving the name of the owner, his place of business, and sometimes even the date. By recording the shapes of dated examples ranging from the 1650s to the early nineteenth century, I might be able to do for post-medieval bottles what Felix Oswald had done for *terra sigillata*. I was not the first to attempt it. In 1914 the antiquary E. Thurlow Leeds had published a simple chronology of bottle shapes based on dated examples from Oxford. The need, as I saw it, was to refine both shapes and manufacturing details to a point where a fragment from a bottom or part of a neck could be datable. To that end, I began by laying out and drawing all the specimens in the Guildhall collection. While I was doing so, the museum received an unexpected visitor—Jean Carl "Pinky" Harrington, the archaeologist from Jamestown, and Oswald's American counterpart in the study of tobacco pipes.

In 1948 Harrington had excavated the early seventeenth-century glass factory near Jamestown and was now in England looking for anyone who knew anything about glass of that period. He had called at the museum at the beginning of his tour and learned that I was out on the building sites, but being a persistent individual (and having had very poor luck in finding anyone to help him), Harrington returned at the end of his itinerary. I have only his travel journal to prove that he met me and that I showed him what I was trying to do with the bottles. As it turned out, lights should have flashed and rockets exploded as Harrington came through the door, for this was to be the most important encounter of my life. But try as I have, I am ashamed to say I remember it not at all.

Throughout the first three months of 1950, the City's rescue archaeology had remained mine to handle as I saw fit. Lysbeth Webb had recovered from her illness and was ensconced in Oswald's old office at the far side of the library, but I saw nothing of her. I was answerable only to the librarian, Raymond Smith, whose supervision of what I was doing was limited to reviewing my monthly written reports. Nevertheless, he remained supportive, and in March he agreed to hire Audrey Baines as my assistant. Her diary entry for Monday, April 3, reads "Committee meeting. My job O.K."

Smith very well knew that if the Guildhall Museum was to regain its stature, it had to be staffed by people with far better credentials than ours, and through the winter months he had been looking for candidates. Audrey's appointment, therefore, coincided with the arrival of an assistant keeper. The keeper would come later.

Ralph Merrifield was thirty-seven, ruddy-faced, and possessed a broad smile and eyes that twinkled with good humor behind thick spectacles. Thinning hair made him look older, and his florid complexion was enough to make a casting agent file him under farmer. In reality, Ralph was a scholarly man in search of something to be scholarly about. He found it at Guildhall, and by the time of his retirement in 1978, and through his several fine books, he would become the twentieth century's leading authority on Roman London. At sixteen he had gone straight from grammar school to a job as an assistant at the Brighton Museum, one of Britain's more eclectic collections of everything from stuffed birds and arcade slot machines to George IV's Chinese pavilion. Apart from the inevitable wartime interruption, Ralph remained there until he came to London in 1950.

Perhaps because he, too, had entered the museum profession without either a university degree or any prior training, Merrifield remained forever helpful and encouraging—even when to do so became politically unwise. From the outset he must have been aware of the ill will emanating from the London Museum, but in the four months that would elapse before the new keeper arrived, he neither did nor said anything to trim my sails. Instead, when pressures from the building sites became too great, he would put on his boilersuit and descend into the maelstrom to do battle alongside us. Although he was never the exuberant teacher that Adrian Oswald had been, I was content in the belief that Ralph would be a willing and wise counselor.

Reading other museums' catalogs of Roman pottery I had often encountered the term Upchurch ware, one that seemed to encompass such a wide range of types and shapes that I had no idea what it really meant. Upchurch is a Kentish village not far from Rainham and stands on the edge of vast marshlands reaching out into the estuary of the river Medway. It was there in the mud of the Upchurch marshes that nineteenth-century antiquaries had found large numbers of complete Roman pots along with evidence of actual manufacturing. The finders' descriptions were vague. Had they really discovered the remains of kilns and if so what were they producing? What, if anything, still remained to be studied? With the Easter holiday coming up and with work on the London building sites temporarily slowed, Audrey and I decided to go see for ourselves.

We discovered that the marshes were owned by an orchard grower, Michael Webb of Sittingbourne, who graciously gave us permission, not only to survey and excavate on the marshes, but also to retain anything that interested us, an extraordinarily generous posture that hardened us in our resolve to make worthy use of his confidence. In 1950 gasoline was still rationed and few people had cars, and so the expedition traveled by train and bus: Audrey and I and two of the Guildhall Irregulars, Don Bailey and Peter Clark—all bowed under rucksacks crammed with rubber boots, paper bags, towels, measuring and photographic gear, and with army picks and shovels strapped to the outsides. We were, to say the least, an odd lot.

Lodged over a pub in Rainham, and using information culled from the nineteenth-century accounts, we spent the first two, fruitless days scouring the creeks, which had reportedly been the principle sources of kiln waste. But we found only a bronze purse bar dating from the fifteenth century. On the third day we spread farther afield and reached an area known as the Kingsferry Saltings across which an eroded causeway led to an island called Slayhills. Early Ordinance Survey maps showed small crosses there labeled "Roman Jewellery Found"—beacons to draw even the most conservative of treasure hunters. What, we asked ourselves, were hoards of Roman jewelry doing out on these marshlands where only potters were believed to have worked?

The causeway linking Slayhills to the mainland was in places barely twenty feet wide and at two points had been severed altogether, making passage impossible until the tide went out, and only then by wading through deep mud. Part of the three-quarter-mile link was natural clay, but part had been built up with London rubbish brought down on barges in the 1870s. Broken crockery, intact bottles of both glass and stoneware, ceramic ointment pots and their decorated lids, and clay pipes created a treasure-house of Victorian artifacts that thirty years later would be dug up from land dumps and sold in antique shops. In 1950 it was just junk to everyone but Audrey. By the time we had gone a quarter of a mile, her rucksack was filled with bottles and jars, and she had to abandon early treasures in favor of later and better examples. As for the rest of us, we trudged and slid onward still vainly searching for the first trace of Roman occupation.

I think it was Peter Clark who found it: a single gray potsherd bearded with green seaweed. We gathered excitedly around to admire it as though we were seeing the Holy Grail. There was no doubting that it was Roman—as were the several other pieces we found a few yards farther on. Each was picked up and bagged, its location roughly marked on our map. Beyond the next hummock of marsh grass we came on more—and more. Before long, like Audrey with her Victorian garbage, we were staggering under the load of potsherds, and took to bagging and leaving them to round up on our return. We never did. The farther we went, the more there were, until in places they stretched out into the mud flats as thickly as pebbles on a beach. As we waded through the mud we could feel our boots crunching them underfoot. Test holes dug into the mud found layers of sedge grass about a foot below the surface, and under it solidly packed potsherds and the burned clay called bricketage that the Romans used as drying pans for the extraction of salt from sea water.

We had found the mother lode, but we were little the wiser. We could find no evidence of structures, nor any indication that the huge quantities of broken pottery were any more kiln related than was the crockery in the London dumps. Two more days of hunting showed that the Roman potsherds extended out to Slayhills itself, but the ground there was so cut up by mud-filled gullies that much more time was spent floundering than finding. Several times one or other of us stepped into deep, mud-filled holes and would have sunk to inconvenient depths had we not learned to lie forward or back and to roll out of the loose onto firmer mud. Only by so doing could one escape without losing one's boots. We later discovered that many of the holes were the result of the marshes having been used as wartime shelling and bombing ranges. We learned, too, that the tide that went out with commendable rapidity to reveal several miles of mud could, in a matter of minutes, return as fast, and that once water-covered, the mud-filled holes could grip us until we drowned.

If we were to accomplish anything useful in this inhospitable yet bleakly beautiful environment, we would need to equip ourselves with safety ropes, an inflatable boat, much better tools, and containers for the finds—and a campaign plan. This, however, was not the only decision reached over that Easter week-end. Trudging mud-boltered back off the marshes, Audrey and I paused to rest in the rusting ruin of an abandoned army hut and there, guessing that she was too tired to argue, I asked her to marry me. In retrospect, I had not chosen one of the great romantic settings; but then we looked less like Romeo and Juliet than a pair of spent mud wrestlers, and anyone finding us there would readily have taken us for squatters.

Neither my decision to ask nor Audrey's to accept was reached as lightly as I make it appear or as irresponsibly as my mother would insist. We had been inseparable for the past three months, Audrey had moved out of her family home in Wimbledon and taken a room near me in Marylebone, we were now employed to work together, and we were totally committed to the task of saving London's archaeological legacy. Thus, marriage seemed as logical and necessary as putting the top on a milk bottle. What Audrey saw in me, heaven only knows; but to me she brought a degree of stability I had never before enjoyed. She had the beauty of Ingrid Bergman and the will of the Iron Duke, and I was entranced by one and needed the other. Though we had no home, no money (not even enough to buy an engagement ring), and singularly dicey long-term prospects, we returned to London in a state of ill-concealed euphoria.

Through the spring, work continued on the Walbrook and Bankside sites, with occasional side trips to Adrian Oswald's No. 11 Ironmonger Lane site where Selborne House was on its way up. Before it was complete Audrey and I would be called on to undertake a task for which nothing had prepared us— stabilizing and preserving the battered Roman mosaic, which the landowners public-spiritedly agreed to preserve in their basement. The pavement was, as I noted earlier, in very shabby shape, having been laid directly on the earth. The only way I could think of to make any sense of the mutilated design was to bed the pieces in a floor of cement and then to paint on enough of the missing elements to connect the surviving bits. This was easier said than done because the mosaic had sunk into hollows leaving some parts higher than others. Besides, neither Audrey nor I knew the first thing about mixing cement and less about achieving a sufficiently smooth surface to take the painted strips. A passing construction worker offered free advice.

"If you really want to get a nice smooth finish, you know what you oughta do?"

"No, what?"

"Piss on it, mate!"

I didn't—at least I don't remember that I did. Nevertheless, for amateur cement layers we can't have done too bad a job. Nearly forty years later, down in the Peat-Marwick basement, the Roman floor was still there.

June brought another and infinitely more nail-chewing commitment. A now sear-edged invitation printed on opulent card is the lasting reminder that on "Tuesday, the 20th of June, 1950, at 12.30 for 1 P.M. Precisely" I was to speak to members of the Bassishaw Ward Club on "Recent Discoveries in the City." I had accepted the invitation over the phone in February (when June seemed eons away), and had given it no further thought until the announcement card showed up in the mail. Apart from my virtuoso dramatization of Pizarro's conquest of Peru before an audience of surprised sixth formers, and a later army demonstration of how to dismantle and reassemble a Bren gun (never completed owing to a surfeit of parts), I had no experience in lecturing to a live audience.

"What nonsense!" said Audrey. "Of course you can do it. What better training could you want than the theater?"

"But that's not the same," I replied. And it wasn't. Learning a part, and being
supported by other actors if you dried, was one thing; standing up scriptless to
try to excite an audience of lunch-filled London businessmen to the thrill of digging up broken pots was quite another.

The clubs are a long-established feature of the City's mercantile life, providing opportunities for senior men working in the individual wards to get together
semisocially for monthly luncheons. This one was to meet at Tallow Chandlers'
Hall, one of the few old guildhalls to have escaped Hitler's bombers. To me,
therefore, even the building was an intimidation. Though I was cleaned up and
in my best suit, any fool could see that I did not belong among the gathering
Bassishaw wardsmen. Tall, gray-haired men with gold watch chains across their
waistcoats looked straight through me, and short fat ones with purple veins in
their noses enveloped me in cigar smoke. They had nothing to say to me nor I
to them, so I retreated to a corner, accepting each offering of sherry while going
over in my mind the various names and dates that had to figure in my talk: the
emperor Hadrian, AD 117 to 138; Antoninus Pius, 138 to . . .

"More sherry, sir?" asked a waiter.

"Yes, thanks very much." Pius, 138 to 161, or was it 151? Then there was the
coin of Postumus from the well. What were his dates, 258 to 268?

"Would you care for a little more . . ."

"Thank you." Each glass brought a new surge of confidence, and soon I was
no longer worrying that mine was the only cheap gray suit in the room or that
my well-worn shoes did not shine like those around them. I even said "Hello" to
somebody and took the answering grunt as burgeoning camaraderie.

The luncheon began as advertised, at one o'clock precisely, and although it
progressed with the speed born of long practice, for me it spanned several eter-
nities. After offering pleasantries about the weather and how jolly it must be to
be an archaeologist, my flanking companions felt that they had done their duty
and left me to eat in silence. Between courses I passed the time taking furtive
looks at the note cards hidden on my lap, going over my dates, and trying to
remember the gestures I had rehearsed at the bathroom mirror.

Augustus—Tiberius—Caligula—Claudius—Nero . . . Then who? Was it
Vitellius, or maybe Galba? The buzz of voices and the clatter of cutlery began to
fuse into a single mesmerizing sound. From a great distance a voice was saying
something that seemed to matter.

"And we're most grateful to the Corporation for allowing our young friend here to set aside his pick and shovel long enough to be with us today. It's a great pleasure to introduce . . ."

I don't recall standing up, but I well remember my horror as my notes slid off my lap and disappeared under the table. I remember, too, the rows of pink faces wreathed in blue smoke, all expectantly turned in my direction, and how as I tried to share with them the thrill of digging in London I found myself seeing fewer faces and more bald heads. I had planned to tell them about two thousand years of the City's history, but before I got past the Romans, coughing broke out, handkerchiefs fluttered from sleeves, and the sound of nose blowing and the sharp click of closing watch covers all made their point.

I had given a lot of thought about how to begin, but none about how to end. "I, er . . . I don't know about you," I mumbled lamely, "but I think I'd better be getting back to work." Then, as a bright but infinitely dumb afterthought, I added something to the effect that perhaps this very afternoon I would make a discovery that would prompt the club to invite me back.

I didn't, and neither did they—which was hardly surprising. As a lecturer I had committed every sin in the book. My audience, like members of business and social clubs the world over, was there not because I was speaking but because it was Thursday. On such occasions even prime ministers recognize the importance of brevity. Lunchtime listeners with afternoon meetings to attend, trains to catch, or mistresses to mollify become demonstrably insecure if the speaker gets within five minutes of his allotted time without flagging the end with a "Now for my last . . ." or "And finally, gentlemen, . . ." Lacking any structure to my lecture (beyond the beginning at the beginning and going on until I was through), I had no means of pacing myself.

Waiting impatiently in line to retrieve his coat, one man snorted, "Damn that feller! Didn't anyone tell him we break at two?"

Although stopping on time would have helped, I doubt whether anything I might have said or done could have turned fiasco into a cheering, foot-stomping, never-to-be-forgotten success. I had been invited as a faceless name representing the Corporation of London's museum, and theoretically someone meriting the attention of people of importance in the City. In reality, I was hopelessly out of my class: too young, too scruffy, and too inexperienced a speaker to be taken seriously. I was also too well wined to respond to the temper of my audience— and heaven only knows what violation I had done to Claudius and Co.

Had Adrian Oswald remained at the museum, he would no doubt have taught me that when asked to speak for thirty minutes, never take more than twenty-nine. He would have taught me much else besides—including a warning never to be afraid to confess ignorance, something hard to do when one is looked to as "the expert" from the City's museum.

A call from the manager of a warehouse at the eastern edge of the Corporation of London's domain took me to Cooper's Row near the Tower of London, where, in the basement, workmen had dug a large hole to seat something or other. In the course of their digging they had uprooted several lumps of Kentish ragstone and two fragments of what looked like part of a sandstone pillar. It was this that the manager thought might be interesting. In the dimly lit cellar I examined the broken stones and noted that the badly flaked surfaces retained what appeared to be the remains of scalelike decoration. A close inspection of the hole revealed nothing datable, and for me the stones' decoration rang no bells. One thing was certain, however; they were much too heavy to get back to the museum on a bus.

"Almost certainly Victorian," I announced. "Probably dumped in as fill when your building was put up."

The manager thanked me and profusely apologized for dragging me across the City on so worthless an errand. Several days later, while thumbing through the London Museum's Roman catalogue I came on a photograph of a scale-decorated column fragment found in King William Street in association with an early Roman mosaic pavement. A little more research (of the kind that should have been done before setting out for Cooper's Row) showed that the warehouse block straddled the foundations of the Roman city wall—the wall whose later bastions contained reused building materials. In 1852 construction work a short distance to the south of the warehouse had encroached on part of Bastion B2 and had yielded fragments of the tomb of Rome's procurator in Britain at the time of the Boudiccan rebellion, Julius Classicianus—fragments which included parts of pillarlike bolsters decorated with similar scale ornament. In his 1965 book *The Roman City of London,* Ralph Merrifield would describe the Classicianus tomb remains as "one of the most important historical documents of Roman Britain."

A call to the Cooper's Row warehouse manager revealed that his Victorian pillar fragments had been rolled back into the hole and concreted over. Gone—but not forgotten. Today a contemporary print of the City wall exposed in 1818 during an earlier Cooper's Row demolition hangs in my hall as an ever-present reminder of what can happen when one is too afraid, or too arrogant, to confess, "I'm sorry, I don't know."

With the Walbrook and Bankside sites having almost run their course, and such finds as we continued to make being insufficiently breathtaking to retain Fleet Street's attention, we settled into a routine anonymity that must have been welcomed by the archaeological profession. Nevertheless, the three months of intense publicity between December and the end of February, coupled with our monthly pot parade, had convinced Raymond Smith's Library Committee that the museum was alive, busy, and important to the City. In retrospect, although only Smith and Oswald acknowledged what we had accomplished, I believe that giving the Guildhall Museum a public face was our most important contribution.

In theory, merging the Guildhall with the London Museum made admirable sense; to have done so in the winter of 1950 while the Guildhall was without curatorially experienced staff could have been chaotic and potentially disastrous. Nevertheless, the merger was a step whose time would come, and the felicitous and carefully planned marriage that brought the Museum of London into being in 1975 ranks high among Britain's postwar cultural accomplishments—even if its entrance has all the charm of an abandoned railroad station.

Knowing virtually no one in the museum profession, the name Norman Cook meant nothing to me. Indeed, I do not recall hearing it spoken until the day he turned up as Smith's choice for keeper. Small, with a cherubic face and a ready if tight smile, he appeared to be a man who, when looking in the mirror, liked what he saw. In contrast to the quiet and scholarly Merrifield, he would prove to be an outgoing and excellent public relations advocate for the museum. He arrived as a man with several missions, not the least of them to play First Murderer to my Clarence, though who bid him to do the deed and where stood Smith withal, were questions neither posed nor answered.

Had I been in the new keeper's shoes I, too, would have recognized the need to ensure that no loose cannons were free to explode into newsprint. It made perfect sense, therefore, that he should instruct me to refer all press inquiries to him. But that was not enough. When I told him that the second part of Audrey's and my paper on the Walbrook pits was ready to be sent to the London and Middlesex Archaeological Society, he declined to let it go. The conversation went something like this:

"There'll be plenty of time for publishing. But now and for the foreseeable future, I want you to concentrate on the sites and leave the report writing until later."

"How much later?"

"Ten years perhaps. It can take that long for the rebuilding to slow down."

This was the antithesis of Oswald's teaching. I tried to argue that unless one analyzed and reported on the key discoveries while they remained fresh in one's mind and while questions arising out of the research could be checked out, much vital information would be irretrievably lost. But it was to no avail. Norman Cook was committed to ensuring my silence no matter what else might have to be sacrificed on the same placatory altar. His decision has to have been one of the most unfortunate and ill advised in the history of London archaeology, ensuring as it did that all but a few of the products of seven years' salvage work performed during the most widespread rebuilding since 1666 would remain forever mute.

It was on this occasion or on another shortly thereafter that Cook told me that having no university degree I would be unwise to count on a career in archaeology. But so what? At twenty-three, the here and now was all that mattered. The sun was shining, I was no longer starving, I was being paid for having fun—and I was about to be married.

15 🖋 *Walbrook to Williamsburg*

R AIN FELL HARD in London on Saturday, September 30, 1950, the day of both my twenty-third birthday and Audrey's and my wedding. It was a big day but a small wedding. Neither of us had any money, and we were hard-pressed to find enough to buy something suitable to wear. The Marylebone Street Registry Office was as no-frills as one could get, but if Audrey yearned for a traditional veil and confetti wedding she never said so. Her mother gave her away; my best man was our senior volunteer digger, Skip Allen, and our official photographer Bill Davis—who came close to being felled by a passing taxi as he stood back to get his shot. After lunch at the Café Royale in Regent Street we retreated to Wimbledon and to the second floor of Audrey's family home, where we were to live for the next seven years.

I recall only two wedding gifts, one a butter dish from Aunt May (which we were convinced had been left over from her own wedding in 1922), and a magnificent set of walrus ivory–handled carving cutlery wrapped in a crumpled sheet of brown paper handed to us by a kindly dragline driver on the Bank-side Power Station site. It did not behoove us to ask where he got it, but both the gesture and the cutlery remain as testimony to the rapport that we were able to establish with the much older and sometimes semiliterate construction workers.

Having no vacation time due to us, there was no honeymoon, and the following Monday we were back in the London mud. The arrival of Ralph Merrifield and then Norman Cook had secured a future for the Guildhall Museum, and in the eyes of the Library Committee there was no longer a monthly need to justify its existence. Consequently, pressure on our attic pot-restoration factory eased and no longer did we have to work late into the evening to turn potsherds into pots. That was just as well. Building sites were opening up all across the city, and two pairs of legs and eyes were stretched to the limit. Week after week our efforts ranged from salvaging the contents of Roman pits to seventeenth-century sewers—to a charnel pit in an old graveyard in St. Mary Axe.

In 1950 my family relationships had taken a turn for the better—or worse depending on one's point of view. In January my mother wrote saying that she had remarried and asked me to come down to Torquay to meet her husband. She was now Mrs. Douglas Reddall, having combined his first and last names into a better sounding surname, the same disservice she had done me so many years earlier. Nevertheless, I did as she asked, and was astonished to find her ensconced in a large house with a grand sea view. Douglas, however, seemed less grand, in his sixties, of medium height, and with no time for archaeology, the theater, or anything else that interested me. My mother appeared less enthusiastic about the marriage than about the opportunity to buy expensive furniture. Poor Dougy had had a rough life, she assured me, and now deserved to reap its rewards. Dougy had money and it was up to her to spend it. But it turned out that Dougy did not have money, and he later told me that he had been led to believe that she did. After that single visit I would never see my mother again.

About six months later I received a call from the Torquay police advising me that Mrs. Douglas Reddall had called them to accuse her husband of trying to strangle her. He, in turn, had claimed that she had assaulted him. The officer wanted to know whether I had anything helpful to say about this embarrassing domestic quarrel. But I did not. Shortly thereafter, a frantic Douglas came to London to plead with me to intercede with my mother on his behalf. But I could not. At the time of my own marriage, Audrey and I had been accepted into my father's family—on the condition that I no longer maintained a relationship with my mother, and it was a commitment I had no intention of breaking. Throughout my seven years at the museum I met my father once a week and ruefully grew to recognize the significance of having lived all those years without a father. Had the divorce judge ruled differently, the course of my adolescent life would certainly have been very different and probably infinitely happier.

My father's weekly visits to the museum invariably found us ragged cuffed and mud caked, in marked contrast to his immaculate business suit and bowler hat. If he inwardly winced, he never showed it. Indeed, I think he was rather proud of seeing his "children" in the *Illustrated London News* or on the picture pages of the *London Times* and *Daily Telegraph*. The association meshed well with his own activities as secretary of the City of London Society.

Within a year of Norman Cook's being hired as curator of the Guildhall Museum it became apparent that our husband-and-wife team made him uneasy,

and by the spring of 1953 he had ordained that Audrey should remain working with the artifacts in the lab while I continued the fieldwork on my own.
It was a decision that pleased neither of us, but I had the solace of knowing
that in an emergency I could rely on Ralph Merrifield to help out. One such
plea brought him to the site of the new Bank of London and South America,
where I was working at a depth of about twenty feet in a Roman wood-lined
well shaft. Standing upright in it was a ladder, its wood sodden and spongy but
still intact—the first Roman ladder found in England. While a historical treasure of great price, it was also a challenge to save. Unfortunately, Ralph and I
were denied the opportunity to fully succeed. The contractors made us desist at
twenty-seven feet, and it was not until several weeks later that we were allowed
back into the construction hole to discover that the midsection of the ladder had
been destroyed, leaving us only the bottom five feet. Remarkable though the
find still was, it was eclipsed by another discovery, a goat-skin bikini bottom
with one of its leather drawstrings still tied.

What came to be known as the "Bikini Affair" would mark a further decline
in Audrey's and my relationship with our boss. On the afternoon of bringing it
to our attic lab, we were about to immerse the garment in neat's-foot oil when
Cook told us that he intended to take it to the BBC's TV studio to display it on
the quiz show *Animal, Vegetable or Mineral?* Knowing that the fragile leather
would shrink and crack if left to dry out, one or other of us (I forget which)
dared to question the wisdom of his subjecting the thin leather to the hot television lights. But Norman Cook was not a man who liked to be challenged, least
of all by his junior staff. As expected, the outcome was that the bikini suffered
damage that could never be entirely rectified.

We resolved that thereafter we would not report important new discoveries
until we had time to give them stabilizing first aid.

Early in 1952 work began on a city block facing Leadenhall Street that was to
be home to a vast new building for Lloyds Insurance. The removal of bombed
basements and the grading of the soil and gravel beneath them went on at a
rapid pace, allowing me time only to uncover, plot, and photograph fragments
of a succession of Roman buildings that ranged from the first to the fourth centuries. Underneath a tile-constructed pier for one of them I found that someone had thrust a pointed stick into the subsoil and filled the resulting hole with
small provincial coins of the fourth century. Known as minims and made of copper, they had fused together into a solid column of green corrosion. Back in
the lab Audrey began the slow process of separating them. After several days of

treatment they were apart but still scarcely identifiable when Cook visited the lab and saw them for the first time. Outraged that he had not been told earlier—though in truth there had been nothing to tell—he berated us for operating like an independent branch of the museum answerable to nobody but ourselves.

To a degree Cook was right. Only once do I recall him visiting a site where I was working. It was about three in the afternoon when he arrived accompanied by two well-dressed City businessmen with whom he had been lunching. I, in contrast, was up to my knees in a seventeenth-century trash pit and had been there throughout my lunch hour, since that was when the builders took theirs. Tired, dirty, and hungry, I foolishly asked, "Have you come to help?" Whereupon my boss answered, "Why keep a dog and bark yourself?" On that occasion, and on many another, I wished that Adrian Oswald had never quit. Fortunately, however, I had the friendship of Ralph Merrifield, whose cautioning words of wisdom helped keep the ship on what passed for an even keel.

My work on the Lloyds site lasted more than a year and included three memorable moments. The first was heralded by the odor of wine so permeating that it drifted out into Leadenhall Street, prompting wine connoisseur businessmen to stop, sniff, and smile. A prewar wine merchant had occupied premises at the west end of the site, and his cellar stock had been buried beneath the debris when the building burned. I was there soon after a dragline bucket broke through a cellar wall to reveal hundreds of still-binned bottles of port and other wines. Within hours of the discovery drunken workmen on the site were sitting, lying, and in one case swinging from the cables of a mechanical grab. Unopened bottles were being hauled away by workmen in bags, baskets, and old cement bags, anything that would get the windfall home. It took several hours for Lloyds' management to discover what was afoot and demand that the clerk of the works restore order and cordon off the treasure chest. Of my six bottles of port, three had been spoiled by the fire and three were as close to ambrosia as I could imagine—and I still have the empties to remind me of one of the great moments in London archaeology.

A few weeks later a second wine cellar was breached, but by then Lloyds knew what had to be done. Insurance had paid for the merchant's loss, and so, legally, the cellar's contents belonged to whichever company had paid out. Rather than trying to find the owner, Lloyd's legal counsel advised that the premises should remain bombed. To that end the dragline operator was ordered to smash his bucket through the cellar, breaking every bottle—hence the renewed aroma wafting over the city.

My second still-vivid memory of the Lloyds dig was singularly unfunny and marked by deferred terror. A pottery-rich Roman pit had been exposed in the wall of the excavation just before the dragline operator quit for lunch, a heaven-sent opportunity for me to work on retrieving the contents. The driver had assured me that I had half an hour before he would be back. But neither he nor I knew that his foreman had elected to change drivers for the next shift. Unaware that I was in the hole, the new operator started up his machine and hurled its bucket in the direction of his predecessor's last cut. Whether he saw me in time or the bucket's reach could extend no farther, I shall never know. But it stopped about six inches from my right ear. So engrossed was I in saving the pottery that I thought only to step back long enough to warn the operator that I was still there. Shortly thereafter, I gathered up the pottery into a sack and made my way off the site to catch the next bus back to the museum. While sitting onboard with the bag of pottery on my lap, I suddenly began to shake uncontrollably. My head spun, my back shivered, and my hands shook so badly that other passengers stared at me wondering what was wrong. The fear that should have gripped me as the bucket swung at my head had been inexplicably delayed.

The third happened a few weeks later. I was working in a safer area at the same western end of the Lloyds site, digging within a timbered caisson about twenty-five feet below the surface. It was a gloomy November afternoon that required electric lamps to enable the workers to see what they were digging. At the bottom of the huge, timber-lined trench the foundation-laying crew had found the last three feet of a Roman well constructed from a square wooden frame with two barrels within it, set one inside the other. Excavating the contents and carefully drawing the well's construction was slow going. Workers who had been busy around me when I began had departed without my noticing, nor was I aware that the noise of machinery had ceased. When eventually I stood up there was not a sound to be heard. I looked up to the lights and saw them defused by swirling yellow fog. The cross-timbers that I would have to traverse to get out were lost somewhere above me in the seemingly impenetrable blanket. Deep below the surface of the construction pit, the fog sagged down into the trench like thick molasses. With my tools slung around me and clutching three intact Roman jugs, I clambered up the ladder to the first stage, and there swung away from it to grab a second ladder, which disappeared into the choking yellow blanket above. Having scaled it, I had next to reach the upper cross-bracing spanning the thirty-foot-wide trench and along whose twelve-inch timber I would have to crawl to safety. I was painfully aware that should I slip, nobody would find me until the next day; but more importantly, I might lose the jugs.

Although I was by then above the lights, I had the advantage of a soft yellow glow below me that enabled me to see a foot or so ahead. Inching across the narrow timber and knowing the depth of the hidden gulf below was a never-to-be-forgotten journey. The trauma of that experience is memorialized by the jugs now in the Museum of London.

In retrospect, my work was archaeology at its most primitive at a time when the opportunities offered as a result of the wartime bombing went largely ignored. In the eyes of the City fathers, its past was being well served by Grimes's random trenching for the Roman and Medieval London Excavation Council, and my puny efforts to clear a well there and plot a fallen wall here were nice but not necessary. Because I had no transportation, tools were limited to those I could take on a bus: the old museum camera, notepad, a handful of six-inch nails, trowel, hand brush, a U.S. Army surplus entrenching spade and pick, a ball of string, a tape measure, and a six-foot transit pole that conveniently came apart in the middle. Surveying with no one to hold the other end of the tape led, I fear, to some less than precise measuring.

On small building sites the clerk of the works would sometimes take an interest and come to my assistance, as one did during clearance of the graveyard beside the bombed church of St. Olave, Hart Street, the burial place of the famous diarist Samuel Pepys. On more than one occasion I would arrive at that site and find the clerk down on his knees carefully scraping dirt from a skeleton for me to photograph. That was in 1951 when Audrey was still helping me with the digging. Her presence generated one of the more memorable London moments. Two Irish laborers coming on the site looking for employment saw her at work, and one said to the other, "My Christ, Paddy, they've got f——in' women workin' here!" Evidently preferring unemployment to the stigma of unisex laboring, they quickly departed. On the same site, a Saturday noontime cessation of foundation digging left a chalk-walled pit beside the church only partially emptied. As the last workman climbed out he told me, "If you find any gold, mate, it's mine!" Moments later I jumped down in his place and picked up a George I gold guinea. "You mean, like this?" I replied. It was one of only two gold coins I found in seven years of digging.

Before the war Audrey had been the fond owner of two tortoises, neither of which survived the bomb that destroyed her Wimbledon home. With the house rebuilt and the first postwar importation of tortoises reaching the Bermondsey street market, she insisted that replacements be purchased and installed in our garden. She bought one and I another. With legs and heads protruding from both ends of brown-paper wrappers, we sat with them on the bus being quizzically eyed by bowler-hatted fellow passengers. We had just reached the Mansion House bus stop when I felt something wet and nasty in my lap. My tortoise had laid two shell-less eggs on my trousers. Thus was I introduced to the hitherto closed book of herpetology.

After her first wet run, Mrs. Calloway (I forget why we called her that) proceeded to lay four properly shelled eggs which we incubated in our airing cupboard. Along with photographer Bill Davis we had acquired several friends in the newspaper world, one or more of whom recognized that the impending birth of the first tortoises in England since the war had popular appeal. Consequently, the sand-filled box in the airing cupboard became the focus of a press vigil. When the first tiny brown head pecked its way out of its shell it must have been surprised to find flashbulbs popping and a newsreel camera whirring to capture the moment of arrival. The proud owners were interviewed at length and became overnight celebrities on the pages of the less reputable newspapers as well as in movie houses around the country. That we both worked for London's Guildhall Museum seemed to add a touch of class to the stories. The previously cited adage that any publicity is better than none was not in the mind of Norman Cook, who was certain that we had embarrassed him personally and sullied the name of the museum.

Undeterred by what we deemed to be unwarranted criticism, Audrey set about enlarging her tortoise family and did so with the help of the world-renowned naturalist Gerald Durrell, who later founded a famed zoo on the island of Jersey. Specimens shipped to us from expeditions to both East and West Africa, along with imports from Australia and South America, made 10 Melbury Gardens an established tortoise habitat and the subject of a nature film that played throughout the United Kingdom as the second feature to Humphrey Bogart and Katherine Hepburn's *African Queen*. Together Audrey and I wrote a slim volume titled *A Handbook of Tortoises, Terrapins and Turtles*, which was to remain in print through three decades and was widely recognized as the tortoise keeper's bible. Later Audrey wrote her own book, *My Family of Reptiles*, by which time the collection had expanded to include caymen, alligators, assorted terrapins, and an incredibly vicious teguexin from South America.

The tegu, whom we named Francis, clearly resented having been brought from Brazil to Wimbledon. Feeding primarily on mealworms and eggs, he was impossible to tame and tended to blow the eggs back in one's eye. One Saturday afternoon we were scheduled to receive two visitors from the London Zoo. In the hope of keeping Francis relatively cordial, we shut him in the bathroom with a bowl of eggs, and only went to return him to his cage minutes before our visitors were expected to arrive. But Francis had vanished. He had escaped down a pipe hole beside the basin and departed between the floor joists. Only the end of his tail remained visible from a point somewhere under the living room where tea was soon to be served. To our dismay, we were still tearing up floorboards in an effort to corral him when the doorbell rang. Any hopes we might have had of being accepted into the world of professional herpetology ended abruptly with Francis, who shortly thereafter went back to the pet shop—as a gift.

The pride of the collection, and certainly the most intelligent and friendly, was a large South American red-eared tortoise whom we called Tigillinus, naming him after the commander of Nero's Praetorian Guard. He had featured in our nature film, where he was shown being courted by an amorous Australian long-necked terrapin, as well as doing his party trick of sliding down a flight of stairs. In the week before commercial television (ITV) began in Britain, I took part in a dry-run, closed-circuit broadcast, taking several of the family on the show. Unfortunately, Tigillinus disgraced himself by mounting Mrs. Calloway on camera, eventually pushing her off the table. He was never invited back.

In 1954, after much lobbying, Norman Cook was able to secure the interior of the Royal Exchange as a venue for exhibiting many of the museum's treasures. At the same time, he moved the museum offices away from Guildhall to the Exchange. Only Audrey and I remained in our aerie in the Guildhall attic. Though out of sight, we were not out of mind. On the contrary, our leader became increasingly nervous that we were now out of easy reach and doing work that he knew nothing about. Late in the year, Cook had "a word" with Audrey suggesting that her growing stature as a tortoise-keeping celebrity could be benefited by her giving up archaeology for herpetology. The writing was on the wall. She read it and quit—soon to be replaced by an American postman.

Bill Rector had been stationed in England with the U.S. Army and had become so fascinated by British history that employment in the U.S. Postal Service lost its appeal. Hired by Cook as my conservation assistant in 1954, Bill was a genial colleague who introduced me to life in the United States. In contrast to the drabness of postwar England, it sounded so like a latter-day Babylon that I found it hard to understand why he'd left.

Earlier, in the spring of 1953, began a saga that became an archaeological circus more bizarre than the herald-led search for Dick Whittington. Grimes's random trenching had sliced through an open basement on the opposite side of the Walbrook road where Adrian Oswald and I had begun our salvage efforts in the early fall of 1949. The property occupied a whole city block that was to be home to a new office building named Bucklersbury House. At a meeting of the Roman and Medieval London Excavation Council on June 25, 1953, Grimes described the discovery of "part of a Roman dwelling" and, adjacent to it, part of a large classical sculpture that "had been thrown down among later and undatable debris," with "nothing to indicate its date or original provenance." Both statements were classic examples of the limitations imposed by trenching, which cannot be more revealing than reading a single line from a page of text. In the spring of 1954 both statements would be proved wrong.

When the clearing of the bombed remains still standing on the Bucklersbury House site began, Grimes's workman were able to return to expand their earlier trench. It turned out that they had dug, not into a dwelling, but into a temple to the god Mithras—the most sensational archaeological discovery to have been found in postwar London. As for the unidentified sculpture, that turned out to be a figure of the god Cautopates (the god of night) which had been retrieved from debris associated with the destruction of the temple in the fourth century.

My salvaging mandate on that site had very little to do with the temple (other than excavating a Roman well located a few yards from it). Instead, my job was to recover such antiquities that might be revealed across the rest of the vast construction site. That it was likely to be immensely rich had been indicated by John Price's discoveries, described in chapter 12, made directly to the north in 1873 when building excavators cut through the bed of the artifact-rich Walbrook river. I had reached the western edge of its peatlike silt (where I found the still-feathered bird) in 1949, but those discoveries were a mere whisper of the excitement to come.

The Walbrook stream had meandered about and had been revetted and channeled several times to allow for Roman building construction in its valley, the timber platforms and pilings for which remained perfectly preserved in the peat. So, too, had countless metal objects, ranging from iron door locks to carpenters tools, and hundreds of nails large and small, all immaculately preserved, thanks in part to the leatherworkers' waste that put tannic acid in the soil.

One morning when I arrived at the site, a workman pointed to an iron hook that was being used to suspend the weight of a powerful pile driver. The workers' own hook had broken, and a Roman hook salvaged from the Walbrook was serving as an adequate substitute. Remarkable though that was, it pointed to a growing problem. The workmen were digging into the Roman levels in their lunch hours and selling what they found in nearby pubs. Shiny brass and copper broaches, coins, toiletry tools, and heaven knows what else were daily leaving the site and disappearing into the hands of souvenir collectors. And there was worse to come.

The limitations of my salvage mandate had been very clear. I could dig where the workmen had more to do, but once they had cut the precisely defined holes to receive the concrete piers, I could not invade the sides no matter how tempting a half-revealed artifact might be. But that restriction was unknown to (or ignored by) treasure hunters who attacked the site at night and, with the aid of flashlights, tunneled into the sides of the contractor's neatly dug holes. Chief offenders were a schoolboy and his dad (their names withheld to protect the guilty) who together retrieved a collection that would be the envy of any museum. But I was blamed for the damage they did, and was barred from the site. Two years later, the boy, by then a maturing seventeen, donated his collection to the Guildhall Museum, where it was graciously and smilingly accepted by the curator, Norman Cook. The *Sunday Times* reported that father and son had assembled the collection from "lower levels revealed by the builders' excavators after professional archaeologists had completed their investigations." No one remembered that the vandalous lad had been responsible for halting those investigations.

It is safe to say that builders the world over shudder at the approach of an archaeologist, and those responsible for construction progress at Bucklersbury House were no different. By the time Grimes had uncovered most of the Mithraic temple, archaeology had become an incredibly dirty word. As soon as the press got wind of the discovery crowds gathered, some people climbing on their friends' shoulders to see over the tall fences, others lying in the street to peer between the boards. Headlines shouted "15,000 at Roman Temple. Hundred are turned away" and "Roman Temple Crowd Clash with the Police." One report had it that Grimes had to be surrounded by five policemen to protect him from a crowd angry at being denied a sight of the God of Light.

The outcome of all this was that no one but the construction crews were allowed onto the site, and all I could do was watch departing trucks piled high with Walbrook peat in which small brassy objects glistened in the sunlight on their way to a dumping place said to have been somewhere in the North Sea.

In spite of increasingly dismayed and angry letters to newspaper editors calling for the new building's owners to preserve the temple remains, not even a member of Parliament's House of Commons question in support could delay the march of progress. I must add, however, that the MP had not then visited the site, and that when he subsequently did, he reportedly said "he did not think it was worth a lot paying to save it."

Nevertheless, it was saved—after a fashion. When the construction workers attacked it with pneumatic drills and sledge hammers, the stones and tiles were thrown into skips and trucked to an adjacent bomb site where a measured plan of the temple had been laid out. As each load was dumped, other laborers arranged the stones to simulate the walls—which was fine as far as it went. But the temple's foundations turned out to be far larger and deeper than predicted. Consequently, the skips of rocks kept arriving—and arriving—until the wall piles fell over and the rest of the rubble was heaped on top, creating a shapeless rock pile that soon sprouted weeds. Years later the pile was dismantled and from it a simulation of the temple was erected in the forecourt of Bucklersbury House, albeit facing in the wrong direction. The landowners had the satisfaction of knowing that they had done their bit for London history, and for his work at the temple site Grimes was made a Commander of the British Empire (CBE). So all was well that ended well—well, wellish.

Such is the relentless march of time that in 2007 Bucklersbury House was torn down, leaving the lowest levels of the temple's foundation, which escaped the salvage effort, to be restudied—albeit without the media circus that surrounded the first Mithras moments.

In the spring of 1956 with Bill Rector's help I excavated the remains of a Roman building in Cheapside about as large as the Mithras temple, but by no means as spectacular in its recovered artifacts. Described by the *City Press* as a "Giant Roman Bath under New Insurance Building," it was more complex than the paper suggested, having separate rooms for the various steps in Roman-era bathing ranging from the cold plunge of the *frigidarium,* through the *tepidarium,* to the hottest of all, the *sudatorium.* Outside the building rested a ten-foot-square wooden box that I identified as a holding tank for water to be used in the bath house. From it, said the newspaper, came several wooden writing tablets and leather shoes as well as a couple of slightly damaged pottery jugs. The paper did not list another relatively large object—because I didn't know what to call it. Made as a thick-ended, rectangular wooden box, with several holes drilled through it, I guessed that it might have had something to do with the building's hypocaust heating system. Like all the other finds, Bill and I conserved the wood and stored it away still unidentified. Thirty-five years later, Ian Blair, my successor in London archaeology, would find two more of these square vats and in one of them more of my previously enigmatic boxes. But this time they lay beside a series of iron links identifying them as part of a sophisticated water-raising system whose working reproduction is now an impressive feature of the Museum of London. Both Ian's boxes and mine were reunited when we appeared together in a British television program chronicling the reproduction process. If nothing else, this demonstrated that in archaeology no one should ever throw anything away.

Old newspaper clippings from 1950 remind me that within weeks of Norman Cook's arrival at the Guildhall Museum he gave some of my Roman finds from the Walbrook to the University of Western Ontario's museum in exchange for "a gift of Indian tools, arrow heads and skinning knives to a group interested in archaeology in England." Such trading really benefited nobody, since my London artifacts had nothing more than curiosity value to Canadian students even though they included "part of a shoe believed worn by a Roman about A.D. 120." Years later while visiting the archaeological collection at Plimoth Plantation in Massachusetts I came upon several pots that looked familiar. They had Guildhall Museum numbers on them, having been given to the then president of the reconstructed plantation.

From school geography classes I knew approximately where to find Western Ontario, and from history I had learned something about those self-righteous Pilgrims who buckled their hats and chased turkeys, but my knowledge of American history (other than that the United States had once been ours) was woefully deficient. Consequently, I knew nothing of Williamsburg in Virginia, and would have been astonished to know that my name was being uttered there.

Promoted by the history-obsessed rector of the Episcopal parish church, the Reverend W. A. R. Goodwin, and bankrolled by John D. Rockefeller Jr., the restoration of Virginia's colonial capital had been in progress, off and on, since 1928. By 1955 its architects and historians were beginning to look beyond bricks and mortar to the lives of the eighteenth-century citizens who had lived there. With tourism growing and Williamsburg's fame spreading, it seemed a good time to bring in a consultant from England. I have never entirely understood the logic of that proposal, but it may have had something to do with hands across the sea, or letting Revolutionary bygones be bygones. Be that as it may, Pinky Harrington of the National Park Service, who had visited Audrey and me at the

Guildhall Museum in 1950, was being asked whether he knew of anyone over there who might know something useful.

Harrington remembered our meeting and my interest in the evolution of glass wine bottles, and indeed half the artifacts dug up at Williamsburg since the restoration began were broken bottles. Why not bring that guy from London to work on your broken bottles? he suggested. Although the management of Colonial Williamsburg was not enamored of bottle bits and from time to time debated throwing all that junk away, Harrington's proposal filled the bill and certainly could do no harm. Consequently, Williamsburg's director of architecture, Mario Campioli, was instructed to invite me to pay Virginia a three-month visit in the summer of 1956.

Along with the invitation came several promotional books and pamphlets, among them a 1937 offprint from *National Geographic* extolling the beauty of the town's architecture. Illustrated in color, the gardens and avenues were discreetly peopled with strolling couples in white wigs, knee britches, and ball gowns. It appeared to be a halcyon world in which there were neither busy nor poor people. Only in the Governor's Palace kitchen was there a black person, "'Mammy' explaining to visitors the use of cooking utensils." Lastingly memorable, however, was an image of two Revolutionary-era soldiers watching modern black children eating watermelon over a caption explaining that "forebears of the pickaninnies who are up to their ears in watermelon probably received a similar treat from the soldiers of the Revolution."

"Can this place really be real?" Audrey asked as she handed me the magazine. "I mean, really . . ."

Not being readers of London's *Daily Mirror* we had not known that in April 1954 Ralph Champion, its American correspondent, had voiced a comparable (and equally uneducated) response to Rockefeller's Williamsburg. He called it a "fake city" whose people "spend their days in uncomfortable period costumes" for the benefit of "the students, tourists and women's clubs who arrive in reverent droves." The Ameriphobic correspondent had sneered at Rockefeller millions being "poured into creating a phony all-American sort of Stratford," its interiors furnished with British "heirlooms, tapestries from hard-up peers," and "irreplaceable national treasures shipped over from our country." Daisies can grow on a dunghill, and it is possible, even likely, that my invitation was inspired by Colonial Williamsburg's desire to rebut Champion's charges.

True, in our austere and threadbare postwar English experience the idea of a town inhabited by people with nothing to do but wander around looking decorative was hard to believe, but the invitation was real enough. "Three months in never-never land" could be, well, interesting. "Besides," I added, "one never knows where something like this might lead."

However, there was more good news to be considered. The theater company that owned the Q Theatre at Kew was willing to showcase *House to Haunt,* but it needed me to be on hand to work out the kinks. To do so would mean quitting my job at the museum. Audrey's response was terse and to the point. "Do that and I'll leave you," she said. And I'm sure she meant it.

In the New World

IN 1956 FLYING ANYWHERE was considered a rare adventure, and crossing the Atlantic in one of those huge TWA Super Constellations was akin to a later generation flying aboard the Concorde. Stewardesses were still hired as much for their looks as for their tray dexterity, and at the flight's end (after stops at Shannon in Ireland and Gander in Newfoundland), they gave you a full-color parchment certificate of achievement—fit for framing.

Colonial Williamsburg had agreed that Audrey should accompany me, but she was unable to secure a visa in time. So I traveled alone, seated in relatively luxurious coach class alongside a middle-aged and rather austere woman who said that she was an anthropology professor bound for somewhere called Poughkeepsie. Being accustomed to simple English place-names like Brighton or Bath, I thought Poughkeepsie a very odd name for anywhere. I had much, indeed everything, to learn.

I arrived in Williamsburg on July 3, and the next day being the Fourth of July holiday, I was left on my own to get my bearings—clad in a worsted English suit under a scorching summer sun. From beneath the shade of a Market Square tree and amid a happy crowd of more appropriately attired tourists, I watched a company of musicians in colonial uniforms fifing and drumming their way down the main street behind American flag bearers. A few minutes earlier I had watched the British flag being hauled down from the cupola of the Capitol building accompanied by a good deal of good-natured cheering from the crowd. Although I could see no cine cameras I supposed that somebody was making a movie. Nobody was, and I would soon learn that sort of thing went on all the time in restored Williamsburg.

Unlike the empty streets portrayed in the *National Geographic* photographs I'd seen, on this day Williamsburg was crowded with patriotic Fourth of July tourists. Liveried black coachmen drove happy families in carriages hither and yon up and down Duke of Gloucester Street. Everything and everywhere had an English ring to it, yet to my eye it looked very much like Hollywood's idea of cute British settings for movies starring the likes of Walter Pidgeon and Greer Garson. The immaculate, white-painted clapboard-sheathed houses shone in the sunlight, as did their dairies, kitchens, and smokehouses, all perhaps too clean to be real. Every fence was white, not a pale out of place. The sidewalks were equally pristine—no garbage to be seen, no laundry hanging on lines across yards—and neatly trimmed matching shrubs stood sentinel beside front doors. Emerging from the Ham Shop a young woman tourist wearing an attractive floral dress and a small white hat on the back of her blonde head could have been on her way to church. Turning to her dutifully following daughter, she asked in an unexpectedly grating voice, "Do you have your quill, Miranda?"

This insignificant incident became for me the defining image of Williamsburg in the 1950s. The Norman Rockwell mother (perhaps from New York?) and her quill-holding daughter spoke to national pride and respect for their history—a world apart from the tank tops and crotch-clutching shorts of future tourist generations. But what, I wondered, had any of this to do with the down and dirty work of archaeology?

The next day I was introduced to Williamsburg's archaeological laboratory and its staff of three: Moreau B. C. Chambers, its chief; John Van Ness Dunton, its lab technician; and an aging black man named Sandy Morse whose job was to paint numbers onto artifacts. The trio worked out of a long brick building without air conditioning. The oppressive atmosphere was conducive to afternoon lethargy, its silence broken by occasional snores from Chambers and the buzzing of irritated flies trying to exit through the screened windows. John Dunton was as vigorously full of ideas as Chambers was sluggish. Born at another odd-sounding place, Birdsnest on the Eastern Shore of Virginia, John had been employed as a student under Chamber's predecessor, Minor Wine Thomas, and together they had developed methods of preserving excavated iron that fifty years later left their end products still in immaculately good condition. My arrival as one who knew something about conservation and archaeological methodology provided John with a friend and a sounding board—and the possibility of injecting fresh ideas and new vigor into a moribund office. Such stirring naturally was watched with suspicion by Chambers, for whom sustaining the status quo was challenge enough.

I quickly learned that the lab was far from the mainstream of Williamsburg's activity, and that archaeology did not aspire to department status. It was simply a subsection in the department of architecture, whose hierarchy ruled everything and everybody. At the apex stood senior vice president A. Edwin Kendrew, who in 1928 had begun his career as a draftsman in the office of the Boston architectural firm hired by John D. Rockefeller Jr. to head his restoration project. Under Kendrew came the director of architecture, Mario Campioli, and below him the director of architectural research, Orin M. Bullock. It was Orin who presided over the archaeological office and its only field archaeologist, James Knight.

Jimmy was a draftsman in the architectural office who supervised a local crew employed to dig trenches across open lots in the hope of finding brick foundations whose remains could be transformed into reconstructed buildings. The trenches they dug were oriented on a diagonal to the street lines and were a shovel's breadth wide and a shovel's length apart. The narrowness of the trenches precluded any investigation of the soil's stratigraphy or the recovery of artifacts from meaningful contexts. Jimmy Knight explained that one needed none of that stuff when finding footings was the sole name of the game.

Orin, Knight's supervisor, had never given much thought to archaeology's potential and was content to know that some of the artifacts thrown up onto the dirt piles along the sides of the trenches would be rounded up and sent to the lab. What became of them afterward was of no great concern. In truth, most of them wound up, unwashed, in large wooden fish crates stored in a nearby garage. Since I had been contracted to write a study of Williamsburg's wine bottles, it was necessary to sort through the contents of the boxes, separating bottle bits from old tractor parts and relatively new mouse nests. It was, to say the least, a depressing and unrewarding process. None of the material retained any cultural context, having been salvaged from unspecified trenches somewhere on each half-acre lot.

When I explained this to Orin, he seemed relieved and allowed that he had been thinking of ways to get all that junk out of the garage. "Maybe," he suggested, "we should dump it all in the York River." This I advised against, arguing that the collection might be statistically useful to future researchers. I could see that Orin was not persuaded, but since I was the imported "expert," my advice had to be heard with politeness before being quietly forgotten.

Orin was then in his early fifties, with crew-cut gray hair, a ruddy complexion, and a bow tie for all seasons, and imbued with a bubbling enthusiasm—particularly for amateur theatrics. On Thursday evenings he and his wife, Christine, hosted others with thespian yearnings at bourbon-laced parties in the basement of their house on Duke of Gloucester Street. It was an event widely known as Bullock's Underground, at which plays were read—or rather, half-read, the flow of whiskey rarely allowing progress beyond the second act. Bourbon was new to me and took some getting used to, as did participation in readings that rapidly became slurred and eventually incomprehensible. It would turn out, nevertheless, that my future career had its roots watered by the libations in Bullock's Underground.

Orin's ambition was to found an amateur theater where he could be involved at every level of production—including acting. In 1955 Williamsburg's historic area had been transformed into a Hollywood movie set when famed director George Seton was hired to make a promotional film titled *The Story of a Patriot*. Anybody in town who wanted to be involved in its production was encouraged to do so. Even inmates of the neighboring Eastern State Hospital for the Insane had been conscripted to don wigs and tricorn hats to play Revolutionary-era burgesses cheering Patrick Henry's florid address to the General Assembly. Orin, too, had played a role. As a burgess in a Raleigh Tavern scene he had a memorable line to speak, a privilege allowed few nonprofessional actors. "There is grave danger, but so few are aware of it!" he declared. The fact that his line was cut and dubbed in later with another's voice was to be often and cruelly recalled by his Williamsburg colleagues.

I had been in Williamsburg a month when Audrey finally arrived and, owing to crossed signals, landed in Richmond while Orin and I were at Newport News looking for her plane. Having no American money, she was unable to buy a cup of coffee or, more importantly, to make a phone call, and so languished for five hours in the sweltering Richmond airport before we finally arrived to rescue her. Had I been on my own, I would have been the recipient of colorful vituperation, but with Orin in the lead an explosion was skillfully averted. Among his many wonderful qualities, Orin Bullock had an enviable way with women.

Orin's librarian, Anne Parrish, took both Audrey and me under her motherly wing and was responsible for much of our indoctrination into American life. It was she who took us to Virginia's most impressive colonial ruin. Located on the north bank of the York River in Gloucester County, the four-story Rosewell mansion had been built around 1725 by planter John Page and burned in 1916, leaving only a brick shell that slowly disappeared amid climbing vines and falling walls. The south wall had collapsed during a hurricane, but the other three stood to chimney height, their vacant window openings vandalized by souvenir hunters who threw bricks at them to break loose the elaborately fluted keystones.

While beating our way through the vines and trees that had grown up around the ruin in search of the circular icehouse featured in an old photograph, I came upon a large groundhog burrow that disappeared under the roots of a tree. Lying in the spoil at its tunnel's mouth were several fragments of eighteenth-century bottle glass, a few potsherds, and a brass harness buckle. The animal had evidently made its home in a late colonial trash deposit. Here, I explained to Anne Parrish, was just the kind of association that had to exist around the houses of Williamsburg and that, if found and excavated, could open a door to the possessions of their inhabitants.

Being anxious to show Orin Bullock how soil layers could be interpreted to reveal the passage of time, I spent many fruitless hours walking around town in the hope finding an open utility ditch or drainage gully that might provide the necessary demonstration. Orin and his fellow architects humored me by listening to my explanations of what modern archaeology could do for them, but continued to insist that the only artifacts that interested them were bricks and builders' hardware.

Frustrating though that was, I had much else to think about, often through the slightly fuzzy outlines of martini glasses. Four-thirty was the time to head for Orin's house or to that of the architectural historian Howard Dearstyne, whose martinis created the night before were now matured and chilled for the happy hour. It being time for what Orin called "a toddy for the body," I soon learned that my new and wonderful friends had long since mastered the art of relaxing and letting tomorrow take care of itself. It was all a far cry from the roar of London draglines and the antlike crowds of office workers rushing in or out of subways. Life in Williamsburg in the 1950s seemed as close to paradise as any mortal could hope to get.

With John Dunton as our constant companion, we visited Jamestown, where Pinky Harrington had excavated the glasshouse that had brought him to London. He was overall head of continuing excavation at Jamestown, which was led by his affable field director John "Jack" Cotter, who showed us through the National Park Service's archaeological collections. To my surprise they included waste products from a stoneware kiln that looked identical to some I had found on the Bankside Power Station site. These, however, came not from Jamestown but from Yorktown, where a stoneware potter had been at work in the second quarter of the eighteenth century. Neither Cotter nor Jamestown's curator, Paul Hudson, knew anything about stoneware factories and were surprised and pleased that I had something to offer. More surprising yet was the sight of a wine bottle fragment bearing an applied seal marked RW, the letters seemingly identical to seals on two broken bottles given to me by Grimes's assistant, Dr. Bellerby (who died shortly afterward from an unidentified disease while opening coffins in the vaults of Fleet Street's Church of St. Bride). Walking through the City one Saturday afternoon, Bellerby had been drawn to the sound of breaking glass and saw workmen amusing themselves throwing bottles against a wall. That the Jamestown RW seal, which came from a lot that had belonged to the mid-seventeenth-century colonist Ralph Wormeley, should match the London bottles was a coincidence so improbable as to defy belief. Thus, in our visit to Jamestown Audrey and I found two transatlantic connections that only we could have recognized.

The Jamestown excavations were a prelude to the 350th anniversary of Virginia's first settlement in 1607, to which end the state government was in the process of reconstructing the first English fort, an Indian village, the three ships that had brought the first colonists to Jamestown island, and Harrington's glasshouse, which was being rebuilt to demonstrate seventeenth-century glassmaking. On visiting that almost completed reconstruction we caught sight of the nearby palisaded fort. It was a Sunday afternoon in October, a time when no one was around, and although a sign on a chain read "No Entry" we ignored it and went inside. The tools of joiners and thatchers lay where they had been left when the workmen quit for the weekend. It was easy to imagine that when they returned they would be wearing the clothes of 1607 and talking about the savages watching them from the woods. Although I would visit the Jamestown Festival Park many times in the years to come, never did I recapture the sense of being transported in time that I experienced on that silent Sunday afternoon in 1956.

For Audrey and me, the October clock was ticking all too fast. Orin had promised that before we left he would find us an opportunity to visit an eighteenth-century plantation. Those, he told us, had been the lifeblood from which Williamsburg drew its colonial strength. Although the closest plantation was only seven miles away, being allowed to see the house itself had the makings of an insurmountable problem. The owner, Mrs. Archibald "Mollie" McCrae, liked men but hated women and was unlikely to let Audrey inside. Orin therefore decided that a more senior escort might have better luck, and so it fell to Williamsburg's architectural director, Mario Campioli, to lead the way. "It might be better," he said, "for us to just walk around outside." Which we proceeded to do.

"Who's there? Who's that?" barked a female voice from behind the screen door of the adjacent plantation office.

When Campioli identified himself, the door opened and a small woman in a somewhat ill-fitting red wig emerged into the sunlight. It was Mrs. McCrae. "How nice of you all to come to see me," she declared, thereby giving the lie to her women-hating reputation. For close on two hours we sat at a large horse-shoe-shaped table while she plied us with scarcely water-splashed bourbon and told stories about the house and its history. She told us about pirates buried in the basement, and how, in what she called "the refusal room," Thomas Jefferson proposed to his "fair Belinda." She showed us the notches in the banister of the great staircase where the villainous British Colonel Tarleton had ridden his horse up the stairs, slashing at the banister as he went. I refrained from asking why he would do such a thing, but admired the metal fragment protruding from the newel post which we were told was the tip of his blade broken off as he rode. Nor did I mention that marks around the relic suggested that it had been driven in with a hammer.

Gratefully and reluctantly we bade farewell to Mollie McCrae, storing away the experience in our memory bank, expecting never again to see the house called Carter's Grove.

October found the American electorate taking sides between President Dwight D. Eisenhower and challenger Adlai E. Stevenson, prompting Williamsburg wags to threaten to vote for me in the guise of "Candidate Dunmore," the last British governor of colonial Virginia. Along with a campaign button created by Orin Bullock we received from Howard Dearstyne a copy of his book *Shadows in Silver* inscribed:

> To the Candidate, Dunmore (alias I. Noël Hume) and his gifted Lady—though his campaign failed to secure him the necessary electoral votes, he (and she) won the hearts of their (alienated) former countrymen.
>
> He (and she) return to their motherland with our fond good wishes, which are mixed with a feeling of melancholy, since their sojourn here was so very short.
>
> Williamsburg Oct. 26, 1956.

We were deeply touched by Howard's words and by all the expressions of friendship that sent us on our way. A two-day stopover in New York found us in Times Square on the night of October 28 watching the illuminated news bulletins coursing their way across the Chrysler Building: *British and French Troops*

Invade Port Said after U.N. Resolution Vetoed by Britain and France. So immersed had we been in the farewells and business of leaving, we knew nothing of the events of the previous week and were astonished that Britain had gone to war with Egypt. More astonishing was the lack of interest being show by Times Square bystanders. Seeing us staring at the bulletin, a man standing next to me asked, "Port Said, where the hell is that?" We suddenly felt very foreign and as far from Williamsburg as we were from England. And there was a chill in the New York air.

My return to the Guildhall Museum found nothing changed, though I was warmly greeted by Bill Rector, who had spent the past months alone in our attic laboratory. In my absence a young man named Charles Rosser had been added to Norman Cook's Royal Exchange staff, and it was he who assumed the task of construction-site salvage. But being unused to getting his hands dirty, his efforts were limited to gathering whatever artifacts the workmen cared to give him. For me, it was to be business as usual, my salvage efforts focusing on a site adjacent to Grimes's Dick Whittington fiasco of seven years earlier. The ground had been the churchyard of St. Martin, Vintry, and yielded several graves, one of them containing a male skeleton over whose pelvic area rested an inverted and intact delftware plate of about 1680. Adhering to the face of it was a tuft of the deceased's pubic hair. Why this splendid, chinoiserie-painted plate was placed where it was has never been determined. It was, nonetheless, to be my last memorable London discovery.

On November 20, Orin Bullock, writing from "Colonial Williamsburg in the Colony of Virginia," began, "Dear English Cousins, Noël and Audrey. This letter will completely disrupt your life!" And it did. Orin was about to be authorized to offer us both jobs, my position initially to be that of Archaeological Records Writer. The title, he assured me, was simply a means of bringing me back under the mantle of preexisting positions, but in reality to "organize and run the Archaeological program." An immediate need, however, was to design an archaeological exhibit for the new information center that was to open in the spring. Not stated in the November letter, but made clear in another written just before Christmas, was Orin's hope that I would help him run his newly created Little Theater. Indeed, had it not been for my theatrical rather than archaeological background, I very much doubt that he would have pushed to bring us back.

Trudging the city gray with cement dust and caked in mud could not compete with Williamsburg sunshine and Howard Dearstyne's martinis. Although Orin was hoping to have us back by the year's end, it took three months to find good homes for forty-two tortoises and terrapins, two caimans, one lizard, a hedgehog, two crows, and a minah bird. Obtaining permanent visas to live and work in the United States wasn't easily accomplished and required prolonged string-pulling at the State Department to get it to accept the premise that, although a foreigner, I was the only individual in the length and breadth of the United States capable of writing Colonial Williamsburg's archaeological records.

When eventually we were called to the U.S. Embassy to obtain our visas, I cautiously asked the immigration officer what I was committing myself to by signing. He smilingly replied, "Nothing really—other than that you're prepared to die for us." As he handed me my stamped passport, he brightly added, "But I shouldn't worry too much. It looks like the peace in Korea is going to hold up."

"And what if it doesn't?"

"Then it'll be up to your draft board. Good luck."

As Audrey and I left the embassy steps on a freezing cold January morning, I remember asking her, "What in God's name have we just done?"

17 🪶   *Putting on a Show*

Although living above one's mother-in-law had been less than ideal, leaving Wimbledon was hard to do. The closer the time came to pack our library and our collection of antique bottles and to give away the furniture, the more uncertain we became.

But the decision had been made, and that was that. Audrey's friends in the London press came to see us off and to photograph the departing tortoise that had made her famous. Tigillinus was coming with us, and was photographed again as Audrey carried him aboard the plane. We were, to say the least, an odd trio.

In accepting the Williamsburg job I had made two stipulations, both of which Orin Bullock assured me were no problem. The first was that Colonial Williamsburg had to provide us with somewhere to live at a rent we could afford. It seemed a reasonable request because we knew that many of the smaller restored and reconstructed houses were rented to employees. My second requirement gave me pause, but it had to be demanded, namely, that lab supervisor Moreau Chambers be moved to another department. I was certain that I could accomplish nothing as long as he remained. But when we arrived in Williamsburg, we had no house and Chambers was still at his desk. Orin had been too busy, he said, to get to grips with either commitment.

Anne Parrish had found us a room in a rundown house in a Williamsburg side street whose female proprietor took an instant dislike to Tigillinus—who responded in the only way he knew. Moreau Chambers, on the other hand, did not respond at all. Although John Dunton knew and approved of what had been promised, the unfortunate Chambers had no idea that he was to be replaced. Having had no instruction on how to behave toward us, he was unsure who was in charge, and so did nothing—as did I. The awkward standoff lasted two weeks until Orin finally bit the bullet. Chambers had half a day to clean out his desk and be gone. The ruthlessness of his ousting and my involvement in it have always plagued me. Today, of course, such terminations are the rule rather than the exception, but in those sunny days in Williamsburg such brutality seemed entirely foreign.

As soon as the deck was cleared, I began the task of turning a roomful of artifacts into the makings of an archaeological department. We were fortunate in having been moved into a newly constructed building that we shared with the commissary, from which odors both fine and foul emanated upward into our quarters. We were under no pressure to accomplish anything spectacular beyond designing an archaeological exhibit to be installed in the new Information Center. Between the time when we learned of the job offer and our actual arrival, both Audrey and I had been corresponding with John Dunton about our mutual futures. He was as committed as I to bringing Williamsburg's archaeology out of the Dark Ages into the light of Stratification. We both knew that to succeed we had to teach our superiors that the earth of Williamsburg was a book whose pages were waiting to be turned—and read. To that end, John created a styrofoam mock-up of one of my London soil profiles, rightly believing that if something like that could be made at full scale and installed in the Information Center both tourists and the architects would get the idea.

With massive slabs of styrofoam, quantities of fish glue, and even greater quantities of soils and paint colors, a section through an imaginary Williamsburg site was created. Beginning close to the surface with modern drain tiles, descending through nineteenth-century foundations, an eighteenth-century cellar, down to a seventeenth-century ditch cutting across precolonial soil dappled with Indian potsherds and arrow points, it was a gratifying achievement. Although all three of us worked to build the ten-foot-long profile (which included a section through a brick-walled well shaft), the concept was John's. Artifacts of successive ages protruded from it, providing dates for the ditch, the cellar, the foundations, and the drain tiles—among which was embedded a Wendell Willkie campaign button.

The exhibit drew enthusiastic responses from "those at the top," but I doubt they realized that they were witnessing the prelude to an entirely new approach to looking at the buried past of Colonial Williamsburg. Orin built an equally spectacular cutaway of a colonial house which, to my novice eye, looked authentic in every detail, even down to the weathering of the window frame and the wear on the wide floorboards. I asked whence they came, and I was told that most of the parts came from houses in town that had to be dismantled while they were being restored.

Several weeks later, John, Audrey, and I went on a tour of potential archaeological sites in the surrounding counties, and came to a sad-looking story-and-a half house on the Pamunkey River. Evidently abandoned, but still restorable if given the Williamsburg treatment, we were appalled to find that someone had been at it with a chainsaw and carried off several of the floorboards. The saw, it turned out, was Orin's. In those days, salvaging from abandoned houses was thought to be legitimate "research" and doing the past a service—until an architectural draftsman was caught removing a door lock from a house that was not as abandoned as he thought.

We soon discovered that behind its picket fences and painted shutters, Williamsburg had a darker side. In 1928 the Ku Klux Klan had donated a flagpole and a public bench to the College of William and Mary, which continued to be sat on until finally removed in 1955. With racial segregation still in effect, many of the waiters and gardeners lived in a dormitory block just outside the restored area. Adjacent to this well-constructed brick building was a short row of old clapboard houses occupied by "colored folks." When Mrs. Prentis, the owner of a Duke of Gloucester Street bookshop, reported seeing her stolen bicycle outside one of those houses, the police chief replied, "That's a pretty rough area. Let's wait till they ride it up town." None of this would have much relevance to two starry-eyed new arrivals were it not that we were about to meet the seamy side face to face—or rather eyeball to eyeball.

Within a year of our joining the staff we had advanced from one small reconstructed dwelling to another, until we ended up in a narrow, three-room house on Nicholson Street called the William Randolph Lodging. One evening Audrey came out of the bathroom convinced that someone had been watching her between the slats of the window blind. I told her I was sure she was mistaken, until I saw eyes peering through the bedroom blind. Wearing only my undershorts and carrying a sword (found in the Thames), I charged out into the night and chased the Peeping Tom up the street into the arms of the police, who apparently had been watching him. In the midst of taking notes the cop observed that had he been me, he'd have blown the bastard's head off.

"I don't have a gun," I lamely replied.

"Take my advice. You should get one," the policeman laughed.

"Where?"

"The jailer sells them. Go tell him I sent you." So I did. Nearly fifty years later I still have the gun, still in its box, and fast becoming an antique.

During the first months of our arrival, two endeavors occupied all our time, the first being to prove by example how important archaeology could be to

Williamsburg. The second was to fulfill my obligation to Orin and his fledgling Little Theater. I was to have the privilege of directing what would be its second production. When I confessed that I had never worked with amateurs, Orin assured me that he would be there to ease the way. All I had to do was name the play of my choice and audition the local talent. The play was to be *Gaslight*, one that I had stage-managed but never directed, nevertheless a staging that I knew pretty well. What I did not know was that the pool of auditionable talent was insufficient to cast all the parts. Consequently, with the exception of two policemen to be added later, I handed out scripts to everyone who wanted one. I was soon to discover that my amateurs, unlike professionals, only came to rehearsals when they could fit them into their proclaimedly busy schedules.

Getting the cast to show up for rehearsals was difficult enough, getting the leading man to learn his lines was worse. Ten days before we were to open, he quit. Playing *Gaslight* without its villain was not an option, which left me no other choice than to play the Charles Boyer role of Mr. Manningham myself. The best that could be said for my performance was that I knew the lines. The reviewer for the *Virginia Gazette* found my performance insufficiently diabolical but thought the second policeman totally convincing, which was hardly surprising as he was played by Williamsburg's own police chief.

Gaslight had proved an inauspicious step toward bringing professionalism to Williamsburg's amateur theater. However, the early stumble did not prove lastingly disastrous, and for more than half a century the Williamsburg Players have given the town the quality productions that mine so dismally lacked. Needless to say, even before we opened, I had resolved that having paid my theatrical dues to Orin Bullock I should henceforth confine my talents to promoting archaeology. The problem was how to do that in an attention-getting way.

The half-finished excavation I inherited from Jimmy Knight lay across Duke of Gloucester Street from Bruton Parish Church and focused on the remains of Peter Scott's cabinet shop, a building inadvertently burned by billeted British troops in January 1776. We found the proof of that in the ashes on the cellar floor, clues that ranged from burned chicken bones to a Virginia copper halfpenny of 1773. But before the dig was finished, Colonial Williamsburg architect Ed Kendrew had changed his mind. He preferred to reconstruct another cabinet shop, that of Anthony Hay, whose business was on the back street and spanned a stream which might or might not have provided water power for his lathe. For that and other reasons, the Peter Scott reconstruction was aborted, the site backfilled and grassed over—and so it remains fifty years later.

The Peter Scott cellar's sole contribution to Williamsburg's archaeological education was my refusal to fully excavate it, arguing that were I to take out the last quarter of its colonial fill, nobody could ever return to reinterpret my evidence. Archaeology, I insisted, was a destructive process and had led to many an uncheckable assertion dating back to Heinrich Schliemann's misreading of the stratigraphic evidence at Homeric Troy. Since the Scott project had already been put onto the architectural back burner, neither Orin nor Ed Kendrew saw any point in challenging their newly imported expert.

Archaeology aside, 1957 was a year of great activity in and around Williamsburg. The new Information Center opened, along with the premier of *The Story of a Patriot,* and at Jamestown the Festival Park celebrated the 350th anniversary of the first English landing. The National Park Service built a curiously triangular visitor center for Jamestown (complete with equally curious triangular exhibit cases), Harrington's excavated glasshouse was rebuilt, and in October Queen Elizabeth II and Prince Philip came to add a touch of British luster to the celebrations. Amid the crowds lining the streets of Williamsburg were two young Britons who obtained their first close-up glimpse of their monarch. "She waved to us!" Audrey rejoiced. "She really did!" I wasn't so sure about that, and thirty-five years later I would have the opportunity to remind Her Majesty of that moment. Unfortunately, her recollection was noticeably less vivid than ours.

The royal visit coincided with the last of the 1957 big events, namely, the reenacting of the Battle of Yorktown and the ignominious British surrender on October 18. The Queen wisely left on the 17th.

The Yorktown Day celebration was the biggest such event since the Centennial celebration of 1881 and involved reenactment regiments from New York, Rhode Island, Pennsylvania, and most of the other colonies, plus a contingent of "French" troops provided by the U.S. Second Army based at Virginia's Fort Monroe. Along with the marching bands and parading patriots there was to be an audio element with actors providing the voices of the original participants. The British commander, General Cornwallis, had called in sick on the day of the surrender and so the symbolic handing of the sword fell to General O'Hara. I was to deliver his lines via the public address system from a concealed bunker at the edge of the battlefield. When it came time for our on-site run-through, much of George Washington's and Rochambeau's army was still milling about the field admiring each other's uniforms. Consequently, our audio rehearsal went ahead on its own. My simple instruction was to wait until I saw General O'Hara ride up to the waiting General Benjamin Lincoln (substituting for Washington) and then to deliver the words of surrender. But there were snags.

The battle reenactment was to end with the British yielding to the American assault on Redoubt No. 9, the staging orchestrated via landline phone from our bunker. But someone had broken the wire—leaving the garrison to fight bravely on while the Americans awaited their delayed cue. Eventually a costumed horseman was sent galloping through the smoke of battle telling the British to quit. For several long minutes it seemed likely that Cornwallis would win.

The dignitaries from Washington and ambassadors from foreign governments sat huddled against the wind and chill of that October afternoon, doubtless wishing that the whole thing were over. It had taken considerable effort and much shouting to get the twenty-two colonial regiments and five Connecticut fife and drum corps into position for the grand finale. I found a company of French infantry parading directly in front of our bunker and completely obscuring the surrender taking place at the opposite side of the field. I had no alternative but to scramble out from our bunker and crawl between the feet of the surprised contingent, hauling my microphone cable behind me. Fortunately, I was able to reach the front rank before the sword was passed, but unfortunately, my plug had pulled free of the amplifier and nobody heard my spirited, voice-over interpretation of Irish General O'Hara's speech of surrender.

Despite this further proof that Thespis was not in my corner, showmanship became the name of the archaeological game. I put artifact exhibits wherever I could find an empty case, be it in our Motor House motel or in the august Williamsburg Inn. Later, I even managed to put one in the house of Colonial Williamsburg's president, Carl Humelsine. For an archaeologist to tell hotel managements what he intended to install in their cases was not as audacious as it would appear in the twenty-first century. In those days benefactor Rockefeller was still alive and paying. Williamsburg was still an architectural project ruled by the architects, and what their men said carried weight.

The colonial Court House in Market Square had served as an archaeological museum since 1934, but its exhibits, once installed, had remained unchanged through the years. They had begun life in the architectural drafting room, where selected colonial builders' hardware could be laid out in pleasing designs. It probably never occurred to the installers that an archaeologically challenged public would see only hinges geometrically arranged and anchored to a burlap-covered backboard. When it had seen one hinge, that was enough. The same was true of hasps and padlocks.

Treading cautiously, and one at a time, I began to change the exhibits; the new philosophy was that every artifact should say something about itself or its colonial owners. Just *being* was no longer enough. If we were to show hinges, we would need to show different types for different purposes and where possible to draw parallels with those that the viewers would find in their own homes. Knowing that the public has a taste for human skeletons, I exhibited a surgically trepanned skull found in a grave in the Revolutionary War cemetery beside the Governor's Palace. With it I displayed the eighteenth-century trepanning tools that had belonged to Williamsburg's Dr. Minson Galt, and alongside them an engraving from Diderot's encyclopedia showing how they were used. Today, of course, I would have to use a fiberglass replica of the skull and would have to say so in letters large and clear. Nevertheless, the original skull remained on exhibit until 1975 when the museum was shifted up the street to the James Anderson House.

The house had been the home of the senior vice president architect, Ed Kendrew, who in 1959 allowed me to install an archaeological lab in his basement. That may seem a little odd, since we already had half a building for that purpose. I thought it important, however, that the products of any digging we planned on sites outside the Colonial Williamsburg properties should be kept separate and not be processed on company time. And we did have such a plan.

In an effort to demonstrate the interpretive value of stratigraphically associated artifacts, we returned to the Rosewell ruin, which we had first visited in 1956, to see what other treasures the groundhog had hidden in its bed. But first there were necessary formalities. One does not intrude, shovel in hand, onto private property without formal written permission to do so. Equally important was the need to establish the artifacts' ownership and their ultimate fate. Permission was readily granted by the heirs to the colonial Page family, and thanks to my friend Malcolm Watkins, curator of cultural history at the Smithsonian Institution (whose Secretary had made me an honorary research associate), it was agreed that the artifacts would go there and, better still, that the Smithsonian would publish our report on the excavation.

The Rosewell groundhog had five entrances to its burrow, prompting us to lay out an area in the underbrush that extended beyond them. By modern standards this was not a big excavation, since it covered an area measuring only twenty by twenty-eight feet. But working only on weekends, we took the best part of two years to clear the area. Our work began auspiciously on the first day with the discovery of a still-shining silver coin of 1719. Then—and perhaps still—the largest silver coin found in Virginia, it was a French half ecu from the reign of Louis XV. Hopes that the coin defined the date of the pit and that more such treasure might lie deeper proved wrong. Nevertheless, the excavation yielded an impressive trove of Page family–related artifacts from the early 1770s. There is no need to provide a boring list of all that was found—that's what published reports are for. It is pertinent, however, to quote from the report's introduction where I expressed my gratitude to our tiny team: "My commiserations go out to my wife Audrey Noël Hume and to John Van Ness Dunton, who suffered through snow, frost, rain, heat, and mosquitoes to help me with the excavation, an operation that was really too large for three people to handle."

The report did not mention that progress was frequently halted or delayed by an assortment of problems, not the least of them the fear that while we were at work in Williamsburg vandals would rob the excavation. As I noted in the previous chapter, Rosewell had become a magnet for souvenir hunters, who hurled loose bricks at the window openings in an effort to break loose the fluted stone blocks that decorated their caps. We could see the rock throwers through the jungle of trees and vines, but we knew that chasing them away would reveal where we were and what we were doing. To keep hidden, we dispensed with metal buckets and substituted U.S. Army surplus canvas water carriers, but even then, on a windless day the scraping of a trowel on an oyster shell seemed loud enough to waken John Page. We were slowed, too, by my insistence that we should film the progress of the excavation in the hope that, even though it was shot on 8 mm film, someone would be interested in seeing how a real Williamsburg dig should be dug.

Part of the resulting film was shot in Williamsburg, thereby ranking it as the first such record of its archaeology. Fifty years later the frail film remains in its can, the means of projecting it and its taped sync sound having long since become as obsolete as 78 rpm phonograph records.

The Rosewell report was published by the Smithsonian in 1962 and proved to be a landmark in the evolution of historical archaeology insofar as it did what we had hoped: demonstrate how the study of artifacts contributed to our knowledge of the family's eighteenth-century lives. We had seen their possessions, studied their food, recognized their taste for mineral waters, identified improvements made to the mansion, and even found physical evidence of the Pages' political leaning. Back in Williamsburg the Powers that Were had begun to take notice.

The Rosewell project was followed by another, closer to home. Logging on

Colonial Williamsburg property on Tutter's Neck Creek in James City County had yielded traces of colonial occupation. Once again our weekend trio set to work, this time uncovering the remains of a plantation datable to the first quarter of the eighteenth century. Among the recovered artifacts was the pedestal base of a delftware salt container decorated with the face of a turbaned Turk. Seven years earlier on the Thames foreshore I had found another such base, broken in exactly the same way. That such until-then-unique fragments should be found by one person half the world apart was a coincidence that might have been thought unbelievable had we not already found the Wormeley bottles at Jamestown. Another no-less-unbelievable coincidence would follow several years later when an amateur archaeologist working at Pemaquid in Maine would find a very corroded brass "coin" and send it to me for identification. Its condition was so poor that only a few letters and traces of its decoration were discernable. Indeed, identifying it as a counter from the reign of England's Queen Anne would have been impossible had I not had its twin in my collection of coins from the Thames. I had found it hidden in the toe of a leather shoe that had preserved it in shining "as new" condition. I have never since seen another.

Like the Rosewell artifacts, the Tutter's Neck collection went to Malcolm Watkins at the Smithsonian, and the report on the excavation was published as a United States National Museum Bulletin in 1966. Shortly afterward a third extramural excavation took us back to a Gloucester County site at Clay Bank, not far from Rosewell, where a fallen tree had exposed a late seventeenth-century cellar. The property, named Ardudwy, was owned by the novelist and inventor William F. Jenkins, whose house stood less than twenty feet from the cellar. Unlike our previous ventures, located far from a telephone or a source of water, the Jenkins family insisted that we stop work to share their Sunday lunches and, when the day was done, to enjoy their liquor. This was archaeology at its most enjoyable, and when it came time to scrape the last dirt from the cellar floor, the thought weighed heavily that there would be no more weekends with the Jenkins family. The sadness was tempered, however, when the last pan full of oyster shells in the remaining corner of the cellar yielded the stem of a magnificent candlestick in English lead glass. It remains to this day without parallel and can justly claim to be the finest example of early English glass found in America.

I argue that any excavator who does not thrill to the Eureka! moments lacks the humanity to reach out to the people of the past and to see beyond quantitative analyses and computer printouts. Plus, the spectacular artifact, if properly exploited, can lead to the funding of future work or publication.

All three of our Smithsonian-published extramural projects provided a basis for future studies of the remains of eighteenth-century material culture. They presaged, too, the creation of the American Society for Historical Archaeology, fostered by Wilcomb E. Washburn, the Smithsonian's director of American studies. But that was still some years into the future.

In 1961 my 1956 work on Williamsburg's broken bottles reached print in the Corning Museum's *Journal of Glass Studies*. This was the first Colonial Williamsburg publication of its archaeological collections, and it was greeted with surprised satisfaction. Why not get Noël Hume to write a whole book about Williamsburg's archaeology? suggested Carl Humelsine. Ed Kendrew somewhat hesitantly agreed—with the proviso that no word of it should be seen as critical of the way things had been done when Ed alone dictated how, when, and where digging was authorized.

This cautious recognition that archaeology was being allowed into the mainstream of Colonial Williamsburg's research seemed a vindication of all our weekends at Rosewell, Tutter's Neck, and Clay Bank, and I eagerly set to work on the manuscript, which was to be titled "Williamsburg's Buried Treasure." Along the way, chapter by chapter, I received helpful hints from the architects, historians, landscape architects, and anyone who Kendrew thought might have something useful to inject. But by the time I was through, the text had received so many injections that it bore scant resemblance to the story I had tried to tell. Besides such picayune quibbles as whether I should call a bush a shrub, the necessity to include the names of every employee who had any role in the development of the town's restoration resulted in something akin to a roll call. When the Kendrew-approved manuscript eventually went to Humelsine, he called me into his office and shoved it back at me across his desk saying, "This isn't what I had in mind!"

I agreed, and said so. The book's abandonment was disappointing, but as so often happened in the course of my career, one thing led to another. In partnership with Colonial Williamsburg, the College of William and Mary sponsored the highly respected Institute of Early American Studies, to whose board the New York publisher Alfred Knopf had been appointed. When I put on an exhibit of recent discoveries for the institute's 1962 meeting, Knopf heard that I had already published four books before leaving England, and asked whether I had thought of doing a book on Williamsburg. When I told him about the failure of "Williamsburg's Buried Treasure," he asked to see the manuscript. Several weeks later he offered me a contract to rewrite the book and to expand it from Williamsburg digging to archaeology at Jamestown and elsewhere in Virginia. The result, first published in 1963, became *Here Lies Virginia*, a book that was to remain in print for more than thirty years.

The exhibit that had captured Alfred Knopf's interest was set up on Nicholson Street adjacent to the site of Anthony Hay's colonial cabinet shop. It was yet another of the many sites that the architecture department's Jimmy Knight had trenched, meaning that it had been considerably mutilated. Nevertheless, lying as it did in a valley through which a stream still flowed, considerable silting remained undisturbed. In the winter of 1961 the architects decided to go forward with sinking pilings on which to erect the stream-spanning cabinet shop. From an archaeological point of view, the timing could not have been worse. The ground was frozen, and ice formed as soon as the muddy silt was reached. For weeks, therefore, John Dunton and I worked up to our knees in freezing mud and water to salvage an incredible array of objects relating to the cabinetmaking trade. Among them were examples of most of the brass furniture hardware types in use in the colonial eighteenth century, as well as examples of unfinished or discarded table and chair legs and rails, all preserved in the silt. In its modest way the Anthony Hay stream was doing for Williamsburg what the Walbrook had done for Roman London.

Cabinetmaker Anthony Hay had also been the proprietor of the town's premier tavern, the Raleigh, on Duke of Gloucester Street. Some of his squirrel-decorated delftware plates found their way to the cabinet-shop site and would later be reproduced for service in one of Colonial Williamsburg's operating taverns. Copies of tile and pine shingles found in the stream would be used on the roofs of the reconstructed shop. In short, our artifacts were beginning to play a significant and visible role in the future appearance of restored Williamsburg. There is, however, one artifact from the Hay stream that no one has been inspired to exploit: the sheet-iron back from a colonial orthopedic corset. Remembering my previous discovery of the Roman bikini, I began to think that I was fated to become an expert in ancient underwear.

My association with Malcolm Watkins and the Smithsonian, as well as with the Corning Museum of Glass, led to my being asked to direct the excavation of a 1780s glass factory near Frederick, Maryland. The site had been the workplace of one of America's most famous glassmakers, John Frederick Amelung, who had emigrated from Germany in 1784 and operated the factory until felled by a stroke ten years later. Ours was to be a joint Corning–Smithsonian–Colonial Williamsburg project with labor picked up off Frederick street corners augmented by curators from Corning and an amateur acquaintance of Malcolm's named Richard Muzzrole.

Dick was one of those remarkable people who have dotted the pages of archaeological history and whose very real contributions nevertheless cause professionals to turn puce with rage. He was myopically dedicated, incredibly lucky, but eventually self-destructive.

After the successful completion of two seasons at the Amelung site, Malcolm Watkins took Dick onto the Smithsonian staff when the institution accepted a watching brief over urban renewal in downtown Alexandria. Working with a corps of volunteers, Dick excavated the contents of numerous Alexandrian privies and toted back to the museum bushel baskets of ceramic and glass from the 1790s to the 1850s. His problem was that to do so, he had to trudge mud caked and privy footed through the galleries and curatorial hallways of the museum. In Smithsonian parlance, curators were the archaeologists who sent others out to do the dirty work. Dick, whose background was that of a stevedore and a veterinarian's assistant, was a law unto himself. He brushed off mild-mannered Malcolm's relayed complaints as foolish interference with his work. He could see no reason why he should not brew soup in his lab next door to his mentor's office. After all, coming back from all day in a privy one could hardly be expected to go to a restaurant to eat. The logic was there, but acquiescence was not, and eventually Malcolm could no longer protect him. Nevertheless, Dick Muzzrole left behind a legacy of carefully recorded stratified sequences, and countless unparalleled examples of exported English pottery that eventually became the property of the city of Alexandria. Volumes of Dick's photographs and his handwritten notations continue to be among the most used in my library, while his tragically ended career remains a constant reminder that *amateur* should not be a dirty word.

I N 1958 Carlisle H. Humelsine became president of Colonial Williamsburg on the retirement of Kenneth Chorley. I scarcely knew Chorley and had met him to shake his hand only twice. On each occasion he informed me that we had something in common in that he had been born in Bournemouth. I remember him best, however, as the president whose aides issued numbered tickets to the staff to hear him lecture on his visit to the King of Morocco. By taking the tickets back at the high school entrance he would be able to know who did and did not take advantage of this once-in-a lifetime opportunity.

Humelsine's administration represented the highwater mark of the Restoration as it was originally conceived. He would often joke that he considered himself the last of the big spenders. However, with the long-established senior vice president Ed Kendrew still at the architectural helm, restoration and reconstruction plans went forward to fill in the missing pieces of the dream of Dr. Goodwin and John D. Rockefeller Jr. Mr. Junior, as he was known, was to die in 1960, but the Restoration retained close links with the family and would continue to do so through the rest of the century. Part of the plan entailed erecting a new "colonial compatible" post office on the southwest corner of Francis and Henry streets. Initially launched by the architects with Jimmy Knight and his cross-trenching method (albeit using a backhoe), the remains of two buildings and a well shaft were located. The machine had sliced through the middle of a cellar largely filled with broken wine bottles from the mid-eighteenth century, at which point I intervened and told Orin Bullock that this was not an example of Williamsburg's new archaeology. Thereafter, John Dunton, Audrey, and I took over the work both in the cellar and down the well—which proved to be earlier and unrelated to the bottle-rich cellar. From the brick-lined shaft came fine delftware plates of the 1720s, a well-preserved pewter porringer, and parts of a sidesaddle, this last a unique reminder of female riding in Virginia at the beginning of the eighteenth century. It is artifacts such as this that bring the past glowingly alive for those of us who dare to romanticize. Who was the woman who sat that saddle? What did she think about as she rode into the colony's still-under-construction new capital? Did she see it as a city (as we are wont to do) or only as a muddy or dusty village woefully short of big-city potential?

In the spring of that year I had taken Audrey fishing in our boat (which she did not enjoy), and at her bidding I let her ashore a mile or so above James-town Island to let our dachshund walk along the beach. No sooner had the bow touched the shore than we saw it was littered with red earthenware potsherds, many of them evidently kiln rejects. They were coming from the eroding cliff edge of a large wooded tract called Pine Dell. In October we learned that the land was about to be cleared for development, and I persuaded Orin to authorize the use of landscape crewmen to help in a rescue excavation, which we carried out over five December days. Thousands of waste products were retrieved from a land surface that had become buried under rotted leaves and held in place by a blanket of poison ivy. We were to learn at Pine Dell that poison ivy has a long shelf life: its sap, having been absorbed into the potsherds, raised blisters on every hand that touched them. We used the same canvas buckets we had employed at Rosewell, and years later when the buckets were touched, the poi-son was still active. Nevertheless, apart from recurring poison ivy rash, the site yielded information about a pottery-making operation active at the end of the seventeenth century on land then owned by colonist Edward Challis.

We abandoned our lab in Ed Kendrew's basement once the Challis kiln site project earned Colonial Williamsburg approval, but it remained our intent to donate the collection to the Smithsonian in exchange for publication of the re-port. I am chagrined to confess, however, that the report was never finished, and more than forty years later the boxes of potsherds remain in storage in Colonial Williamsburg's archaeology department. My excuse for such negligence is that the quantities of pottery were so great that they had to be boxed before they could be fully analyzed, since we needed the space to complete work on the Anthony Hay and Post Office artifacts.

The problem of how to keep pace with ever-increasing demands on our time steadily grew as each year went by. More and more excavations were required to meet the needs of the Restoration architects, one sometimes following on an-other with scarcely a month's respite. It is an old archaeological axiom that three months in the field generates nine in the lab and in the library; but although I frequently pleaded for time to finish one project before starting another, the wheels of progress continued to grind. I was reminded of my years in London when Norman Cook had ordered me to keep digging, saying that writing reports could wait for ten years or more—reports that never got further than my daybook notes.

In March 1962, with the Challis pottery hastily cleared away, we embarked on the architecture department's next big project. Across Francis Street from the still-under-construction Post Office stood a large frame house that had been moved there from Duke of Gloucester Street, where in the 1930s it had served as a restaurant. Now the architects wanted this, the Travis House, back on its original foundation, from which it had been moved to Duke of Gloucester Street. To that end I imported the latest thing in high-tech archaeology, namely, a soil resistivity meter. This instrument passed a small electrical impulse from one electron to another planted in the ground four feet away. The charge passed in an arc through the earth, its depth penetration depending on the spacing of the probes. The technique had proved wonderfully successful in locating substantial rock-walled Etruscan tombs but did nothing for finding shallow brick foundations. Nevertheless, our probes, trailing wires, and magic box with its oscillating needle impressed passersby, who could see that we were astride the cutting edge of archaeological technology.

I said it then, and have continued to insist, that no electronic device can, by itself, be an adequate substitute for human eyes and a digging trowel. At the beginning of the present century, however, the National Park Service favors what it is pleased to call "noninvasive archeology" that uses remote sensing and avoids the effort and cost of digging and then dealing with the resulting artifacts. Such studies are a valid first step, but knowing *where* is useless without learning what and when, which only excavation can reveal.

In October 1962 the Cuban Missile Crisis found Audrey and me piling sandbags into the basement bulkhead entrance to our house on Duke of Gloucester Street, fearing that we, archaeology in general, and Williamsburg in particular—located as it is amid several U.S. naval installations and atomic stockpiles—were about to disappear in the blinding flash of atomic fusion. With our cellar entrance theoretically protected from radiation, we chanced to look up and saw light through the wide gaps between the colonial floorboards and realized the futility of our efforts. We were still in the same house a year later on the day we signed the papers that enabled us to begin building our own home beside the James River barely a hundred yards from where we had found the Challis kiln site. November 22, therefore, was a landmark date in our lives. It was also the date that Lee Harvey Oswald carried a rifle upstairs in the Texas School Book Depository.

The Travis House dig initially called for finding out everything we could about its environment, and that we did. A row of outbuildings ran down the east side of Henry Street and would make an ideal screening to separate the colonial property from the modern Post Office. But the architecture department's plans changed yet again, and the outbuildings were never reconstructed. Nevertheless, the Travis site excavation went on until February 1964, save for a brief diversion in April to salvage what we could of the Saunders Plantation, which was inconveniently in the way of a new fourteenth green for the Williamsburg Inn Golf Course. Four months later the fourteenth fairway called again. The architects, led by historian Paul Buchanan with support from Jimmy Knight, encountered what they thought were the burned clay remains of a colonial brick kiln. Our team hurried to the site (which showed no postholes or brick fragments) and began to search further while being watched over by puzzled landscapers. At the end of the day, having found nothing, one of the watchers came up to me and asked what we were looking for. When I told him, he replied that the burned red clay we had been so carefully scraping had been the site of a bonfire the landscapers had used to burn brushwood. My report on this exploit read, "Further evidence of reddening was noticed in the faces of the embarrassed excavators who thereupon folded their tents and crept away."

The Travis excavation ended on February 15, and on the afternoon of the same day we began at the house then known as Captain Orr's dwelling, so fast did the architecture department's requirements change. In this instance, the life tenant had died, enabling the Foundation to tear down an unauthentic modern addition. Although much new evidence was recovered, no colonial-style reconstructions followed. Of special archaeological interest, however, was a pathway paved with more than four thousand clay tobacco pipe fragments that enabled Audrey to carry Harrington's quantitative study a step further. We never proved where so many pipe fragments came from, but deduced that they were part of a shipment broken in transit and were used to help in the walkway's drainage.

Like the sorcerer's apprentice, my efforts to create enthusiasm for archaeology in Williamsburg resulted in an increasingly disruptive call for lectures and television appearances around the country. Colonial Williamsburg's public relations department happily sent me forth to appear on midday talk shows that I dubbed Lucy Locket's Ladies Hour. Touting my book *Here Lies Virginia* on shows like Washington's *Inga's Hour* did nothing for its sales. But then, neither did lectures. The most dispiriting of 1963 was an appearance at Higby's Department Store in Cleveland, Ohio, to help launch both my book and Colonial Williamsburg's "Craft House" store within the store. After standing for an hour in the book department without signing a single book, I was ushered up to the top floor to deliver my standard Williamsburg lecture. The huge room with its rows of folding chairs was empty. Two old ladies who had missed Apparel on the escalator took advantage of the chairs to rest. By the time I finished, fourteen or fifteen other lost souls had overshot the bra department and dropped in to rest their feet.

When I returned to Williamsburg I swore that never again would I accept a department store booking. And I never did. Nevertheless, requests for lectures in more appropriate venues continued to grow. In November 1963 I reported that the lecturing load was getting in the way of report writing, and added, "It might be argued with some truth that these lectures which publicize the authenticity of Williamsburg and the depth of our research, are currently more valuable than is the continuance of the research itself. Nevertheless," I concluded, "this is a matter for some thought, and one which needs to be debated."

There can be no denying that in more recent years archaeological projects that garner widespread or national publicity are those most likely to be funded. But there comes a point when the pursuit of publicity can have an adverse impact on the progress not only of report writing but also of the excavation itself—an expressed concern that would prove my undoing years later at Jamestown. But in 1963 I had more immediate concerns. Our friend John Dunton, Audrey's right hand in the laboratory, was leaving to become conservator for the great new Canadian restoration of the Fortress of Louisbourg in Nova Scotia, leaving Audrey to deal single-handedly with the constant flow of artifacts reaching the lab from the Orr site.

The Louisbourg project was to be on a scale scarcely smaller than the restoration of Williamsburg and a magnet for ambitious archaeologists, or so it was presented to me when I was offered the job of directing it. I had just arrived in Macon, Georgia, to speak at a conference on Historic Site Archeology, when a persistent Canadian, over late-night drinks, invited me to take the Louisbourg job. "I'm just fine where I am," I told him, then added rather lamely, "Besides, I've just bought a boat . . ."

"We'll ship it up there for you. No problem," said my new friend. "Have another drink."

When I continued to decline (not the drink, which I accepted), he asked whether I would then and there fill out the job application form so that he could take it back to Ottawa just as an example of the kind of individual Parks Canada should be seeking. "Let's have another, while you're doing it," he laughed. So I laughed too, filled out the form, went to bed, and thought no more about it. Four months later, I got a call from Ottawa congratulating me on my appointment as archaeological director for the Fortress of Louisbourg. My caller's tone changed abruptly when I told him why I had filled out the form.

Several years later Audrey and I went up to Louisbourg to visit John and found him emerging from the ice and snow of a Nova Scotia winter. We both agreed that the boating season would have been too short.

John Dunton's departure was both a departmental and a personal blow because I felt that I had failed to justify the high expectations he had voiced when we first arrived seven years earlier. Previously, John had been Williamsburg's voice of archaeological reason, echoing in the wilderness of architectural indifference. But after my arrival it was always I who led the charge, I who was writing books, appearing on national television, and being cited in the newspapers. It was not that I sought the exposure, but it's a simple fact of media life that it always wants to hear from the top gun. John, alas, was being pushed into the background, and with Audrey in charge of the lab, he could foresee no opportunity for advancement in the department.

Just as draftsmen in the architectural office never get to cut the ribbon at the opening of a new building, so in archaeology the people in the field rarely get credit for their years of back-breaking toil. That is also true of archaeological directors who fail to find anything that excites anyone but themselves. Without the Eureka! discovery to propel them into the limelight, they head quietly away into dusty retirement.

Today, like archaeological foremen in Egypt, who fall into two classes, known as a working or an ornamental *reis*, there are directors who actually work and others who are mere figureheads, whose names as "principal investigators" on grant applications are sufficient to bring in the bucks. Having earned my spurs as a lone soldier in the Guildhall Museum's war on progress, throughout my career I wanted to be down in the dirt assessing every soil layer, posthole, or emerging potsherd, and throughout the 1960s I was trying to do so—lecturing intrusions notwithstanding.

Early in 1963 Ed Kendrew and his architects informed me that we should next turn our attention to a four-acre lot on the south side of the town, one of the few areas not previously affected by Jimmy Knight's cross-trenching. The intent was to reconstruct an early house that had burned around 1810, but one of whose brick-walled outbuildings survived and bore the tantalizing name of Martha Washington's Kitchen. The house had been built around 1714 by the wealthy colonist John Custis III (Martha's father-in-law from her first marriage), who reportedly had modeled it after the still-surviving 1665 Jacobean-style mansion built by Arthur Allen in Surry County. Erroneously named Bacon's Castle, it stands as the only mid-seventeenth-century dwelling remaining in Virginia. Consequently, the opportunity to replicate something like it in Williamsburg was too inviting to be ignored. It would provide an opportunity to rebuild a house very different in character from the familiar story-and-a-half clapboard dwellings to be seen up and down the central Duke of Gloucester Street. Equally important, John Custis had been Williamsburg's foremost horticulturist, and his published correspondence with a fellow gardener in London, Peter Collinson, suggested that the remains of the Custis gardens lay waiting to be archaeologically revealed.

The block known in the eighteenth century as Custis Square was occupied in the latter years of the nineteenth century by support buildings for the adjacent Eastern State Lunatic Asylum. The latter's forbidding, turreted complex dominated the southwest corner of the town and was the successor to the colonial Public Hospital, built there in 1770 and dismissively described by Thomas Jefferson as resembling a brick kiln. It, and all its ancillary buildings, burned in 1885, to be quickly replaced by an even uglier complex. Colonial Williamsburg bought Custis Square in 1960, but not until its Victorian asylum buildings were torn down could archaeological work begin.

Digging began in March and immediately ran into trouble. Instead of carting away the remains of the demolished hospital buildings in 1885, the rubble had been spread as much as eighteen inches deep across the Custis Square site and seemingly rolled flat into an almost concretelike mass that took a heavy toll on the humor of pickax wielding archaeologists more accustomed to the trowel and the whisk broom. Beneath it lay the cellar of the Custis House and a brick-vaulted drain in whose tunnel I became embarrassingly stuck. That exploit was recorded on film—along with my ungentlemanly expletives. However, more worthy of media immortality were the contents of John Custis's well. The Williamsburg subsoils comprise layers of clay and sand overlying beds of marl laid down when Tidewater Virginia was still under the ocean. Wells dug during the wet months could be expected to draw water at a depth of about twenty feet. But because that water was the product of rain, in the summer such shallow wells would dry up, and a deeper shaft would have to be dug. And this Custis did in 1737. To his friend Collinson, he wrote: "I send you some things which I took out of the bottom of a well 40 feet deep; the one seems to be a cockle petrefyd one a bone petrefyd; [this?] seems to have been the under beak of some large antediluvian fowl."

We reached the bottom at a depth of forty feet one inch, and there found a thick bed of marl from which we recovered shells and fragments of whalebone that equated with Custis's antediluvian fowl. Much more significant, however, were the artifacts from the later filling—which brings us back to Custis the man. He was given to feuding with anyone from the governor on down and had a particular dislike for fellow planter John Dandridge, whose daughter Martha married Custis's son Daniel Parke in 1749 in spite of his father's vehement disapproval. Shortly before his death, John Custis gave a quantity of silver and pewter ware to the wife of the innkeeper Mathew Moody. When Daniel Parke sued to get it back, Anne Moody testified that she had been given the plate because the old man did not want it to fall into the hands of "any Dandridge's daughter." Custis himself had described her as "much inferior to his son."

What, you might wonder, had this to do with John Custis's forty-foot well? The answer was to be found on a glass wine bottle, one of many found in the shaft with a seal on its side stamped either *John Custis 1713* or simply *I Custis.* One of the latter had had his name carefully and firmly ground from the seal until only a white scar remained. Custis died in the same year as his son's marriage to Martha, and eight years later Daniel, too, died, leaving the house to his widow, who at twenty-six was the wealthiest widow in Williamsburg. In 1759 she gave her hand and her £23,500 estate to Virginia's most eligible general, George Washington. Before the year was out she stripped the Custis house and auctioned off its memories, including 135 of the family's pictures, and then (perhaps with a thin-lipped smirk) rented the house to her brother Bartholomew Dandridge. Thus, in the Custis well archaeology was to find a graphic reminder that there may have been more to Martha Custis than the attribute of "an infectious gentleness." The mutilated bottle pointed instead to a spite and hatred that still lingered ten years after Martha's father-in-law died.

Although the Custis project was proving immensely informative, it was halted in December when the architecture department required us to shift gears yet again and prepare to embark on another project that was almost as big. As Colonial Williamsburg's annual report for 1964 claimed, the Foundation's archaeological program "was the most intensive of its kind ever attempted in

America." But it added somewhat ominously, "Our future program will be intimately connected with archaeology, which will go on at an accelerated rate as new projects are undertaken."

Two Williamsburg families had balked at selling out to Rockefeller and the Restoration, one of them members of the Haughwout Estate, which owned the large Duke of Gloucester Street house known in Colonial Williamsburg parlance as the Bland-Wetherburn House, but to the estate as the Richard Bland Tavern. Fiercely independent and opposed to what was perceived as the Rockefeller takeover, the owner made her point by hanging Mr. Junior in effigy from her signboard! Nevertheless, in 1964 the estate agreed to a ninety-nine-year lease of the building. The lease required that the building eventually be returned in the condition in which it was transferred, but since the year 2063 was far-off in somebody else's future, that did not deter the Foundation from tearing down a row of ratty modern outbuildings and beginning the process of taking the building back to the state during its ownership by tavern keeper Henry Wetherburn (1743–60).

Because the tavern was the last major clapboard building yet to be restored, Ed Kendrew decreed that every step of the process, both architectural and archaeological, should be recorded on film with a view to making a scholarly documentary on the art of restoration. I was less than enthusiastic, having learned that the uncovering of an archaeological something-or-other that should take five minutes would take at least twenty when being filmed. However, there was consolation in the expectation that eventually there would be a prizewinning celluloid legacy.

Every inch of the restoration of Wetherburn's Tavern was recorded, from peeling away layers of woodwork paint to reveal the colors used in the mid-eighteenth century, to uncovering rows of cherry-filled wine bottles buried beside the building in Henry Wetherburn's era, to removing a nineteenth-century flight of cellar steps to expose the clay matrix left after an earlier set of steps had been removed. This last called for very careful scraping to avoid the risers crumbling away before they could be measured and photographed. We were just ready for the photography when a shadow and silhouette loomed in the sunlight above. It was Ed Kendrew. Fearing that he might assume the clay steps sufficiently strong to walk down, I asked him not to do so.

"Who has a better right?" Ed demanded as he trod on down into the cellar.

The restoration of Wetherburn's Tavern was completed in 1967 and has ever since been among the most visited of Williamsburg's exhibition buildings. If you wonder why you have never seen the completed documentary on television, the answer is simple. It was never finished. The miles of raw footage went into temporary storage until architectural historian Paul Buchanan and I should have time to edit it and record bridging commentaries. But the ever-pressing demands to embark on new projects never allowed time to return to the Wetherburn film. Paul Buchanan died, I retired, and 16 mm film became obsolete when videotaping took over, to be followed in turn by digital photography.

The sobering lesson that what you don't do now rarely gets done is an adage that should be printed in large type on every archaeologist's office door. Sponsors of archaeological projects, be they Colonial Williamsburg architects, private foundations, or state agencies, are usually satisfied to be shown or told the information they are seeking. On the basis of a drawing or plan, the walls go up, the planting goes in, or the highway rolls on. Nobody allows the time or the cost of writing scholarly reports, which perhaps few people read, but which are the true end products of every archaeological endeavor. I managed a better-than-nothing solution by writing a series of booklets outlining what was found on each site and illustrating them with images of the most interesting (and complete) artifacts. I designed the publications to have illustrations on virtually every right-hand page—usually bleeding to the edges, thereby giving the casual thumber the impression that the book was worth a buck. Consequently, I called them "thumbers' books," and most are still in print forty and more years later—though no longer selling for a dollar.

The 1960s saw the birth of a discipline at first defined as historic sites archeology—no second "a" because this was a National Park Service term and the fiefdom of its anthropologists who considered digging for history a distant second cousin to prehistoric studies. Historians, on the other hand, mistrusted and dismissed the cultural, non-site-specific work of anthropologists. Having no anthropological training, I believed that it was the historians I should strive to reach. After all, there is not much point in digging up history if historians have no use for it. Consequently, with my *Here Lies Virginia* having enjoyed favorable reviews, I embarked on a series of books to try to show that artifacts properly excavated could successfully challenge the written work. It was a tub I had been thumping ever since my arrival in America, and in the title of a lecture delivered in Raleigh, North Carolina, in December 1963, I dubbed the new discipline "archeology: handmaiden to history." I hasten to add, however, that I was not its father. That designation belonged to my mentor J. C. Harrington, who eight years earlier had stood before the American Anthropological

Association and dared to claim archeology as an "auxiliary science to American history." Although Harrington was preaching to the wrong choir, when I came along and added my voice to his, a handful of both anthropologists and historians began to take notice.

For me, as I have said, the target was historians, to whom I directed my 1966 book *1775: Another Part of the Field*. Taking that year in Virginia, I reassembled it from the events, attitudes, and opinions voiced in contemporary newspaper reports and columns. I wanted to demonstrate that, like fragments of pottery that could be excavated and reassembled, the detritus of a year in history could be put back together to provide an impression of what it was like to have lived at that time. It was, in short, an archaeological approach to social history. In retrospect I continue to think that this was one of my better books. However, in reviewing it one well-established historian observed that in discussing with colleagues whether or not archaeologists should attempt to write history, their conclusion was "not necessarily."

Although 1965 had been primarily devoted to excavations at Wetherburn's Tavern, an originally extramural project had intruded to the point of becoming a mainline endeavor. It began with a visit from the developer L. B. Weber, who was starting clearance of a tract adjacent to the Warwick River. His backhoe had turned up a cache of late seventeenth-century wine bottles. Precisely where they came from or why they had been buried, we never discovered. Nevertheless, they drew us to Weber's property and to a major Jamestown-era plantation named Mathews' Manor. Weber's own interest in history was such that he provided whatever heavy equipment we needed to explore the site and his own surveyors and draftsmen to record what we found. Rarely, if ever, does one have this level of cooperation from a developer, and we made the most of it.

We uncovered the brick foundations of the manor house as well as the post-constructed imprint of a much larger house built after the original manor house burned in the 1650s. From pits, ditches, and an icehouse came a large quantity of ceramic and metal artifacts from the second quarter of the seventeenth century, the most spectacular being a copper watering can for which no parallel exists outside Dutch genre paintings. Although Mathews' Manor was the earliest plantation to be excavated in Virginia, as so often happened in Williamsburg, the demands of newly imposed projects prevented our being able to publish the results more fully than was possible within the pages of the December 1966 issue of *The Magazine Antiques*. Failure to complete the study of the Mathews' Manor material still hangs like a black cloud over my career. Mr. Weber, on the other hand, was well-satisfied. He published a handsome, lot-promoting brochure constructed around the Mathews site illustrated with drawings of the watering can and several other artifacts. In consequence, he won a national preservation award, which made up for the fact that he learned the hard way that archaeology is only modestly useful in selling real estate.

The busy summer of 1965 had led to my hiring several short-term excavators, among them a young man who was then a local history teacher and football coach. His name was William Kelso, and over time he matured from a dirt scraper to become the state's commissioner of archaeology, and subsequently director of archaeology, first at Thomas Jefferson's Monticello, and then at Jamestown. When asked for advice about becoming a professional archaeologist I invariably answered, "Don't!" Yet I confess to having derived much satisfaction from the subsequent careers of people like Bill Kelso who chose to ignore that counsel. Another young man from the summer of '65 came to us as an unpaid intern and worked extremely well on the Mathews' Manor project. Cary Carson would later return as director of Colonial Williamsburg's research and eventually an influential vice president.

The year ended with work at Wetherburn's Tavern far from finished, but in the hope of impressing our leaders I was able to report the recovery of more than 65,000 artifacts. In truth the figure was meaningless to all but the unfortunate lab technician who had to write a catalog number on each of them. Besides, in another year the figure would rise to 156,000—"excluding nails, bones, and architectural remains."

It was to be a busy one both in the Williamsburg dirt and in front of my attic typewriter. Believing that artifacts are to the ground what words are to the written page, I produced two books that had started out as one until Angus Cameron, my editor at Knopf, thought otherwise. The first, *Historical Archaeology*, was a guide demonstrating how to do it, and the second offered a means of identifying what it reveals. The latter, *A Guide to Artifacts of Colonial America*, was universally well received and is still in print, but *Historical Archaeology* promptly ran afoul of the then often strident women's lib movement and became a rallying cry for anthropological bra burners. In writing about the merits of volunteer excavators I declared that on an archaeological site "high heels and low décolletage are a lethal combination."

Today I reread those pages and shudder, but the comment stemmed from two examples. The first happened to Audrey when she was working on a Roman villa near Bristol and suffered from volunteers wearing high heels who when treading across a mosaic pavement punched the individual tesserae through into the ground beneath. The second was my own experience at Wetherburn's Tavern, where tourists found the archaeological discoveries less revealing than the absence of a bra worn by our ever-stooping drafting person. One has to remember that in 1963 female archaeologists were a rarity, even though I was married to one, and two of Britain's foremost excavators were Kathleen Kenyon at Jericho and Tessa-Verney Wheeler at the Iron Age fort of Maiden Castle in England. Besides, three of my London Irregulars were women.

It is an entrenched supposition that no one, whether politician, media pundit, or simple archaeologist, has a right, over time or through experience, to change his or her mind. Evolution, Darwinian or otherwise, remains a theory unrelated to contemporary reality. Within ten years of writing the offending chapter the face of American archaeology had changed. Not only were women working alongside men, in several important instances they were giving the directions.

INETEEN SIXTY-SIX was to be a year in which the discipline of historical archaeology came of age. In the spring the Smithsonian Institution
hosted a three-day conference to promote the setting up of an archaeological
department within the institution. Headed by the historian Wilcomb E. "Wid"
Washburn, the gathering included most of the names then prominent in American anthropology, among them the Smithsonian's own senior curator, Malcolm
Watkins, who had previously played a contributing role in the Amelung glass
factory excavation. Although creating a new department proved too grandiose
an aim, the conference did endorse a proposal to create a national and interna-
tional society for historical archaeology to be formally constituted a year later at
Southern Methodist University. Among those assembled in Dallas the following
January to chart the future of historical archaeology in America were our host Ed
Jelks; Pinky Harrington and John Cotter for the National Park Service; Bernard
L. "Bunny" Fontana from Arizona; Charles Fairbanks from Florida; and from
the Smithsonian, Wid Washburn and Malcolm Watkins, who also represented
New England.

Many weighty issues passed back and forth, not the least of which was
whether to add an extra "a" to archeology, and whether to call ourselves fellows, directors, members, or the like. The "a" went in—we were officially the
Society for Historical Archaeology—and I emerged as a director (after "fellows"
had been nixed as too pretentious) and was charged with the responsibility of
hosting the new society's first annual meeting, to be held in Williamsburg. Simultaneously, a comparable society was being formed in England, to which
I was appointed the first American vice president. It could not have the same
name as ours because "historical" in Europe went back through the classical
centuries, so since England already had a Society for Medieval Archaeology, the
name became the Society for Post-Medieval Archaeology. In the editorial to its

first published volume, the author expressed the hope that the society's links to America would "provide tangible benefits in the research field with a free interchange of knowledge and ideas." And they have.

Following in the wake of countless reports from the Society of Antiquaries of London as well as papers published in the journals of county archaeological societies, the new British society elected to publish studies on specific sites and artifact categories and so was immediately and continuously a source of practical knowledge. The American society, on the other hand, would in time become increasingly theoretical, and socially and politically oriented. There is nothing wrong in that save for the fact that those of us who rely on careful artifact drawings no longer get them. Draftsmanship, alas, has become too expensive and time-consuming, a contention usually voiced by those who have little interest in the specificity of artifacts and are satisfied with fuzzy photographs of scarcely identifiable potsherds. Nevertheless, the creation of the American and British societies (quickly followed by another in Australia) and their published annual journals laid the ground for all that has since been achieved.

With that said, however, 1966 also saw a major step backward.

Following the publication of my *Here Lies Virginia*, with its plea for the creation of a Virginia state museum to house the results of excavations such as those at Mathews' Manor and elsewhere, a local potter, James E. Maloney, and his brother Andrew decided to do something about it. Jimmy and Andy were as unalike as it is possible for brothers to be—Jimmy, in his battered baseball cap, tennis shoes, and coated with clay dust, and Andy, the impeccably dressed Richmond lobbyist on first-name terms with everyone on Capitol Hill. When we first met Jimmy in the summer of 1956, he was already making stoneware for sale by Colonial Williamsburg at his own salt-glazed stoneware kiln on Richmond Road, the start of a multimillion-dollar empire. Augmenting his own output in stoneware and slipware with bulk purchases from other potters and glassmakers in West Virginia, and advertising them with huge roadside signs reading "Acres of Seconds," he was soon attracting more customers than walked the streets of Williamsburg. He became a good friend to Audrey and me, and from him we learned the art of reproducing the kinds of stoneware we were finding in our excavations. Thus, the brothers Maloney were inspired to encourage the governor and the General Assembly to vote funds for creating a Virginia museum of historical archaeology. A local developer quickly offered land on Richmond Road on which to build it, and the governor appointed a study commission to put together a budgeted master plan, to be chaired by Dean Melville Jones at the

College of William and Mary. As vice chairman I thought this an excellent idea, particularly when Mel offered land on the campus in preference to the smaller tract on Richmond Road.

Shortly thereafter the whole plan began to unravel when the college's anthropological faculty got wind of it and demanded that prehistory be included and awarded comparable space. But there was no time to incorporate that requirement before our report went back to the General Assembly, and besides, I had no enthusiasm for allowing the museum to lose its historical focus. In the end only one opinion counted, that of Governor Mills Godwin, who failed to include the funding in his budget while apologizing and hinting that the proposal might be reintroduced in 1968. But with the original plan in shreds we had no stomach for a battle with the college anthropologists, particularly since the gentle Mel would necessarily bow to his own people. Nevertheless, out of this disappointment emerged a state commission for archaeology with Bill Kelso at its head. Although the new agency was to be located on the campus, as Mel had proposed, it was not to be housed in a grand new building but rather in a handful of subterranean offices in the cellars of the college's Wren Building. Promises from Virginia politicians of better things in the future went no further than that, and as we launch into the twenty-first century there is still no state museum of archaeology, be it historic or prehistoric, and thousands of artifacts languish in drawers and boxes closed to the public.

Although I had put a good deal of time into designing a museum and lobbying for its creation, I had more immediate concerns, primarily the completion of the Wetherburn's Tavern excavations, which did not end until April 1967. Exactly a year earlier another of those wrench-throwing interpolated projects intruded into the orderliness of our labors. The architecture department launched into the reconstruction of a metalworker's shop behind the James Geddy House on Duke of Gloucester Street. At the outset this did not seem likely to involve us, since the property had previously been archaeologically studied, first in 1930 when the house was restored, and again in 1952 by Jimmy Knight and his trenchers. At that time they also uncovered a foundation to the east of the Geddy House and reconstructed it as a story-and-a-half shop. It was also at that time that they found the remains of what they took to be the metalworkers' forge site.

The first James Geddy was a gunsmith and brass founder who died in 1744. Subsequently, on behalf of their widowed mother, his sons David and William continued in the trade until 1760 when their brother James took over the property and worked there as a silversmith until 1777. Straddling two lots and subject to numerous expansions and rebuilding, the James Geddy complex proved to be a far greater archaeological challenge than the restoring and reconstructing architects had imagined. That something was amiss became apparent when trenches were dug to install foundations for the new exhibition workshop. Exposed in the sides of the trenches were large numbers of artifacts related to brass working and quantities of clinker and ash. That the spread extended both inside the new building and outside toward the Geddy dwelling made it abundantly clear that the workshop being reconstructed had not been the one that generated the waste.

Reconstruction of the workshop went ahead while we were still at Wetherburn's Tavern, but the architecture department did agree that perhaps we should take another look at the Geddy property in 1967. The results were spectacular. We found the ground plan of a workshop complex behind the house that had straddled both lots, complete with one forge and lead patterns for casting brass buckles, for the handle of a silver sauceboat, and for brass gun parts. Along with the patterns were spoiled and rejected castings. Buried in a sand pile beside the well lay five of James Geddy's silver teaspoons, probably left there by playing children.

More important was evidence of renewed gunsmithing during the early days of the Revolutionary War. The presence of the firing mechanism for a seventeenth-century matchlock musket was graphic evidence that very old weapons were being renovated for war service by the local militia. Dating for this activity was provided by a fragment from one of Governor Dunmore's armorial-decorated Chinese porcelain dinner plates, which I suspect had been looted from the Governor's Palace after his precipitous flight in April 1775. More signs of martial activity on the Geddy property at that time were provided by a small barrel sunk into the ground containing three cannon balls, a quantity of still-sticky tar, and an attached feather. A simple coincidence? Or was this evidence that the tar and feathering of an arrested Tory in Isle of Wight County in August was a fate shared by someone in Williamsburg? If true, the Geddy site's lump of tar and its feather survive as the sole relics of one of the Revolution's least humane moments.

Although a tar-soaked feather was not something that could easily be shared with or sold to the public, the Foundation's merchandising department was always on the lookout for something new to reproduce, and found it in one of the Geddy site's principal artifacts, namely, an earthenware bird-nesting bottle made in the 1730s at Yorktown. Such bottles were anchored under the eaves of Williamsburg houses to encourage occupation by mosquito-devouring swallows. First reproduced by Jimmy Maloney in 1968, the Geddy bird bottle has been one of his factory's and Colonial Williamsburg's best sellers.

The early 1930s rush to restoration generated decisions that were not always sound. At the Geddy House, a lean-to addition running across the back had been torn down as "postcolonial," and in 1952, as I have noted, the east sales area was reconstructed as a story-and-a-half building. However, the documentary evidence showed that it had been single-storied, shed-roofed, and one with the demolished rear addition. That this last was actually a colonial work area was revealed by narrow east-west lines of dirt littered with pins and silver scraps that had fallen between its floorboards.

But these discoveries came too late. The restoration was essentially complete before we started, and no one had a mind to tear down the 1952 shop or to rebuild the demolished rear shed addition. James Geddy's long forge workshop was not reconstructed because the later rebuilt structure had already been assigned as the Geddy foundry, and clearly they had not coexisted. Enormously informative as archaeology can be, it all too often opens closets that its sponsors would prefer left shut. Thus 1967's somewhat embarrassing Geddy revelations went unobserved by any but the architects, and would remain one of the Foundation's little secrets.

Not so Sunday, November 12, which put Williamsburg on the front pages of newspapers across the country and as far away as Australia. It also brought Audrey and me into the lab on extraordinarily short notice to greet an important visitor, America's First Lady, Lady Bird Johnson. Owing in large measure to Carl Humelsine's close ties to the State Department, distinguished foreign heads of state frequently spent a night in the retrospective and beguiling atmosphere of Colonial Williamsburg before being subjected to the rigors of Washington's pomp and politics. Such dignitaries were known to the staff as "the king of the week." In this instance, however, the head of state was our own President Lyndon Johnson, who had come to Williamsburg to address the Gridiron Club. On Sunday afternoon we were assigned to show Mrs. Johnson the Geddy artifacts and anything else that could pass the time until she was scheduled to rejoin her husband. She made the appropriate noises of amazement and appreciation, albeit in a somewhat abstract way, as though her mind were elsewhere. Not until that evening when we watched the NBC news did we learn why.

That morning the Johnsons, Humelsines, and other assorted dignitaries had attended the eleven o'clock service at Bruton Parish Church and heard a sermon by the locally beloved Reverend Cotesworth Lewis. Cotesworth had endeared himself to Audrey and me by attending my lectures and volubly expressing his fondness for our archaeological work and its contributions to his parish. But that Sunday, and completely out of character, his peacenik sermon lambasted the president and his government for its shameful continuation of the war in Vietnam. Johnson was furious, the Humelsines were embarrassed, and Colonial Williamsburg's previously self-congratulatory public relations staffers were close to cardiac arrest.

Autobiographies are supposed to propel the reader from the nursery to the grave, preferably in that order. But there are moments when deviations and re-grouping are permissible—at least by me. The visit of President and Pat Nixon is one of them.

In April 1981, seven years after resigning the presidency, President Nixon and his family revisited Colonial Williamsburg as private citizens. Carl Humel-sine, by then retired as chairman, hosted a small black-tie dinner for them at Carter's Grove plantation to which Audrey and I were invited. Needless to say, being staff, we thought it wise not to be late, an endeavor that inevitably resulted in being early. Rather than drive up to the mansion ahead of the guests, we decided to turn off, driving the wrong way onto the single-lane Country Road to wait there until the minimotorcade had passed us up the main driveway to the house. It never occurred to us that Carl would bring the Nixons down the Country Road. But he did, and we found ourselves facing the oncoming lights of the motorcade which left no doubt that it was heading straight for us. I hastily tried to reverse and instead slid into the roadside ditch, where for what seemed an eternity the wheels spun and the mud flew as the headlights got ever closer. In, as they say, the nick of time, the tires gripped and we were able to escape in a shower of mud that flew upward into the lights of the pursuing limousines. Had they arrived a few seconds earlier to find us still straddling the road the Secret Service might very well have construed that we were planning an assassination attempt and should be shot just to be on the safe side.

Once clear and out of the way, we sat aghast imagining how close we might have been to making our last headline: "Williamsburg Archaeologists Gunned Down in Botched Attempt to Assassinate Ex-President."

Why, out of all the citizens of Williamsburg, Audrey and I should have been chosen for a dinner of only ten people, we never discovered. We could only guess that not being American citizens, we were least likely to refuse the invitation or accept it and usurp Cotesworth Lewis's bully pulpit. No such affronts spoiled the evening; instead, we were privileged to question the president and listen to him talk openly about his relationship with China, the fiasco in Vietnam, and much else. Although the visit did not make it into the printed Colonial Williamsburg Foundation Chronology, for Audrey and me the memory of that candlelit evening at Carter's Grove would remain one of the great moments of our lives and left us with a lasting impression of Richard Nixon as a brilliant international statesman whose gifts were not entirely engulfed in the mire of Watergate.

The next day the Nixons spent the afternoon with us in the archaeology lab reviewing all that we were finding. His inscription to us in the flyleaf of his memoirs thanked us for our hospitality and for our "extraordinary contribution to American history and scholarship." And we were vain enough to believe that he meant it. Back now to the Johnson era.

Because American history extended to the Caribbean and because I had been an armchair pirate from childhood, in the summer of 1966 I decided that a vacation at Port Royal in Jamaica would be both educational and fun. The town had two claims to fame, one for having been home base for the duplicitous Henry Morgan (governor and allegedly reformed pirate), and the other for having sunk into Kingston Harbour in the earthquake of 1692. That date remains forever in my mind—or rather on my cuff links. A gift from a Jamaican architect, they are made from brass studs from the coffin of one Lewis Galdy, who was sucked down into the earthquake's fissure, ejected into the harbor, and lived to tell about it until his death in 1733.

For our first visit to Port Royal we booked a room at the Morgan's Harbour Hotel, then a popular berth for yachtsmen heading south. On making the booking, I received a letter from the owner, Sir Anthony Jenkinson, who said he knew me and was a business associate of my father. He wrote that he was anxious to pick my brains, but did not say for what purpose. We soon found out. Jenkinson was at the Kingston airport to greet us and drive us out to Port Royal. Before we even arrived at the hotel he was taking us to the points of interest in the town and telling us how he was planning to turn Morgan's Harbour into a Williamsburg in the Caribbean. I would be his bridge to Colonial Williamsburg, and as archaeology would be needed, I was just the chap to lead the archaeological part of the project.

Audrey tried to tell Jenkinson that we were on vacation and not there to work. But his steely-edged enthusiasm brooked no demurral. There were to be gift shops, a colonial-style bank building, a restaurant with tavern atmosphere, a swimming pool behind it—and on and on. It was immediately obvious that this was a strictly commercial venture and that history was no more than bait to attract romantics like ourselves. Nevertheless, I did agree to dig a four-by-four-foot hole to try to determine how much of seventeenth-century Port Royal had failed to plunge into the harbor. The answer was quick in coming. About a foot down in a layer of sand we found a man dressed in the kind of clothing that would have been worn by Henry Morgan—long buttoned coat, lace stock, and full Carolian wig. I must add that he was only four inches tall and molded in pipe clay, but he was clearly telling me that as much of the old pirate port remained on land as did later layers deposited by eighteenth-century occupation and subsequent hurricanes and earthquakes. Port Royal was an archaeological gold mine and something needed to be done before Jenkinson began to tear into it. Still in my youthful, white-knight-to-the-rescue mode, I thought it my duty to take up the archaeological sword.

Pinky Harrington had already advised me that one cannot save everything and shouldn't try. Fight the battles you can win and shun those you can't. That had been his sage counsel, but it took me another fifteen or twenty years to accept it—and not always then. At Port Royal, I should have known from the outset that Jenkinson was not on the side of the angels. At lunch on the Morgan's Harbour terrace, I asked him whether there were stinging insects, biting spiders, and such like to be avoided. "Nothing like that here, I assure you," he replied. The words were scarcely out of his mouth when I felt a sharp and searing pain in my right foot. Anchored to it was the largest yellow centipede I had ever seen or could have imagined. "Oh yes, there are those," Jenkinson admitted.

The submerged Port Royal had already been subjected to quasi-archaeological excavation, which had hinted at the riches that lay amid its rubble under the waters of Kingston Harbour. In 1959 the inventor and oceanographer Edwin A. Link dove on the site and used an air lift to suck goodies up onto the deck of his boat. His wife described in the *National Geographic* how a pocket watch rocketed up, and when Link pried it open "a handful of delicate brass gears and other parts rained into his palm." When I read that brightly descriptive sentence my initial response was not condemnation of Link for his vandalism but rather dismay that the revered National Geographic Society would publish it.

Beginning in 1966, the Jamaican government had hired diver Robert F. Marx to renew excavations on the site of the sunken city, and he was hard at it by the time we arrived. He had already brought up an astounding array of objects which were then in storage at his makeshift lab in Port Royal's nineteenth-century naval hospital. Although I had never been underwater any deeper than a snorkel's tube, Marx's invitation to dive with him to see what he had uncovered was irresistible. This was not a free-dive experience, however, air being provided from a hookah leaving one umbilically linked to a surface pump, but it was a great way to learn what diving was like. In a word: wonderful! Far less wonderful was what awaited me on the bottom. Rather than finding houses standing as high as the ruins of bombed London, all I could see were modern beer bottles and cans, old tires, and assorted weed-covered trash. In one of Marx's trenches I could spot a few bricks but not much else. For me, diving at Port Royal was a tremendous disappointment. Nevertheless, Bob Marx's recovered artifacts were clear evidence that I was not seeing the site at its best—indeed, scarcely at all, since every touch of the bottom stirred up silt that reduced visibility to inches.

In later years Marx would be roundly criticized by academian divers for his use of rough-and-ready methods, but reviewing his records forty years on I remain impressed by his diligence and single-handed mapping.

Besides my diving with Marx and spending two days digging a test hole, Jenkinson wanted me to meet and talk to his architect, Tom Concannon, as well as members of a wealthy group of Jamaican businessmen who called themselves the Port Royal Company of Merchants and were, I supposed, potential investors in the Williamsburg of the Caribbean project. I showed them what we had found in our test hole and impressed upon them the need for thorough archaeological work to precede any building construction. I stressed that it was theirs, Jamaica's, heritage they would be disturbing and destroying. This they clearly understood, and agreed that archaeology was an essential first step. I added that I thought it important that Jamaican nationals (perhaps from the University of the West Indies) should be prominently involved. This, too, they accepted. Jenkinson, on the other hand, said little or nothing.

By the time we were about to leave for home most of our visit had been expended on Jamaican archaeology and preservation goals. Although not the vacation we had envisaged, I think both Audrey and I believed that we had sown seeds from which worthwhile things would grow. There remained, however, a farewell dinner for us on the lantern-lit terrace at Morgan's Harbour. It was the night of April 1, the party hosted in part by the Company of Merchants, several of whose members joined Jenkinson in expressing gratitude for our contributions to the island's heritage. Finally, late in the evening, under a starlit Caribbean sky came my turn to speak.

I was enthusiastic about Port Royal's historical potential, called for restraint in developing it, and then made my grand offer. I would welcome two or three archaeologically inclined Jamaican students to Williamsburg to spend a summer working in my department. This would prepare them for working under a yet-to-be-contracted historical archaeologist—if the government and the Company of Merchants would underwrite the cost. The offer was received with a round of applause and a good deal of happy handshaking that left us even more certain that we had done something good. After the party broke up, Audrey and I stood alone looking out over the harbor toward the twinkling lights of modern Kingston and historic Port Henderson across the bay. Suddenly the Hollywood-style closing shot was shattered by the irate arrival of Jenkinson. In a voice steeped in venom he barked, "By God, if you want to take [expletive] to Williamsburg, that's your affair! But I'll have no part of it!" And that was the last we saw of him.

"Well," sighed Audrey, "so much for April Fool's Day."

But useful seeds had in fact been sown. In August, I was invited back to Jamaica by Edward Seaga, the government's minister of finance, to meet with him and the director of the Institute of Jamaica to formulate plans for the excavation and reconstruction of Port Royal, an element of which was bringing at least one student to Williamsburg. Sir Anthony Jenkinson and his Morgan's Harbour were scarcely mentioned, and I believe that it was not long after that he left the island. UNESCO funds were later secured to embark on land excavations after I had been able to help find a respected British archaeologist to direct them. But there our association ended. We never returned to Jamaica for that promised real vacation. As for a Williamsburg in the Caribbean, to the best of my knowledge, it was a vision that left Jamaica with Sir Anthony.

I N 1967 the still-continuing digging and filming at Wetherburn's Tavern became the genesis of a separate archaeological film. The idea had been on and
off the table for eighteen months, during which time the audiovisual director,
Arthur L. Smith, had hired two successive scriptwriters who, knowing nothing
about colonial archaeology, failed in their assignments. In the process it had
become apparent that I was the only person who knew what we were trying to
achieve, and so it fell to me to write the script and direct the film. Titled *Doorway to the Past,* it tried to show how events of the colonial century left their
traces in the ground that could be recovered by archaeologists and ultimately
reconstructed for the edification of the public.

The film opened with a sequence showing Thomas Jefferson addressing a
meeting of the Society for Useful Knowledge at the Capitol and explaining the
stratigraphy of the Indian mound he had excavated at his Shadwell home. The
action then shifted to the Raleigh Tavern, where the narrator filled in the historical background as the camera focused on the Apollo Room's furnishings, specifically on bottles, a punch bowl, and other artifacts whose parallels would later
be seen being excavated. We hired the veteran actor Hugh Franklin as narrator,
someone well-known on the midday soap opera *Days of Our Lives.* Hugh was a
pro who never once snarled at his novice director. Not so some of the others. No
one actually growled, but when clustered together they made it clear that as professionals they were unenthusiastic about being directed by an archaeologist.

The film ended with a re-creation of a violent scene in the Raleigh Tavern
where the crockery and glasses were broken and tobacco pipes trampled under
foot. We then dissolved from the eighteenth century into the present as a ball-
gowned hostess guided a group of tourists through the same room, explaining
the serenity her ancestors had enjoyed there. Although the message was that
the truth is not necessarily what we claim it to be, I got away with the heresy,

perhaps without the Powers that Were recognizing it. The film ended with what I considered my Orson Welles "Rosebud" shot. A bored child listening to the hostess twiddled a button free from her sweater, causing it to roll across the floor and drop between the boards. We followed it in a tight shot under the floor to see the button land on a brick where, as the credits rolled, accumulating dust and cobwebs slowly covered and obscured it. Unfortunately, projectionists and video watchers have all too often cut the credits, thereby denying me my moment of artistic brilliance.

Doorway to the Past subsequently earned two documentary awards, and more than thirty years later it is still available on DVD. Its premier, however, was less than stellar. I took it for screening at the 1969 annual meeting of the American Anthropological Association in New Orleans. The audience could see no merit in archaeology being used to reconstruct a Colonial Williamsburg–style interpretation of history. Actors in wigs and tricorn hats did not promote the seriousness of anthropology. So the anthropologists booed it. Pinky Harrington's seminal speech to the same group in 1955 had fallen on no more receptive ears. Historical archaeology still had a long way to go before anthropologists would accept it as a legitimate discipline. Historians were even slower.

Along with the major excavation projects, the late 1960s involved a plethora of other smaller sites, all of them generating a continuous flow of artifacts into a laboratory whose staff was only large enough to handle one site at a time. We had planned to devote 1968 to editing the Wetherburn film and to completing reports on previous fieldwork. It did not turn out that way. Instead, four sites were worked on, the largest of them the vast Custis Site. Unless we were to drown in artifacts and unfinished reports, something drastic needed to be done. At the year's end I wrote that "if Colonial Williamsburg were to abandon its digging program forthwith, there would be enough museum-oriented duties to keep the present staff hard at work indefinitely. . . . The completion of the reports on all significant artifacts recovered in the past ten years would alone take seven to ten years to complete." I was still ringing that doleful bell in 1970 when I outlined a new ten-year plan in a report to my new leader as head of architecture, Charles Hackett. Reluctantly, I accepted that archaeology would "continue in the role of a service department with its own goals primarily geared to the needs of others"—the others being the assorted directors and vice presidents of Colonial Williamsburg's various divisions.

One such need prompted our involvement with the Carter's Grove plantation, an involvement that would continue on and off for thirteen years. Following the death of the owner, Mollie McCrea, in 1960 and its purchase by the Rockefeller Brothers' Sealantic Fund, Colonial Williamsburg had become the property's steward, a task that involved little more than its maintenance. In December 1969, however, ownership was transferred to Colonial Williamsburg. Plans for the plantation's ultimate future were needed—and quickly.

As early as the 1950s, John D. Rockefeller Jr. had agreed with Ed Kendrew that the story of life in eighteenth-century Williamsburg could only be told in tandem with the source of its prosperity, namely, the outlying plantations. Another site much further away was considered, and so was the closer Kingsmill Plantation, which Colonial Williamsburg bought but later sold to Anheuser-Busch to create the Busch Gardens theme park. Carter's Grove lay seven miles from Williamsburg and was easily accessible to visitors. But it had a problem. The alterations made by Mrs. McCrea in the 1930s had so enlarged the mansion that it would cost more than it was worth to return it to its colonial appearance. The decision, therefore, was to let it remain as she had left it, and to interpret it to visitors as an eighteenth-century house that had evolved through time. Around the mansion would be reconstructed all the since-vanished support buildings essential to the operation of a colonial plantation. It became my responsibility to find them.

Certainly, out of small holdings many great plantations grew, their additions both in land and buildings stretching out from the central core. But Carter's Grove was an atypical plantation. It had been put together from several failed seventeenth-century farmsteads by the great Virginia landowner Robert "King" Carter. For twenty years he operated it as an absentee landlord before giving it to his daughter Elizabeth at the time of her marriage in 1738 to Carter Burwell. It would have made no sense for the newlyweds to build themselves a mansion in the midst of the daily dirt of a plantation economy already successfully operated by King Carter's overseers and gangs of slaves. Consequently, Burwell built his house apart from all that activity. Result: there were no agricultural and social activity sites for us to find in the immediate vicinity of Mrs. McCrea's big house.

Although the Carter's Grove acreage had shrunk from about 1,500 acres when the Burwells owned it to the 522 acres when we were confronted with it, the search called for a very different approach than I had developed for half-acre lots in town. It is true that much of the acreage was woodland and some of it swamp, but the agriculturally cleared fields alone posed a formidable challenge. With too much going on in town, I hired a separate crew headed by Bill Kelso, with David Hazzard, another experienced archaeologist, as his assistant. After determining that the arable fields had been plowed down to the subsoil, the only economical recourse was to use machinery to cut wide trenches to try to expose the tops of ditches or foundations that cut into it. The method was crude but effective. Unfortunately, its revelations were not as Colonial Williamsburg had hoped.

Apart from traces of a brick kiln, a group of burials found behind the twentieth-century stables assumed to be those of eighteenth-century slaves, and a cluster of rectangular pits first identified as tanning vats, most of the artifacts dated from the seventeenth century. To me, however, whose London interest had been in that century, these potsherd discoveries were an exciting portent of the area's archaeological potential. My architect colleagues were not impressed, but they were placated by Bill Kelso's skillful exposure of the postholes for successive garden fences leading from the mansion toward the river. Equally impressive was his discovery of the large brass disk that linked Carter's Grove to the Revolutionary War's legendary Banastre Tarleton.

Legendary, too, was the belief that somewhere in the Carter's Grove area there had once been a thriving seventeenth-century community named Martin's Hundred. A state highway marker (subsequently stolen) told us that it had embraced eighty thousand acres and that seventy-eight people had been killed there in the Indian massacre of 1622. With traces of seventeenth-century occupation all around the McCrea mansion, it seemed likely that it stood in the midst of Martin's Hundred. The realization that when King Carter owned the land it had been called Merchant's Hundred came close to confirmation. Unfortunately, although Bill Kelso's excavations had suggested a time frame in the second quarter of the seventeenth century, he had found no evidence of contemporary structures other than a rectangular pit close to the river. Rotted sticks at the bottom of it led him to tentatively identify it as a duck blind. Twenty-two years later that conclusion would be dramatically reevaluated.

Archaeology anywhere and focusing on any time relies heavily on educated guesswork, a caveat particularly true when beginning work in a period about which one knows very little.

Outside Harrington's and his successor's digging at Jamestown and our rescue effort at Mathews' Manor, the artifacts and architecture of the seventeenth century were virtually unopened books—and in the eyes of eighteenth century–focused Colonial Williamsburg they could safely remain so.

At the conclusion of Bill Kelso's survey my own crew, working under the supervision of senior archaeologist Neil Frank, resumed excavations in the immediate vicinity of the McCrea house that would continue into 1972. Although its eighteenth-century well and the brick foundations of both a dairy and another neighboring building were exposed, nothing was rebuilt. Meanwhile, the debate on what to do with Carter's Grove continued unabated. When a wealthy donor asked that the 1930s exterior shutters be removed, the architects complied, thereby leaving the brick walls starkly naked. The unity of Mrs. McCrea's colonial revival mansion had been impaired without returning it to its eighteenth-century size and shape. Audrey was inspired to lead the charge to have the shutters replaced, and eventually they were.

We were both still of a crusading age, and having been instrumental in creating a national society of professional archaeologists, we believed that we had a parallel responsibility to promote professionalism among amateurs, a view not readily embraced by the pros. We therefore proposed conducting a summer school for social studies teachers across the state. To find suitable candidates, we sent out application forms to school systems calling for essays from teachers explaining why they wanted to be part of the program. We received about fifty responses, from which we selected twenty-eight students. That number was determined by our budget, which, naively, undertook to pay the students to attend.

Paying the students to do what they should have been paying us to do was an incredibly stupid idea, for very few of the selectees came with a burning desire to include archaeology in their social studies courses. However, my decision to saddle us with a crew of twenty-eight totally raw excavators was based in part on the knowledge that my department had been given the biggest project of my career. With a view to reconstructing the last of eighteenth-century Williamsburg's public buildings, we were to excavate the remains of the lunatic asylum of 1770.

Since the buildings had been razed after the fire of 1885, it was naive to expect that the digging would turn back the clock to the eighteenth century. Instead, the students, who I had expected to teach how to separate one period layer from another, spent their summer hacking their way through tons of brick rubble that filled the cellars from top to bottom and end to end. Fortunately for the toiling student laborers, their afternoons were spent indoors listening to lectures by high-caliber imported speakers, but that meant that we were only getting half the laboring hours needed to keep the digging on schedule. Among the speakers, incidentally, was young Cary Carson, who had done such yeoman service at Mathews' Manor.

The summer school experiment at the Public Hospital taught us an important lesson. One must never lose sight of the fact that students are there to learn and not to provide slave labor. Consequently, progress on the dig has to be subservient to the slowest student. In short, research and schooling are not necessarily the best of bedfellows. Besides, when the staff crew goes home the day is over. But not so when the students are housed in a college dorm and generate complaints that running naked through the corridors is not to be tolerated. The summer experiment of 1972 would not be repeated. Nevertheless, the exercise was worth it in that two of the twenty-eight teachers in the program received lasting value from what they had learned. One of them, Martha Williams, went back to her Fairfax school and developed archaeological classes that undertook professional-level excavations of their own. She eventually retired from teaching to become a professional historical archaeologist. Under the circumstances, two out of twenty-eight was not too bad an average.

Had I been an academic archaeologist or one relegated to the basement of a museum I might have paid less attention to the task of wooing the public, but as Colonial Williamsburg daily reminded us, its mission was to enable the future to learn from the past. Surprisingly, therefore, our archaeological museum, its exhibits installed in 1933 in the Court House of 1770, was just about as dull and uninformative as it was possible to be. Although John Dunton and I had done some sprucing up in the first years of my tenure, there was little one could do with a roomful of oversized glass cases with canvas-lined and permanently stained interiors. In 1974, however, there came the first stirring in the underbrush of Colonial Williamsburg's administration. The Bicentennial of the American Revolution was only two years away, and thought needed to be given to handling the crowds, crowds who would need a ticket office in the center of town. There being nowhere closer than the Court House of 1770, the archaeology museum would have to go.

Ed Kendrew had recently retired, vacating the large and imposing James Anderson House on Duke of Gloucester Street, and I was able to persuade Carl Humelsine to let me have Ed's house for a new museum. The plea was all the more effective because we had already begun excavations in its backyard preparatory to reconstructing Anderson's blacksmithing forges. I proposed that the museum be designed to prepare visitors to view the excavations and later to tour the reconstructed buildings. Having rung all the right bells, I received a relatively generous budget, and Ed Kendrew's handsomely paneled interior quickly disappeared behind walls of sheet rock and plywood. Ed would almost certainly have suffered aesthetic convulsions had he come back to find us sinking a reconstructed well shaft through his living room floor.

My intent was to introduce visitors to every aspect of colonial archaeology. To that end I built an exhibit I called "The Traveler's Room." In it were more than forty objects, ranging from window glass and fireplace tiles to the blanket on the bed and the chamber pot under it. The room was as it might have been had the traveler just gotten out of bed. His shoes were on the floor, his brass-buttoned coat hung on the bed frame, and the remains of last night's smoking and drinking lay on the table in the middle of the room. The lantern clock on the wall was ticking, there was glimmer of fire in the grate, and the stubs of two candles burned on the table and mantle shelf. The light level was such as would be provided by those candles, and so when modern visitors entered the room from the daylight outside, they could scarcely see that it was furnished. But in a brightly lit case across the front of the room were the buttons, clock parts, shoes, tiles, wall plaster, window glass, blanket fragments, and potsherds that provided the precedents. Beside each artifact was a large, back-lit color transparency of the appropriate detail within the room. Thus, for example, alongside mug and medicine-bottle fragments was a photographed detail of the mantle shelf on which a matching mug and bottles were standing. Hence the room had been broken down into a jigsaw puzzle of artifacts and images. After the visitors spent a few minutes studying them, they became sufficiently accustomed to the low light behind the case to take in the room as a whole. A voice-over narration helped visitors to focus on specific objects while stressing that what they were experiencing was what archaeology does for the architects and curators of restored Williamsburg. Having absorbed that, the narrator said, let's now go on through the museum to see how archaeologists go about their work.

The Anderson House archaeological museum opened in January 1975. From the outset visitors responded well, and averaged fifteen thousand a month in the summer and eight thousand in the off-season. The curator Graham Hood was generous enough to declare that the Traveler's Room was the most authentic room in Williamsburg, and the British archaeologist Peter Addyman allowed that it had given him the idea for his immensely successful Viking Center at York.

For Audrey and me, the early 1970s had been years of much activity both in the department and on the home front. Seeking a break from archaeology I wrote two novels for an English publisher, one about chicanery in the Caribbean, and the other a satire on the forthcoming 1976 centennial celebration of the American Revolution. Getting ready for '76 was already high on Colonial Williamsburg's horizon, and a report in the *Washington Post* that three million tourists would be descending on Williamsburg was both mouthwatering and alarming. How could the restored buildings withstand the stampede? How could the Information Center handle the ticketing? How many more employees would be needed?

Spreading the load became the mantra. A new and shorter introductory program replaced *The Story of a Patriot* movie, which was ousted from the Information Center theaters and relegated to the old downtown movie house. The vacated seating was stripped out and replaced by cattle rails against which the moving multitude could lean. That decision did not sit well with one of Colonial Williamsburg's wealthiest supporters, DeWitt Wallace, founder of *Readers' Digest,* who each year had sent senior employees down to see the movie and thereby recharge their patriotic batteries. How much would it cost to build a new theater to house *The Story of a Patriot,* he wanted to know? Somebody promptly came up with a figure of $4 million, to which Mr. Wallace said, in effect, "You've got it."

The problem of threading the endless ribbon of arriving visitors through the Information Center was but the first of the challenges facing the staff. What was to be done to prevent gridlock on DOG street—our irreverent sobriquet for Duke of Gloucester Street? The answer, as we shall see, was Carter's Grove.

It was while all this was in the planning stage that I came up with what I considered archaeology's lasting contribution to the Bicentennial. Remembering the stacks of fish boxes loaded with broken bottle glass from earlier excavations, I figured that we could get a modern glass factory to melt it down and reshape the glass into accurate reproductions of wine bottles appropriate to the period. To their sides would be affixed a glass seal inscribed "1776 Williamsburg 1976." Each bottle would be handsomely gift boxed, supplied with a numbered certificate of authenticity, and sold at an appropriately immodest price. Our merchandising department smiled on the project and so did the architecture department, which was delighted to be rid of the dust-gathering crates of broken glass. I assured them that we could easily sell the intended run of about three hundred bottles, and was confident that if the demand was such, there was plenty more old glass where that came from.

I barely had time to savor the prospect of creating a great Bicentennial souvenir when the manufacturer informed me that he could use no more than 20 percent of the old glass in his mix, the other 80 percent had to be new. Thus my sales pitch claiming that the souvenir bottles were made from those actually used in eighteenth-century Williamsburg would, at best, be only marginally true. But worse was to come. The first samples bore little resemblance to authentic eighteenth-century bottles. Their bases were too thick or their necks the wrong shape, and some of the seals were illegible. Over the next several months my office filled with unacceptable prototypes. When the bottoms looked right, the necks were wrong, and vice versa. The manufacturer insisted that one could not expect uniformity in hand-blown glass and did not appreciate my insistence that if it could be achieved in the eighteenth century, it should surely be possible in the twentieth. In the end, out of the several hundred made, only about twenty-five were of more-or-less acceptable shapes. The rest were consigned to the reconstructed Palace cellars where their shortcomings are hidden in straw-filled bins, an enduring reminder of my great Bicentennial idea.

It is an axiom that nothing prepares one for the unexpected, and I had no idea that writing a letter of complaint about a TV show would plunge me deeper into the Bicentennial frenzy. The program had aired on Hampton's WVEC Channel 13, or to be more correct, had not aired. The series *The Strauss Family* had been abruptly canceled in midseason, and having enjoyed it, I was incensed at having been deprived of the closing episodes. Consequently, I wrote to the station and said so. A few days later I received a phone call from the station's owner and president, Thomas P. Chisman, suggesting that we should lunch and talk about his programming policies. Thus began one of my life's most enjoyable associations that only ended when I delivered the eulogy at Tom's funeral in 1992.

Tom Chisman was a small man with an infectious enthusiasm for everything he did. His family had lived in what is now called the Lower Peninsula since the 1640s, yet he had grown up in relative poverty. When he returned from service in World War II he started a radio station in Hampton (though he knew virtually nothing about radio) and, seeing the potential of television, soon expanded into it. Eventually he would become chairman of the ABC affiliates and a powerhouse in the industry. More to the point as far as Audrey and I were concerned, he had a love of England and the English that extended to part ownership of a British pewter manufacturing company whose products he peddled in America. Always on the lookout for a sweet deal, he imported scores of obsolete London street lamps as well as dozens of coal-miners' pit lanterns. The outcome in each case found him saddled with quantities of goods that nobody was eager to buy. That he himself was not above personally hawking them to stores and individuals was very much the measure of the man.

Before our first meeting, Tom had been to the BBC in London to propose his great idea of promoting the forthcoming Bicentennial by daily airing on radio four minutes devoted to the corresponding date from April 1775 onward. Two minutes would be provided by the BBC, the reading of contemporary eighteenth-century news in England, while the matching American minutes would chronicle events in the colonies. Would I write the American minutes? Tom wanted to know. Having already published my book on Virginia in 1775, the prospect did not seem all that daunting. Unaware of what I would be getting into, I agreed.

The research proved more arduous and protracted than I had expected. And after four months the BBC dropped out. But by that time we were syndicated through 146 stations across the country and Tom had his contracts to honor. Therefore, until the end of 1976 I was saddled with writing both the American and the English reports as well as providing the English voice from London. Tom received a national award for his contribution to the Bicentennial, and I inherited all the tapes, which slowly degraded as the scripts turned yellow with age. The celebration of '76 was ancient history by '77.

Tom, being a wheeler-dealer and on first-name standing with every politician in the region, prevailed upon his cousin Senator Hunter B. Andrews to appoint me to the board of his Jamestown-Yorktown Foundation, which had evolved from the 1957 celebration to lead the charge for '76. As chairman of the state's finance committee, Democrat Andrews was as close to being king of Virginia politics as one could get short of being crowned. He and another patrician Democrat, Senator Lewis McMurran, were the powers behind the Bicentennial in Virginia. Both were unabashed Anglophiles and assured me that they would look kindly on a museum for Virginia's historical archaeology once the big show was over. Indeed, the multimillion-dollar Victory Center being built by the Commonwealth at Yorktown could be ours for the asking. I did ask, but the best we achieved was to extract Bill Kelso, by then the state archaeologist, from his cellar under the College of William and Mary's Wren Building and into part of the post-Bicentennial Victory Center. This was by no means the equivalent of what had been promised, but it gave Bill exhibit space—until the Jamestown-Yorktown Foundation had him evicted as a potential fire hazard. The state archaeologist's office then moved to Richmond into the building occupied by the Historic Landmarks Commission. In 2010 there is still no museum, but the Victory Center continues to serve the revolutionary purpose for which it was built, and I had learned that politicians' promises and honeyed words had a short shelf life.

Nevertheless, I had been given an entrée into the circle of people who made things happen, and it gave me an opportunity to start thinking about the next great national event—the 400th anniversary in 2007 of the first British landing at Jamestown. Over lunch with Hunter Andrews I suggested that once the Bicentennial was behind us perhaps it would be a good idea to start thinking about it. Hunter replied with a laugh, "Noel, forget it! We'll both be dead by then!" He was half-right. Hunter Andrews died in January 2005. Tom Chisman, on the other hand, embraced the 2007 idea with the enthusiasm he applied to any new project.

In the run-up to the 1976 celebrations the Commonwealth of Virginia had created for itself a slogan that would resonate from coast to coast. Buttons, T-shirts, coffee mugs, bumper stickers, and any other promotional material would be emblazoned with the assertion "Virginia Is for Lovers." The slogan certainly had a ring to it, at least to the extent that it included two *v*'s, but what it had to do with the Bicentennial of the American Revolution left me baffled. Tom agreed that for 2007 something similar, but better, was needed to get our ball rolling. To that end I coined "1607 Virginia Is Forever 2007," and glued the lettering around a coffee mug.

"That's it!" Tom exclaimed. And I thought so too. Before long the Tom Chisman 2007 express was getting up steam. He ordered "Virginia Is Forever" T-shirts, tote bags, and coffee mugs. I took one of the T-shirts to a Jamestown-Yorktown Foundation committee meeting, where it was received with unbridled delight and declared a great send-off for the foundation's future involvement with 2007. Such was the enthusiasm that at our next meeting one committee member had "Virginia Is Forever" buttons made to distribute to us all. In the meantime, however, Tom had taken it upon himself to copyright my slogan to ensure that he reaped all profits from its usage, so I had to tell the committee that it would have to clear the slogan's use through Tom. Hunter Andrews angrily rejected so crass a proposal, and thereafter my relationship with him became significantly less cordial. But had the slogan not been copyrighted, it would almost certainly be as familiar across the nation at the beginning of the twenty-first century as is the tired and still enigmatic "Virginia Is for Lovers."

Aʟᴛʜᴏᴜɢʜ Aᴜᴅʀᴇʏ and I had become almost exclusively immersed in the seventeenth and eighteenth centuries, we still retained an affection for a "bit o' the old Roman," and so we took ourselves to Italy in the winter of 1968. At a black-tie dinner in Rome I told my host that we were on our way to Pompeii. A fellow guest (a cardinal as I recall) asked whether I planned to dig there. Before I could say "Of course not!" he assured me that he could arrange a permit for us to do so. My point is this: even the educated public assumes that anyone calling himself an archaeologist is fit and free to dig anywhere and into any time. I would be reminded of the Pompeii offer when I received a phone call from the National Geographic Society asking me to authenticate a site in Haiti reputed to be the settlement Christopher Columbus called La Navidad. I explained that I had no experience of Spanish sites, but was assured that that was not necessary, since all I was being asked to do was to review the validity of work already under way there. Again I demurred, saying that if I were to be released to go to Haiti somebody very senior at the National Geographic Society would have to check with my boss, Carl Humelsine.

Came the rather plaintive response, "But I am somebody very senior." And he was. John Scofield, editor of the *National Geographic,* had been writing an article on Columbus when he received a letter from Dr. William H. Hodges, resident physician at the Hospital of the Good Samaritan at Limbé on Haiti's Atlantic coast. Hodges believed from cartographic and documentary evidence that he had found the La Navidad site. He had cut a trench across it that seemed to provide supporting evidence. This was the bait that drew John Scofield and the Noël Humes to Haiti—or at least toward Haiti. First, we had to deal with a reported bomb on the plane.

Having flown several times into Jamaica's Pallisadoes Airport, I thought our approach unusual. From our forward seats we could see the water of Kingston Harbour rising alarmingly toward us. For a few seconds it seemed that we were diving straight into it, but then the plane leveled off and touched down on a sandy strip as far from the airport buildings as it was possible to land. Instructions from the cockpit were terse and to the point. "Everybody off as quickly as you can. Leave your possessions. There's a reported bomb on the plane."

Nobody lingered, and for half an hour we stood on the windswept sandy edge of the tarmac while a Jamaican lieutenant urged an unenthusiastic squad to enter the plane to hunt for the bomb. They were still at it when we were hustled onto a bus and taken away to the main terminal. Two hours later we were returned to find all our baggage spread out along the runway. With bayonets at our backs we were ordered to open the bags for inspection, an exercise performed with the points of the blades. When nothing was found and everyone's luggage had been rooted through, we were herded back to the plane to watch the luggage being reloaded, much of it with sleeves and underwear dangling. Not until we were airborne did John Scofield provide an additional piece of helpful information. Dr. Hodges's peasant diggers had been intimidated by machine gun–wielding government thugs who believed the workers had found gold and so were ready to shoot them if they declined to reveal it. This was the era of the dictator Papa Doc Duvalier, and the men were members of his feared Tonton Macout. It was possible, said Scofield, that they would be waiting for us.

The National Geographic Society had a long history of dealing with tiresome foreigners and supplied its adventurers with authoritative documents rich in impressive but meaningless ribbons and stamps, irreverently known as Dago Dazzlers. John Scofield had no such lifesavers, but Dr. Hodges had enlisted the support of the local mayor, who would supervise our endeavors. And that he did throughout the three days of excavation. Wearing a top hat and black coat, the mayor of nearby Limonade sat beside the excavation brewing something in a tin can covered by a palm frond. The men with guns were there too, but kept their distance, which was just as well, since we had much else to worry about.

Dr. Hodges's trench had been no more than a foot wide and too narrow to read the stratigraphy in its sides, but it had yielded brickbats. However, the charcoal that John Scofield hoped would provide carbon 14 dating for the ground had nothing useful to contribute. After harvesting, Haitian farmers burn off the stubble and dig it in to enrich the soil for the next crop. Such slash-and-burn agriculture had been common practice for countless generations. The bricks, on the other hand, were evidently part of a structure, and being set in clay rather than mortar, their age was not immediately apparent. To me, they did not look very old, but then I had no knowledge of Spanish brick making.

Out of earshot of the eager Dr. Hodges, Audrey asked, "Don't you think it odd that Columbus's wrecked crew knew how to make bricks?"

She had a point.

The plan, as John Scofield had outlined it, was simply to look and evaluate. Consequently, we had brought no equipment and could stay no more than three days. It was immediately apparent, however, that if we were to make any sense of Hodges's "evidence" we would have to launch into an excavation of our own. He could supply shovels, but dustpans had to be made from cut-down gasoline cans, and brushes from palm fronds, and only Audrey and I knew how to lay out an archaeological grid. By the time we got started, our three-day window had shrunk to two and a bit.

Although we had sterling support from Dr. Hodges and his family, as well as from John Scofield and Frederick Mangonés, the son of Haiti's conservator of historic sites and monuments, no one knew what was expected of them. My instructions to them were at best baffling. We had to dig fast but at the same time we had to be extremely careful. Just how that was translated into Spanish by Fred Mangonés I had no idea, but as the locally recruited crew was reluctant to work either slow or fast, it made little difference. Nevertheless, by dusk on the third day we had done enough to prove that the bricks had nothing to do with Columbus and instead were part of a fairly substantial building related to a late eighteenth-century French plantation. Indeed, Dr. Hodges had previously found a brass military button inscribed Département de Norbiran and attributable to a date between July 14, 1790, and January 1793. One could not ask for closer dating than that.

We were a glum and tired trio as we took an ancient cab out to the Cap Haitien airport, and our spirits were not buoyed when we saw the plane that was take us across the island to Port au Prince. An arrow pointed to dotted lines painted on the fuselage and beside them the message "In case of accident cut here." On board a fellow passenger pulled out his seat belt only to have it come away in his hand.

"Now what do I do?" he asked anyone who would listen.

Came a voice from the rear, "Repeat after me. Our Father who art in heaven . . ."

So ended my first brief involvement with the National Geographic Society. Not being clairvoyant, I had no way of knowing that another would soon begin and last more than a decade.

Carter's Grove had been open to the public since 1970 but had remained an ugly duckling on the corporate pond until, as I noted in the previous chapter, the *Washington Post* raised the specter of three million flag-waving tourists descending on the town in 1976. In the face of that prospect Carter's Grove suddenly became a swan. It could be used to relocate in-town crafts such as coopering, wheelwrighting, and shingle making into a cluster, even a temporary village, somewhere on the Carter's Grove acres. An obvious choice was the large field behind Mrs. McCrea's stable building, which was already being used as a visitor center. The only impediment to progress was the presence of five slave burials that Bill Kelso had encountered in the middle of it. With civil rights on the national conscience, one could not risk being accused of being disrespectful. My instruction, therefore, was to find them, see how many there were, and cordon them off.

There turned out to be twenty-three burials, none of them the remains of eighteenth- or nineteenth-century slaves. Bill Kelso's limited digging had led us to an early colonial burial ground, and to the remains of a large and equally early plantation complex. For me, this was cause for ill-concealed delight, but not for Colonial Williamsburg. I insisted that having uncovered what I believed to be the earliest complete plantation layout in British America, we could not walk away with it only partially explored.

I got a grudging nod from the Powers that Were and a firmly phrased request to get finished as soon as I could. Carter's Grove was the tourist safety valve and it had to be ready for '76. But excavating graves is not something you do with a shovel; it is slow paintbrush-and-scalpel work. Having bared the bones, unless one is a forensic specialist, an expert osteologist is needed. Fortunately, we had one in the Smithsonian Institution's renowned Dr. Larry Angel. Before asking him to come down I had told him that we suspected that the graves were those of nineteenth-century slaves, but when he arrived I neglected to tell him that they were not. Consequently, he began his assessment of each individual with that preconceived assumption still in mind. The fault was mine, but the results raised interesting questions. Larry initially concluded that the graves located by Bill Kelso were those of black slaves, based on the physical evidence of one that made him report that in his "opinion she is not white . . . and could possibly compare with examples of the West African Ebo and Gaboon tribes." In later conversation Larry allowed that the woman might have been a mulatto. But as he had given her age as about twenty-eight and we had determined that she died before about 1640, the racial mixing would have had to have occurred before she came to Virginia—which seemed extremely unlikely. The moral, of course, is that scientific judgment should never be swayed by the opinions of others. Besides, in the 1970s forensic anthropology was not an exact science. Larry Angel himself put it this way: "Determination of race is chancy on a single individual. Only comparisons between groups are safely protected by statistics."

As invariably happens in archaeology, digging is likely to pose as many questions as it answers, and this certainly was true on the plantation we called Site A. Not the least of them was tantalizing evidence of a potter working nearby to produce earthenwares every bit as sophisticated as those made in England in the second quarter of the seventeenth century. We had the waste but no sign of a kiln, and time was running out. The site had to be backfilled to provide the acreage for the proposed craft exhibits. We had almost finished doing so when late one Friday afternoon I received a phone call from Carl Humelsine.

"Are you doing anything interesting?" he wanted to know. Before I could answer that in my mind I was always doing something interesting, he went on to explain that an important visitor had arrived to go sailing with him but had come on the wrong weekend. "Can you keep him happy while I clear my decks? Take him down to your dig at Carter's Grove."

I explained that it was too late. The site was already covered. But if the visitor came down to the department I could show him slides of what we had found.

"Good. Do that."

"But who is the visitor?" I asked.

He was Melville Bell Grosvenor, chairman emeritus of the National Geographic Society. He and his wife sat through my hastily composed slide show, but said absolutely nothing. By the time I had shown the last slide I assumed that they were asleep.

But Mel Grosvenor was not asleep. "Didn't you say that there's a pottery kiln to be found?"

I allowed that I thought it was nearby. And, yes, it would be a tremendous first to find the earliest potting venture to be discovered in Virginia.

"Is it a matter of money?"

I knew that there was no budget to continue at Carter's Grove, but I also knew that Colonial Williamsburg wanted us out of there before the Bicentennial. Nevertheless, I agreed that we lacked money, but said nothing about the other issue.

"You have to find that kiln," Grosvenor said firmly. "Let me talk to Carl about it."

And he did. By the time the sailing weekend was over Mel Grosvenor had committed the National Geographic Society to funding the Carter's Grove archaeology program for a full year in 1976, a commitment that, as it turned out, extended across five years as more and more discoveries were made.

In those days the National Geographic Society was a family business— though I doubt if any member of it would so describe their venerable institution's contribution to world geography. Mel Grosvenor knew that if he said something would be done, it would. No vice presidents or committees would say him nay. That is no longer the case—more's the pity.

When Carl called me to his office to tell me of the National Geographic's commitment, my immediate response was not very gracious. "That doesn't mean, does it, that we'll be restricted to giving the magazine all rights to what we find?" I had heard that other beneficiaries of National Geographic grants had been hog-tied by the magazine's requirement that every news item or photograph be approved by its people. Carl assured me that it would not. But a few days later I received a formidable package affording the Society every right from first photo to first born.

"Leave it to our lawyers," was Carl's response. So I did, and that was the last I heard of it. Instead, there developed a warm relationship between myself and the Society's magazine and personally with Mel Grosvenor. While sitting next to him at a senior staff luncheon he leaned toward me and asked, "What do you think I've been doing?" I had no idea. "I've been scuba diving in Lake Champlain looking for Benedict Arnold's fleet. At my age, what do you think of that?" I expressed awe and amazement before he went on. "And there, right there was a ship. I broke a lump off it and brought it up and sent it to the Smithsonian to have it authenticated. What do you think they told me? It was just an old coal barge!"

I'm sure I did not admit to relief that Benedict Arnold's wreck had escaped the attention of this grand old man of the National Geographic Society, but the escapade immediately brought to mind Ed Link's salvage of the Port Royal watch and the tiny parts that "rained into his palm." A good picture and a colorful story were the stock in trade of the Society, and that lunchtime saga was to be a constant reminder that blind gratitude for Mel's support had to be tempered with caution.

There was no denying that, carefully controlled, publicity would be beneficial both to Colonial Williamsburg and to the *National Geographic*. One of the questions Mel had asked at the beginning of our association was whether we were keeping a film record of the excavation. The answer was, no, we were not. We had been so anxious to get as much done on our seventeenth-century plantation site as we could before being called back to town that any Wetherburn's Tavern–style filming was unthinkable. But now, in the wake of Mel Grosvenor's unscheduled visit, the rules were changing.

Testing of the soil in the woods east of the plantation site had turned up fragments of locally made earthenware that gave reason to suspect that it was there that the pottery kiln would be found. With Site A covered over and available for whatever use Colonial Williamsburg chose to put it to, we had the money to keep on digging at the woodland site we were to call Site B. Consequently, the pace could be slow, making filming both possible and desirable. Even though my *Doorway to the Past* had won no Oscars I was anxious to try again, not just to shoot footage to store away in a can, but to make a documentary that would chronicle the hopes and disappointments of archaeology. It would be a "warts and all" record of what we were about to do.

In the previous year I had made a film on the history of archaeology in Williamsburg for the BBC's prestigious *Chronicle* series. Called *The Williamsburg File*, the film was anchored by one of Britain's premier archaeologists, Professor Glynn Daniel of Cambridge. He had come into the public eye as the result of his chairing the museum-related quiz show *Animal Vegetable or Mineral?* which, if you remember that far back in my story, was the one to which my boss Norman Cook took my Roman bikini and fried it. Glynn Daniel was also the editor of the British science magazine *Antiquity,* and though a prehistorian with a reputation as an expert on Megalithic France, he became enthusiastic about our Williamsburg work and said so in the pages of *Antiquity*—the first time that historical archaeology had been seen in such venerable company. I hasten to note that I was neither the director nor the writer of *The Williamsburg File.* Indeed, there was no formal script. Glynn and I simply ambled round Williamsburg talking off the cuff about previously agreed topics. The program became the BBC's salute to the American Bicentennial and was repeatedly aired on PBS. It was *The Williamsburg File*'s success that prompted Carl Humelsine to commit Colonial Williamsburg to making the Carter's Grove movie, for which I would be the writer and the on-screen narrator.

Most archaeological programs are patched together from a combination of "wild" footage and talking heads coupled with reenactments of the discovery that created the interest that, in TV terms, made the project worthwhile. No one could afford to have a union-strapped film production company on hand throughout an excavation just in case something photogenic turned up. But we had that luxury. Colonial Williamsburg's nonunion film unit, affectionately known as "18th-Century Fox," had already produced my *Doorway to the Past* and a widely praised series of films on colonial crafts, and had several shelves of statuettes, plaques, and testimonials to prove it. Thus, when we began our search for the Carter's Grove potter, the old firm was back in business, the crew on call whenever I thought something interesting was about to happen.

Directing an archaeological project while at the same time planning to turn it into a movie requires a degree of clairvoyance or educated guesswork and can lead to embarrassing surprises, and it did on Site B. Our procedure was simple. I would write an outline script for the day and on the basis of it I would describe what we were doing as I worked. On one such day I was removing fill from a pit that had the shape of a kiln and describing on camera our reasoning for believing that it dated from around 1620 and the earliest days of settlement. The tobacco pipe fragments, I explained, were giving us that close date when, at the bottom of the pit, I came upon part of an upturned dish. As I prepared to turn it over, as if by magic, a shaft of sunlight suddenly poured down on it through the trees, spotlighting the date inscribed in yellow slip on the red clay. It was the first dated fragment we had found and is still the earliest dated example of Virginia-made pottery. The problem was that the expected date of 1620 turned out to be 1631, making nonsense of virtually everything I had been saying.

Digging in the woods had the advantage of being relatively cool, but in early June the mayflies came out in such numbers and with such vicious intent that I had to pull the crew out before it mutinied. However, the clock was running and the National Geographic's money being spent. I decided, therefore, to investigate several spots closer to the James River where Bill Kelso's 1970 digging had turned up fragments of seventeenth-century pottery.

The area I had chosen set us down inside the 1620 fort erected by the colonists of Wolstenholme Towne as the centerpiece of their Martin's Hundred settlement. Immediately Sites A and B were swept from center stage as we uncovered more of the fort and the buildings inside it. But in the summer of 1976 our mandate was to justify the National Geographic's investment by finding the potter's kiln at Site B. Reluctantly, therefore, we went back into the woods.

We didn't find the kiln, but we did find the potter's workshop, and several years later a letter was discovered that was written at Martin's Hundred on May 20, 1625, and signed "Thomas Ward, Pottmakerr."

The National Geographic board of trustees met in Williamsburg in October and in a soaking rain came out to Site B. There wasn't much to see, but the members happily slogged about in the mud and declared themselves well satisfied with our progress. More important, they agreed to continue to finance the work at Wolstenholme Towne. Their confidence proved well justified. Nineteen seventy-eight saw the entire fort cleared as well as other buildings of the village, the unearthing of two helmets of a type never before discovered in the New World, and the grave of a man scalped in the Indian massacre of 1622.

The man's identity has never been confirmed, but there is reason to believe that he was Lieutenant Richard Keane, who was in command of the fort at the time of the attack and listed as being among the massacred dead. He had been felled by a blow above the right eye with a sharp instrument like the corner of a spade before being scalped and having his head beaten in from behind. This last was a ritualistic reslaying of an enemy to prevent his returning in the afterlife. My theory that the man was killed with a spade gained credence when, in England, Margaret Chapman murdered her transvestite husband. She had killed him with a spade, and the pathologist who identified it at the trial subsequently viewed photographs of our massacre victim's skull and agreed that the wounds were similar. Although the murder of Lieutenant Keane went unavenged, on December 5, 1979, Margaret Chapman and her accomplice were sentenced to life imprisonment.

Documentation is the weft of archaeology. Without it one is digging in the dark. At Martin's Hundred we were blessed with several contemporary letters and, most important, a list of the dead in the massacre. Among them was Martin's Hundred's leader John Boise and his family, which included his wife, a maid, and four male servants—which brings me back to Bill Kelso and the duck blind.

The summer of 1978 had been as hot as any I could remember, baking the clay of Wolstenholme Towne so hard that it could only be excavated when sprayed with water from a hose run down the hill from the Carter's Grove mansion. I was ready to conclude that we had done all we could in the area of the village, but our ever-astute field supervisor Eric Klingelhofer suggested that before we dismantled our water supply we should reroute it around the head of a small ravine to the area of the duck blind. I was not enthusiastic. We had already dug test holes there but had found nothing, and yet there remained that nagging question: Why would anyone dig a rectangular hole to create a duck blind? And why would there have been seventeenth-century potsherds in the half of it that Bill had excavated? All in all, it was worth another look.

I must prefix what happened next by repeating that archaeology is heavy on guesswork and that when Bill was digging at Carter's Grove he was expecting to find evidence of eighteenth-century occupation. In that context one would not be thinking of four men buried head-to-toe in the seventeenth century. The brown stains previously identified as sticks were actually the legs of two men and the heads and torsos of their companions. On uncovering the other halves of the four we found that one was wearing a workingman's hobnailed shoe. These men almost certainly were John Boise's four servants killed in the 1622 massacre. It followed, therefore, that the Boise homestead could not be very far away. And it wasn't. In the woods beside the ravine we uncovered the house site and more graves, one of them we believed to have been of the family maid. We concluded that she had been scalped and escaped to die from loss of blood in a nearby refuse pit.

The woman had lost her lower molars and so was of middle age. We called her Granny and thus she remains on the pages of January 1982's *National Geographic*. The previous discovery of Wolstenholme Towne had led to my writing a lead article for the magazine in 1979, and with artwork by Richard Schlecht and photographs by Ira Block, its publication launched Martin's Hundred into living rooms around the world. We already had our share of promotion in the United States, the grinning skull of Lieutenant Keane having graced the pages of newspapers from coast to coast. Although the *National Geographic* rarely ran two articles on the same subject, the discovery of Granny was dramatic enough to warrant another. In addition to the articles in 1979 and 1982, the Society mounted an exhibition of the artifacts in its main gallery at Explorers Hall which ran for nine months and is said to have drawn more than half a million visitors. All this publicity brought a surge of pilgrims to Carter's Grove and disappointment that none of the artifacts were exhibited there.

At the end of the 1976 dig and the finding of Site A—which we subsequently determined had been the home of Martin's Hundred's governor William Harwood—I had proposed building a museum at Carter's Grove and went as far as designing it and its exhibits. However, with everyone waiting for the Bicentennial millions, no support was forthcoming from Colonial Williamsburg. It was still waiting for the tourist crowds when the magic year ended—either the hordes had insufficient interest in the event or had stayed away until the town was less crowded. Either way, the proposed temporary exhibits that had taken us to Carter's Grove in the first place never materialized, and we were left to get on with our excavations, interrupted only by the need to accommodate our own visitors. In retrospect, the discovery of Martin's Hundred and all that came after it were the result of two fortunate events over which I had no control: the expected Bicentennial hordes and Mel Grosvenor's mistaken date to go sailing. From such disparate threads is history woven.

I DON'T REMEMBER who first thought Wolstenholme Towne might have had Irish parallels. It may have been field supervisor Eric Klingelhofer, who already had an archaeological interest in Irish castles. But regardless of whose notion it was, he (or even she, if the credit belongs to Audrey) was right. The layout of the Wolstenholme settlement followed a pattern already established in Ulster and known as "bawn villages," a bawn being a defensible livestock enclosure separated from the homes of the villagers.

Ever since one community felt the need to defend itself from its neighbor, it chose either of two methods: it built a wall to enclose it as did most medieval cities—and as was done at Jamestown—or it erected a formidable castle in which the leader and his followers lived. The latter was the lord's preferred solution. It kept him safely inside while leaving his serfs, tenants, and other grubby people outside and regrettably in harm's way. In theory, the villagers would abandon their homes and flee into the castle—always supposing they got there before the drawbridge went up and the portcullis dropped down. The bawn village was slightly more democratic in that the bawn needed to be no stronger than a palisaded enclosure into which the settlers' livestock would be driven at night. At Wolstenholme Towne the stockaded compound was built at the landward side of the town, which stretched away from it toward the James River. The governor's house was inside the bawn, which had a watchtower at one corner and a light artillery projection at another. When attacked, as the settlers were in 1622, they would run with their muskets into the fort and shoot from behind the palisades. But because the Indian attack was unexpected and the houses scattered, seventy-eight people failed to reach the safety of their modest castle.

In October 1978, while we were still working at Wolstenholme Towne, I accepted an invitation to visit and lecture at the new University of Ulster in Londonderry, more specifically at its Magee University College, which housed the archaeology department. To be able to see surviving Irish bawns and the artifacts that had been found in them was an opportunity not to be missed. We were, of course, well aware of the persisting sectarian strife that divided north from south, but for several months nothing dramatic had made it into the newspapers. Nevertheless, we were a mite apprehensive when we landed at Belfast airport.

No sooner had we passed through customs than we (and three other inoffensive-looking couples) were ordered aside to be subjected to an intensive baggage search. The police were polite but firm—all our luggage was to be opened. While Audrey fumbled with its locks, the senior policeman thrust a pad at me. "Please sign here," he ordered.

When I demurred at signing an affirmation that our property had not been damaged in the search—a search that had not yet begun—Audrey nudged me and whispered, "Sign the damn things!" If I didn't she could see us being hauled away and cast into the dreaded Maze prison.

So I signed and began to write my address. When I got to "Williamsburg" the senior policeman stared hard at it and then at me. "Williamsburg, is it!" he exclaimed. "I know you!"

I remembered my experiences in police lineups and decided that somehow I was being taken for an IRA terrorist.

The policeman peered closer. "I've seen you on the television!" And so it proved. The officer had seen the BBC's rerun broadcast of *The Williamsburg File,* not once but twice.

On the seventy-mile drive to Londonderry in the limousine of the University of Ulster's vice-chancellor, the chauffeur, a Catholic living in a Protestant area, told us at length about the feelings of peace-loving people unwillingly caught up in the violence. British troops were not as much in evidence as we had expected. A major roadblock outside the airport, a few helicopters sweeping the countryside, and machine-gun muzzles sticking provocatively from watchtower slits defending local police stations were about the extent of it. As for the "enemy," its presence was manifest only through the countless graffiti spray-painted on walls. "Most of the IRA ringleaders are in prison in Belfast," our driver explained. "And it'll be a long time before they get out."

As we drove through the rich green countryside, past laborers harvesting wheat and potatoes, and on over the rolling hills toward Londonderry, it was hard to realize that for more than a decade this beautiful land had been torn by civil war. More than 25 percent of the city we were approaching had been destroyed, rebuilt, and partly destroyed again. In the villages, however, there was no escaping the animosity. Walls shouted at each other in red paint, cursing Protestants, Catholics, and above all the British troops. Here and there flew a defiant Protestant Union Jack, its thin stick tied to a chimney pot, frail and vulnerable in the brisk wind that sent lowering clouds buffeting the hilltops and kept the sunlight constantly on the move across the valleys below. It was not a placid landscape, but as I wrote in my travel journal, "By God it was beautiful!"

We found that we were to be housed, not in Londonderry itself, but across the river Foyle in a new American-style motel inappropriately named the Everglades and decorated with allegedly Seminole artifacts and motifs. We were uncertain whether it had been chosen to make Americans feel at home or to keep us safe from potential IRA activity. We had barely settled in when we were greeted by the university archaeologist, David Lacy, who drove us around Derry (the locals omit the London) where we ended up at a current archaeological site near the city center which seemed curiously deserted. On returning to his car we found a British Army truck parked on the opposite side of the square. Out of it emerged a robust corporal, flak-jacketed and heavily armed, who bore down on us like the wrath of God. He towered over the diminutive Irish Catholic, telling him in tones that may have been acceptable in colonial India that he had committed a crime worthy of six months in jail and a four-hundred-pound fine—at the very least. Had Lacy not seen the notice forbidding the leaving of unattended cars in restricted areas? Could he not read? Did he not know the law?

It would have been hard to imagine a better way of alienating the local population. Had I been Lacy I would have been praying to St. Columba that the next unattended car would explode in the corporal's face. Instead, I was embarrassed, angry, and disappointed that the soldier was one of our guys. Lacy, however, held his tongue and took the abuse, pleading only that the car was never out of sight and therefore, technically, not unattended. The corporal eventually ran out of steam, marched back to his truck, and drove off in search of better violations. We breathed a collective sigh and drove back to the motel more or less in silence. We had seen the face of a defender of the faith and it was not pretty.

We spent the next morning examining Lacy's archaeological collections and found that they closely matched the artifacts we had been finding from the same period in Virginia. But my hoped-for visits to surviving bawn-related villages never materialized. Our hosts thought it more important for us to meet people of prominence who could be inspired to throw their weight behind local archaeology, or support a still-embryonic plan to erect an Ulster farm village in Virginia under the aegis of the Jamestown-Yorktown Foundation. The presence of a press photographer left us with no doubt where our hosts' priorities lay. Those included a civic reception for us at Londonderry's Guildhall, an event hastily inserted into the university's planning less than a week before we left Williamsburg. Not knowing how formal this was to be, I took the precaution of writing a ten-minute speech lauding the opportunities for Virginia and Ulster to work together to explore their shared British plantation-era roots. Just to be safe I mailed a draft to my host, Professor Hugh Sockett. He, being English, was well aware of the delicate balance of civility in the city and so shared my proposed speech with Colm Geary, Londonderry's town clerk. In an abrupt reply handed to me on the evening of our arrival, Geary wrote that the Irish Society had been the first to point out the similarities between the development of Londonderry and of Williamsburg. As I was to be talking about the seventeenth-century plantation at Martin's Hundred which had nothing to do with Williamsburg, I was unsure how to benefit from Mr. Geary's advice. He added, rather cryptically, "No doubt Mr. Hume is aware of other similarities although it may not be diplomatic to presume that the results of the plantation in both towns was necessarily similar. This I would suggest," he added, "is a topic best left untouched by Mr. Hume."

What, I wondered had I let myself in for? I couldn't imagine that a discussion of two-hundred-year-old history could be untouchable in 1978. But uncertain how thin would be the ice I was to walk on, I decided to scrap the prepared speech and settle for off-the-cuff platitudes. But ad-libbed responses can get you into trouble, and they did when Councillor and Mayor Thomas Craig presented me with a wooden plaque bearing the arms of the city on whose box were the words "Painted by Hand"—seemingly more in apology than in praise. Dominating the shield was a human skeleton seated on what appeared to be a moss-covered egg. I had not seen the city's arms nor did I have any idea of its symbolism, but I did know a skeleton when I saw one. I therefore began my grateful response by telling the assembled city fathers that I thought it particularly appropriate to an archaeologist that the plaque's principal device was a human skeleton. I don't remember what I said next, but I do recall the looks of shock, disgust, or dismay on the faces of my audience. After I was done, Mr. Geary took me aside and pointed out that the mayor had misunderstood my reference to the bones and thought I was making some oblique comment on the recent bloodshed in Londonderry. I was, of course, referring to the relationship between archaeology and bones, and specifically to our recent discoveries at Carter's Grove.

I explained all this to Mayor Craig, a local farmer who felt that as a rural outsider he stood a chance of bringing the opposing factions together. He showed us round the Guildhall, which itself had been gutted by a bomb, rebuilt, damaged again, and repaired again, and it was clear that another round of terrorism was rarely out of the mayor's mind. Two days later, early in the morning of Friday, September 22, the IRA's silence was shattered by three bombs exploding at Londonderry's airport, their blast wrecking the control tower, a hanger, four planes on the ground, and Derry's hopes of developing the airport as a means of encouraging industrial expansion. The bombs also wrecked Mayor Craig's dream of peace in his time.

Having failed to visit as many bawn sites as we had hoped, in September 1979 we accepted an invitation to return to Derry to attend a conference and to continue our relationship with Magee College and its archaeologists. One might think that in the days of relatively civilized air travel, getting there would pose no problems. But one would be wrong.

When we changed planes at Shannon, we were assured that our bags had been checked all the way to Belfast. When none of the baggage appeared there, Aer Lingus people expressed confidence that it would be on the next plane up—except that it wouldn't be until Monday. It was now Thursday.

Since our suitcases contained all our clothes as well as my lecture texts and slides, I was—not to put too fine a point on it—in a state of some agitation, a condition not one wit alleviated when I called the airport on reaching Londonderry to be told that a check at Shannon had shown no record of any of our bags being there.

We had been promised a copy of the program for our stay in Derry, but it had failed to reach us before we left Williamsburg—for the very good reason that it did not exist. Having been thwarted in 1978, I had stressed our need and desire to visit the seventeenth-century bawn sites at the beginning of our stay and before a proposed seminar devoted to plantation period archaeology. It turned out, however, that the only plan so far established was that the seminar would be held tomorrow—with or without my slides.

It turned out that the Magee conference's list of participants embraced the spectrum of Northern Irish historical thought, thirty-four people who had very little idea why they had been invited. With no agenda, Hugh Sockett opened by discussing his desire to see more accomplished in the field of historical (there known as post-medieval) archaeology and hoped that the assembled scholars would help Magee College in its attempt to get something going. Following Sockett's lead, each speaker agreed that somebody should do something. Some added that our work on Martin's Hundred could be a catalyst to promote similar studies in Ireland—both north and south. I noticed, however, that one elderly man, who seemed to be due a degree of deference by his fellow attendees, remained grimly silent throughout. At the lunch break Sockett told me that the silent scholar was the keeper (curator) of antiquities at the Ulster Museum, and a southern Irish Catholic of explosive disposition. Of much more immediate concern to me, however, was the strike at 12:30 p.m. of the Londonderry telephone operators, precluding further information about our bags from Shannon.

At this point there was nothing more to be done; besides I had a scheduled interview with a radio reporter from the BBC before the conference resumed. It was to be a ten-minute discussion about the Magee meeting. At home in Virginia the questions would have been easily handled, but remembering last year's Derry Guildhall experience I figured that I had to be extremely careful about saying anything that could suggest that an archaeological program might lead to the glorification of British colonial history. I knew that I had to be equally cautious about answering questions on the direction the conference was taking (though none was apparent) and what might result from it. I therefore did my best to sound keenly optimistic without defining my reason for being so, and to make what I hoped were appropriate sounds about the value of a better understanding of the past. In reality, I had but one thought in mind: where in St. Patrick's name was our luggage?

Had the conference ended with lunch, all would have been well. Instead, the afternoon session began and ended with vitriolic observations from the antiquities guru from the Ulster Museum. Though he was conservatively attired, I was told that until recently he had worn his hair to his waist and was given to wearing purple shirts open to his navel. But whatever he had sacrificed to sartorial sobriety he made up for in oratorical flamboyance. He told us that his peers had been talking nonsense when they said that little attention had been paid to sites of the plantation period. On the contrary, they were all recorded on file cards in Belfast. A professor from the University of Ulster replied that there was no point in having file cards if they were not available to others. Someone else, who had seen the cards, declared that they were old, incomplete, and unreliable!

There being nowhere else to go but down, the Belfast curator took the floor and announced that Magee College should leave American studies to Queen's

College, which was already developing its own program, and that nothing was to be gained by courting American money and letting fleets of American students loose to dig up Ireland's heritage—something that no one had proposed. He then went on to attack a recently published paper, "Vernacular Housing in Ulster in the Seventeenth Century," by a noted folklore scholar whom he knew to be in the audience. Its author, a mild and intelligent man, had made sensible suggestions regarding the role archaeology could play in the study of the plantation period, and we were all shocked by the sudden attack on his paper, which few if any of us had read. Our moderator, Hugh Sockett, realized that as moderation was out the window, he should wind up his conference before it dissolved into an Irish barroom brawl.

Hugh explained to us later that in Northern Irish academic life there was little agreement on anything. Underlying it all were the opposing religious persuasions of the faculty at Magee, which that had earlier been a Catholic college. The Northern Irish Parliament had chosen to move Protestant elements to the nearby town of Coleraine, which displeased those members of staff who had to commute from their homes in Londonderry. In addition, there was distrust between English and Irish faculty and between faculty and administration (we were guests of the latter), teachers charging administrators with interference and insensitivity to their needs while the administration considered the faculty lazy and often childish.

In the course of five days in Londonderry we listened to all these points of view—new sounding boards always being welcome—and came to the conclusion that five days amid this academic and simmering, subsurface religious turmoil would be enough. And our luggage was still missing. On the morning of September 15, the IRA reminded us of its presence, setting off three firebombs in Derry's best paint and wallpaper shop about a quarter of a mile from our Magee lodging. The store was still burning when at lunchtime we drove past it on our way to the long-delayed bawn village tour. Shortly thereafter, another bomb went off in a butcher's shop.

The Derry telephone operators' strike had ended that morning, and so we were able to discover that our luggage had been found in Dublin and for unexplained reasons was being sent back to Shannon rather than to Belfast. Later in the day, we learned that the transfer had been accomplished, but found the people at Shannon unwilling to have the baggage shipped overland to Londonderry. The suitcases were locked, they said, and therefore could not cross the border without being opened. The best Aer Lingus could do was to send them to the harbor town of Sligo to which we would have to drive with the keys. And the next day we did, having been driven across the border by Hugh Sockett. Sligo was still at the forefront of most Irish and British minds, for less than three weeks earlier Earl Mountbatten's yacht had been blown up in the harbor, killing him and members of his family. If we needed a reminder, we found it carved into the mountainside behind Sligo: BRITS OUT. Being part of a hated minority was a new and uncomfortable experience, and we were relieved to secure our luggage and get back across the border into somewhat less hostile territory.

The affair of the lost luggage had had an adverse impact on virtually every day of our second foray to see the bawn villages of Northern Ireland. No less pervasive was the sectarian divide, its fissure evident even in Londonderry's Protestant cathedral. A verger was there to take us through the building. He was a man in his midseventies, a coach painter by trade, and renowned for painting Protestant drums used in the Orangemen's parades—as well as painting Williamite murals on walls. The country is in a state of war, he told us, adding that ten years ago the Protestants and Catholics lived side by side like brothers. As an example of this filial relationship he told how, as lead drummer for the Orangemen's parade, he once found his drum broken and so borrowed one from the Catholics' drummer. "That was how close we were in those days," he said. "Mind you," he added with a broad grin, "there I was out front in the parade with that Catholic drum with the Pope's face right there on the side, an' me bangin' away on it."

The rancor was there, yet softly swathed in humor and regret. Was this, I wondered, how the vergers and citizens of Williamsburg felt in 1775 as Virginians talked themselves into war with their mother country? Whether or not the parallel is justified, it served to remind me that though the lessons of history are repeated over and over, learning from them is a task that nations tend to shun. Nevertheless, in our Ulster travels the lessons of its archaeological history were not hard to read: the plantation period villages did have their parallels at Wolstenholme Towne, whose palisaded bawn was of comparable size to those stone-built in Macosquin, Dungival, and elsewhere.

23 🖋 *Following the Pharaohs*

THE PAINTED SIGN on the door of a Williamsburg gas station read "Toot-an-kum-in." The date was 1923 when the world press was agog with reports of Howard Carter's discovery in Egypt's Valley of the Kings. Finding the undisturbed tomb of the boy king Tutankhamen proved to be the most spectacular archaeological discovery of the twentieth century. In its wake, public interest in the treasures of the Nile reached a height unparalleled since Napoleon's savants began to study and publish the art of the ancient Egyptians in the 1790s. Amid Tut songs, Tut dances, and Tut cartoons, it was only to be expected that even the sleepy citizens of Williamsburg would want to go with the flow—albeit slowly. This was, as one local wag described it, a town dominated by its eighteenth-century lunatic asylum, where "five hundred lazy lived off five hundred crazy."

James Breasted, professor of Egyptology at the Oriental Institute of the University of Chicago, had persuaded John D. Rockefeller Jr. that he should fund the building of a new museum in Cairo to house Egypt's archaeological treasures. Were it not for the short-sightedness of the Egyptians and the machinations of their French advisers, he would have done so. Instead, Rockefeller listened next to Williamsburg's Reverend Goodwin and committed his philanthropy to saving and restoring at least part of the colonial town. Had Breasted prevailed, there would have been no Colonial Williamsburg—and I would have had no American career.

For both Audrey and me, the ancient world still beckoned, as it had when I carried Gaston Maspero's book into my Uncle John's office. It stirred again in 1961 when UNESCO called on museums and other educational institutions to join the U.S. National Committee for the Preservation of Nubian Monuments, monuments threatened by the damming of the Nile at Aswan to create Lake Nasser. Professor John Wilson at the University of Chicago invited me to serve on the U.S. committee. Though as a British citizen I could not accept, I did give a couple of fund-seeking lectures drawing on the promotional package, which included a set of color slides which were already turning purple. Nevertheless, my concern for the survival of the temples at Philae and Abu Simbel was unlikely to fade. Audrey and I made up our minds that we had to see the threatened sites for ourselves—a promise delayed by the unrelenting demands of Williamsburg's archaeology. Thirteen years slipped away before EgyptAir decanted us onto the Cairo tarmac and into a roach-sharing room at the airport hotel.

By 1973 the days of sailing the Nile from Cairo to Aswan in one's private dahabeeyah were long since gone. Instead, one took a well-appointed tour boat. In our case, it was the *Delta*, directed by Swan Tours of London, which lay moored off the famed Shepheard's Hotel in Cairo. For us, the Swan Company's appeal (as opposed to the more famous Cook's Nile Tours) lay in the fact that its chairman was Audrey's old tutor Sir Mortimer Wheeler. However, he was not to lead our adventure; that role fell to a much-published Egyptologist, Cyril Aldred, whose knowledge was vast but whose social graces were in need of burnishing. He probably assumed that he would be casting his pearls before a shipload of idiots—which was almost certainly true, since most of us were seeing Egypt for the first time.

We began with a tour of mosques, which many of us thought a dull prelude to visiting Tut and his treasures in the Cairo Museum—the one that Rockefeller had been on the brink of replacing. Once inside we could quickly see why Breasted had pushed so hard for a new museum. The Cairo Museum had been improved scarcely at all since the French had built it in 1910. Acres of unlit cases filling the galleries contained thousands upon thousands of wood, alabaster, fabric, and metal objects whose curling labels were largely in French and Arabic. The already dim light level had been further reduced by the leaking sandbags piled in the windows for fear of Israeli air strikes.

I need not discuss and wax enthusiastic over the temples that punctuated our journey up the Nile. Suffice it to say that any architect or archaeologist who has not visited the Hypostyle Hall at Karnak has no yardstick against which to measure man's creativity. Although the temples are unrivaled in their majesty, some of the smaller tombs are as remarkable for the quality of their murals, particularly those of the Middle Kingdom in the necropolis of Beni Hassan, cut into the terraced limestone cliffs back from the east bank of the river. The painters showed us how their contemporaries made household goods, laid siege to their enemies, wrestled and hunted. A short distance further upstream our guide, Aldred, suggested a hike inland up onto the escarpment above the cliffs to get a look at the real desert. Audrey and I, who were among the young and mobile, thought that a great idea—until our progress was halted by half a dozen armed men who looked as though they had been extras for Peter O'Toole's *Lawrence of Arabia*. Their shouting and gesticulating left no doubt that they thought our presence undesirable, and the rifles and muskets pointing at us added colorful emphasis. On our way back to the *Delta* Aldred suggested that the men might have been tomb robbers and that it was best not to argue with them.

Older passengers who had not attempted the trek were already gathering for lunch, which was hurried forward when we returned so quickly. Buffet lunches on the *Delta* sundeck were a highlight of days spent chugging upstream. White-turbaned servants dressed in red robes hemmed in gold added to the splendor of the arrayed food, and kept us all fed and happy. But then an American woman looked over the side of the still-moored ship. Below her, sitting and standing in the sand at the water's edge, were a dozen black-swathed Arab women who had apparently materialized out of nowhere. "Those poor, poor people!" wailed the American lady. She demanded to know how we, in good conscience, could sit there on the sundeck with all that food around us? I muttered to Audrey that if we refrained from looking over the side, we could manage just fine, but the seeds of compassion had been planted. The ship's manager was summoned and told that the leftover lunch must be given to those poor, needy, and probably starving women. In spite of his protestations, Swan's bounty was loaded into baskets—fish, fruit, bread, vegetables, all mixed together—and carried down the gangplank by crewmen who hesitated, then dumped the food onto the sand in front of the women, whose number had by now doubled. Our Good Samaritans barely had time to congratulate themselves before a wailing sound came from the beneficiaries, followed almost immediately by a fusillade of food being hurled back at us. Some bread rolls even made it back onto the sundeck, so robust and well fed were the outraged Arab women. The *Delta*'s crew hastily cast off and we lurched back into the river in a hail of garbage.

The lesson to be learned from this incident is simple. Neither tourists nor archaeologists should presume to impose their mores and standards onto the people of host nations. It took Audrey another Nile journey to get the message. At several of our stops children came to the boat waving schoolbooks and shouting, "Pencil! Pencil!" Next time, vowed Audrey, she would bring large quantities of pencils, enough for every kid who needed one. And she did. Smiles and happy laughter were her reward. Then one of crewmen pointed to a man standing in a village doorway. One by one the boys were handing their pencils to him. "He sells them in Cairo," the crewman explained.

We had a great deal to learn. For me, however, it was not the deviousness of small boys but my inability to connect with all that we had come to see. To be confronted with walls carved or painted with written information that I was unable to read was immensely frustrating. It was like listening to a concert with the sound turned off—until we reached the majestic Ptolemaic temple at Kom Ombo. On one of its walls, along with the usual hieroglyphic cartouches and letter-equating symbols, were what looked to me like the kinds of Roman medical tools I had found in London's Walbrook silt. I remarked on the similarity to Cyril Aldred, who curtly replied, "Of course. This is the second-century Roman part of the temple." On that he walked away, probably wondering how many more stupid questions he would have to answer in the course of the morning. For me, however, this was one of my life's Eureka! moments. I had seen the writing on the wall and I had begun to read it. I was resolved that we would be back next year and that by then I would have learned to read much more.

Kom Ombo lies about sixty miles below Aswan, and it was there that we learned that there could be trouble ahead. We had been without off-boat contact with the outside world for a week, during which time the Israelis had shot down a Libyan airliner, killing a hundred passengers. The American ambassador to the Sudan had been seized by Palestinian Black September militants. Two days later, after the guerillas surrendered, the body of the ambassador (whose named happened to be Cleo A. Noel) was found in the embassy basement along with those of two other diplomats. The possibility that farther up the river more Black September marksmen might be waiting for the *Delta* became a hot topic among the more imaginative passengers. The *Egyptian Gazette* also reported that an American cruise ship leaving Beirut had been "holed by a mysterious explosion" resulting in the evacuation of 250 Baptists bound for the Holy Land.

We docked at Aswan without incident. The next war involving Egypt would not break out until September and be over in seven days, with much the same results as the Six Days' War. With that settled, Audrey and I had no hesitation in booking a second Nile voyage aboard the *Delta* for September 1974. This time we were careful to avoid lecturer Aldred and went instead with Veronica Seton-Williams, of whom we knew nothing. At the first assembling of our motley group I assumed that she was the large Eton-cropped woman talking to an elderly and baggy-trousered man, and deduced that he was a friend who had come to see her off. I was wrong. The short-haired woman was Joan du Plat

Taylor (another distinguished Egyptologist) and the baggy-trousered man was Dr. Seton-Williams herself. I found her wonderfully informative, always ready to answer questions, and able to mix easily with the group.

Most tour companies provide their buses and boats with two shepherds. The lecturer is there to answer why Nefertiti only had one eye but not to tell us whether Egyptian toilet paper is safe to use. Such practical questions are directed to the courier, who on this voyage was known to us simply as Tracey. An attractive, blonde-haired person in her early thirties, she evidently bore the hidden scars of dealing with tiresome tourists. In her introductory welcoming speech she informed us with steely conviction that time and tide waited for no man—and neither did buses, donkeys, or camels. When the bell summoned, she said, we would have five minutes to get off the boat and into our vehicle. No-shows would be left behind.

Tracey meant what she said. When, on the first day out, an Australian couple failed to board the bus, she gave them five minutes' grace, and then in spite of protests from the passengers, she instructed the driver to go without them. As the bus lurched up the dirt road, the missing Aussies were seen running behind us in a cloud of dust. Someone shouted, "Stop! Here they come!" But Tracey refused. The dusty duo was left with the boat while the rest of us went off on a daylong trip to Sakkara, Memphis, and Meydum.

The next day I had a chance to talk to Tracey about the incident. She insisted that she had no choice. If she gave way at the beginning, by the end the group would be uncontrollable. I thought she was right, but the antis became either bellicose or sullen and vowed to write letters of complaint to Swan. And they did. Alas, mine in support was not sufficiently persuasive to save Tracey's job. She was fired, and when I last heard from her she was working somewhere in South America.

The trip had gone badly from the outset. We found that the relatively well-appointed *Delta* had run aground, bent its propeller shaft, and lay stranded at its Cairo berth. Its replacement, the *Nefertari,* had been rented from another Egyptian company and so hastily put into service that its still-wet paint attached itself to already complaining boarders. The crew spoke virtually no English, as we discovered after being repeatedly told "Mind your 'eads" when there was nothing overhead but sunshine. Later, a deck swabber gave the same warning when he wanted us to move our feet. Unlike the *Delta,* the *Nefertari* had no air conditioning, no fans in the cabins, and no awning over the afterdeck. In consequence, the passengers carried the deck chairs to wherever shade could be found on any of the boat's three decks. Though a practical solution, it did not sit well with the Nubian at the wheel, who complained to Tracey that he could not steer the boat with all its passengers over on one side. Tracey posted a notice saying that all chairs must be replaced and never more be moved. It turned out later that shade-seeking passengers were not the helmsman's only navigational problem. He was found asleep in the wheelhouse stoned on cocaine, requiring the ship's manager to take over much of the navigation—which explained why we frequently ran aground with bottle-bouncing crunches.

Tracey warned us not to tip the bartender Dmitri (a Greek who resembled the actor Adolphe Menjou playing a spy) on behalf of the crew, since they would never get it. She also did her best to offer other practical advice about avoiding contaminated food and drink, but before long half the group was laid low with Pharaoh's Revenge, myself included. Audrey escaped, but took her own hit from an oversized hornet. While posing as my photographic scale beside the temple at Dendera, she heroically bore its sting without moving. Later, her foot blew up like a bright red strawberry and left her in agony for thirty-six hours. Those hours, as it turned out, included the time that we had to tramp through the Valley of the Kings, torture which Audrey bravely accepted on behalf of the gods.

We had traveled by bus to Luxor while the *Nefertari* struggled upstream to rejoin us before nightfall. But when we arrived, there was no sign of our ship. Tracey helpfully suggested that those of us with swimsuits could keep cool in the pool of the New Winter Palace Hotel, but they found it filled with enormous, rubber-capped Russian women who sat glumly and silently staring at each other. We learned that they were red-star workers who had been sent on a compulsory vacation at Egyptian expense as part of the USSR's price for building the Aswan Dam.

Night fell with no news of the lost *Nefertari*. By ten o'clock Tracey's chicks were either in the Winter Palace bar getting belligerently anti-Swan or had wandered away all over Luxor. But being our resourceful mother hen, Tracey decided to rent a local ferryboat, herd us all onto it, and set off down river in search of the probably grounded *Nefertari*. My journal noted that "this seemed likely to be a particularly dicey adventure in pitch darkness" down a river renowned for its dangerous eddies, rocks, and sandbars. A newspaper story vividly made the point: the picture showed divers recovering suitcases from the sightseeing boat *Nubia* "which capsized in the Nile near Edfu on Wednesday," with nineteen Italians still missing after the bodies of ten more had been recovered. Fortunately, as we boarded the ferry the lights of the belated and benighted *Nefertari* came round the bend below Luxor.

It was a measure of Tracey's dedication that after all the drama of losing her ship she came immediately to our cabin armed with basins, lotion, ice, and whatever it took to tend to Audrey's still-swollen foot. This, I wrote, "was service to the troops beyond the call of duty, and knowing how fed up and tired Tracey was, I was tremendously impressed by her." If for no other, that was reason enough to write to Swan in her defense.

While in the ruins of the mortuary temple of Rameses II in the Theban necropolis, I was approached by a persistent Arab clutching a newspaper-wrapped parcel containing a painted wooden figure. Without weighing the consequences, I gave him ten Egyptian pounds for it. I afterward explained to Audrey that I did so to get the salesman to go away. "But supposing the figure is genuine?" Audrey demurred. "You'll be guilty of exporting a stolen antiquity—you of all people!" With its painting partially concealed by fragments of mummy wrappings, the figure did look convincingly ancient. I was still agonizing over what I had done when I passed the window of a Luxor antiquities dealer and saw an identical figure (sans wrappings) that looked as though it had been aged down one side with a blow torch.

In Luxor the strand below the Winter Palace is lined with the shops of antiquities dealers, one of whom not only offered tea but was willing to talk—in English. Hassani el Galeb admitted that 80 percent of his stock was fake, most of it made in the village of Gourna in the Theban necropolis and ranging from simple painted limestone slabs to well-made bronzes coated with fake patina. The large pieces, he said, were no longer being made, since tourists now traveled by air and not by sea. I neglected to ask him who made the painted wooden figures, but he did tell us that the itinerant sellers in the necropolis bought directly from the Gourna factory. I was satisfied that I was not about to illegally export an ancient treasure. When we got back to London, just to be on the safe side, I took my purchase to the British Museum for identification and there was told that it was probably genuine and dated to the late Ptolemaic or Roman period. "There, you see! I told you so!" said Audrey.

Remembering the unwrapped twin I had seen in Luxor, I remained unconvinced, and later took our figure to the Brooklyn Museum, where a curator of the Egyptian collections needed no second look to assure me that it was as wrong as a three-dollar bill. Being used to telling museum visitors that their treasures are only worth their weight in wood or copper, he was surprised that his bad news was so well received. He might also be surprised that the face peering out from behind its wrappings is still beside me as I write, a reminder of a treasured chapter in my married life and of the skill of a Gourna forger.

Before leaving the ill-starred *Nefertari* I was able to sit down alone with Veronica Seton-Williams to question her about her distinguished career as an Egyptian and Near Eastern archaeologist. Like Audrey, she had begun her archaeological career as a student of Sir Mortimer Wheeler—albeit decades earlier—and dug with him at the Iron Age fort in Dorset known as Maiden Castle. It was there that she met another of his students, Joan du Plat Taylor, who remained her lifelong companion until her death in 1983.

I took the opportunity to ask Veronica whether she knew anything about Williamsburg's first archaeologist, and my predecessor, Prentice Van Walbeck Duall. Duall had come to Williamsburg from teaching classical archaeology at Bryn Mawr College. His presence in Williamsburg had been short-lived, however, and was limited to supervising work at the Wren Building at the College of William and Mary, and to the excavation of the Governor's Palace. He left before the latter was complete, having made a prior commitment to Breasted to become the Oriental Institute's field director at Sakkara in Egypt—but his credentials in that area were no more impressive than those that had brought him to Williamsburg. I asked Veronica whether he really should be identified as an archaeologist. "No," she firmly replied. "Prentice Duall was a fine draftsman, but he was not an archaeologist. He was a deliniator. A good draftsman accurately draws what he sees; but he does not interpret. Without interpretation, there is no archaeology."

That statement made so long ago has remained with me as firmly as had Uncle John's "archaeology is an avocation, not a profession" assertion. Both were fundamental ideas to impart to any would-be archaeologist—one of which I rejected and the other of which I believe to have been the cornerstone of my career.

Although drawing the murals and monuments of ancient Egypt might not make one an archaeologist, drawing *on* them certainly made one a vandal. And there have been plenty of those. Indeed, the graffiti that mutilate the murals are so numerous that they provide a history of European and America travel from the sixth century BC Greeks onward to the father (or mother?) of "Susan Westmacott Age 2 1974." I was embarrassed to find that too many of the visitors were Englishmen—who should have known better. James Mangles and the Honourable Charles Leonard Irby were there in 1815 and carved their names wherever

they went. At the Ramesseum at Thebes they inscribed them on the same column that bears the name of Belzoni and his mentor (and British consul general
in Cairo) Henry Salt. In that temple alone we found several Frenchmen, a Bel-
gian, a German, dozens more that had become unreadable, and a Mr. Dixon of
Boston who wanted us to remember that he was there in January 1843.

Who, we wondered, was another Bostonian who had sought immortality by
scribing through one of the most beautiful murals in the Beni Hassan necropolis, and then had his name erased by someone else? Our growing fascination
with this catalog of infamy was enough to send us back to Egypt in 1986 with
the specific intention of photographing the graffiti, each one discovered with the
kind of delight enjoyed by bird-watchers and collectors of automobile license
plates. The identity of the eminent travel writer Amelia Edwards, whose name
we found at Abu Simbel, needed no research, but who, in the 1840s, was T.
Lowell of Boston, and who were the Bushnells from Ohio who disgraced themselves in the tomb chapels of Beni Hassan? We had no answers for most such
questions, but they led to a lecture for the National Geographic Society which
I rather tritely titled "Gods, Gold and Graffiti." In it I addressed the question,
why? Why did these evidently wealthy and educated people travel so far to see
the wonders of Egypt only to mutilate them? The answer has to be an over-
whelming desire to be remembered, specifically in the place where our civilization was born. I confess that Audrey and I were not immune to that ambition.
Before leaving for Egypt in 1986, we persuaded Colonial Williamsburg's silversmith to engrave a small label reading:

Audrey & Ivor
Noël Hume
Williamsburg, Virginia
Were Here
February 20, 1986

We chose that date knowing that we were scheduled to be back then at Dendera, where, between two stones in the foundation of a "birth house" of the god
Horus, we slid our silver message. Having paid our respects to him, we prayed
that in some distant, future age our offering would be discovered and prompt the
finder to wonder who were those weird people—and where was Williamsburg,
and where was Virginia?

THE 1976 BICENTENNIAL year had not provided the expected visitation bonanza that Colonial Williamsburg had hoped for, but for me it had been
the best of times. The Martin's Hundred film, *Search for a Century,* was close
to completion and would air several times on PBS and on the BBC. It won a
Gold Medal at the 24th Annual Film and TV Festival in New York and a Cine
Golden Eagle in 1981, and much later the Palme d'Or at the International Film
Festival of Archaeology and Ethnology at the Louvre in Paris. Carl Humelsine's
credo that his people should have the latitude to succeed but not to mess up was
holding good.

An honorary doctorate from the University of Pennsylvania enabled me not
to have to deny it if someone inadvertently addressed me as "Doctor." Later
another was awarded from the College of William and Mary, but it rendered
me no more worthy of academic accreditation than the first. Of more practical
value was Carl's elevating me to the ranks of the Foundation's officers, which
thenceforth afforded me all the social and financial advantages of the vice presidents—without actually being one. No similar appointments had been made in
Colonial Williamsburg's history, but now there were three of us: Beatrix Rum-
ford, director of the Folk Art collection, who would later gain the full mantle of
vice president; the Foundation architect, Nicholas Pappas; and myself. In the
course of nineteen years, archaeology had risen from a drawing board in a corner
of the architectural drafting room to the board room. But while archaeology's
star rose, that of architecture lost some of its luster. Where once the Foundation's architect was its senior vice president, now the architect no longer rated a
place on the masthead. For those of the staff who read tea leaves, something was
happening that boded ill for the Rockefeller legacy.

In November 1977 I received a call from Carl to help him sail his yacht
from the Rappahannock to the Elizabeth River at Norfolk. This was the kind

of invitation that made many of his senior staff cringe. Anecdotes about sailing with Carl were legion, and his transformation into Captain Bligh when the wind dropped or one of us ran him aground was the stuff whereof legends are made. Needless to say, one did not decline such invitations. This one found the weather so foul that we had to moor overnight at Gwynn's Island before heading out under engine power into the Atlantic. In retrospect that trip through stormy seas (Audrey was a very reluctant sailor) was to mark the last of our halcyon days at the top. At the end of that year Carl resigned as president of Colonial Williamsburg and became chairman of the board. In his place came New Englander Charles Longsworth, previously president of Hampshire College in Amherst, Massachusetts. Tall, lean, and austere in appearance, he lacked the bonhomie that was the Humelsine trademark. With him, and from the same college faculty, came a new vice president for education, succeeding our good friend and previous boss James R. Short, who died after a long illness in August 1980. James's replacement was a horse of a very different hue. Audrey once likened him to Othello's Iago or Joe McCarthy's Roy Cohn, but regardless of the appropriateness of the analogy, Iago had a hatchet and meant to use it to cut me down to size.

At one of our first meetings, he told me that there was no place in this organization for a renaissance man, and that the new management viewed Colonial Williamsburg less as an ongoing restoration project than as a university campus. To ensure smoothness in its operation, everything would be run by committees, and no individual would be free to chart his own course. To this Iago added a parable: A professor of astronomy at a university had the ear of the trustees and could get a new telescope for his department while others languished within their allotted budgets. The result: jealousy and interdepartmental feuding. We want none of that here, I was assured. It was true that one wealthy friend of Colonial Williamsburg had given my department a truck, but if there had been opportunities for entrepreneurship, they had come from Carl Humelsine's office. It was clear, nevertheless, that the new order would work very differently from the old.

Whereas Carl sized up his staff from the cockpit of his yacht, Charles "Chuck" Longsworth got to know the caliber of his officers by inviting them to spend a weekend at Rosegill, his rented house on the Rappahannock. Though largely dating from the nineteenth century, it stands on or close to the site of the house built by Ralph Wormeley of Jamestown and the owner of the mid-seventeenth-century bottles marked RW given to me in London. It is, as they say, a small world.

In a house as sparsely furnished and as bleak as its new tenant was cold, the weekend was memorably chilly. It began by my losing a fistful of brownie points. Pointing to a small rock outside the rear door, Chuck asked, "What can you tell me about that?"

I had long ago learned that when you don't know the answer you should say so. If I was to say anything I should have prefixed it by saying that I was an archaeologist and not a geologist. But this question seemed so simple that I answered without hesitation that I thought the rock looked like the esturine quartzite nodules common in the Tidewater Virginia clays.

"Well, it isn't," Chuck replied with a wry smile. He had brought it with him from Massachusetts. I neglected to ask why, but I knew that I had failed the test. It was too late to apply the escape clause about archaeology and geology being different disciplines. Audrey tried to convince me that I was making more of the incident than I should. But the memory of Chuck's triumphant smile told me that the damage to my credibility had been irreparably done. Never again would I spend quality time with Colonial Williamsburg's new president.

Some projects were already out of the starting gate when the new collegiate era began, one of them being to use deceased chairman Winthrop Rockefeller's legacy to construct a museum at Carter's Grove to tell the Martin's Hundred story and to exhibit its artifacts. As I noted in chapter 21, in 1976 when Site A's plantation was excavated, I developed a plan to build a small museum adjacent to it; but once we discovered Wolstenholme Towne and all that was in it, I realized that the story was much bigger and that my proposed museum would have been too small and in the wrong location.

One has to recognize (as visitors soon did) that the remains of a wooden fort are no more than a lot of round holes in acres of yellow, sun-baked clay. We therefore put wooden fence posts in the holes and linked them together with cords of different colors, red for the palisades and blue for the buildings. However, from a distance and in the eyes of the short-sighted, the site looked like a forest of matchsticks. Passing a disappointed tourist on her way back from the fort I heard her remark to her companion, "Well, I must say the Park Service didn't do a very good job of that!"

I did not disillusion them.

The problem, of course, was what can you do with a field full of matchsticks? We did not know enough about the original appearance of this early seventeenth-century village to give it the full eighteenth-century Williamsburg reconstructive treatment. After prolonged cogitation, I came up with what I considered my most brilliant idea. The *National Geographic* artist Richard Schlecht had painted the scene from a vantage point on the hill behind the site, so why not find a way to project that image onto it from a museum buried into the hillside? Visitors would enter behind the hill, see the exhibited artifacts, and then enter an auditorium to view a short introduction to Wolstenholme Towne, the last image being Richard's painting blown up and projected at life size. But this would be no ordinary screen. It would be backed by a matching window that would be revealed as the projected seventeenth-century image began to vanish and the screen slid downward into a slot below the floor. Slowly the painted sky would be replaced by the real sky outside, and the painted trees by real trees. By the time the transformation was complete the audience would see only the vacant site but retain in memory the vision of what might have been there.

Had I had this idea during Carl Humelsine's reign I might have risked taking it directly to him. Instead, we built a small model in our lab and found that in principle it seemed to work. The next step was to erect a frame on the hill to simulate the window. Once that was done, it was time to try it on the rest of the Foundation's officers. I had expected derisive laughter but was surprised to find that several colleagues thought it a neat idea—but not for long. Several days later I was told by vice president Peter Brown, who was in charge of Carter's Grove, that digging out the hill to seat the museum was not an option, and that having the window visible from the Wolstenholme Towne site would be a distraction. He may well have been right on the last count. Besides, to have gone ahead only to find that we had an enormously expensive failure would probably have cost me my job. Nevertheless, a museum there would be, and $4 million from the estate of the late Winthrop Rockefeller had been assigned to the project.

A New York architectural firm was hired to plan and build the museum, and after reviewing all the options it concluded that the hill behind the site should be dug out and the building buried beneath it. That novel concept was unanimously applauded and adopted.

The exhibit design firm of Staples and Charles of Washington, D.C., was hired to design the interior and its exhibits. With several high-profile projects in their portfolio, notably the Coca-Cola exhibit in Atlanta and the Kennedy assassination gallery in Dallas, a museum for Carter's Grove should have been a breeze.

It had been my experience that exhibit designers are happiest when the client shows them what is to be exhibited and then goes away until the job is done. But that was not the way it was to be. First, there had to be the mandatory committee chaired by the vice president for education, and in the second chair

Peter Brown to protect the virginity of Carter's Grove. Neither had much idea of what had been found or how it should be interpreted. Although seated several chairs down, I was to have that responsibility. Since I had already planned how I wanted to tell the story and how to exhibit it, my principal task was to discourage Staples and Charles from doing something else. It wasn't easy nor was I always successful. Since the designers were being paid big bucks to do the designing—and I was not—I also had to convince the committee that advice it was being offered gratis was preferable to what it was paying for. Peter Brown found himself with the unenviable task of being the referee.

My original design for the smaller museum beside Site A was to set it on the side of a ravine and dig out to seat a basement-level research center for seventeenth-century archaeology. I argued that a museum without a research element was no more than a static exhibit devoid of any intellectual heart. Consequently, when the larger museum was in the planning stage, the basement research element was part of the design—until the price estimates started to come in. A basement would add $2 million that wasn't in the budget. It was hardly surprising, then, that the research unit was the first to go. Bit by bit the exhibit space eroded to be replaced by the necessary utilities, electronic controls, and so on. It was a sobering experience, but I learned a lot. An example: I did not know that if you hung urinals on the wall of the men's room, the wall had to be no less than five inches thick, but if you stood them on the ground you could get away with three.

Because Carter's Grove was both a quick, maybe one-hour stop for tourist buses and also a stay-as-long-as you-like destination, the museum had to cater to both. My plan, therefore, was to have a central U-shaped spine down the middle of the gallery whose exhibits told what was found, how it was found, and what it meant. That was the short tour. On the outer sides of the gallery would be what I called enrichment pods, minigalleries amplifying the main theme. These pods were to be sufficiently enclosed so that the sound of recorded narrative could be retained within them. But it did not work out like that. The U-shaped spine was there, but the enriching pods were no more than exhibit cases along the outer walls. Consequently, although the introductory narrative talked about the short and long tours, there was no visual distinction between them. Since most of the compelling displays were on the outer walls, the short-tour visitors were lured away from the primary message into the enrichment exhibits, and having done so wandered at random through the museum. Furthermore, when sound was employed it spilled out to intrude on the attention of visitors trying to absorb something else.

If I was to be denied my minigalleries, could I at least have the walls painted different colors to identify differing subjects and themes? Absolutely not, I was told. The walls had to be off-white throughout, but as a concession the exhibit titles could be in different colors. Like most compromises, this one achieved nothing. The titles were so high on the walls that viewers standing in front of the cases could not see them. Besides, the subtlety of words in different colors on banners nine feet up was too obscure to be meaningful.

Most exhibit designers have to make do with whatever gallery space is assigned to them. But we had the luxury of constructing a wholly new building around the exhibit concept. This should have allowed everything to be snugly integrated, but unfortunately the architects designed the building without regard for the elongated U-shaped exhibit layout. Consequently, the ceiling electrical grid was erected at a right angle to the cases, seriously limiting the lighting's flexibility. Nevertheless, in spite of these and other shortcomings the Winthrop Rockefeller Archaeology Museum was deemed a great success. My plea to Chuck Longsworth that the name should be "Archaeological" rather than "Archaeology" was dismissed as semantic pedantry and quickly rejected. To this, Audrey dryly observed that he who pays the piper calls the tune.

In addition to the Winthrop Rockefeller legacy, the National Geographic Society contributed funding for a small theater in which to show a video presentation of the recovery and conservation of the Wolstenholme helmets, and to depict the process of replicating them. In a case at the entrance to the theater were the actual helmets and behind them the reproductions, which were only briefly visible when a button was pushed. Why, colleagues asked, are the reproductions not continuously on display? My answer was simple: the shiny new helmets would upstage the rusty originals.

There had been many skirmishes, if not battles, to be fought before the museum finally opened, not the least of them being committee disagreement over a diagrammatic display showing how an archaeologist peels away the layers of the ground to reveal the sequence of structures cutting into and through them. Far too erudite, I was told. Children wouldn't understand or take the time to try. I argued (a) that children's minds are far more agile than some of us think they are, and (b) that there is no point in having an archaeological museum without demonstrating how archaeologists do what they do. That was one battle I won, and subsequent experience showed that young people are far more inquisitive and willing to stand and learn than are their parents.

The museum, as I have said, was constructed as a prelude to a yet-to-begin

Wolstenholme Towne experience, to which end my recorded lecturettes in the gallery were continued at nine locations along the tour. The treatment of the site itself had developed beyond my matchstick and string marking of the postholes to the complete reconstruction of what we believe to have been the fort's watchtower. But standing alone in the middle of the field I thought it looked remarkably like a French privy. While we were still at that stage, Audrey and I made our second visit to the Nile, and there got the idea of how to interpret Wolstenholme Towne.

The courtyard around the Ptolemaic temple at Dendera is enclosed within mud brick walls pierced by massive gateways of Aswan granite that have survived the millennia virtually intact. The once-towering walls, however, have eroded away until sections of them stand only two or three feet tall, barely high enough to outline the enclosure. Standing on the roof of the great Hypostyle Hall shortly after dawn we could clearly see the lines of the crumbled enclosure walls outlined in shadows cast by the rising sun. It was immediately evident that what was wrong with Wolstenholme Towne's strung posts was that they cast no linear shadows. We resolved to give our 1620 wooden Virginia fort the Dendera treatment. Like the Egyptian stone gateways, our wooden gates would be reconstructed to their full height, while the curtain walls between them would be irregularly raised to a height of about two feet.

At Jamestown in the 1950s the National Park Service had installed a series of tape-recorded scene setters voiced by not very convincing "English settlers" to indicate where one was in the town. They were mounted in brick pillars that were not particularly anachronistic, since nothing there had been reconstructed above foundation level. Nevertheless, over the objection of Colonial Williamsburg's architect, who liked the brick pillar idea, I proposed putting the speakers inside barrels of the kind that would have been used at Wolstenholme Towne in the 1620s. By raising the open-bottomed barrels three inches off the ground, the sound emerged from beneath them and thus remained in the immediately surrounding area. The scheme worked, and became known as "Noël in a barrel." However, it got off to a rocky start. The tape players were located in the Carter's Grove mansion from which a network of audio and electrical lines fanned out down the hill and into Wolstenholme's nine barrels. On the first weekend the system was activated, lightning struck in the middle of the archaeological site and fried the entire system, including the recorders in the mansion. The damage was estimated at $22,000, give or take a cent or two.

Several years later the fort's watchtower took a direct lightning strike that shredded its bark roof. Subsequent discerning visitors might have noticed the lightning rod protruding in a less than 1620 manner from its apex. In 2004 the watchtower again graced the local newspapers when a deer hunter using it as a blind accidentally shot himself and thus became the first person to die in Wolstenholme Towne since the Indian massacre of 1622. It was, perhaps, appropriate that the ball that killed him came from a black powder gun.

How long could one expect a tourist to stand listening to Noël in a barrel? The answer was provided by a visit to the Army Museum in London's Chelsea, where several video screens were running clips from past battles. I found that the first of them would hold arriving visitors spellbound for a maximum of four minutes, but after that, their attention span ran out at three minutes and on down until some people simply pressed the start button, took one look at what they decided was more of the same, and walked on. I figured, therefore, that most of my barrel texts should run no more than three minutes, and that when it was necessary for one to run longer, a bench should be provided to sit on. The problem, of course, was that having pressed the start button, the listener would not know how long he or she was expected to remain there. Again, the answer was simple. One attached a printed plastic plate to the top of the barrel giving the running time, thereby allowing the button pusher to know what to expect. The device worked admirably until vandalous or souvenir-hungry visitors took to prying them off and stealing the plates.

Sometime after the losses were discovered, the then director for Carter's Grove decided that rather than replace those missing at a dollar or so apiece, it was more cost effective to remove all that remained and replace none of them. Although the director's tenure was short, the timing plates were never replaced, probably because no one remembered that there had been such plates or knew why they were needed. If I seem to belabor a small detail, it serves to demonstrate how, over time, standards of excellence slowly decline as new managements, unaware of the reasoning behind previous decisions, unwittingly settle for less.

Later yet, a subsequent Colonial Williamsburg management opted to save even more money by closing the Winthrop Rockefeller Museum and putting Carter's Grove and Wolstenholme Towne on the real estate market.

WHILE THE MUSEUM at Carter's Grove was still under construction I happened to arrive at the site before the rest of the committee showed up. To fill the time I walked northward along the ridge behind Wolstenholme Towne and found that graders had turned up a scatter of colonial brickbats and mortar. There could be little doubt that they came from a building that preceded the mansion, which was not completed until 1755. This, I thought, had to be the site of the "old house" referred to in the records, and probably the home of the Burwells while the mansion was being built. Although it is unlikely that they coexisted for any length of time, the old house site would serve as a marker for the first half of the eighteenth century. This was not the time to embark on a new excavation, however, and so nothing was done. In truth, the last thing Colonial Williamsburg wanted was another chapter to further detract from its focus on the mansion. Indeed, there were some in the front office who wished we had never found Wolstenholme Towne and thereby forced the Foundation to pay attention to the wrong century.

In 1983, when excavations at Carter's Grove ceased, several important archaeological sites remained unexplored, the earliest being an Indian burial ground farther along the ridge from the "old house" site. East of the visitor center a major domestic site dating to the second half of the seventeenth century had been only peripherally examined. Two more to the east of Site B (the potter's house site) had been found during a woodland survey by crew chief John Hamant, but I decided that they should be reserved for excavation by a future generation of archaeologists whose techniques and knowledge would be better and greater than our own. Consequently, I was content to have them marked on the Foundation's property maps to ensure their preservation. The subsequent leasing of that tract for logging demonstrated my naïveté in the business of efficient land management.

Believing in Colonial Williamsburg's mantra "That the Future May Learn from the Past" can be applied to its own past, Audrey and I were grateful to President Longsworth for having proposed that a brass plaque be installed near the exit from the museum recognizing our contributions both to it and to the archaeology of Martin's Hundred. I was grateful to him, also, for his awareness that Audrey had too long toiled in my shadow without proper recognition for her talents and knowledge. To make amends, Longsworth appointed her to chair the committee overseeing the conversion of the Duke of Gloucester Street house called Marot's Ordinary into an operating restaurant named for a later proprietor, James Shields. This ambitious project would be served by subterranean kitchens supplying both it and the existing King's Arms tavern farther up the street. The engineering aspects, however, were beyond the purview of Audrey's committee, whose responsibility was to design and approve the furnishings. With the able support of her friend the historian Patricia Gibbs, Audrey nevertheless ventured beyond the committee's mandate into architectural territory. In England Audrey had purchased a Liverpool delftware tile depicting a fat and jovial English butcher with a tankard in his hand, and this became her design for the Shields Tavern sign. But her principal coup was to install a leaded casement window in recognition of the fact that until the mid-eighteenth century those were common throughout Williamsburg. Although fragments of the lead and diamond-shaped panes of glass have been found on most excavated sites, Ed Kendrew's original architectural team had ordained that Williamsburg's restored and reconstructed houses were to be demonstrably Georgian and, therefore, fitted only with the newer-style sash windows. But old architectural office prejudices were not easily overcome. If Audrey was to have her window it could not be visible from the street. Consequently, the window was set into an interior wall and hidden on its exterior face by a later addition to the building.

The casement window was Audrey's supreme contribution to the authenticity of Colonial Williamsburg, and she was justifiably proud of it—although she was the first to admit that logic dictated that no colonial renovator in his right mind would neglect to remove and plaster over an unwanted window opening. The idea was to instruct the tavern's waitstaff to explain the symbolism to diners occupying the adjacent table. Several years later I did just that.

"Why," I asked the serving wench, "is there a window here when it's backed by a wall?"

"Beats me," she replied. "But now you ask, it is kind of funny."

The 1980s proved to be watershed years in the evolution of Colonial

Williamsburg. Under the Longsworth regime, it was evolving, as he intended, from a restoration project into an educational campus. In October 1981 the previously all-powerful architectural office merged with the department of construction and maintenance, separating the resident architect from the day-to-day control of the restored buildings. The change was subtle but significant, and it would not be long before my department felt the same cold wind of change. There is no denying that I had myself to blame, if blame there was. As I have noted, as early as 1970 I was growing fearful that we were becoming swamped by unfinished and inadequately recorded projects. I suggested in a memo to Vice President Hackett that there could be merit in drastically cutting the fieldwork "to allow a diminished staff to undertake long needed studies of the collections, and to write survey reports on the scores of inadequately recorded excavations undertaken during the past 40 years." Consequently, when another decade slipped by with no scaling back, I took advantage of administrative and philosophical changes in the Foundation to propose that no new excavations be embarked on until we had done justice to those already in progress, notably at Carter's Grove and at the Public Hospital site. Management's response was that as the Foundation had no plans to stop digging, I should step aside and cede responsibility for the continuing fieldwork to another experienced archaeologist. It seemed like an ideal solution. Audrey and I would move our offices to the Semple House on Francis Street. This eighteenth-century building, whose design had been attributed to Thomas Jefferson, would become the office of the resident archaeologist. I would continue to direct excavations at Carter's Grove, but the in-town digging would be under the wing of a new man or woman. But finding that person proved harder than expected. I interviewed several keen but unqualified candidates, always hoping that Bill Kelso would step forward to seize this golden opportunity. He had worked for me at Wetherburn's Tavern and had supervised the early test at Carter's Grove. He had directed work at Kingsmill Plantation and had earned his PhD at Emory University. Bill had also served as Virginia's state archaeologist. There could be no better candidate.

Audrey and I emitted sighs of relief when Bill agreed to apply. But by the time the top management interview was over, Bill had refused the job. I ruefully assumed that he had doubted my assurances that my successor would be in day-to-day control of his own program. Years later he told me that that was not the reason. The vice president for education had made it clear to Bill—though never to me—that he wanted to make archaeology a teaching rather than a practical, down-in-the-dirt research department, and that was not what Bill had in mind.

During the months that the search went on, I had come to realize that I was no longer paying sufficient attention to in-town excavations. With my focus firmly on the continuing Martin's Hundred work I had lost control of the rapidly expanding Public Hospital excavation; I knew that the day a director leaves his site without giving clear directions for the next step he is falling down on the job and it is time to fold his tent. Gone, therefore, was my insistence on finding a fully experienced successor who would continue the same methodology I had established. With the hospital site getting ever larger and more scattered as clearance for its reconstruction got under way, I was ready to settle for anyone who would be constantly on hand to keep the archaeological balls in the air.

That candidate was Marley Brown, from Brown University, whom I had met while lecturing there, although I knew nothing about him except his anthropological credentials. He had no previous experience of fieldwork in eighteenth-century Virginia, of that I was sure, but a few months on one's knees in the dirt assessing the artifacts emerging from it can be a rapid and invigorating learning experience. It remained only for Marley to leave his interview with a smile on his face and the job in his hand. And he did.

The subsequent years were not easy for either Audrey or me. Although as Foundation archaeologist I was nominally in charge of the department, I had been effectively sidelined and my staff dismantled. John Hamant, my excellent and dedicated field supervisor, found that he was not in tune with the new direction and quit. So did the young woman whom Audrey had been grooming to replace her in the lab. My totally reliable excavation foreman, Nathaniel Smith, who had been with me since we began work at Carter's Grove and was the only black member of my team, lacked academic credentials and was ousted. Audrey and I, who had arrived together in February 1957, retired together at the end of 1987 and received a plaque and a pair of handsomely mounted silver trowels to mark the occasion. In spite of a retirement dinner at Carter's Grove and a shallow tide of honeyed words, like Nate Smith, I lacked the credentials to fit snugly into the by then firmly entrenched vision of Colonial Williamsburg as a university campus. Within weeks of our departure management dismantled our archaeological museum in the James Anderson House and converted it to offices. For the first time in fifty-four years Colonial Williamsburg got by without an in-town archaeological museum and would do so for the next twenty years.

In 1992, five years after we retired, and accompanied by Audrey, I was summoned to London for Queen Elizabeth to name me an Officer of the British Empire in recognition of my services to British cultural interests in Virginia. Much as we appreciated the silver trowels, the Queen's award meant a great deal more. It seemed fitting—so we thought—that careers that began in the bombed rubble of London should end on the red carpet of Buckingham Palace. But as it turned out, there was more to come.

Olonial Williamsburg's ploy to expunge employees with fond memories of the Humelsine era by offering early retirements was for Audrey and me a blessing not even thinly disguised. Coming as it did with a five-year contract to finish the Martin's Hundred archaeological and historical studies, the opportunity gave us everything we desired. It also freed us to focus on other projects associated with the approaching 400th anniversary of the founding of the Virginia Colony.

As North Carolinians are quick to point out, the first English colonizing attempts were made in 1585 and 1587 on Roanoke Island, and not in 1607 at Jamestown. Pinky Harrington had excavated on Roanoke Island in 1948 and found the remains of a small earthwork fort. Having confirmed it to be the "traditional fort site" built by the 1585 leader Ralph Lane, the ditch and rampart were reconstructed in 1950 to become the interpretive centerpiece of the Fort Raleigh National Historic Site. Although the fort was much smaller than the surviving documents suggested and evidence of English habitation was lacking, the National Park Service elected to sidestep the problems and identify the reconstruction as part of the "Cittie of Ralegh." For half a century that assumption remained unchallenged.

Nine years after the reconstruction was in place, workmen laying a utility line ran into a scattering of bricks west of the fort. Five years later still, in 1964, Harrington resumed excavating. Identifying and uncovering numerous postholes, he determined that these were part of an "outwork at Fort Raleigh." Uncomfortable with that interpretation, the park historian, Phillip Evans, recognized a similarity between the "outwork's" posthole pattern and that of the watchtower at our Wolstenholme Towne fort.

The prospect that there could be a structural parallel between Fort Raleigh and Wolstenholme Towne was too intriguing to be ignored. Encouraged by

Evans, we secured a permit from the Park Service to expand the outwork site beyond the perimeter of Harrington's dig. The park's splendidly cooperative superintendent, Thomas L. Hartman, agreed to provide some of the labor, and with that assurance, plus a grant from the National Geographic Society, I put together a blue-ribbon team of faces from Colonial Williamsburg's archaeological past to begin where Pinky left off. They included Bill Kelso, Nick Luccketti, John Hamant, Nate Smith, Eric Klingelhofer, David Hazzard, Jamie May, and Martha Williams, our surviving graduate from the Public Hospital field school.

Before describing what we found, I think some background is in order: In June 1586 Ralph Lane and his all-male colonists, having fallen out with the indigenous Indians, packed up and were taken home by Sir Francis Drake. The following year the first expedition's sponsor, Sir Walter Ralegh, sent out another parcel of colonists, this time led by the artist and scholar John White, who stayed only a few days before going home to England for additional supplies. However, his return to Roanoke Island was delayed by Spain's attack on Britain in 1588, as well as by a lack of funds or manifest concern in London over the fate of Ralegh's people. When White finally reached the island in 1590, he found the colonists gone and only the word "Croatoan" carved on a palisade gate as a clue to their fate. Thus, John White's settlers entered American and British folklore as the "Lost Colony."

Because she gave birth to the first English infant born in America, John White's daughter Eleanor Dare became the embodiment of pioneering American motherhood. That her daughter was baptized Virginia further cemented the bond with all the Daughters of This, That and the Other, whose societies blossomed in the nineteenth century. Nobody much cared where Lane's people had lived on Roanoke Island, but everyone wanted to consecrate the hallowed ground inhabited by the Lost Colony. A granite marker was erected in 1898 after Talcott Williams, an amateur archaeologist from Philadelphia, dug a trench within the undulating area believed to be the site of the fort and found confirming "small fragments of iron." Thereafter, the historic site was outlined with markers, first by a rail fence and then with concrete posts. A full-scale timber palisade was erected in 1934, complete with an interior log-constructed blockhouse reminiscent of those erected by the U.S. cavalry to protect them from other Indians considerably farther to the west. This imaginatively reconstructed stockade survived until 1944 when a hurricane blew enough of it down to warrant its removal, clearing the way for Pinky Harrington's 1948 excavation of the fort's ditch and such traces of its rampart that had survived from previous digging and construction on the site. Broken Indian pottery, iron tools, and other obviously colonial artifacts found in the silting of the ditch enabled Pinky to report that he had found the grail. How, then, did the reconstructed earthwork relate to the "outwork's" postholes?

It fell to our team and our two-week excavations in 1991, 1992, and 1993 to provide the Park Service with the answer, albeit one that was not particularly well received. The fort had nothing to do with Ralph Lane or with Virginia Dare. Its ditch had been dug through the ground that had yielded Pinky's Elizabethan artifacts. Our digging found that the artifacts had come from the 1585–86 workplace of Ralegh's scientists, key members of the Lane expedition. Thomas Hariot and the mineral expert Joachim Ganz from Prague had been sent along to determine whether America's natural resources were worthy of English investment. Consequently, I dubbed the site America's First Science Center. Pressed into its dirt floor lay fragments of crucibles, chemical glassware, antimony, brass waste, and other artifacts associated with chemistry—but virtually none relating to the living quarters of Hariot, Ganz, or anyone else. In short, we had found where they worked but not where they lived. Similar soil layers and their chemically related artifacts continued inside the reconstructed earthen fort, leaving no shadow of doubt that the Science Center ground had been cut through by later fort builders. So who were they? A likely candidate was Virginian Samuel Stephens, who was in command of the island in the 1660s.

From Hariot's gleanings and experiments emerged his report, *A briefe and true report of the new found land of Virginia*, which told English investors that America was indeed worthy of their attention. Although little more than a four-by-four-foot square of the Science Center's working floor had escaped Harrington's and others' excavations, enough survived to show that on that spot in North Carolina the future of America had been decided. Had Hariot's report been negative, Virginia might never have existed and its modern inhabitants would almost certainly be conversing in Spanish. It is extraordinary, therefore, that seventeen years after this tiny piece of hallowed ground was identified, the National Park Service had not seen fit to mark its location.

Telling the man who had been instrumental in bringing me to America that he had reconstructed the wrong fort was one of my life's most difficult tasks. But it was the measure of Pinky Harrington and his archaeologist wife, Virginia, that when presented with the evidence they graciously accepted it. They were even resigned to that fact that the Science Center and the story of its discovery would soon be in the hands of every subscriber to the *National Geographic*.

Once I secured a National Geographic Society grant, the next step was for the Society to sponsor artwork and photography to accompany an article. First, I needed to get editor Wilbur E. "Bill" Garrett's endorsement. While in Washington to give a speech to the Daughters of the First Colonists, I won Bill's approval. Four days later the Society's chairman, Gilbert Grosvenor (Mel's son), fired him. Such a dismissal of a hitherto prestigious editor seemed totally out of character at the staid old National Geographic Society. Ousted, too, were Bill White, Garrett's driver, with whom I had stuck up a easy friendship, and the associate editor, Joseph Judge.

In one master stroke Gil Grosvenor had cleaned out the magazine's establishment, a clearance that would soon be followed by the retirement of my mentor at the magazine, Mary Griswold Smith, as well as that of her husband, Tom, who had been a long-time illustrations editor. With my connections severed, my Roanoke article became no more than a notice in the magazine's front matter.

The three brief seasons of excavating at the Science Center site had been remarkably productive, adding, as they had, a new page to the first chapter of Anglo-American history. Although the reconstructive artwork by Richard Schlecht and the photography by Ira Block were of the highest order, I could not escape the fact that no helmets had been found, no golden chalice emerged from the blue waters of Albemarle Sound, and the artifacts we did find were small and had a low gee-whiz quotient. "Ira is a truly fine photographer," wrote the new editor, Bill Graves, "but the images just weren't there. And without them, for the *Geographic*, no text could carry the package." My text, Ira's photographs, and Richard Schlecht's artwork subsequently ran as a lead story in Colonial Williamsburg's quarterly magazine, and offprints were still for sale at the National Park Service visitor center at Manteo in 2008.

In retrospect, the promotional boost that a *National Geographic* article could have provided would have availed us little. The sad truth was that the Science Center, née Harrington's outwork, failed to point the way either to Lane's fort or to the Lost Colony. For my part, however, finding the Science Center was the high point of my archaeological career, for unlike Wolstenholme Towne, the digging at Rosewell, Tutter's Neck, Clay Bank, or the houses of Colonial Williamsburg, the Roanoke Island discovery really contributed something solid to the foundation of Anglo-American history.

With the Roanoke achievement behind us, it was time to look again at the first permanent English settlement at Jamestown. The commonly held view (by that I mean the National Park Service's view) was that the last traces of the 1607 fort had long since eroded into the James River, and that only the site of the later town remained to be exhibited and interpreted. When the historian Philip Barbour published his 1969 book *The Jamestown Voyages,* he felt sufficiently confident to state that the first fort "is a site now under water some 175 yards west of the Old Church Tower and 300 yards south of a partly submerged cypress tree (36° 12' 30" N., 76° 47' 0" W.)." Unfortunately, the landmark cypress was washed away in 2003 by Hurricane Isabel. By then the "lost to the river" theory had also been swept away.

The only colonial structures still standing on Jamestown Island are the shell of the burned, eighteenth-century Ambler House and the tower of the church, whose date is uncertain, but it's generally thought to have been built in the 1660s. The tower probably belonged to the fourth church built at Jamestown and not the one in which John Rolfe married the precocious Pocahontas. That was in 1617 in a structure within the confines of the fort, which, as the National Park Service archeologist John Cotter ruefully noted, was "now possibly off-shore in the James River." In a somewhat bizarre attempt to find it, he used a barge-mounted clamshell bucket to delve for it in the riverbed. Since the fort was built entirely of wood and stood on ground at least twelve feet above the bottom and with posts set no more than four feet deep in the earth, the chances of pulling anything up in the bucket were remote. According to the Park Service report, "The results of the search were inconclusive."

In the 1930s a Richmond antiquary had suggested that the original James Fort had been located at the east and not the west end of New Town in an area defined as the Elay-Swan Tract where a small number of seventeenth-century artifacts had been found in earlier digging. In 1987 I was invited to make a study of the tobacco pipe bowls found throughout the Jamestown area and concluded that, though few in number, the earliest came from the vicinity of the brick church tower and an adjacent Confederate earthwork. At the same time I re-viewed the artifacts found in the Association for the Preservation of Virginia Antiquities (APVA) 1901 excavations of graves in the chancel and found that they included artifacts of a strictly secular nature. They looked to me to be clear evidence of colonial occupation before the church was built, and possibly related to the wooden fort in one or other of its configurations. I said as much in my 1998 book *The Virginia Adventure.* Whether that assertion in any way influenced the APVA to launch its own excavations is hard to say. It was more likely that the association wanted to make its mark on the hallowed ground that fourteen years later would be the focus of the 400th anniversary of the first English landing on the island.

The APVA's executive director was Peter Dun Grover, but its driving force was a formidable but lovable Richmond lady, Mary Douthat Higgins (we knew her as Mary D), who had long been an enthusiastic supporter of anyone's archaeological efforts. More important, she was past president of the association and chairman of the Virginia Historic Landmarks Commission, on which I sat. It was Mary D who urged Peter Grover to put the association's financial eggs in its Jamestown basket and embark on a major program of excavation to prove whether or not the first fort and settlement had been lost to the river. In August 1993 she invited me to lunch at the local country club. I demurred because Audrey was then in a Richmond hospital having knee replacement surgery and I wanted to be there to give her encouragement. But Audrey cared for Mary D as much as I did, and so urged me to accept.

Back in July, Bill Kelso, who was then directing excavations at Monticello, had written to me about something he called the Jamestown Rediscovery Archaeological Project, whose "excavation and analysis will be guided," he wrote, "by the APVA's Archaeological Advisory Committee, chaired by the foremost expert of British Colonial archaeology, Ivor Noël Hume, and directed by the APVA's archaeologist William M. Kelso." This was the first Audrey and I had heard of the project, and no one had approached me to chair its committee, which, as far as we knew, did not exist. And what, we wondered, was implied by the words "advisory" and "guided"? According to Webster's, "advisory" meant "having or exercising power to advise and often recommending action to be taken," but "to guide" implied something more authoritarian, "to direct a way or course," "to direct, supervise or influence to a particular end." The terms were not synonymous, and we questioned whether a committee could muster sufficient on-site knowledge to either advise or direct.

On the way to the country club, Mary D told me that she had talked to Audrey about my coming to lunch. She also said that she had invited Peter Grover to join us. I at once suspected that this was something more than a social invitation. And I was right. Mary D asked me to accept the chairmanship of the advisory committee. Remembering Audrey's reservations about the kind of advice and guidance Bill Kelso envisaged, and her urging that I accept no more responsibilities from anyone, I was surprised when Mary D said that she had already talked to Audrey, who had agreed that I should accept. So I did.

With that settled, Grover explained that my primary task would be to assemble a blue-ribbon group of advisers whose names would promote confidence when the APVA applied for grants. The committee would meet once or twice a year to comment on whatever might be going on at that time. Although its mandate was no clearer than that, I assumed from Bill Kelso's July missive that he expected me to provide the advice and guidance that the committee's far-flung members could not.

Back at the hospital I reported to Audrey all that had transpired, and wanted to know why she had not told me what Mary D had in mind or that I should accept the offer.

She angrily retorted, "I said no such thing! Mary D only said that she wanted you to lunch with her! You didn't accept, did you?"

"Well, yes," I lamely replied. "I mean, as you'd talked to her about the project, I thought . . ."

"Then you're a damned fool! They don't want you. They just want to use your name!" Audrey told me. "You're too easily led and a lot too naive." She went on at considerable length, telling me that she did not trust Grover, and that Kelso didn't want anybody's advice, least of all mine. Audrey was not a loud person, but opinionated and determined, and in all our years of marriage rarely had we endured a confrontation of such intensity.

The day before I took her to the hospital she had pinned a note on the refrigerator that she had apparently cut from some magazine. I had not taken the time to read it before we set out for Richmond. She had been suffering from ever-advancing arthritis, which she had kept it in check with quick-fix cortisone shots which in time had lost their effectiveness. Two days after the knee surgery she had a spinal injection to alleviate pain resulting from lying on the hospital bed. The next day was her birthday, which we celebrated with a cake and a visit from her closest friend (and previously my secretary), Carol Grazier. To pass the time we played board games, one of them involving opposing armies on a checkerboard whereon each side planted mines. Minding the mines, therefore, became a key to the players' strategy.

On Saturday August 21, 1993, the day after the lunch with Mary D, I brought Audrey home from the hospital still in pain from the surgery but in renewed good spirits. As she stepped out of the car onto the checkerboard of flagstones in front of our porch I warned her, "Mind the mines!"

"I think I'm going to faint," she replied and fell dead at my feet.

Audrey was sixty-six. We had been married for forty-three years, companions in life and also partners in our profession, which made her sudden death all the more devastating. With Hurricane Emily bearing down on me, and with plywood shutters all round the house, I felt entombed, and resolved to follow Audrey as quickly as pills or bullets would allow. Later that evening on going to the refrigerator I saw her note. It read: "One of these Days is None of these Days."

As it turned out, the hurricane missed me and I pulled myself together by writing a daily journal pouring out my misery. Friends urged me to seek a psychiatrist's help, but when I did and showed him what I had written he told me that I had no need of him. I was curing myself. In truth it was the ministrations of good friends that pulled me back from my emotional abyss. One of them was the Reverend Richard Tinker, a Thames mudlarking friend from New York who generously came down to be with me. I thought that through him I might mend my atheistic ways and find God. I was to discover, however, that Richard's faith was fragile—but his help was solid. "Get on with life," he said, "Mourning is a sickness. Get over it." Six months later he officiated at my marriage to Carol Grazier. She had worked alongside Audrey in archaeology at Colonial Williamsburg and was currently office manager of its conservation department. Knowing me better than anyone else, Carol now enabled me, if not to start a new life, at least to begin putting the old one back on track.

27 ❧ Plunging to the Deep Ocean Floor in Bermuda

ROM MY FIRST VISIT to the unfinished Jamestown fort in 1956, the fate of Virginia's earliest colonists has frequently intruded into my eighteenth-century archaeological studies. Sir Walter Raleigh's failed settlements of 1585–90, the massacred people of Martin's Hundred in 1620–22, and the ruined Mathews' Manor of about 1630–40, all were leading me back to Jamestown and its fractious, starving, and doomed inhabitants. The legacy of one group, more fortunate than most, landed on my Williamsburg desk in April 1980.

The truism that one thing leads to another is never more so than in archaeology. It should have come as no surprise, therefore, that the publicity afforded Wolstenholme Towne should have brought to my office a suitcase-carrying man from Bermuda. The visitor was Allan J. "Smokey" Wingood, a professional diver who believed he had found the wreck of the *Sea Venture,* the most famous ship from the pages of early British New World history. Bound for Jamestown, the *Sea Venture* had grounded on a reef at Bermuda's eastern extremity in June 1609. Passenger William Strachey's account of wreck, telling how the survivors built two vessels out of the old and sailed on to Virginia in 1610, is one of the great annals of the sea.

As Smokey opened his suitcase, he asked, "Could these date to the *Sea Venture* period?"

They could, and did. The fragmentary earthenware jars he showed me were identical to others from Wolstenholme Towne that we had identified as West of England butter pots manufactured at the north Devon port of Barnstaple at the beginning of the seventeenth century.

Smokey went on explain that the jars came from a wreck that had been found more than a decade earlier by another Bermudian diver, Edmund Downing, who had brought up a cannon as evidence of the ship's age. But when he sent pictures of the gun to experts at the Tower of London, they told him that it dated from the eighteenth and not the seventeenth century. Consequently, Bermuda lost interest in the wreck until Smokey Wingood returned to it. Ironically, Downing had proof of its age all along and could have settled the matter had he not chosen the cannon as his confirming artifact. Instead, the key was a fine German jug of about 1580–90, and anyone who knew anything about European stoneware would have told him so. But in those days—the 1950s—nobody in Bermuda did.

I learned from Wingood that there were other quasi-archaeological divers scouring the island's reefs, and that in the 1960s, one of them, a man named Edward Bolton "Teddy" Tucker, had allied with the Smithsonian Institution curator Mendel Peterson in an underwater survey of Bermuda's wrecks. In the process they had recovered an amazing array of artifacts from the sixteenth to the twentieth centuries. "Maybe," said Smokey, "you could learn something from looking at them." He also suggested that I should dive with him on the *Sea Venture*.

Two months later, in June 1980, I was there, but not exactly ready to plunge into the deep. My only underwater experience had been the hour spent at Port Royal with Bob Marx. Nevertheless, I had only one day to get ready. A diving instructor at the hotel agreed to give me a crash course in the hotel pool. But that was not enough to let me loose on the offshore *Sea Venture* site. First, I had to experience an open-water dive. Two hours later, I found myself bobbing about in an open boat on a choppy sea half a mile south of the island. Perched on a gunwale looking and feeling like a frightened frog, I reluctantly obeyed my instructor's call to "just flip over the side."

Suddenly I was in heaven! All the weight of the gear had vanished. Unlike in the dirty water of Kingston Harbour, visibility seemed endless, and fish were smiling at me. I could see two or three not very old bottles lying on the yellow sand and behind them the multicolored edge of a coral-covered shelf. As I came abreast of it I saw what looked like a rusty drainpipe nestling under it, but on feeling around it I realized that it was the muzzle of a cannon. I had made my first underwater discovery!

The following day, still buoyed by my find and confident that I was now a competent (albeit uncertified) diver, I set out with Smokey Wingood for the *Sea Venture*. There were five of us on the boat, Audrey, Smokey, myself, and two men who were to do their own thing attached to the same type of hookah hoses that I had used at Port Royal. Their air was pumped down to them from an extremely noisy compressor seated in the well of the boat. Smokey did not have a boat of his own, and this borrowed cruiser had a high freeboard and was not well suited to diving—as I was to discover.

It turned out that our air tanks were also borrowed and mine lacked an air gauge. But that was of small concern as Smokey and I dove down into a V-shaped break in the reef in which the wreck rested. The day was not of the azure blue variety that one sees on Bermuda's postcards. The sea was still choppy, a wind was blowing, and the sky only intermittently allowed that there was sun above the clouds. Consequently, the water was a gray green, and silt stirred up against the reef reduced visibility to about ten yards, and less as soon as Smokey began to fan the sand to expose the *Sea Venture*'s timbers. Although thrilled at being there, I had to swim hard to keep Smokey and the wreck in sight, and thus was using up large quantities of my air. Whereas Smokey emitted only a trickle of bubbles, mine were streaming out as I tried to stay down. Eventually I was able to signal to him that I did not have enough weights to keep me there. Back we went to the boat, where Smokey added another eight or ten pounds of lead to my belt. "Do we have enough air to go down again?" I asked.

Smokey checked his gauge and assured me that we had another fifteen or twenty minutes. But we had only been back on the wreck for four or five when I found I was inhaling nothing. My tank was empty, and Smokey was nowhere in sight.

My only recourse was to surface as quickly as I could—which wasn't easy with all my added weights. I remembered my instructor's warning that in such an emergency one should not shed one's mask but continue to try to suck air even though the tank was empty. A break in the clouds came when I was still about twelve feet down, and the sudden brightness made me believe I was at the surface. I stripped off my mask—then felt as though my head was about to explode.

I came to the surface about forty yards from the boat, and dog-paddled to try to keep from sinking. "Help!" I yelled, waving frantically to Audrey, who was alone on board. But the pounding roar of the compressor made it impossible for her to hear that I was in trouble and so she happily waved back.

I was sure I was about to drown as I strove to rid myself of my weight belt. Once having done so, I was able to reach the boat, only to find that the freeboard was so high I did not have enough strength left to clamber aboard, and so hung on the side with my head still reeling. Smokey, finding that I had disappeared, came up and helped to heave me aboard, where I lay in a heap beside the pounding compressor. Audrey, still not understanding that I had damn near drowned, brightly asked, "Well, did you have fun?"

I had a lot to learn about diving, but even more to learn about Bermudan divers. Driven by the search for treasure they were fierce competitors and would stop at very little to prevent diver B from poaching on a wreck found by diver A. One even boasted that he had sand poured into the engine of a rival. A misleading coin could be dropped onto another's wreck to make him think it was more recent than he supposed, and markers could be shifted or stolen, all in the name of one-upmanship. But piratical at sea, they were jovial good fellows ashore and ever ready to congratulate each other on their discoveries or commiserate over mishaps and disappointments. There was something of the nineteenth century about these men, and Audrey and I found their company exhilarating and a far cry from the corporate calm of Williamsburg.

Whereas my visit to the 1609 *Sea Venture* did nothing to advance our study of Wolstenholme Towne's 1620 artifacts, another wreck was squarely in our time frame. Dating from 1619, the *Warwick* had been at anchor in St. George's Harbour when a hurricane drove her onto cliff-hugging rocks. It was thanks to the *Warwick* that we came to know its discoverer, Teddy Tucker, who had found it in his 1960s survey with the Smithsonian's Mendel Peterson. In contrast to the tall and reserved Smokey Wingood, Teddy was short and flamboyant, and he exuded an infectious bonhomie. Behind it, however, lay an incredible depth of knowledge of oceanography, seamanship, and nautical architecture. He also knew a great deal about colonial-era artifacts. In spite of coming from a well-known Virginia family, Teddy had been asked to leave several private schools in Virginia, and so had little formal education and less respect for academics. His attitude toward accredited diving graduates was equally dismissive—as he demonstrated on the *Warwick* when he leapt over the side of his boat without a diving harness and only a tank tucked under one arm.

Tucker had been working on the wreck off and on for several years. His interest was purely historical, since the *Warwick* was known to have had little of value aboard. Nevertheless, Teddy was dubbed a treasure hunter by archaeologists for having found gold on the 1594 wreck of the Spanish *San Pedro*—a reputation not helped by his calling his 1964 book *Treasure Diving with Teddy Tucker.* The book closed with the claim that he and his partner had "hauled up nearly $250,000 worth of treasure from the sea bed round Bermuda." Thirty years later I would do what I could to erase the resultant stigma by publishing a small book titled *Shipwreck! History from the Bermuda Reefs* featuring Teddy's other discoveries. I knew that in doing so I would irritate the underwater archaeological profession, which claimed that only it should excavate shipwrecks.

In 1981 Audrey and I became close friends with Teddy, his wife, Edna, and their daughter, who gave her name to the *Miss Wendy*, their dive ship moored below their handsome house at the west end of the island. A shed beside the house was loaded with boxes and tanks containing all manner of artifacts from all sorts of ships and dates, while in the shallow water behind the *Miss Wendy* rested half a dozen cannon of various ages. From time to time Teddy had loaned artifacts to Bermuda's Maritime Museum, but when that institution hired as director an archaeologist from England who immediately distanced himself and the museum from the local divers, Teddy became his foe and planned to build his own museum. That was no idle threat. Teddy had rich and powerful friends who enjoyed his hospitality and diving with him on his wrecks, among them Bostonian Edward "Ned" Johnson, chairman of Fidelity Insurance; Sir John Swan, Bermuda's prime minister; and Peter Benchley, the author of *Jaws*. Audrey and I would help design the exhibits for Teddy's proposed museum. But that was some years in the future and called for many an evening of planning and imbibing dark and stormys (rum and ginger beer) on the Tuckers' veranda watching the sun go down and the moonlight turn the sea to silver.

On my first dive on the *Warwick*, Teddy and I were accompanied by the National Geographic Society photographer Joe Bailey. The magazine had already agreed to my writing a second article on Martin's Hundred that would include dating evidence derived from shipwrecks, notably the jars from the *Sea Venture* and tobacco pipes from the *Warwick*. To that end, and barely a week after sitting on the *Warwick*'s keelson communing with remarkably friendly fish, I found myself in Sweden standing on the orlop deck of a much more famous shipwreck, that of the *Wasa*, which sank in Stockholm harbor in 1628. Raised in 1961, and still undergoing the long process of conservation, the ship was to all intents and purposes sufficiently restored to enable us to walk her decks, visit her cabins, and go below to inspect her brick-lined galley. Memories of boyhood fantasies of sailing the Spanish Main with Errol Flynn and Captain Kidd came flooding back as I imagined the *Wasa*'s crew singing sea chanteys (albeit in Swedish) as they strained at the capstan and their officers shouted, "Avast ye lubbers!" or words to that effect. They were not destined to do that for long, however, since the newly built pride of the Swedish navy capsized and sank before her well-wishers had time to leave the quay.

Audrey and I were accompanied on our National Geographic-sponsored tour by another photographer, Ira Block, who was to become a long-time friend. Ira is a small man with a big heart and boundless energy who refuses to take himself seriously. At our first meeting he claimed to have been the first Jew to reach the North Pole, having flown there to shoot a whiskey commercial. The National Geographic Society's preference for pictures over text was manifest when it sent Ira to travel first-class while Audrey and I were in steerage, although he would come aft to share the free drinks and goodies that he was enjoying up front. It was a measure of Ira's friendship that when Audrey died he and his wife, Madelain, had a tree planted in Israel in her memory.

The second *National Geographic* article was as successful as the first, and I became the subject of a press conference of the kind that the Society reserved for its star attractions. In an attempt to inject a modicum of drama into the event I demonstrated how to fire a matchlock musket. I don't remember whether the assembled reporters were impressed by such theatrics, but I do recall that one of them wrote that I was "a large pink person," a description that embarrassingly lingered in the memories of Geographic Society friends.

In the same blizzard of publicity, I was invited to give my Martin's Hundred lecture to the Geographic Society's Washington membership in Constitution Hall, the auditorium of the Daughters of the American Revolution. Following in the footsteps of so many of the Society's luminaries, I was awed, nervous, and intimidated by the vastness of the hall and its history, a condition that did not pass unnoticed by the sound engineer, who advised, "If you're going to drop dead, remember to fall upstage to avoid disturbing the audience." The booking director, Joanne Hess, must have thought that I had some facility as a lecturer, for she later scheduled me into the Society's new Grosvenor Auditorium to lecture on seventeenth-century Virginia, graffiti on ancient Egyptian monuments, and on the iconography of mermaids! This, my last lecture for the Society, was made memorable by the arrival of a live mermaid carried to her seat by a male minder. She turned out to be Rhonda Jean Gazda, a harmless collector of mermaidiana, but not wishing to miss a photo op, the auditorium manager summoned a staff photographer to immortalize the encounter. She subsequently posed on a courtyard rock for the benefit of lunchtime Washingtonians, and was last seen trying to hail a cab on M Street.

My interest in mermaids had been born long ago during my Jamaican involvement with the archaeology of Port Royal. In 1970 a London antiques dealer who knew of it called to say that he had a powder horn that he thought might be of interest to me. It had been engraved by J. Mitchell, a soldier of the 33rd Regiment of Foot, while stationed at Stony Hill barracks near Kingston in the 1820s. I bought it "sight unseen" and found that Mitchell had been an amateur naturalist who decorated the horn with critters he had encountered on the island, among them the kind of huge centipede that had greeted me on my arrival at Port Royal. Also depicted was a scorpion, an African green monkey, and a mermaid. She had the obligatory comb in one hand and mirror in the other, but had the flat face of a manatee. There, I remain convinced, was the first rendering of a mermaid drawn from life. Mitchell had seen a manatee basking in a Jamaican lagoon, and like explorers from Columbus onward, he believed that he was seeing a real live mermaid. From that first revelation I became fascinated by what others had seen around the world from Scandinavia and the river Niger in West Africa to the Maldive Islands in the Indian Ocean.

Unfortunately, I could find no mermaid lore in Bermuda, but Teddy Tucker could tell tales of monstrous creatures that lurked in the deep and in the fertile mind of his friend Peter Benchley. Teddy had pictures to prove that part of one had beached near his house at King's Point. Although a shapeless mass of what looked like blubber, the prospect that it might have come from a giant squid prompted a National Geographic Society expedition in 1990 in search of the immense creature which could be seen in nineteenth-century engravings wrapping its tentacles around a sailing ship and dragging it down to its lair. I went along on one of Tucker's sweeps of the deep accompanying the Smithsonian's giant squid expert, Clyde Roper. For six hours we sat staring at a nine-inch television monitor watching a bait fish dangle in front of a camera a thousand feet and more beyond the Bermuda shelf. In one thrilling moment someone thought he saw a shadow pass across a corner of the screen. I, alas, blinked and missed it.

Teddy Tucker's connection with the *National Geographic* was of long standing. He was the kind of larger-than-life treasure-hunting adventurer that fitted the Grosvenor mold. That Teddy was also of the kind the archaeological profession thought worthy of strangulation at birth mattered little to the Society's "expeditions editor" Bill Graves. A photograph of a diver breaking the surface of an azure sea with a gold cup gleaming in his hand would be received with cheering among picture editors. Consequently, Teddy could call on *National Geographic* associates like Clyde Roper, the shark expert Eugenie Clark, and the marine biologist Gregory Stone to join him in creating the Bermuda Underwater Exploration Institute (known as BUEI or Beewee). In 1991 Audrey and I were asked to represent archaeology, but being terrestrial and not underwater archaeologists, we recruited Margaret Rule, CBE, the raiser of the 1545 *Mary Rose*, her achievement even greater than that of lifting the *Wasa*.

Even though I shared Teddy Tucker's dream of putting his collection on public display, I had naively supposed, at least at the outset, that the purpose of the Underwater Exploration Institute was to pursue oceanographic research at every level, hence the blue-ribbon roster of its advisers in the relevant fields. With more than $22 million invested in the building and its design, and with an experienced firm of exhibit designers on board, the omens looked propitious. But once the exhibit plans began to take shape, and the designers and committee began to talk about "gee-whiz facts, hooks, and eyecatchers," I began to have my doubts.

The heart of the museum was to be "The Dive," enabling tourists to enter "a dive capsule for a simulated dive [to] 12,000 ft." In reality, this was an elevator containing a small tier-seated screening room that rocked just a bit as it descended. The voice-over dive commander whipped up tension as the lift went down, monitored by a depth gauge and helped by a video of sharks and other deep-water critters of the kind one can see any day on television. On touching down, the not-visibly-shaken tourist adventurer emerged into a darkened corridor on whose floor were projected the words "Deep Ocean Floor."

To make matters worse, the descent simulator provided the only access to the lower-level galleries, and the size of the capsule severely restricted the flow of visitors. I told Ned Johnson, whose money was invested in the project, that reliance on the dive with no means of bypassing it would be a terrible mistake. Perhaps because Peter Benchley and his hit movie *Jaws* were to be the bait (he wrote and narrated the pre-dive video) nothing was changed. As the brochure declared, "You've made 'The Dive,' now get the T-shirt!"

My role, along with that of Margaret Rule, was to create artifact exhibits for predesigned cases. From the start, Teddy wanted to display his gold, some of which had been found elsewhere than in Bermuda. His argument was that the *National Geographic* reading public is disappointed if it does not get to see gold, preferably in mind-blowing quantities. My answer was that this was to be a research institute whose duty would be to educate the public to the idea that knowledge is more valuable than bullion. To that end, I designed a pyramidical exhibit with one gold coin and an earring at the apex, and below it on the four sides single artifacts ranging from a porcelain cup to clay pipes and a ship's brass nameplate; the captions claimed that these and a multitude of artifacts like them were the sea's real treasures. Teddy was neither convinced nor happy.

One of the largest exhibit cases contained artifacts from a French ship wrecked in about 1760. There had been no gold on board, but a considerable quantity of pewter from the officers' quarters, along with much earthenware and faience bound for French Canada. It was the largest and finest assemblage of French ceramics whose date could be almost precisely determined. The ship had settled on a coral ridge between two large sand holes, eventually breaking its back and scattering objects such as the rudder gudgeons originally at the stern forward into the bow's sand hole. As Bermuda law required, Tucker offered to sell the artifact collection to the government for the price of his investment in the recovery process. On the advice of the Bermuda Maritime Museum, however, not having been found by a professional archaeologist, the collection was deemed worthless. As I had been involved in the analysis and drawing of the hundreds of objects, Teddy offered the collection to me as a gift. Having no wish or facilities to take him up on the offer, I advised the Mariners' Museum at Newport News that Teddy was prepared to give them the collection. The gift was declined for the same unreasonable reason. A disgusted Teddy Tucker at one point threatened to throw the whole lot back into the sea, but with BUEI on the horizon he thought better of it.

This story of the ship nicknamed "The Frenchman" dramatizes the ongoing war between the academically accredited maritime archaeological profession and amateur salvagers, who, no matter how carefully they do what they do, and regardless of the information that can be derived from their discoveries, are all condemned as looters and desecrators of the world's underwater heritage. Margaret Rule and the Noël Humes believed that lambs could lie down with lions and thereby tame them. We were to learn, however, that BUEI's lion was a leopard that had no intention of changing it spots.

More than twenty years later I was approached by a highly successful wreck-diving company that had retrieved the specie and part of the cargo from the SS *Republic*, which in 1865 had been lost in a hurricane off the coast of Georgia. Would I go down to Odyssey Marine Exploration's Tampa headquarters to review the results of its work? I suspected that Odyssey was more interested in my name than in my opinions, but the offer was too tempting to refuse. In the time between Bob Marx's shallow scuba diving at Port Royal and the discovery of the *Republic*, underwater salvage had gone from the Dark Ages to the space age. The wreck lay in seventeen hundred feet of water, a depth far beyond the reaches of diving archaeologists, yet modern technology was capable of safely retrieving something as fragile as a pane of window glass or as small as a single coin. Had the *Republic*'s cargo been remembered as a load of crockery and lumber, it would have had no investment appeal to the Odyssey company. The lure, instead, was a cargo of specie valued in 1865 at $400,000 and whose twenty-first-century retail value could reach $75 million. Fifty-one thousand coins were recovered along with thousands of common bottles and other artifacts.

Although an excellent preliminary study of the bottles was quickly published under Odyssey's aegis, it was the specie—the gold and silver treasure—that stuck in the craw of archaeological purists. The objections are twofold: First, since no archaeologist is physically capable of descending to the seabed to supervise the work, no one should do it. Second, allowing the wrecks' cargoes to underwrite their recovery as an unavoidable business expense is philosophically unacceptable. Nevertheless, after long soul-searching, I concluded that while retrievals from the *Republic* and other deep-water wrecks cannot be sufficiently total to satisfy shallow-water and land-bound archaeologists, some gained knowledge has to be better than the alternative. Having publicly said so, and having taken a stand different from that of the Society for Historical Archaeology's directors, I was appalled when Odyssey made a Discovery Channel series titled *Treasure Quest* and allowed its archaeologist to mug for the camera wearing a pirate's hat. Archaeology, it seemed, was no more than a self-serving veneer to cover a greed for gold, and I had taken the bait. Similar concerns had been much in mind when Audrey and I agreed to design the Bermuda Underwater Exploration Institute's archaeological exhibits.

In the aftermath of Audrey's sudden death, Carol took her place in planning and installing the BUEI exhibits, but Teddy and Edna Tucker had been such close friends of Audrey's that the transition was not as smooth as we had hoped. When Carol took professional charge of exhibit record keeping, Edna was even less entranced. I did not help the situation by insisting on shaping the exhibits around historical significance, while Teddy continued to repeat that the public wanted to see treasure and not history. Indeed, on the evening the museum opened, and while the champagne was still flowing, he told me that he had been given $70,000 to redo the exhibits to reflect his ideas, and that he intended to start doing so as soon as Carol and I were off the island. I therefore resigned from the BUEI board, feeling that I (along with Margaret Rule) had done what I could to inject a level of professionalism into the public face of Bermudan underwater archaeology but that as long as the artifacts belonged to the Tuckers it would be useless to continue to oppose them.

Had Audrey lived, the Tuckers might have been less easily riled, and our friendship (in which I put great store) might have endured. In truth, however, in spite of the millions poured into it, the museum was poorly designed and poorly located to capture the cruise-ship tourist business. With no research staff and no collections beyond those exhibited, it had no hope of becoming the bona fide underwater research institute to which its name so grandly aspired. Ironically, the place might have had greater tourist appeal had it called itself Teddy Tucker's Hall of Treasures—which was how he imagined it all along. The moral to this sad story is both simple and old: in trying to appeal to every audience level one is in danger of satisfying none.

Another Tucker treasure, less visually exciting but in its way of greater historical value, was contained in a folder Teddy handed me while going through a desk filled with drawings. He asked me what I could make of the stained and faded, handwritten document. Ten pages long and written with a steel-nibbed pen on both sides of quarto and legal-sized sheets sewn together with cotton, the document dated from the mid-nineteenth century. It began like this:

> The following account of a shipwreck—less interesting from concomitant calamities than from the turbulence of the crew and its ultimate consequences, is contained in a letter from one of those whose safety was endangered. Though we are not acquainted with his peculiar capacity on occasion of the voyage, both his experience and intelligence are sufficiently conspicuous.

The following transcription began: "Late on Friday evening, the second of June, our fleet consisting of seven good ships and two pinnaces; weighed anchor from Plymouth Sound . . ."

Amazingly, I had read those words many times before, or something very like them: "Know that upon Friday late in the evening we brake ground out of the sound Of Plymouth, our whole fleet then consisting of seven good ships and two pinnaces . . ." Thus began William Strachey's celebrated 1609–10 account of the voyage and loss of the *Sea Venture* on the reefs of the Dread Bermudas. All that has been thought to survive was a copy published in 1625 by the editorially suspect Reverend Samuel Purchas. From my first reading of the Tucker manuscript I assumed that it was a second version of Purchas's publication and of only modest interest. But in time, and after prolonged research, I became convinced that the Tucker manuscript was copied from Strachey's original draft, one probably written on the pages of his commonplace book. I deduced that the copy was penned in Ireland and that the original book may still survive unrecognized in an ecclesiastical library in or near modern Londonderry.

The nineteenth-century transcript, which had been found in a Tucker family trunk, was passed to me in 1983 with instructions to learn all I could about it, find a publisher, and then sell it on the family's behalf. None of these tasks were easy, but the text was finally printed in the admittedly obscure *Avalon Chronicles* published in 2001 by the Memorial University of Newfoundland. Four years later the Irish transcript was purchased by the historian and philanthropist Dorothy Rouse-Bottom, of Hampton, Virginia, who subsequently presented it to the Library of the Mariners' Museum at Newport News. To complete the gift, in 2009 Dorothy republished the Irish document along with my new introduction in a small book we titled *Wreck and Redemption.*

There is, perhaps, an element of irony in the fact that the discovery and saving of the Strachey manuscript may well be considered my most important contribution to Anglo-American history—and yet it owes nothing whatever to my decades of archaeological digging.

I N 1994, with me remarried, and with Carol as secretary to the Jamestown Re-discovery archaeological committee and Audrey's disapproving ghost watching us from the wings, Virginia launched into the most important excavation ever undertaken in the state, or anywhere else in America for that matter.

Walking along the levee between the James River and the ruined church, Bill Kelso asked me where he should begin digging. I pointed to a shallow depression in the grass and replied, "If I were you, I'd start there." That advice was not entirely a guess. Pinky Harrington's 1939 excavations had included a trench in front of the church that yielded several early artifacts. A utility cutting in the same area had previously turned up fragments of crucibles similar to others we had found on Roanoke Island. Either way, the hunch paid off. The first square opened led to the remains of a basement inside the southeast corner of the fort. Virtually from day one, therefore, it was evident that the fort was not lost to the river; instead, at least three-quarters of it remained on land, albeit partially under a Confederate fort. Needless to say, the APVA was ecstatic.

In April the newly created board met to bestow its blessing on the freshly opened excavation and to attend a launching ceremony at the Dale House, which was serving as an artifact display area and conservation lab. The event was staged by the APVA's public relations officer, but my diary for that day noted that "the handling of the press conference was outrageously sloppy. David Evans from the British Embassy came but was not invited to speak, likewise, chief Oliver Perry of the Nansemond Indians." My embarrassment was evidently not shared by the board members, who went on to be wined and dined, first as guests of Tim Sullivan, president of the College of William and Mary, and then at the board dinner in Williamsburg. My diary adds that "Peter Grover cut out before the board dinner," leaving me to give a trite and platitudinous speech about the APVA and the future of Jamestown. "Home at 11.30 very, very tired"—and with much to think about.

Most of the board members were experienced archaeologists and capable of directing a major excavation; some even had experience of digging seventeenth-century sites. But at this first meeting they had nothing to contribute, nor would they the next time. It was highly unlikely that they would be able to correct or direct a future course of action unless they had been down on their knees in the dirt following the excavation's daily progress. In short, they were ornamental rather than useful. I had known from the outset, of course, that they had been chosen as letterhead embellishments. My problem was that as the on-site chairman I could and should be in constant touch with what was going on—albeit on the board members' behalf.

Since Bill Kelso's staff was small, he had arranged to run a field school of the kind he had found beneficial as archaeological director at Monticello, a decision he had made with APVA approval before I was brought on board. As I've mentioned before, I firmly believe that one cannot run a strictly research-oriented excavation and at the same time teach at the pace of the slowest student. I saw the Jamestown excavation as a research project and worried that areas would be opened and only half-completed when the students left. This proved to be true, and I urged Bill to expand his permanent crew to finish the opened squares before bad weather turned them to mud. He replied that he had no money. Would he like me to go to Grover to plead for more funds, I asked. He would, and I did. But Grover saw this as interference in an area beyond the purview of an advisory committee.

The responsibilities and limitations of the chairman had not been spelled out. Where, I had to ask myself, lay the dividing line between help and interference? In the field, should I advise if I saw an excavator digging with a shovel when a more delicate approach was needed? Should I express dismay when I saw metal artifacts exposed and left rusting in the ground in case press photographers should happen by? I was guilty on both counts. When a helmet was found in the cellar, Bill invited me to help in its excavation, but having successfully lifted the two helmets from the clay of Wolstenholme Towne, I slipped easily into both doing and directing the excavation. Although Bill acquiesced, it was natural that he would grow to resent such practical advice and begin to doubt whether he was really in charge. He was, after all, the director of the Jamestown Rediscovery program and officially answerable only to Grover. So where did the chairman of the advisory board fit into the chain of command? Answer: he didn't.

It also became apparent that APVA public relations "opportunities" were becoming a major factor in the excavation's progress. In July an early morning

TV show that was part news and part exercise session got me up at 4:00 a.m. to be at Jamestown by 5:00. My diary called it "a dreadful show, made a mockery of Jamestown and archaeology." But I had not been consulted in the decision whether to do the show or not—and even if I had been, I would have been outvoted. I had learned long ago to be wary of TV producers, whose job is to fill air time regardless of content. Even when they would agree and shoot sequences that were archaeologically acceptable or historically correct, the scenes could be cut by editors who knew nothing about the subject and whose only concern was to fit the time slot and hope that it looked okay on screen. The painstaking slowness of archaeology does not make good television. When in doubt, cut to the treasure!

I was discovering that I would have been better off as a chairman who only appeared one or twice a year along with the rest of the committee to listen, nod knowingly, drink, and dine.

At the same time that I was railing against the notion that any TV is better than none, I was taking a contrary stance by embracing accuracy's ultimate ogre—Michael Eisner's Disney Corporation. It came about like this:

Several years earlier, when Audrey and I had been designing exhibits for our Martin's Hundred museum and while I was lecturing at UCLA, we visited Disney's exhibit-construction plant at Burbank and met its director, Van Romans. His "imagineering" team was then designing a Roy Rogers museum, and being impressed by what we saw and heard, we invited him to help us. Later, when we began talking budget, Van called me and said that to avoid subsequent embarrassment he would tell me up front that we couldn't afford Disney's services—which I am sure was true.

In 1994 the Disney people unveiled a plan to construct Disney's America, a history-related theme park, in northern Virginia on land adjacent to the Manassas battlefield. Civil War buffs were outraged, although in reality the land was five miles from the historic site. The State of Virginia was unconvinced by the supposed sacrilege and, smelling tax revenue, was prepared to assist Disney with funding. Van Romans was to lead the charge and naturally sought the endorsement of the APVA. As chairman of the Jamestown advisory committee, I met him on the excavation site. Over lunch I came to believe that Eisner intended to honor rather than exploit the American past, and that serious attention would be paid to the advice of as many historians as could be persuaded to help. Few, if any, were forthcoming. On the contrary, the most prominent launched a "Protect Historic America" campaign and in a *New York Times* ad damned Eisner as "the man who would destroy American history." Robert Wilburn, then Colonial Williamsburg's president, attended an Eisner meeting in Florida and reputedly left it volubly unconvinced. In spite of the mounting opposition, I continued to believe in Van Romans's assurances of historical accuracy, and discounted Colonial Williamsburg's fear that Disney's America would cut into Williamsburg's tourist revenue.

I countered that Manassas was too far from Williamsburg to adversely affect its tourist trade, and that if Disney's America created an interest in American history among the inhabitants of urban Washington, D.C., that had to be a plus. Furthermore, with interest aroused, visiting Williamsburg and other historic places to see "the real thing" would be an obvious next step. I continued in a naive belief that Eisner really meant, as he said, "to tell important stories about our history" while at the same time providing an "enjoyable experience for our guests . . . without either one diluting the other." But soon after Disney's animated movie *Pocahontas* was released I learned that the Native American consultants hired to ensure the movie's authenticity were soon fired after their help was deemed unhelpful. I had evidently backed the wrong horse, as had Eisner, whose Disney's America never broke ground.

Meanwhile, back at Jamestown, the departed field school students had left their excavations open and incomplete with only Bill Kelso and his field supervisor, Nick Luccketti, to continue. This, in my view, was absurd, and I said so. At dinner with the APVA president, Mrs. Catesby Jones, she asked for my assessment of the progress at Jamestown. It was, I said, understaffed and underfunded. Would I be willing to take a more active role, she asked? I replied that if Kelso so desired, I would do what I could to help the project. On the strength of that response, Mrs. Jones reported to Grover that I was seeking the directorship. As I later pointed out, my health was such that I was barely able to visit the site let alone direct it, but Mrs. Jones's poisoned seed quickly took root, and Bill Kelso, who had complained to Grover that I was trying to micromanage his project, now demanded my ouster as chairman. I had, in any case, intended to resign at the end of 1995, and so the APVA's decision to terminate me after one year in office was no disappointment. However, the Machiavellian behavior of the committee and the bad blood it created were wholly regrettable. Nick Luccketti, who had urged my retention, was subsequently "let go," and APVA's treasurer, and my good friend, Tom Wood, resigned in protest. Somewhere in the back of my mind I could hear Audrey whispering, "I told you so." At Mary Douthat Higgins's instigation, the Dale House laboratory had been named in memory of Audrey. In 1995 the identifying sign was quickly and quietly removed.

In retrospect, I should either have declined to serve or have recognized that success as chairman required nothing more than smiling acquiescence, in short, an ornamental *reis*. Although the Jamestown Rediscovery project got off to a stuttering and contentious start, its fortunes improved when funding greatly increased and the APVA's leadership changed. Equally advantageous was the interest shown by Virginia's then first lady, Roxane Gilmore, and her friend, the best-selling author Patricia Cornwell. The latter's bountiful generosity (and purple helicopter) gave the project public support that sustained it through the lean years. No less valuable was the hiring of curator Bly Straube, the retention of archaeologist Jamie May, and an increasingly strong team of conservators, technicians, and excavators.

As I had predicted, most of Jamestown's fortified compound had escaped the James River's erosion, and once the Confederate earthwork was removed, its triangular plan emerged pretty much as I had drawn in it in my 1994 book *The Virginia Adventure*, and as colonist William Strachey described it in 1610. Several human burials were found inside the fort, one of whose skeletons was hailed as a first colonist who may have been executed, a gunshot to one knee having led to his death. As intended, the press received the news with glee and trumped *National Geographic*, which claimed that it had first photographic rights, thereby creating a temporary rift between the project and that influential supporter. Had I still been chairman I would have urged against saying too much too soon, an opinion that would have brought me into open conflict with the APVA, for whom publicity was the prize. Nobody questioned why an executed colonist would have been shot in the knee, a wound that I believe was the result of a hunting accident. I was relieved, therefore, to be able to watch from the sidelines and later to offer Bill counsel when he sought it. Bill Kelso's Jamestown Rediscovery excavations would go on to become the most productive in the history of historical archaeology. When Queen Elizabeth II visited the site as part of her 2007 tour (en route to the Kentucky Derby) and met Bill and his team, the accolade could not have been more deserved.

Like Roanoke's Science Center, the fort at Jamestown is a national treasure and ranks as "historic" rather than merely "historical," the former being important in history and the latter not necessarily. Martin's Hundred and Wolstenholme Towne, on the other hand, had no lasting impact on the flow of American history. In spite of their popular appeal, derived from the publication and exhibition of their artifacts, the Carter's Grove sites are only footnotes in historical time. Nevertheless, they deserved better than the fate that befell them in 2002 when Colonial Williamsburg closed the plantation, ostensibly for renovations. In reality, the closure was based on Carter's Grove's profitability or lack thereof, but an economic study of the property concluded that the shortfall in ticket sales was the result of an accounting policy that credited to Carter's Grove only those tickets which were actually purchased there. The rest of the tickets sold—the vast majority—which were bought in town, were not. Had they been, there is little doubt that Carter's Grove and Martin's Hundred could have been a successful self-sustaining historical attraction. Left unsaid (and sometimes denied) was the ultimate intent to sell the plantation. Not believing that Colonial Williamsburg's trustees would compromise the Foundation's famous commitment to the future learning from the past, I helped voice the concerns of the many who wanted the renovations done and the plantation reopened. At several meetings with board Chairman, CEO, and President Colin Campbell, I put forward proposals to better integrate the four centuries of history that it represented. He heard me with smiling politeness, just as he listened to pleas by others, including Mary Humelsine, the widow of Carl Humelsine, whose baby this had been. In speaking up in defense of Carter's Grove I knew that I risked being tarred as opposed to Colonial Williamsburg's management, but as Vice President Ed Kendrew had asked so long ago, "Who has a better right?"

As I explained in chapter 20, the mansion's 1930s renaissance into what Colonial Williamsburg called a "Georgian-style mansion" seriously compromised its colonial integrity and in doing so had set it apart from the Foundation's "focus on the story of citizenship and becoming Americans in the 18th century." Thus, added a 2006 press release, "Carter's Grove with its multiple stories spanning some four centuries, is not essential to this strategic focus." When Campbell told me that the museum was to be stripped, I requested that the brass plaque installed by the previous president, Bob Wilburn, to recognize Audrey's and my work be given to me to be a part of my personal archive. He agreed to do so, while expressing surprise that I would want it.

Had there been no Martin's Hundred to intrude into the story of the Burwell family and its eighteenth-century mansion, perhaps the Powers that Were would eventually have given Carter's Grove the Williamsburg restorative treatment, and Williamsburg would own it still. If that is so, then all our years of archaeological toil and public acclaim for the wrong century did the land a crippling disservice.

Put on the market, the plantation remained for sale for more than a year while I watched nervously from the wings. The prospect of its being bought as a trophy by a wealthy celebrity or sports hero was disconcerting. Although a developer's dream property on the James River, preservation restrictions imposed to protect archaeological sites prevented it from achieving its commercial potential. In January 2008, however, it was sold for a modest $15.3 million to California-based but Virginia-rooted entrepreneur Halsey Minor, founder of the highly successful CNet, Inc. Colin Campbell assured the press that there was "a clear indication that [Minor] will be a fine steward of Carter's Grove." When the sale was announced a worried correspondent from Kentucky wrote me asking, "What is going to happen to all of your work at Martin's Hundred?" He added, "It would be such an educational and historic shame to cut the public off from such an important part of Virginia's history." However, in a brief meeting with the genial Mr. Minor I was convinced that all would be well and that the plantation and its history were safe in his hands.

A year later, when rumors began to circulate that all might not be well, I turned to the Internet and found that not everyone was as confident as I had been. One contributor mused that "there's got to be some sort of sinister snake in Mister Minor's real estate grass," adding that "the Midas-like entrepreneur has a bit of a thing for trophy properties." In a long interview with Minor in August 2008, *Fortune Magazine*'s Jessi Hempel asked him about his recent purchase of Carter's Grove and was told, "I had the archaeologist who did all the work here over for dinner, and he said 'I just want you to know you have the most historic property in America,' and I said, come on, how about the White House?" To that assertion a small corrective footnote is in order: Carter's Grove is *not* the most historic property in America—and Mr. Minor never invited me to dinner.

29 🌿 *A Really Big Party*

IN SPITE OF Senator Hunter Andrews's pessimistic forecast, I was still alive as Virginia's 400th anniversary bore down on us. Bill Kelso's excavations on the Jamestown fort were expanding and yielding one newsworthy discovery after another, and the APVA's plans for building a museum in which to exhibit them were going ahead and boded well for the big celebration. Nearby, the state-operated Jamestown-Yorktown Foundation, with multimillions of appropriated dollars to spend, was busily replacing its fifty-year-old Jamestown Festival Park buildings with a huge exhibit structure whose brick exterior looked remarkably like a prison. At the same time the National Park Service was erecting a new visitor center to replace the triangular one flooded in 2003's Hurricane Isabel. That building, too, had been a survivor from the 1957 festival. One might think that all three endeavors would have been joyously integrated. But they were not, each jealous of its fiefdom and intent on making its own splash without the help (or sometimes the knowledge) of the others. At one point, Roxane Gilmore, the wife of Virginia's governor, asked me to try to seek further cooperation between the Jamestown-Yorktown curators and Bill Kelso's archaeologists, but a polite meeting led only to empty assurances. Later, when Bill said that he planned to reconstruct the frame of one of his fort buildings, he was advised that he should not do so lest it compete with the Jamestown-Yorktown's fort reconstruction. He did it anyway, and very instructive it proved to be for visitors.

Two years before the great opening, employing logic that was lost on me, Colonial Williamsburg announced that it was taking planning charge of the seventeenth-century celebrations—this the same organization that had closed Carter's Grove and the Martin's Hundred museum because the foundation's interests were restricted to the eighteenth century, subsequently narrowed to the revolutionary years. I was, needless to say, vastly relieved that my chairmanship of the Jamestown Rediscovery project had lasted but one year.

With the approach of 2007 and the first creaking of a public relations band-wagon, the ghost of Pocahontas reemerged, as did the legend of her love affair with the bristly-bearded and rough-edged Captain John Smith. More vocal than the surviving Virginia Indian tribes, however, were the state's African Americans, whose arrival in 1619 marked the beginning of black slavery in British America (overlooking the 200 slaves shipped to Roanoke Island by Sir Francis Drake in 1586). It seemed to me that it was the Indians who were most in danger of being shortchanged. In an attempt to do something about it, I returned to my earlier love of writing for the cinema, and wrote a script focusing on the year 1610 and the violent new regime of Lord Delaware, which followed the presidency of the injured and ousted John Smith. I titled it "Civilized Men" and tried to show that the English were as barbarous as those they called savages. The Virginia Film Office makes an annual award for screenwriting, and in 2005 it gave first prize to "Civilized Men," so with 2007 in the offing, I felt sure that the state office would steer the script into the Hollywood mainstream. But my timing could not have been worse. Hollywood already had its hooks into the Pocahontas story and was about to build its own Jamestown on the Chickahominy River. It had given the Smith role to actor Colin Farrell and the Pocahontas part to Q'Orianka Kilcher, a hitherto unknown young actress from Peru.

Touted in advance as "a sweeping exploration of love, loss, and discovery," and directed by Terrence Malick, *The New World* had its premier in the little movie house in Williamsburg, where, amid polite applause, the invited audience debated whether the film would prove sufficiently boffo at the box office to boost Virginia's tourist industry in 2007. I sat with Deanna Beacham, the Virginia governor's Indian representative, and neither of us gave it high marks for anything but the local scenery. The film was, as we had feared, a rerun of the old love story complete with romping in the reeds and marginally prurient attention to barely buck-skinned buttocks. I knew my "Civilized Men" script would have treated the Indians with more dignity and with much greater accuracy.

While the film was still being shot I decided that my script was not entirely dead and so rewrote it as a novel, which I dedicated to our old archaeological friend Oliver Perry, retired chief of the Nansemond tribe. Helped by Deanna Beacham, *Civilized Men* was well received by the other Virginia tribes and in 2007 was nominated for a best book award by the Virginia State Library. It did not win, but its acceptance by Chief Steve Adkins of the Chickahominy tribe (who bought several copies) was satisfaction enough. Centuries of decimation and confinement had led in 1924 to the Virginia General Assembly's rejection of the Indians as a race; henceforth, they had to be either black or white. Though reinstated more than fifty years later, in 2008 the eight remaining Virginia tribes continued to appeal for the federal recognition enjoyed by most tribes in other states. I would be flattering myself if I claimed that my speeches and writing on the Indians' behalf had any effect, but it was gratifying that in the following year the House of Representatives passed a bill in their favor.

In a further attempt to set the Smith and Pocahontas story straight I wrote a two-act play titled *Smith! Being the Life and Death of Cap'n John* and set it in a London inn in the last hour of his life. He was not the central character, however, and was to remain hidden behind the curtains of his deathbed until the final seconds of the play. Smith's manservant, Jack Porter, was to be the narrator, augmented (and often contradicted) by the tavern keeper and others who were to speak for assorted colonists. Although it called for a good deal of concentration on the part of an audience, I felt sure *Smith!* would play. Others were not convinced. Two Washington theater companies had rejected the script before I mentioned it to my Strachey manuscript friend Dorothy Rouse-Bottom. She asked to read it and offered partial production funding to a locally based professional theater company. The producers, who had a live-performance contract with Colonial Williamsburg, saw it as an opportunity to stage something appropriate during the 2007 summer season and so agreed to present the play. At last I was to see my circle complete. I had begun in the theater and now expected to end my career in the same way. I remembered my first play in the village schoolhouse at Courteenhall in 1943 and the thrill of an audience's applause. But then I remembered, too, my Williamsburg production of *Gaslight*, Orin Bullock's inability to round up an adequate cast, and my own dismal performance in the leading role. But that was an amateur production. This was to be professionally acted and directed—a horse of a very different hue.

To the producers it was the package and not the content that mattered. My name was sufficiently well-known to draw an audience, and this was to be John Smith's year, so it did not matter that the play was far too long and had too many people in it. All that could be fixed.

I signed a contract with the theater company in June 2006, reassured by clause 7, which stated that the "Producer will make no alterations to the text of the Play without prior consent, either written or oral, of Playwright." Several days later I lunched with the producers and for the first time met the director, who told me, "I see this as a musical." I replied that I hoped she was joking, Then the senior producer came to see me and explained that lectures belonged in lecture halls and entertainment on the stage. I saw his point, but argued that this play was intended as a history lesson in theatrical guise. He had written earlier to tell me that there were a couple of (previously unmentioned) factors that needed to be addressed: First, time considerations meant that the play would have to be cut from two acts to one with a running time of no more than ninety minutes. Second, the cast would have to be reduced from seven to two to "accommodate both financial and cast restraints," the latter because "casting any reasonably decent actors who reside in this area is extremely difficult." In short, regardless of clause 7, the play would have to be extensively rewritten.

In the light of all that was to come, I should have torn up the contract, but with Dorothy Rouse-Bottom's investment already committed, I felt trapped. Besides, as the producer very well knew, I was eager to see my play staged no matter how butchered it might become. After prolonged debate I was able to increase the cast from two to four—the largely silent Smith, Porter, a doctor, and a serving wench (who would later be transformed into Pocahontas)—but casting remained a problem. Actors who did well in early readings became unavailable when better-paying parts were offered elsewhere, and the man who read for Porter was not sufficiently commanding to carry the show. However, before its public reading in November, a savior came to my rescue. He was my old friend John Hamant, who had been a theater major at the University of Arizona before he took his archaeological job with me in 1977 and remained my right hand until I left the field. Thereafter he had shouldered a variety of administrative and performing duties on the theatrical side of Colonial Williamsburg. Reluctantly, and only as a favor to me, John accepted the challenge of the part of Porter, which would keep him on stage from beginning to end. The public reading left no doubt that John and Porter were made for each other.

Our second strength lay in Colonial Williamsburg's own peripatetic "Thomas Jefferson" in the person of the actor Bill Barker, who was to play Doctor Davenant. Although he did splendidly in the November reading, by early 2007 Bill realized that his Jeffersonian duties would not allow him to commit to a play that was to run all summer. This was beginning to look like *Gaslight* reignited.

John Smith was a small man, barely five feet four inches tall, a fact that was brought out in the play. Casting thus called for an actor of small stature with a voice tuned to croaking out Smith's dying words. We had him in November, but lost him before rehearsals started in March. The only available replacement, I was told, had the right voice but was a good six feet tall; he should be okay if he scrunched up in the bed. Our wench was wonderful, but with Bill Barker out, we still had no Dr. Davenant and rehearsals were about to begin. I had nightmare visions of having to try out for the part myself, but mercifully the director had another solution. She conscripted her husband, a classically trained opera singer. Perhaps she had been serious when she said she envisaged *Smith!* as a musical.

Even the most famous playwrights have railed against philistine producers and directors who lacked reverence for the sanctity of their words, and now it was my turn. With my contract's clause 7 long since forgotten, I found myself called upon for multiple rewritings, each version getting further and further from my original concept. Smith's visual absence until the last moments of the play was directorially compromised, leaving me convinced that I had been guilty of turning a truly tragic historical figure into a theatrical buffoon. More dispiriting was the fact that audiences appeared to neither notice nor care.

The play ran through the summer with smallish but appreciative audiences, and by the time it got to within days of its closing, the cast had gelled around Porter, as it should have before it opened. After the penultimate performance, Carol and I hosted a party for the cast and stage crew at which everyone said nice things to each other, and amid hugs and kisses expressed the hope that they could eventually reassemble to stage another Noël Hume winner. They had no such expectation, of course, but adversity and disappointments have steeled theater folk always to look on the bright side. Closing the door after the last car had pulled away, I turned to survey the abandoned glasses, napkins, paper plates, and Dorothy's emptied Champagne bottles, and remembered lines from a Noel Coward song:

> The party's over now,
> The dawn is drawing very nigh,
> The candles gutter,
> The starlight leaves the sky . . .

Carol later noted that the cost of the party had exceeded all the summer's royalties, but that was not the point. The play had been staged. It ran through the festive summer, and audiences chuckled where they should and remained through John Hamant's final exit to give him the sustained applause he so richly deserved. In 2008 the play was restaged by a professional company in Maryland and there gelled to a degree it never had in Williamsburg.

For me, in the fall of 2007, it was time to take stock, count my many blessings, and prepare to quit the stage. Although endowed with a loving wife, a happy family, and an enviable home, at the age of eighty no ambitions were left. Most of my friends were dead; so was my longtime literary agent. The archaeological profession had moved on to be led by new generations straight from graduate school more interested in quantification than stratification.

Strangers comment on my apparently appealing British accent, and marvel that I retained it after fifty years in Virginia, but I am sadly aware that even in that I am an archaic anomaly. What had been known as the King's and later the Queen's English is rarely heard in modern Britain, where the ruins of its language are all that remains of its empire.

Change, politicians tell us, is progress; but looking back to the days of my arrival and my memory of Miranda and her quill, I am not so sure. I entered Norman Rockwell's world and grew to embrace it as my own. The name Williamsburg was known from coast to coast as the nation's historical holy of holies and anyone lucky enough to work there was eyed with admiration and envy. For those of us who enjoyed the luxury of smugness, the small salaries (John D's millions were frugally spent) were eclipsed by the pleasure of living in that magical place. A contemporary called them halcyon days.

But with the retirement of Carl Humelsine, the focus shifted, first to a collegiate mode and then to a healthy mind-and-body concept in which the company doctor offered physicals to the wealthy and a spa in which to soak their overworked bones. The shrine could be marketed as a resort, a tourist destination conveniently close to Water Country and Busch Gardens—all three available on a single, fun-promising ticket. Visitors once identified as guests became tourists and eventually customers. In this metamorphosis the beauty of the restored architecture became a backdrop for street theater in which microphone-aided actors play out scenes from the Revolution. The gracious tranquillity of the 1950s has evolved into the confrontational, in-your-face "Revolutionary City," and in the minds of some Williamsburg retirees, Colonial Williamsburg's revered motto has changed from the noble intent "That the Future may Learn from the Past" to the corporate hope that the future must earn from it. The need to appeal to the iPod and video-game generation with its taste for violence and instant gratification set the new formula apart from the aging and declining number of visitors who were content to listen to gracious hostesses and admire old furniture.

Like growing old, a society's evolution is a slow process that creeps up unnoticed. For me, with my head deep in the dirt of archaeology rather than mercantile philosophy, the changes either went unnoticed or were none of my business.

With my wife Audrey at my side, we lived in our own Little England, letting Elvis Presley, the Beatles, and the Woodstock generation pass us by. Over time our annual visits to England to see family and friends made us increasingly aware that the changes there were more extreme than here, all America's economic and societal problems being duplicated and crammed together onto one small island. Enoch Powell, a wise but often vilified British politician of the 1960s, wrote that the inevitable always takes longer than one expects.

Reading and writing are becoming lost arts as we watch more and absorb less. Handwriting, which began with a stylus scratching on tablets coated with wax, gave way to quills and parchment, then to paper and steel-nibbed pens, from dip pens to fountain pens, thence to ballpoints, and now to key-pad iPods and Blackberries—poked with a stylus. We are kept alive by chemicals in the shape of pills of every size and color while clinging to memories whose recollection evokes more sadness than joy.

Were Aesop alive, he would have a thought-provoking moral for this archaeological fable. It behooves me, therefore to offer one of my own. But first some questions: How does one become an archaeologist? And should one? Was grim Uncle John correct when he told me that archaeology is an avocation and not a profession? In my case, I can only say that were it not for a string of coincidences and improbable strokes of luck, he would, indeed, have been right. Archaeology, as I have tried to demonstrate, is less a profession than a tool, a procedure used by antiquaries, be they historians, anthropologists, ethnographers, classicists, indeed anyone who seeks answers from the earth. My Aesopian moral, therefore, is that the road to a career that uses archaeology is not to follow me through the back door while trying to be a playwright, but to secure a formal education in a field that now and again lets one out to play in the dirt.

It is wise to remember, however, that when recession grips the financial world, its bean counters look to separate bread from circuses, the necessary from the nice. In that climate Colonial Williamsburg sold Carter's Grove, eliminated its director of archaeology, turned his collections over to the antiques curators and its department to the director of architectural research—from whose predecessor I had rescued it fifty years earlier. On September 27, 2008, the usually supportive *Virginia Gazette* published the requiem headline, "CW Buries Archaeology." I can but hope that time will prove it wrong. Nevertheless, having spent my career in the passionate pursuit of the past, it is sobering to realize that, like the dodo, the great auk, and the passenger pigeon, I have become part of it. But in time so must we all.

When, more than half a century ago, I stood muddy-footed, penniless, and jobless on the banks of the river Thames, the future looked just as bleak. But you have seen how it turned out, a working lifetime of excitement, literary satisfaction, archaeological successes, and wonderful people who have supported me, loved me, and honored me. And who could ask for more? Piquant as always, my namesake had the best curtain line:

> Let's creep away from the day
> For the party's over now.

INDEX

BOOKS BY THIS AUTHOR

Non-Fiction
Wreck and Redemption (2009)
Something from the Cellar (2005)
If These Pots Could Talk (2001)
In Search of This and That (1996)
Shipwreck! History from the Bermuda Reefs (1995)
The Virginia Adventure (1994)
Martin's Hundred (1982)
English Delftware from London and Virginia (1977)
All the Best Rubbish (1974)
A Guide to Artifacts of Colonial America (1970)
Historical Archaeology (1969)
1775: Another Part of the Field (1968)
Here Lies Virginia (1963)
Great Moments in Archaeology (1957)
Treasure in the Thames (1956)
Archaeology in Britain (1953)

With Audrey Noël Hume
The Archaeology of Martin's Hundred (2001)
Handbook of Tortoises, Terrapins and Turtles (1954)

Fiction
Civilized Men (2006)
The Truth About Fort Fussocks (1972)
The Charleston Scheme (1971)

Play
Smith! Being the Life and Death of Cap'n John (2007)